THE GREAT AMERICAN
WOLF

THE GREAT AMERICAN
WOLF

BRUCE HAMPTON

A JOHN MACRAE / OWL BOOK

Henry Holt and Company I New York

Henry Holt and Company, Inc.
Publishers since 1866
115 West 18th Street
New York, New York 10011

Henry Holt® is a registered trademark
of Henry Holt and Company, Inc.

Published in Canada by Fitzhenry & Whiteside Ltd.,
195 Allstate Parkway, Markham, Ontario L3R 4T8.

Library of Congress Cataloging-in-Publication Data
Hampton, Bruce.
The Great American wolf / Bruce Hampton
p.   cm.
"A John Macrae book"
Includes bibliographical references and index.
1. Wolves—North American.   I. Title.
QL737.C22H35   1997   96-16298
599.74′442—dc20   CIP

ISBN 0-8050-5528-2

Henry Holt books are available for special promotions and
premiums. For details contact: Director, Special Markets.

First published in hardcover in 1997 by
Henry Holt and Company, Inc.

First Owl Book Edition—1997

A John Macrae / Owl Book

Designed by Michelle McMillian
Illustration by Barbara Smullen

Printed in the United States of America
All first editions are printed on acid-free paper. ∞

1   3   5   7   9   10   8   6   4   2

CONTENTS

It is man's earth now. One wonders what obligations may accompany this infinite possession.
—Fairfield Osborn, 1948

1

THE LAST WOLVES

At Custer, South Dakota, on a crisp, late October afternoon in 1920, sunlight streamed across a crowd of ranchers and townsfolk gathered to witness a death most of them had begun to believe they would never see.

Altogether, it proved a great disappointment.

What surprised onlookers the most was that the executioner, Harry Percival Williams, displayed so little pleasure in the killing.

Posing for photographs, the forty-four-year-old Williams did nothing to allay that impression, his long, gaunt face shadowed by a gray Stetson in the evening light. The only hint of his profession was the Springfield rifle he still carried loosely in his hand. Local residents couldn't recall seeing Williams without it during the past seven months as he trailed alone among the Black Hills in patient and determined pursuit of his quarry. Now, as the sun vanished behind surrounding hills, that chase had ended and grateful citizens assembled to view the famous killer as much as the body of the villain that had ravaged their lives for the past nine years.

At someone's request, Williams reached down and propped up the carcass stiff with rigor mortis, legs splayed and head bowed low to the ground in what some noted was an appropriately submissive posture. As a camera shutter snapped, Williams grimly looked on, strange behavior for the man who had just killed the most notorious wolf in the history of North America.

If the audience found Williams enigmatic, they were even more disenchanted with his prey. Just an ordinary wolf, someone said, nudging the carcass with his boot—barely six feet long from head to tail, weighing ninety-eight pounds, an animal so aged that its pelt had turned white. It didn't seem possible that this was the Custer wolf, assassin over the years of five hundred horses, cows, and calves worth $25,000, losses said to have caused the ruin of several ranchers. The beast had also savaged the reputations of many would-be hunters who had attempted to collect the $500 bounty, an irresistible sum to cowboys and ranch hands whose monthly salary was no more than $25. Other professional wolf hunters had tried and failed. One had tracked the wolf for five years, another for four years, before giving up.[1]

With each killing the legend grew. One newspaper called the wolf "the cruelest, the most sagacious, and most successful animal outlaw" the West had ever known, and "the master criminal of the animal world." Another claimed he was the result of a mating between a wolf and a mountain lion, possessing "the craftiness of both and the cruelty of hell." Depredations had continued for so long that ranchers became convinced they would have to patiently endure livestock losses until the animal died a natural death. Yet, here was the monster—at long last dead.[2]

Despite his somberness, no one was more relieved at the wolf's demise than Williams. Seven months before, in early spring, he had received a telegram from his supervisor at the U.S. Biological Survey in Washington, D.C., directing him to go to South Dakota and stay until he had killed the Custer wolf. Even with his many years as a top government hunter in which he had trapped, shot, and poisoned over a thousand wolves throughout the West, Williams knew when he arrived in Custer that he "was in for it."

He began by learning everything he could about the animal. Like most of the last wolves holding out in scattered pockets across the West, the Custer wolf was a loner. Five years earlier, the wolf's mate and pups had been killed, and it never again ran with other wolves. Unfettered by normal pack responsibilities or territorial constraints, the wolf was believed to regularly range over three hundred square miles of southwestern South Dakota. It was even reported to have shown up in Wyoming and Nebraska.

The wolf's hunting behavior was equally aberrant, often killing or maiming far more than it needed to live. During one week the previous spring, it had killed or crippled thirty cattle, many of them with their tail sheared off at the rump, or with huge chunks of flesh torn from around their anus or vulva. Lately, the creature had developed a taste for unborn calves. Pregnant cows were found dead but otherwise intact, with the sole exception that their bellies had been ripped open, their fetus gone. In an attempt to understand such ghoulish behavior, ranchers cast about for explanations. Most agreed it could be only one thing: revenge against humans who had killed its pack mates.

Three days after he began looking, Williams discovered fresh wolf signs along a narrow ridge. The following day he returned, and with his boots covered with the scent of a female wolf, he set out steel traps designed specifically for wolves. He did this without much hope of success, having learned that over the years the Custer wolf had "sprung enough traps to stock a trading post." When Williams had first begun working for the government, wolves had been relatively easy to poison and trap. But the last ones had become extremely wary of human scent or traps. Williams believed he had a better chance of shooting the animal, as he had done with most other wolves. During his last assignment in Wyoming, he had become so expert with a rifle that ranchers joked that the initials of his first and middle name stood for "High Power."

Williams prepared the traps with extreme care. First, he boiled them for half a day, buried them in cow manure for several more days to extinguish any lingering traces of human odor, and then placed them in a cowhide bag. Approaching the trap site on his horse, he threw down a piece of cowhide with the hair side down and dismounted, being careful to step only on the hide. Then he donned leather gloves and, using a small trowel, carefully removed a disk of surface soil and placed it on one corner of the hide. Next he scooped out a shallow hole for the trap, chain, and drag hook. Using a clamp, he screwed down the trap spring until the jaws opened and he could set the trigger against the metal notch. Then he backed off the clampscrew and placed a handful of dry grass under the trigger pan. The grass prevented a lighter animal from springing the trap, which easily compressed with the weight of a wolf. He next laid a small square of beeswax-covered paper over the pan to keep out dirt, and covered the trap with soil from the deer hide, carefully brushing the edges with an old wolf tail to blend it with the surrounding soil. After he had set several traps in a similar manner, Williams remounted his horse, opened his vial of female wolf scent and sprinkled the mixture around the site. Then he rode away, being careful not to brush against the low limbs of ponderosa pine trees close to the trail that might capture his scent.

In the parlance of trappers, wolves might be caught along a commonly used trail, called a wolf run, or near a scent post—a small tree, bush, or other object where they stopped to urinate, defecate, or rub in order to mark their territory. The method Williams used was a blind set, in which traps are scattered about randomly in the hope a wolf accidentally steps into one. Once caught in the spiked teeth of the trap jaws, a wolf would run away dragging the heavy steel contraption. Eventually the drag hook fouled on brush or tree roots, bringing the animal to a tangled and exhausted halt.

Williams returned two days later to find that the wolf, as expected, had "ignored those traps like they weren't there." But the female wolf scent was another story. A short distance away, the hunter discovered that the odor had inspired the animal to tirelessly excavate a former den. Thinking the wolf might be inside, Williams crawled into the darkness with his rifle, but the den was empty.

For the next few weeks, Williams trailed the wolf. He caught a glimpse of it once from a ridge top, but while maneuvering for a shot, he spooked two nearby coyotes and the wolf fled. Several weeks later he was startled to see the wolf and coyotes again, the animals maintaining a relatively close but respectful distance from one another. Williams had observed coyotes following bears before, but never wolves, although their purpose was probably the same in either case: they had been attracted to the abundant leftovers at the wolf's kills and followed in hope of more. Instead of overcoming only one set of sharp eyes, ears, and a nose, the hunter now faced two more.

After several months, Williams began to detect a pattern in the wolf's travels. It seemed to favor one particularly isolated mountain ridge and a nearby creek. Traps he set along trails always turned up empty, although once he caught a tuft of fur when the wolf attempted to roll in a fragrantly scented mixture that Williams concocted out of the urine, gall bladder, and anal gland of another male wolf. After that close call, the wolf disappeared for ten days. When it finally reappeared, Williams decided to give up trapping and simply observe the animal, searching for a weakness in its behavior.

Through binoculars, one day he saw it surprise a small herd of horses, scattering the animals in all directions. As Williams watched in disbelief, the wolf expertly "rounded them up like a sheep dog." When they were all bunched together, the predator stared at the horses for several minutes, then, as if having accomplished what he had set out to do, calmly trotted off. Another time Williams discovered an empty beer bottle in a dry creek bed. The sand around the bottle was covered with wolf tracks. It took the hunter a few sobering moments to realize that the wolf had spent hours playing with the bottle, its sole purpose being that of standing it upright, "because that's how it was when I saw it."

Before long the animal began to watch the man. Sometimes when Williams trailed it on horseback, he would look up to see the wolf following a parallel path several hundred yards away. When he halted, the wolf halted. When he moved on, it did also. If Williams reached for his wallet or tobacco, the wolf sat down and watched. If he reached for his rifle, it disappeared before his fingers touched the gunstock.

As the months passed, Williams realized the hunt had become a game, one which he believed the wolf fully comprehended, and in truth, controlled. He began to despair of ever killing the animal, particularly when the pair of coyotes was nearby. Then one day from afar, he saw the wolf playing with an old carcass of a steer it had killed weeks earlier. The wolf soon wandered away, but the trailing coyotes lingered to investigate. Williams dismounted, crawled closer, and shot them both. Because he didn't want the wolf to discover he had killed the animals, he carried their bodies some distance away and dumped them in a deep ravine. Then he returned to the steer and set traps around the carcass. The next day he found that the wolf had discovered the coyotes and—in a feat the hunter had believed physically impossible—dragged them both out of the ravine and left them at its edge. Williams rode on to the steer. There, as if to taunt him further, the wolf had pulled the carcass over the traps, springing every one.

It gave Williams an idea, and he pulled the steer several hundred feet away. The following morning he found the carcass back in its original location. He moved it away again, making blind sets in a circle around the carcass and along the path. The next morning he returned to find where the wolf, intent on moving the carcass back again, had carelessly stepped into a trap with its left forefoot. Williams quickly followed the trap drag marks to some nearby brush. There he found the hook and chain caught on the exposed roots of a tree, but no trap and no wolf. In its great terror and speed, the animal had caused the chain's steel swivel to part, and it had run on dragging the six-pound trap.

The trail was easy to follow. Three miles away the hunter found the wolf panting, exhausted, attempting to hide in the brush, its mouth dripping blood from teeth cracked and broken in an attempt to gnaw off the steel trap. As he approached, the wolf made a final lunge away and Williams shot it dead.

Forty years later in an interview, Williams—now frail and on the verge of his own death—spoke of his feelings that day as he stood cheerless before the cameras, the carcass of the dead wolf leaning against his leg. "I remembered all the trouble and grief he'd caused. But I tell you I'd built up such a respect for the old devil that, if he hadn't had a trap on one foot, I just might not have killed him." The old hunter reflected a moment and then said, "I really think I might have let him go."

When Harry Williams killed the Custer wolf that autumn day in 1920, North America was coming to the end of the longest, most relentless, and ruthless persecution one species has ever waged against another. Altogether it was a killing like there had never been before.

It had begun in earnest three centuries earlier, directed against an animal—unlike the whale, buffalo, or passenger pigeon—not for the value of its hair, skin, or meat, but because that animal preyed upon other animals that humans desired for their own consumption. Along the way, the wolf became the object of a passionate, often irrational, sometimes brutal hatred that humans ordinarily reserve for members of their own kind. Hundreds of thousands of wolves were trapped, poisoned, shot, or dynamited in their dens, while some suffered deaths that had every visage of revenge. Caught alive and soaked with kerosene, wolves were set ablaze; others were scalped, had their mouths wired shut, or had their eyes pierced with branding irons before being released to starve to death. Still others were bound with ropes on their upper and lower jaws, tied to horses, and ripped apart.

Although wolf hatred did not originate in North America, it was here that it reached its zenith early in the twentieth century. By then, world populations of the wolf, which along with humans were once the most widely distributed land mammal on earth, had drastically declined due to human encroachment and persecution. Now federal governments themselves took up the chase. What followed was a determined, subsidized, and well-organized crusade to wipe out the final remnants of the species from a vast portion of the planet.

That this effort largely succeeded attests to the depth of human enmity toward wolves; that it ultimately failed is due partly to a reversal of this enmity, but perhaps more to the incredible tenacity of the animal itself. Nevertheless, before it ended, wolves—having once left tracks from Florida's coast to the beaches of Puget Sound, from Aztec ruins in Mexico to the boreal forests of Saskatchewan—vanished from over half of their original range. In numbers, for every twenty wolves that once roamed North America, by the mid-twentieth century less than one remained.

What made this pogrom particularly effective was the dedication and determination of the men who carried it out, almost all of whom by the end were professional government hunters like Harry Williams. Unlike ranchers and farmers who suffered wolf depredations, few hunters actually hated the animal. In fact, as they pursued the final animals, many of them developed lasting respect for their victims. As with the Custer wolf, near-human characteristics were often assigned to them. In turn, these qualities earned certain wolves notorious—some would say mythic—reputations as "outlaws," "thieves," "monsters," "killers," "criminals," or "beasts." Often they were the final wolves of a particular locale, but sometimes they were only the best known. Wolves who were highly secretive and avoided preying on domestic stock may have managed to survive a little longer. Eventually, however, the hatred and attention drawn by the more infamous wolves also doomed these animals. Today the human hunters are long forgotten, and the obscure and colorless names of some of the last hunted—Rags the Digger, Bigfoot, Snowdrift, Three Toes, Phantom, Old Lefty—belie the great fear and hatred these animals once evoked, ghostly but vivid memories that today still haunt stock owners generations removed from the wolves' depredations.[3]

It's difficult to separate truth from fantasy in many of the stories told about the last wolves, but nearly all of them were said to share certain characteristics: exceptional intelligence, long life, excess killing and maiming of prey, extended territories, and the trait that made them so difficult to track down and kill, solitariness.

Wolves are highly social animals. Under normal conditions, they usually live in groups of two or more, yet lone wolves are not uncommon. Often these are dispersing subadults or wolves that for unknown reasons have been ostracized from a pack. By contrast, the last wolves were frequently alone because all other wolves of a particular region had been eradicated. But strangely, some wolves—often in close proximity to others—were believed to prefer to live alone, particularly after a mate or fellow pack members had been killed.[4]

Without the companionship of those of its own species, the loner abandoned the single most vulnerable behavior so successfully exploited by their human pursuers: orderliness. No longer did the wolf range methodically and therefore predictably over the same territory and trails. Nor did it confine its activities during late winter and early spring to a restricted denning area where it could be more readily located. Instead, a lone wolf was almost constantly on the move, rarely killing or sleeping twice in the same place, often ranging randomly over an ill-defined territory that had doubled, tripled, or quadrupled in size now that boundaries maintained by former packs had disappeared. One of the last Oklahoma wolves, Traveler, was said to be particularly adept at evading human pursuers by killing, eating rapidly, and then traveling as much as forty or fifty miles before repeating its performance the following night.

What provoked (and still provokes) the most outrage from stock owners, and perhaps more than any other trait sealed the fate of the last wolves, was their penchant for excess or what some biologists today term "surplus" killing. Wolves, as well as certain other predators, occasionally kill beyond their immediate needs. Under natural conditions this behavior is relatively uncommon but can occur when wolf packs are confined to limited hunting territories during denning season and are in need of a continuous supply of food for their young. It may also happen for no apparent reason when prey animals are particularly abundant and vulnerable.[5]

Judged by turn-of-the-century stories, surplus killings appeared more frequently when wolves preyed on domestic stock. Often victims went uneaten or only partially so. Sometimes this was the result of the carcass being discovered by humans before the wolf returned, but often the predator simply never came back. During one night in 1919, the Aguila wolf of southwest Arizona was said to have killed sixty-five sheep, at another time, forty sheep. Three Toes, a wolf of northwest South Dakota who had previously lost a toe to a trap, allegedly killed twenty cattle during a single night and sixty-six sheep during a subsequent two-night rampage. By the time it was finally trapped in 1925, ranchers claimed it had destroyed hundreds of livestock worth $50,000, the greatest economic loss ever attributed to a single wolf.[6]

For many years after wolves were gone, these and other tales were used to describe their inherently savage nature, as well as to justify the methods deemed necessary to destroy them. Today many people disbelieve them. Stock owners of this period, say critics, exaggerated their losses to gain support for eradication programs. They also point to modern-day studies which show that wolves infrequently kill livestock, or they proclaim that there is no way to prove that a particular wolf was responsible for certain deaths.[7] Probably no one will ever know the truth. Records were kept, if they were kept at all, by stock owners, not dispassionate observers. But circumstances then were vastly different from today. Bereft of their traditional wild prey, pursued tirelessly by human hunters, deprived of the society of other wolves, and wholly conditioned to feeding on domestic animals, the last wolves may have been entirely capable of inflicting such death.

Instead of mass death, sometimes a wolf killed a single victim every day or two, ate only the choicest portions, then abandoned the remainder of the carcass. This behavior proved to be a particularly successful survival strategy. By feeding only on fresh kills, the wolf never risked returning to hidden traps or poisoned meat.

Occasionally a wolf maimed a victim instead of killing it, although the wound frequently resulted in the victim's death. Bobtailing was perhaps the most common injury, but ears, noses, or even genitalia were often special targets of a wolf's slashing canine teeth—cows were found udderless, prized bulls were found with cleanly severed testicles. To the horror of ranchers and the public alike, wolves sometimes fed on their prey while it was yet alive, leaving the victim with disembowled entrails or huge chunks of missing muscle, and hours or even days passed before death relieved its agony.

Another reason why domestic animals may be particularly susceptible to surplus killing or maiming is the manner in which they react to the presence of wolves. Depending on the behavior of a potential prey (interpreted by a wolf as either fear or resistance) the wolf may choose to attack or move on. Author Barry Lopez describes this subtle communication between predator and prey as the "conversation of death." Unlike most wild prey, domestic animals such as sheep appear to have lost the ability to communicate anything but naked fear in the presence of a wolf. The result, says Lopez, is "not so much slaughter as a failure on the part of the sheep to communicate anything at all—resistance, mutual respect, appropriateness—to the wolf."[8]

Unconcerned with how or why surplus killing occurs, or even in what manner human actions may have contributed to this behavior, enraged stock owners saw only wanton carnage. Such a wolf was frequently labeled a "vicious, fanged mass murderer," or a "sullen killer who drew blood for the love of it." Until relatively recently, some biologists added their voices to this defamation by explaining away such behavior as "sport" or "recreation," implying the animals should have known better. It was these "malicious" eccentricities that made the last wolves responsible for their own fate, declared Stanley Young, a top government biologist and administrator who played a major role in their eradication. "Man has won. The wilderness killers have lost. They have written their own death warrants in killing, torture, blood lust, almost fiendish cruelty." When Young published these words, first in 1929 and then again as recently as 1970, they went unchallenged, still so convinced were most people that the actions of wolves were accountable to a standard no different from their own.[9]

Even as the last wolves sometimes killed domestic animals in excess of their needs, they also preferred the taste of some animals over others. Swine, turkeys, chickens, goats, sheep, geese, ducks, dogs, horses, cattle, any one animal might prove to be the pièce de résistance for a particular wolf. But most often wolves, as with wild prey, preferred large animals—sheep, cattle, and to a lesser degree, horses and mules, as well as the young of these animals. Although the Custer wolf's predilection for unborn young was uncommon among the last wolves, this behavior was known decades earlier when buffalo were plentiful. Some wolves could be quite discriminating. Montana's Pryor Creek wolf was described as being especially fond of Shetland ponies.[10]

Most of the last wolves were white, but few, if any, had been white their entire lives—their pelage color was usually due to old age. Under natural conditions today, a wolf rarely survives more than a single decade. Many of the last wolves, however, were said to have lived considerably longer. The Sycan wolf of southern Oregon, twelve years old; South Dakota's Three Toes, thirteen; Rags the Digger and Old Whitey of Colorado, fourteen and fifteen, respectively. Perhaps the oldest was the White Wolf, alleged to have lived for eighteen years and caused $35,000 worth of stock loss to ranchers before it was finally killed in central Montana in 1930. Mounted by a taxidermist, the gaunt, nearly decrepit eighty-three-pound wolf still snarls at passersby from a glass case inside the local county courthouse.[11]

Stock owners and biologists alike determined the ages of the last wolves based on the length of time they were suspected of having killed in a certain area, the victims they favored, and their manner of killing. Signs frequently identified the culprit. Old Lefty of Burns Hole, Colorado, chewed off its left forefoot after being caught in a trap in 1913. Eight years and 384 cattle later, ranchers claimed they had become quite familiar with the wolf's three-legged track. Another Colorado wolf made a print so large that it barely fit inside a no. 2 horseshoe, earning it the moniker Big Foot. Sometimes wolves were identified by how they killed. Older wolves, possessing teeth worn to the gum line and missing canines with which to pierce and tear, resorted to strangling their victims, evidenced by a crushed and saliva-covered throat. Trappers referred to such wolves as "gummers."[12]

Sometimes a wolf was said to have survived into old age despite great physical disability. In 1938 a twelve-year-old, one-hundred-forty-pound Minnesota wolf known as Lobo, the Killer Wolf of the North, was finally killed by a man who had lost the animal to a broken wire snare two years before. The trapper was astonished to discover that the wire was not only still wrapped around the neck of the wolf, but it had partially severed the windpipe, severely retarding the animal's ability to both breathe and swallow.[13]

Although the ages of some of these last wolves may have been correct, such a method of determination was at best subjective, haphazard, and prone to the same hyperbole that often afflicted tales of their depredations. (When modern-day taxonomists recently examined the skull of one notorious wolf, Three Toes, they estimated the animal was no more than six to eight years old when it died.) Today, the most we can say with assurance is that some of the last wolves may have lived to be quite old, a condition that doubtless contributed to the ease with which most of them were finally killed.

But age or, more accurately, the wisdom that accompanies age, is also what kept wolves alive for so many years. With every passing season, they gained additional knowledge of their environment, and that knowledge extended their years even longer. In truth, the extent of their intelligence is what human hunters found most disconcerting about the last wolves. Even as they sought their destruction, many considered them "possessed of near human intelligence," according to Stanley Young, one so refined and subtle that it "at times caused the greatest wonderment."[14]

Wolf hunters reported numerous examples of the animal's intelligence, but its relationship to the raven—arguably the most intelligent bird— serves as an illustration. At times both animals appear to enjoy a mutually beneficial relationship. Ravens may signal wolves concerning potential prey, and wolves often allow ravens unchallenged access to their kills. The two species even occasionally may play a game of tag, the raven pestering wolves and, in turn, being chased by them. This game took an elegant but deadly twist in Alaska during the winter of 1921, when a wolf hunter happened upon three unsuspecting wolves. Above their heads flew a single raven. As the man was about to shoot, he saw one of the wolves "suddenly swerve a little, and his body stiffen, and his legs, seemingly paralyzed, slither from beneath him, and in an instant he was lying stark and stiff on the ice." The other wolves proceeded on without slowing. The hunter lowered his gun and as he watched, the raven landed near the wolf, hopped over, and pecked once at the prone animal. Before it could repeat this action, "the cruel jaws of the waiting wolf snapped upon the hapless raven and he was killed." The hunter then shot the wolf.[15]

Among hunters, wolf intelligence was defined most often as the animal's extraordinary ability to elude capture. Again, the truth of such tales is elusive, since outwitting such a creature inherently reflected the superior intelligence of the captor over the captive—the smarter the wolf, the more respect for the hunter. But the stories appear too frequently to entirely discount them to human vanity.

When traps set along a path managed to catch a lead wolf yet none of the trailing pack members, trappers discovered that the surviving animals quickly learned to give the victim a wide berth and forgo further use of the trail. Trappers also reported setting concealed traps along a trail and later returning to discover wolf tracks leading into the trap location, then mysteriously disappearing. A close examination revealed that the wolf had detected the traps, halted, and carefully backtracked using precisely the same footprints it had used going into the area. Some wolves were even adept at carefully excavating a trap, picking it up by their mouth and removing it from their path, all without disturbing the delicate trigger mechanism. It was also not uncommon for a trapper to carefully conceal a dozen traps one day, only to return the following morning and—it would have been comical had it not been so insulting—find them all sprung, piled in a heap, and freshly crowned with wolf excrement. Of course, wolves may treat any unfamiliar or foreign object within their territory in such a manner, but trappers chose to believe such behavior expressed nothing less than the animal's vile contempt for humankind.[16]

Intelligence plus endurance rendered some wolves seemingly indestructible. In central Saskatchewan during the mid-nineteenth century, a large, dark wolf caught by the hind foot in a steel trap was portrayed as dragging both the trap and a chain attached to a heavy log for some ninety miles through deep snow before being shot. In another instance in Upper Michigan in the 1920s, a dozen men claimed to have trailed a particularly notorious wolf for four days before shooting and wounding it. The wolf redoubled its efforts. After two grueling weeks, sometimes following at night with lanterns, the men finally killed it.[17]

During the spring of 1921, following the demise of the Custer wolf, a government trapper named W. J. Nearing started on the trail of Phantom, a large, elusive female wolf who ranged throughout the White River country of western Colorado. Nearing tracked the animal to its den, dug out its pups, and killed all but one, which he tied alive to a stake surrounded with traps. When he returned, he found the traps undisturbed but the pup dead, having been "ripped to shreds." Nearing claimed that signs showed the mother wolf had carefully stepped around the traps, attempted to sever the collar from the pup, and, failing that, had killed it. A year later during denning season, Nearing surprised the wolf and shot her. She rolled once, staggered to her feet, and then collapsed. As Nearing approached, he stopped to collect her pups and stuff them back into the den, covering the entrance with his coat until he could return to kill them. When he turned to where the wolf lay, she was gone. The following year at another den site, Nearing claimed to have finally killed her, but most sheepherders in the area believed his victim was another wolf, not Phantom.[18]

Ernest Thompson Seton, the early twentieth century naturalist and writer who had also been a professional wolf hunter, preferred to attribute wolves' intelligence to their innate shyness, although he admitted shyness failed to entirely explain why the last wolves were so difficult to trap, poison, or shoot. In the beginning, he said, they were easy to kill and great numbers of them fell until "the species seemed on the verge of extinction." But after 1890, something happened to the survivors. These wolves had survived poisoning or managed to "get into a trap and out again, and thus learn that a steel trap is a thing to be feared." Only a few were so lucky. Yet all wolves seem to have this knowledge about traps and poison, said Seton, almost as if "the information was communicated to them by others of their kind." How this might be done was not easy to say, pondered the troubled naturalist, observing that it was far easier "to prove that it *is* done."[19]

Of one thing Seton was certain. If the last wolves possessed a high level of intelligence, it was "the result of our continual warfare against them." By declaring "bitter, exterminatory war, we have evolved a creature that for long has defied us."

Most stock owners agreed. Quipped one frustrated Colorado rancher in the early 1920s, "Wolves have all been trapped at, shot at, and poisoned at so long that they can damn near speak English!"[20]

None of the last wolves survived long enough to prove Seton right or wrong. To the specter of the rancher, the most we can say today is that wolves have yet to learn the language of humans, while we, if only in the most primitive fashion, have begun listening to theirs.

2

EARLY ENCOUNTERS

The story of the wolf begins with teeth, ones the world had never seen before: specialized, highly adapted, shearing teeth—the carnassials—common to wolves and other carnivores.

To kill an animal, a wolf uses the front part of its mouth. Piercing canines and sharp incisors are a formidable package of death delivered by the muscular force of the bite. After the kill, the bladelike carnassials take over. These teeth first appeared in early mammals, known as Miacidae, some 55 million years ago. They consist of the upper last premolar and lower first molar and are used to shear through flesh and slice off bite-sized morsels of muscle. The carnassials' position is critical, falling about halfway along the jaw, making them a kind of efficient toothy fulcrum. Wolves chew off pieces of meat on only one side at a time, exerting maximum force on the object. Food then passes to the molars for chewing, mixing with saliva before being swallowed. Unlike cats, which lack chewing molars and bolt chunks of meat directly to the stomach, wolves and other canids ingest a variety of foods: meat, bone, sinew, invertebrates, and plants—sustenance that allows them greater versatility and, if their worldwide success is any measure, greater evolutionary advantage.[1]

The wolf family's first recognizable ancestor appeared in the Oligocene between 38 and 22 million years ago. During the following epoch, the Miocene, canids known as *Tomarctus* arose possessing traits unique from those of other contemporary carnivores: a smaller tail, relatively long feet and legs, a reduced fifth digit, and except for its shortened muzzle, a physical size and appearance not unlike modern wolves. *Tomarctus* was extremely long lived, surviving until only a few million years ago. Midway during the Pliocene it gave rise to the genus, *Canis,* which today includes the various species of wolves, jackals, and wild dogs.[2]

Canids appear to have first evolved in North America before spreading throughout the Northern Hemisphere. About one million years ago— nearly midway through the Pleistocene—a coyote-sized canid living in what is now Texas began to develop a larger body with more massive jaws and teeth. Little is known about this first wolflike animal except that it was rather small compared to modern wolves and possessed a longer muzzle and larger brain than its predecessors, probably an animal quite similar in shape and size (and possibly lineage) to the red wolf (*Canis rufus*) of today. After spreading across the continent, this early wolf took advantage of the exposed land bridge, known as Beringia, that occasionally surfaced between North America and Eurasia during glacial periods, and managed to migrate to the Old World. There the wolf evolved into a number of races or subspecies. One of these was a small, buff-colored wolf (*Canis lupus pallipes*) that still exists today throughout portions of the Middle East and closely resembles the red wolf of North America. Another subspecies farther north in Eurasia was the probable progenitor of today's gray wolf (*Canis lupus*). Between 600,000 and 300,000 years ago the modern wolf began its successful diaspora throughout Eurasia. When Beringia became exposed during subsequent glacial periods, *lupus* lost little time crossing back to the New World. There it appears to have gotten a toehold in unglaciated refugia of Alaska. During subsequent warm periods, it ventured through ice-free corridors to the tundra and grasslands just south of the glaciers near the present-day border between Canada and the United States. In that region it encountered another successful offshoot of the red wolf line, one that had evolved in the New World while the gray wolf was developing in Eurasia: the dire wolf (*Canis dirus*).[3]

Despite the ominousness conjured by its name, if the dire wolf were alive today we would be hard pressed to identify it from a modern-day wolf, at least at a distance. Paleontologists had the same difficulty when they uncovered the first fossils on the banks of the Ohio River in the early 1850s. It soon became apparent, however, that *dirus* was some 20 percent larger than the modern-day wolf, with a heavier jaw and tremendous teeth. Somewhat small limbs relative to its overall weight and massive head have led scientists to surmise that *dirus* may have been quicker and stronger at short distances, but lacked the long-distance endurance possessed by its smaller cousin.[4]

The dire wolf appears to have evolved in South America, and its fossil remains have been found as far south as the pampas of Argentina. Eventually it headed north into Mexico, and by some 100,000 years ago it ranged widely and abundantly throughout most of unglaciated North America. Here it encountered gray wolves, but also two smaller native canids: the red wolf and the coyote (*Canis latrans*). By now both coyotes and red wolves had developed certain physical characteristics that readily distinguished them from both gray and dire wolves: a significantly reduced body size, and a longer and narrower jaw. Both animals also killed small-sized prey, occupied a smaller territory, and appear to have hunted either alone or in small packs. Because the coyote and red wolf weren't directly competitive with either the dire or gray wolf, they managed to survive out of their way.

The relationship between gray and dire wolves is less clear, and it's difficult to know how competitive the two species may have been. Where their ranges overlapped, there was a tendency for *lupus* to become smaller, an indication that it gave way ecologically to the dire wolf. The two species may have occasionally interbred, but probably no more than wolves and coyotes today, both of whom under natural conditions generally avoid one another. At the same time, *lupus* appears to have maintained a genetic contact with the Eurasian wolf via Beringia, at least enough to guarantee survival into modern times as a single species. There are also indications that gray wolves from northern North America invaded the southern part of the continent more than once, since fossil remains of both large and small gray wolves have been found as far south as Mexico. Today, the continent's largest gray wolves occur in northern latitudes, while the smallest subspecies are found at the eastern and southern periphery of its range, possibly remnants of the first migrations where gray wolves competed with dire wolves. This relationship between the two species might still be the case today if the dire wolf had not met its demise during one of the most massive and mysterious extinctions in ecological history.[5]

After over a century and a half of investigation, scientists still know far more about the results of this extinction than its causes. During the final two millennia of the Pleistocene, some 12,000 to 10,000 years ago, great numbers of North American mammals—a whopping two hundred species, representing two out of every three large mammals—simply vanished. Many were immense plant-eating megaherbivores: mammoths, mastodons, long-legged camels, giant sloths and armadillos, and a beaver the size of a small bear. But there were also predators of prodigious size and ferocity: the sabertooth tiger, American lion, dire wolf, American cheetah, and perhaps the most formidable terrestrial mammalian carnivore that ever lived, the giant short-faced bear. Some biologists believe that the unprecedented human expansion that followed the Ice Age extinctions could not have happened had the short-faced bear—a swift runner, tall as a modern-day moose, and entirely capable of preying on humans—survived.[6]

Why did these animals disappear? Theories abound, but most point to early human hunting, climate change, or a combination of both. Probably not coincidentally, archaeologists have determined that at the same time these extinctions occurred, North America became occupied by humans whose fluted spear points have been found among numerous mammalian remains. These people, known as Paleo-Indians, were the first to successfully settle North America, although other less robust and less numerous humans appear to have tenuously inhabited portions of the continent many thousands of years earlier. The "overkill" theory proposes that Paleo-Indians crossed Beringia 14,000 to 12,000 years ago and stumbled on a hunter's "garden of Eden" populated by 50 million to 100 million megaherbivores unused to sophisticated human predation. The blitzkrieg that followed enabled humans to spread throughout the hemisphere and left many animal extinctions in its wake. Another theory claims that following a period of relatively stable rainfall and temperature, the climate of North America suddenly turned inclement. Megaherbivores and their predators couldn't adjust quickly enough and died. Still another theory, perhaps the most likely, maintains that the extinctions were the result of both climate *and* human predation, although most scientists believe climate probably played the greater role.[7]

Of the large predators who vanished, the dire wolf hung on longer than most, the last specimens disappearing about 8,500 years ago. Built more for power than speed, and used to preying on relatively sedentary megaherbivores, *dirus* simply may have been unable to catch the smaller and faster ungulates that ascended as larger ones disappeared. The dire wolf also may not have possessed the efficient social behaviorism of *lupus,* being less tolerant and more aggressive toward members of its own species. In terms of modern scavengers, it may best be compared to hyenas. Although no one knows for sure, it appears to have hunted in large packs that were possibly less mobile and far-ranging than modern wolves. As its prey grew increasingly scarce, it may have resorted more and more to scavenging, a survival strategy considered less versatile than that practiced by self-supporting carnivores. If true, scavenging became a dead end when megaherbivores disappeared altogether. A preponderance of dire wolf fossils—1,646—over other predators have been recovered at Rancho La Brea tar pits in California, indicating *dirus* was drawn by trapped animals, and, in turn, became trapped itself. Scientists studying the teeth of predators at La Brea report increased tooth breakage during the period of extinction, implying that as megaherbivores declined, large carnivores like the dire wolf were forced to make increasing use of their bones.[8]

Ultimately, *lupus* may have survived and eclipsed *dirus* because it was fast while the dire wolf was slow. There may be more than a little truth to the Russian proverb: "The wolf is kept fed by his feet."

As extinctions ravaged the great populations of large herbivores and their traditional predators, smaller ungulates like deer, elk, bison, moose, antelope, mountain sheep, and caribou not only survived but began to thrive, filling the ecological niches left by the huge beasts. At the same time, two species rose to the position of top predator: humans and modern-day wolves. In the abundant grasslands of the continent's mid-section each one's primary quarry became the modern bison, while in the tundra and forests to the north, they preyed on caribou, and to the south, east, and west, deer.

Given this potential for conflict, the question arises why humans and wolves were not evolutionarily, and thus literally, at each other's throats. Competition between the two predators doubtlessly occurred from time to time, but it appears to have been minimal. One reason may have been the astonishing abundance of available prey; there was more than enough to go around. The central grasslands alone are believed to have harbored the greatest number of hoofed animals since the mass extinctions of the Pleistocene, perhaps rivaled only by those of the great African savannahs. According to one estimate, over this rich prairie, mountain, and basin biome roamed some 57 million hoofed animals. Bison or buffalo accounted for most (40 million), followed by antelope (9 million), deer (3.6 million), elk and bighorn sheep (2 million each). Although this vast number of prey probably fluctuated periodically during the past 10,000 years, it appears to have remained fundamentally unaltered until increasing numbers of Europeans began arriving on the continent 400 years ago. Today this grassland biome is virtually gone, and only about 8 percent of the hoofed wild animals, primarily deer, still survive. Take away deer and the number drops to less than 2 percent of the original number of wild ungulates.[9]

Until recently, early North Americans were thought to have been simply the lucky beneficiaries of this prairie wealth. But there is increasing evidence that the grasslands were, to a great degree, manufactured. The instrument was fire, much more than can be attributed to lightning alone. Apparently, Paleo-Indians cleared land and drove game herds by regularly torching the prairies, thus perpetuating a rich and successional grassland ecosystem that otherwise would have supported far fewer ungulates. The vast animal herds, predominantly buffalo, simply followed the grass, forever shifting and migrating across the immense prairies. Following closely, their depredations encouraging the herds' unceasing movements, were nomadic human hunters and wolves.

Of course, wolves did not inhabit only the continent's grasslands. Like humans they lived wherever they found suitable prey, from arctic tundra to desert and, in the case of red wolves, the humid subtropical wetlands and piedmont of what is today the southeastern United States. By the time of Columbus, wolves occupied nearly the entire continent with the exception of present-day central California, southern Mexico, Central America, and the Greenland icecap—a nearly 8.5 million-square-mile range encompassing about 90 percent of North America. With the exception of humans, probably no other land mammal inhabited so much of the continent or occupied so many different environments.[10]

Such widespread ecological diversity was reflected in wolf evolution. Based primarily on minor differences in skull measurements and often a limited number of specimens, taxonomists once identified as many as twenty-four subspecies or races of New World gray wolves, and three subspecies of the less numerous red wolf. There is a growing consensus among scientists today, however, that wolves are more peripatetic than previously thought. Thus they are capable of spreading their genes great distances, interbreeding frequently enough with one another to make such a large number of distinct races improbable. More likely, only one species of red wolf and five subspecies of gray wolf are truly valid. In the case of gray wolves, the largest are found in Alaska and western Canada (*occidentalis*), and the smallest in southeastern Canada (*lycaon*) and the Southwest United States and Mexico (*baileyi*). More moderately sized wolves live in the eastern Canadian arctic (*arctos*) and across the central portion of the continent from the Pacific Ocean to Hudson Bay (*nubilus*).[11]

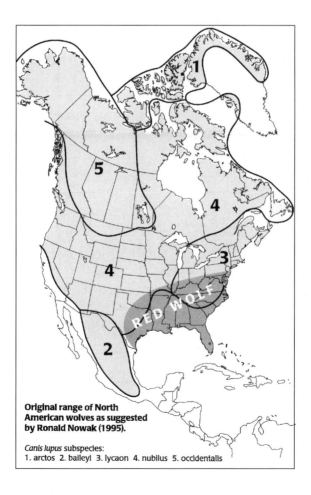

Original range of North American wolves as suggested by Ronald Nowak (1995).

Canis lupus subspecies:
1. arctos 2. baileyi 3. lycaon 4. nubilus 5. occidentalis

The first estimate of the continent's pre-Columbian wolf population was made in 1925 by Ernest Thompson Seton, who set the number at two million. Since offering that figure (one he termed "conservative"), it has often been repeated, particularly by present-day wolf advocates eager to demonstrate how far wolf populations have plummeted during recent times. Seton based this number on his own crude estimate of available prey for wolves, a technique used by subsequent estimators as well.[12] But determining the population of wolves solely on prey numbers—even if those numbers were accurate—is imprecise, for it assumes prey were equally vulnerable at all times of the year. It also doesn't account for periodic prey fluctuations due to climate, seasonal migrations, competition with other predators (including humans), or the tendency of wolves to select prey of a particular species, age, or sex. Above all, it ignores the wolf's innate behavior mechanisms that tend to limit the number of wolves inhabiting a particular geographic area, regardless of prey abundance.

In the decades since Seton, biologists have determined that gray wolf density varies considerably, averaging a low of about one wolf per 61 square miles to a high of one per 10 square miles, with a mean density of about one wolf every 24 square miles. Although today's densities may not be entirely analogous to those of the past, they provide a rough, but reasonable, comparison. The central plains and prairies with their tremendous numbers of large prey animals probably supported the highest density of wolves (possibly as many as 1 wolf per 6 square miles), yet these grasslands made up no more than about one-seventh of wolf range in North America. Less productive areas comprised the remainder of the continent and doubtless sustained far fewer wolves. In the high arctic where prey is generally scarce, for example, wolves are known to inhabit as much as 500 or more square miles per wolf. Based on the range of average densities, North America was home to as few as 140,000 or as many as 850,000 wolves. More likely, however, the continent at the peak of abundance never supported more than about 400,000 wolves.[13]

As top predators, both humans and wolves evolved the most successful means to capitalize on the continent's wealth of prey. In short, by traveling parallel paths, the two species arrived at the same solution of how not only to survive, but flourish.

The resemblance is haunting.

Both humans and wolves lived primarily in small, cooperative family units. Each one's offspring required long periods of learning, spending relatively similar portions of their lives as infants and subadults. Group members shared food with one another, young and old alike. Both species were highly individualistic, with identifiable personality traits. Loners were uncommon, and if they persisted in antisocial behavior were often ostracized by the group. Both practiced elaborate ceremonial rituals, gathering and singing before hunting, after eating, or at other occasions, thus promoting group cohesion. Social order was maintained by a hierarchical system based on the subordination of followers to a leader, but decisions were often made by general consensus with a supreme value placed on overall group welfare. Aggression occurred toward unfamiliar individuals and in defense of territory, yet was rare among group members. Both species were generally self-regulatory in their populations, avoided other groups' territories, and demonstrated great adaptability regarding climate, habitat, and food sources.[14]

As revealing as these similarities are, it is in the hunt that the symmetry between early humans and wolves truly startles the imagination. Besides seeking identical prey, each occupied and repeatedly hunted comparable areas; a pack of ten wolves and an extended family group of twenty-five humans generally inhabited the same-sized territory. Like wolf packs, human groups might break apart to hunt separately and more efficiently at certain times of the year, then re-form later. Each was capable of extreme physical exertion over long periods. Before the development of the bow and arrow, absolute cooperation was the only means for humans to kill large prey. This led to sophisticated hunting techniques shared by both species: ambushing, driving, encirclement, blocking of escape routes, and relay pursuit, all which require a high level of intelligence and coordination among group members.[15]

It's entirely possible that these similar hunting strategies arose separately in each species, the inevitable result of intelligent predators responding to nearly identical environmental demands. But the fact that both wolves and Paleo-Indians spread more or less concurrently throughout North America, while at the same time pursuing the same prey in the same manner, raises the intriguing notion that imitation may have played a role. Scientists who dispute this possibility insist that no direct proof of such a relationship exists. Nevertheless, surviving ancient oral histories and creation myths of several Native American peoples—Caddo, Ojibwa, Sioux, Tonkawa, and Cheyenne—attribute the wolf with having taught their ancestors how to hunt.

The idea of conscious imitation has profound implications that extend beyond similarities in social behavior, going to the very heart of what we humans believe separates us from other animals. Wolves (and several other predator species) possess what some scientists term a "cognitive map" of hunting territory, an intelligence advantageous to any predator who ranges repeatedly over large areas in pursuit of prey. As wolves regularly traverse territory along familiar routes, they may occasionally choose a new and more direct path to a destination, thus suggesting that they possess a "map" of a particular geographic area. Even in unfamiliar territory, wolves have demonstrated an uncanny—almost eerie—ability to rapidly learn new landscapes and select optimum travel routes. Wolves moving south from Canada into western Montana today frequently choose the same "runs" identified as those used by former wolves decades before, suggesting an ability to recognize prime wolf habitat. It's entirely likely, believe some anthropologists, that it was this same selective advantage of cognitive mapping, so critical to hunting success, that fostered the need for ever greater communication in early humans. Lacking the wolf's rich olfactory abilities, humans instead utilized sound, and perhaps to a lesser degree visual signals, to identify and communicate directions, objects, places, and hunting strategies.[16]

In a word, the ways of wolves may well have started humans along the path to a more richly textured language. These and other similarities have led some observers to conclude that, in many respects, wolves are a more appropriate model than primates in understanding the foundations of human behavior.

Looking back, it seems impossible that two species with so much in common could long remain apart. So it happened that wolves and humans came to live with one another. Precisely how this alliance began is the subject of endless speculation. Before they became successful hunters, were humans primarily scavengers? Did they follow wolves, chase them from their kills, and hungrily devour the leftovers? If so, once humans became proficient hunters, the roles reversed. Wolves proved to be as opportunistic as humans, becoming a common sight both at kills and the edge of camps as they hung about awaiting scraps. These wolves may have also alerted humans whenever anyone or anything approached. This relationship may have grown infinitely more complex with wolves learning to lead humans to game, as sometimes ravens in hope of a meal appear to signal wolves the whereabouts of potential prey. Within certain early human cultures, such a mutually beneficial relationship may have been nurtured with wolves protected and revered as totem animals, a liaison not unlike some Native American cultures had in their recent past or still have today. How much wolves and early humans associated with one another is unknown, but it's clear that a human eventually touched a live wolf (likely a captured pup) and a bond was born between two species that forever changed the world.

Just when the first wolves called dogs became domesticated is uncertain, but fossil evidence discovered in the Middle East goes back at least 12,000 years. Domestication appears to have happened at several places and times as well. Three thousand years later, dogs began commonly showing up on both Eurasian and American continents, from present-day England to Illinois. Since the earliest North American dog fossils unearthed in a cave in eastern Idaho are 10,400 years old, most authorities believe that dogs arrived in North America with early Paleo-Indians. Based on rather obscure and circumstantial evidence in Alaska, some authorities believe they may go back even farther, perhaps as much as 20,000 years. By comparison, other early animal domestications—donkeys, sheep, pigs, and goats—didn't appear until some 9,000 years ago. Cattle survived in their wild state a few thousand years more, and horses even longer. All of these latter domestications occurred elsewhere than North America; here only the dog was tamed.[17]

However ancient this relationship eventually may prove to be, anthropologists are fairly certain that overland explorations by early humans, particularly those throughout North America, were carried out mainly on the backs of ex-wolves. When Spanish conquistadors entered the American Southwest in the 1500s, they were startled to discover nomadic tribes traveling about with as many as five hundred dogs. While people walked, dogs carried skins, food, utensils, and all other camp paraphernalia either in packs or dragged in travois. During hunts dogs often chased game and brought it to bay for hunters to kill. At night they guarded the camp, growling and barking at intruders. Surprise gave way to repugnance when the Spanish learned that the meat floating in the stew these nomads offered them was none other than yesterday's beast of burden.[18]

For unknown reasons, the earliest dogs appear to have been smaller than today's average breed. Four 8,500-year-old skeletons unearthed near Eldred, Illinois, indicate dogs were about the size of fox terriers. Soon dogs became larger, the result of selective breeding by humans, but also continuous back-breeding to both wild and captive wolves. The early nineteenth-century explorer Prince Alexander Maxmilian zu Wied observed the near wolflike appearance of some Mandan Indian dogs, remarking that "many of them were perfectly similar to the wolf in form, size and colour" due to the fact that "they partially descend from wolves, which approach the Indian huts, even in the daytime, and mix with the dogs. . . ." During John James Audubon's ascent up the Missouri River in 1843, he noted that the Assiniboin possessed "both wolves and their crosses with the common dog in their trains, and their dog carts were drawn alike by both" animals. Frontier artist Paul Kane described the dogs he saw in Canada as "very like wolves, both in appearance and disposition, and are, no doubt, a crossbreed between the wolf and the dog." In the Pacific Northwest, Alexander Ross observed that Indian dogs "are in general of the wolf-breed, and are said to be vigorous and long winded; a hundred miles a day is a common journey for them." So valued were these animals that Ross and other fur traders bought them for five pounds sterling—double the price of a horse.[19]

Contemporary archaeological evidence supports these and other early observations that dogs didn't remain entirely isolated when they branched off from wolves thousands of years ago, but have been periodically recharged with wolf genes, making re-domestication a continual effort. Although some scientists still consider the dog a separate species, most agree with the Smithsonian Institution's recent reclassification of dogs from their own species, formerly *Canis familiaris,* to *Canis lupus familiaris,* a subspecies of the wolf.[20]

Why Native Americans periodically bred their dogs with wolves remains a mystery, since first generation wolf-dog hybrids can be high-strung and difficult to train, often unpredictable and perhaps even dangerous. One reason may have been that they wanted a larger animal to carry heavy loads. Dogs were strictly work animals, not pets, and their owners were less concerned with an animal's submissiveness than is desired today.

Dogs may be wolves; nevertheless, they differ in important ways: shorter snouts, a jaw with smaller and more crowded teeth, and prominent, broader foreheads—all morphologic changes that modern-day humans have evolved as well. Compared to wolves, dogs have no scent-marking tail gland and usually possess smaller feet. Nor is their bite as powerful as a wolf's, whose jaws can exert a pressure of 1,500 pounds per square inch, compared to a German shepherd capable of only half that amount. Dogs also have smaller brains, and although the measurement of intelligence is arguable, they're generally considered less endowed than their wild cousins. Yet they often exhibit greater fearlessness, a quality that when mixed with intelligence serves up a potentially deadly combination that more than one present-day owner of a wolf-dog hybrid has come to rue. Dogs also are prolific breeders, females reaching sexual maturity at six months and estrus every six months thereafter. In contrast, wolves generally don't reproduce until they are two or three years old, and then they are capable of producing only a single litter each year. Perhaps most important to the success of dogs, however, is the fact that they were able to transfer to humans the social behavior they once displayed as wolves. As many dog owners sense, the bonds between a dog and its human family aren't dissimilar from those found among members of wolf packs.

Until recently, humans have taken a rather one-sided view of this process, maintaining that dogs and other domesticated animals were entirely the result of human artifice, the inevitable subjugation of nature to human purpose. Few people have questioned this view since Thomas Aquinas, Roman Catholic saint and philosopher of the Middle Ages, wrote that God placed animals on earth for the use of humans. Another obstacle to understanding domestication has been science itself. Traditional evolutionary thought tends to focus on individual species in describing their evolutionary journey, often ignoring species interaction.[21]

Scientists today speak of "coevolution," or how species affect one another as they evolve. What they've learned is that domestication is more complex than just one species' exploitation of another. Wolves, as well as other animals which have become domesticated, may have played a more active role in this process than previously thought. In fact, it may have been wolves who initially adopted humans as a survival strategy, not the other way around. At the very least, both species capitalized on their association, one that appears, if numbers are any measure, to have ultimately benefited the descendants of wolves at least as much as their human providers. Dogs have proven immensely successful, resulting in some 140 true-breeding types—from chihuahuas to Irish wolfhounds—that have spread to virtually all parts of the world inhabited by their human care-takers. Today there are 54 million dogs in North America (between 100,000 and 300,000 are estimated to be wolf-dog hybrids), nearly as many dogs as there were once hoofed animals on the Great Plains. Along with an almost equal number of domestic cats, the two animals support an industry believed to be greater than the entire economy of medieval Europe.[22]

Although some wolves managed to favorably exploit their relationship with humans, most of their wild brethren kept their distance. Where humans and wolves closely competed for the same prey, their association was sometimes too close. Bones of wolves have shown up in massive buffalo kill sites. Apparently they were attracted by carrion and early humans took advantage of this fact, although the killing of wolves by this method was relatively uncommon given the paucity of such finds.

The converse—that wolves preyed on humans—persists in a hopeless jumble of fact, fear, myth, and folklore handed down throughout the centuries. Despite the debunking of most of these accounts during modern times, their overwhelming preponderance suggests there is a shred of truth, however slim, in the allegation that during the not-so-recent past wolves may have attacked, killed, and sometimes consumed humans. This appears to be particularly true for Europe and Asia, much less so for North America.

The past suggests several possible explanations. To a great degree, animals learn what is dangerous not by their own experience but through heredity. It isn't difficult to imagine a time before humans became formidable hunters and began their successful expansion across Eurasia and into North America when wolves preyed, if infrequently, on humans. Eurasian wolves may have never entirely lost this behavior when thousands of years ago some humans ceased hunting and turned to pastoralism and agriculture. Old World history is rife with frequent wars and devastating plagues, both of which provided countless human corpses upon which wolves were known to have fed, a behavior which may have encouraged them to regard humans as prey. Also, feral dogs or wolf-dog hybrids may have been responsible for deaths attributed to wolves. Finally, rabies appears to have occurred more frequently in Eurasia than North America. Although rabid animals rarely, if ever, consume their victims, the greater incidence of the disease may explain the higher number of reported attacks in regions such as central Asia.[23]

Regardless how it came about, the fact remains that many Eurasian people continue to this day to exhibit a widespread and cautious attitude toward wolves. Moreover, not all wolf attack tales come exclusively from Eurasian farmers and pastoralists who harbor antipathy toward wolves for obvious economic reasons. Well into the twentieth century, Siberian Evenk hunters believed that when meeting a wolf "one had to step aside, having asked him to leave one alone."[24]

By contrast, when Paleo-Indians and wolves began their simultaneous expansion throughout North America at the end of the Pleistocene, humans were members of vigorous hunting and gathering cultures—a condition that predominated among many Native American peoples until Europeans sailed to their shores only a short time ago. By then many tribes fostered a varied and complex relationship with wolves, perhaps best characterized as respectful coexistence.

All of which may disguise the fact that at some earlier time during the past twelve thousand years in North America, wolves gained a different, but no less lasting, regard for the two-legged creature armed with a sharp, stone-pointed spear.

3

SPEAKING FOR WOLF

Long ago, Sun loved a Crow woman. So great was his love for her that Sun blessed the Crow people with an abundance of buffalo. One day while Sun was away from his lodge, a fool-dog, a Crow man with an evil spirit, raped Sun's wife. Upon Sun's return, his wife told him of her shame and then killed herself before his eyes. So enraged was Sun that he banished the Crow people from their land, promising to destroy them. They wandered for a long time, suffering greatly from hunger until finally, White Wolf, a servant of Sun, took pity on them. Wolf told them of a ceremony, and when they performed it, a bright flame exploded and out galloped ten fat buffalo. Wolf warned the people that they must kill every buffalo, for if one escaped, he would surely tell Sun what Wolf had done. Over and over the people performed the ceremony until they had killed nearly a hundred buffalo. The people tried to kill them all, but with only bows and arrows, a lone buffalo escaped and ran directly to Sun. When he learned what had happened, Sun became very angry, but more with Wolf than the people, whose bravery in the face of starvation had touched his heart.

"Go to the Crow people," Sun said to White Wolf, "and tell them that I shall no longer work to destroy them. You yourself will forever more be a vagabond, an outcast among the animals of the world."[1]

When Europeans first stepped ashore centuries ago in North America, they encountered a people with cultures incredibly rich, diverse, and complex.

They also found them entirely inscrutable.

"As a race, there never was one more unpracticable," fumed Professor Henry Schoolcraft, the continent's foremost ethnologist of the mid-nineteenth century. "They recognize their Great Spirit in rocks, trees, cataracts, and clouds, in thunder and lightning." They believe that He exists within "every possible form in the world, animate and inanimate," and "they see Him in every place that inspires awe." Animals, in particular, are revered. Worst of all, "they can, in a twinkling, transform men and animals."[2]

Such absurdity, declared Schoolcraft, is best evidenced by the Tonkawa of the southern Plains, who believe they came into the world with the help of the wolf. To commemorate this event, they hold a wolf dance. Dressing in wolf skins, the dancers creep about on all fours, howl, and make "other demonstrations peculiar to the wolf," explained the ethnologist. After awhile they stop, smell the earth at a particular spot, howl again, and commence scratching. Soon a Tonkawa man, who has been previously buried, is unearthed. He addresses his fellow dancers: "You have brought me into the world, and I know not what to do for a subsistence; it would have been better to let me remain as I was. I shall starve in this world." Then the dancers put a bow and arrows into his hands, and tell him he must do as wolves do—"rob, kill, and murder, from place to place, and never cultivate the soil."[3]

Despite his chauvinism, the professor was correct in one respect. For Native Americans, human existence was inseparable from the plants, animals, earth, and sky that comprised the great mystery of life. All entities, including humans, were part of an eternal cycle and thus possessed intimate kinship, one that fostered special obligations. Because they ate their flesh and wore their skins, Native Americans held animals in particular high esteem. Hunting was a sacred ritual in which the hunted played an equal role with the hunter. Without their consent, animals could not be killed. They were powerful, mysterious, and sometimes dangerous, but rendered the correct respect, animals might bestow their gifts on humans.

They were the link between the great unknown and human existence, making them a continual source of eternal wisdom. Animals talked with people, protected and taught them, sacrificed their flesh for them, gave them special powers and knowledge, and might even punish them if disobeyed.

A Tonkawa who identified with the wolf, for example, might possess the skills and knowledge of wolves, wear the skin of wolves, understand the language of wolves, learn and be nurtured by wolves, and even dream wolf dreams. In spirit and without actually changing physical form, a person and a wolf became essentially the same. Yet so powerful was this bond that under certain circumstances it transcended the ethereal into the physical; wolves could become humans, and humans, wolves.

In such a world, anything was possible.

For cultures like the Tonkawa, which relied on hunting more than agriculture, the wolf played a prominent role in tribal cosmogony. In the Pacific Northwest, one of the prominent bands of Kwakiutl, the Tsawatenok, claimed that before they became men and women, they were wolves. During a giant flood, four wolves survived the rising waters by climbing a mountain, where they shed their skins and became human. They wanted to learn if any other people were alive, so the oldest one, "Listened-To," donned his wolf skin again and howled from the top of the mountain. On a distant island he heard an answering howl, indicating that at least one other being they called "Howling-About-in-the-World" had survived the cataclysm.[4]

To the Paiute of the Great Basin, Wolf created the earth while floating in a boat on a great expanse of water. For the Cree of Hudson Bay, it was Wolf who, after a great flood covered the land, carried a ball of moss round and round a raft containing the world's animal survivors. Due to Wolf's efforts, the earth re-formed and grew, spreading over the raft until it remade the world. According to the Arikara of the northern Plains, once there was only sky and a limitless lake where two ducks swam eternally at peace. Suddenly, Wolf-Man and Lucky-Man appeared and asked the ducks to bring up mud to make the earth. Lucky-Man made the hills and valleys, and between the two regions, the Great River (Missouri). Then Wolf-Man made a great prairie for all the animals, including humans.

In other legends, the first humans were not created by wolves but instead learned from them how to hunt.

When the Cheyenne (Tsistsistas) moved south from present-day Canada into the Great Plains about 2,500 years ago, they brought with them the Massaum, an ancient, elaborate ceremony depicting the creation of the world, one whose closest roots have been traced to northern Siberia. Serving as messengers, wolves played a prominent role in this ritual, a red wolf the messenger during the day and a white wolf at night. These two sacred animals were instructed by the spirit world to teach the Cheyenne to hunt. As a reward, the grateful people always called wolves to their kills, setting aside a portion for their use.[5]

The Sioux, who later became allies of the Cheyenne, say they learned to hunt from *sungmanitu,* the "animal that looks like a dog but is a powerful spirit," by example. Once, a legend goes, the Sioux lived an impoverished life underground, but Wolf showed them the exit to a cave leading to the surface. As they left the cave, other wolves drove herds of game past in an attempt to entice them to hunt. In this way the Sioux came to inhabit and thrive on the earth.[6]

Still other tribes told subterranean tales of the wolf as trickster. One of those was the Caddo of the lower Red River country of the southern Plains. According to their creation legend, they arose from a cave in a hill they call Chakanina or "The Place of Crying." In those days, people and animals were related and lived together underground. When the first people discovered the cave exit, they decided to ascend. Several people went first, then some animals. All intended to leave, but Wolf closed the hole after climbing out, imprisoning the rest of the people and animals underground. Those who escaped wept for their friends below.[7]

Some Native Americans sought to explain where wolves came from and why they behaved as they did. Winnebagos believed that long ago wolves had befriended humans when they were given permission by the Earthmaker to come to live among them. In the Pacific Northwest, numerous legends—from Chinook to Nez Perce to Coast Salish—involve a triangular conflict in which humans, salmon, and wolves fight over a young Indian girl who is first kidnapped by salmon and then abducted by wolves. Humans battle the wolves and defeat them, after which wolves assume their present animal nature, become harmless to humans, and having given up cooked food, now eat it raw.[8]

During this time when wolves fought humans, according to a Coast Salish tale, a chief's son decided to trick a wolf. The boy lay down on the beach and pretended to be dead. When a wolf approached, he jumped up and cut off the tip of the wolf's tongue. A hundred wolves returned several days later to retrieve the tongue, but by then it had dried up and didn't fit anymore. Furious, the wolves ate everyone in the village except for the chief's daughter, who went to live with the Wolf chief. She bore him two sons—a wolf and a human boy. When the boy grew up, one day he discovered a whale on a beach. He tricked all the wolves, including his half-brother, whom he tried to stop by holding his tail, into entering the whale with promises of meat inside. But his brother escaped to join the other wolves inside the whale, and the boy was left holding only a handful of wolf hair. He was sad that he couldn't save his brother, but he took the hair into the woods and blew upon it, and it became wolves as we know them today.[9]

The Skidi band of Pawnee told how the first wolf came to earth, resulting in the human fall from grace. According to their creation legend, the gods forgot to invite the Wolf Star (Sirius), the brightest star in the heavens, to a great council. For this the Wolf Star was deeply resentful, and sent the first wolf to earth disguised as one of the gods. When people discovered this ruse, they killed the wolf. Upon learning of his death, the god was furious, proclaiming that forever after they would be known as the Skidi or Wolf People. Moreover, since they had killed the first animal on earth, they had brought war, pestilence, and death upon themselves and would no longer possess immortality. The Pawnee also called the Wolf Star *Tskirixki-tiuhats* or Wolf-He-Is-Deceived. They observed that the nighttime howling of wolves increased markedly just before sunrise, about the same time as the appearance of the Morning Star (Venus). During that portion of the year when Sirius rose in the southeastern sky before the Morning Star, wolves prematurely began their howling to greet the day, having been deceived by the Wolf Star.[10]

Another origin story told by the Hitchiti of the Southeast contains a rueful twist. Long ago a shaman struck two pine cones together to create wolves. When they grew hungry, he told them to go along a trail until they met a man. "What he eats, you eat," said the shaman. After the wolves were gone, the shaman felt guilty, saying "I am worthless for having done that." Thereafter wolves preyed upon the same animals as humans.[11]

Native Americans readily explained why wolves looked the way they did and why other animals feared them. The dark markings that some wolves displayed at the sides of their mouths were acquired in Distant Time, according to the Koyukon of central Alaska, when Raven threw caribou innards in Wolf's face. In a Sanpoil myth, an old woman and her grandson were trapped by a pack of wolves on a rocky ledge. They built a fire and threw hot stones wrapped in suet down to the wolves. All died except the youngest who was unable to swallow the stone, although the side of its mouth was burned in the attempt. Why were the eyes of wolves so like those of humans? A shaman was to blame, said the Northwest's Bella Coola, when he attempted to turn wolves into men but succeeded only with the eyes. Why did deer fear wolves? According to the Tsimshian of the Northwest Coast, wolves prepared a feast at the mouth of the Skeena River and invited several deer chiefs. The wolves wanted to see if the deer had teeth like their own, so they joked and laughed, hoping the deer would open their mouths and show their teeth. Finally the deer could hold back no longer and laughed. When the wolves saw how small their teeth were, they immediately attacked and devoured them.[12]

Native people recognized that certain other animals behaved like wolves. The Haida of the Northwest, who called the wolf *gōdj*, told of a man who captured and raised two wolf pups. When they were grown, they swam into the ocean and killed whales. They killed so many that the Great Above Person grew angry and made a storm to prevent the wolves from returning to land. Those wolves, said the Haida, became orcas—the hunters of whales, wolves of the sea. The nearby Kwakiutl had a different explanation: spirits of deceased human hunters of animals of the sea became killer whales, those of the land became wolves.[13]

Because Native Americans believed that the power of the wolf was transferable to humans, they sought to emulate the animal in a multitude of ways. Wolf names, symbols, and icons pervaded everyday life and were used to record an event involving a wolf, invoke the animal's spirit, or generally demonstrate their respect.

The wolf was so admired among some native cultures that it was used to represent particular kinship groups. The Iroquian-speaking Kahnawake were divided into three clans: bear, turtle, and wolf. One of three Delaware clans—the Pauksit, meaning the "animal having a round foot like a dog"—believed that Wolf had led them out of the interior of the earth, for which his name was to be revered forever. Of the three divisions of southern Arapaho, one was known as Haqihana, or The Wolves, while among the ten Caddo bands, the wolf band was known as Tasha.[14]

Several large Northwest tribal phratries chose the wolf to represent their lineage. Perhaps the best known was the Tlingit of present-day southeast Alaska who divided themselves into Ravens and Wolves. The Tlingit admired both animals for their intelligence, socialness, and gluttony, this last trait celebrated in the tribe's overindulgence at ceremonial potlatches. Although they occasionally hunted the wolf, or *gōtc,* for its fur, they also believed during ancient times that an animal could shed its skin, revealing its true nature as a human being. According to one legend, some Tlingit men were out fishing one day when they discovered an exhausted wolf swimming far from shore. The men pulled it aboard and returned to their village. The wolf became human in all but physical form, a constant companion, hunting, speaking, and living with them. It was so mourned when it died that the men carved a giant totem in its honor.[15]

From nine-hundred-year-old Plains Indian rock art along Montana's Yellowstone River to two-thousand-year-old wolf pipe effigies of Ohio's Mound Builders, native cultures sought to summon Wolf's power. Such representations were not just symbolic. Once created, the icon was infused with the animal's spirit; it became Wolf.

In southern Florida the fourteen-thousand-strong Calusa crafted exquisite wooden heads of wolves and other animals, but their precise purpose was not recorded before the Spanish annihilated the tribe in the early 1700s. Three thousand miles distant, the Bella Coola painted the backs of their children with a picture of a wolf gall bladder, for this organ was infused with intelligence and wildness. North of the Bella Coola, the Tlingit carved massive wolf totems and donned huge, fierce wolf masks. During George Vancouver's voyage to this coast in 1793, a Tlingit man wearing a giant wolf mask so unnerved the admiral and his crew that a fight erupted, resulting in the death of several Indians and the wounding of two sailors.[16]

Sometimes icons portrayed a deep level of philosophical sophistication. In Greenland, a wolf mask was worn by an Inuit or Eskimo shaman in order to acquire certain wolf characteristics: quickness, acute sense of smell, and skill at hunting animals. The shaman sang a song, learned from the wolf's *inua* or spirit. Wolf power, however, didn't arise directly from the animal, but from the great omniscient power that was to be found everywhere—in the air, land, sky, and stars. Although this power, known as *tunraq*, was in all things and always present, it was at the same time infinitely remote and therefore could not be fully comprehended. The wolf was only the medium between humans and *tunraq*, but to possess the animal's abilities was to commune, however briefly, with the Great Unknown.[17]

Five thousand miles from Greenland, the Zunis of the Southwest believed that four animals presided over the cardinal points: mountain lion to the north, black bear to the west, badger to the south, and white wolf, master of the east. Zuni children played a tag game where one of them became Wolf and chased the others who were Rabbit or Deer. Other tribes witnessed changes in wolf behavior at certain seasons of the year and named them accordingly. For the Teton Sioux of the Plains, the lunar period with the least daylight and most severe cold was known as "the moon when wolves run together."[18]

An individual who identified with the wolf as a personal tutelary spirit often assumed a wolf name such as: Howling Wolf, Lone Wolf, Wolf Face, Lean Wolf, Mad Wolf, Wolf Lies Down, Trotting Wolf, Wolf Killer, Old Wolf, Leads the Wolf, Yellow Wolf, or Skins the Wolf. Because the wolf was viewed as predominantly male, wolf names usually belonged to men who desired to become hunters or warriors. But in certain tribes, woodworkers took wolf names because their work required honed senses, and among the Coast Salish, the most skilled weavers and blanket makers were women imbued with Wolf's patience. Native American perception even extended to the animal's disposition. The Northwest's Okanagan often named strong-willed children after the wolf, while mild-mannered children were named after a deer, rabbit, or bird. Far from an opprobium, those who possessed aggressive personalities often made the best warriors.[19]

The most common way to obtain a guardian spirit was through dreams and visions. Some cultures encouraged an individual to pursue a vision quest, enduring the hardship of fasting, loneliness, or even self-torture in order to be worthy of association with an animal spirit. A common method of obtaining such a vision among Plains Indians was the Sun Dance. One summer day in the 1850s, Wikis, a Northern Cheyenne youth, retired to a secluded hillside, pierced his breast with wooden pins, and without food or water walked around a pole tethered to the pins with sinew. As he completed each circle, Wikis lunged backward in an attempt to rip the pins from his breast, but failing to do so by darkness, a companion had to sever the pins from him with a knife. Wikis collapsed, fell asleep, and that night a wolf appeared, saying, "Look at me, and consider well my ways. Remember that of all the animals, the wolves are the smartest. If they get hungry, they go out and kill a buffalo. They know what is going to happen. They are always able to take care of themselves. You shall be like the wolf. You shall be able to creep close to your enemies, and they shall not see you. You shall be a great man for surprising people. In the bundle that you wear tied to your necklet, you shall carry a little wolf hair, and your quiver and your bow-case shall be made of the skin of a wolf." The wolf stared at Wikis and then trotted off. After recovering, Wikis became an accomplished hunter and warrior, and was remembered as being particularly good at sneaking into camps and stealing horses.[20]

Sometimes Wolf simply appeared and offered itself without a vision or dream. Sitting Bull claimed he owed his fame to such an encounter. When he was fifteen years old, one day along a tributary of the Missouri River he discovered a wolf wounded with two arrows. "Boy," cried the animal, "if you will relieve me, your name shall be great." Sitting Bull pulled out the arrows, washed and dressed the wounds, and saved the wolf. Then he composed a song about the encounter which came to exemplify his life:

> *Alone in the wilderness I roam*
> *With much hardships in the wilderness I roam*
> *A wolf said this to me.*[21]

Individuals who received Wolf's favors possessed unique powers as well as certain obligations. Owl Friend, a Blackfoot warrior, claimed he was befriended by four wolves who taught him a dance, which he later conveyed to fellow tribesmen. Soon the dancers became known as Wolf Soldiers, and were said to have danced on fire without being burned. The wolves told Owl Friend to never let the sun catch him sleeping when it rose, just as they themselves never slept past dawn. Throughout his life, Owl Friend obeyed this dictum until he grew old. One morning his wife saw that the sun had risen. She ran to the lodge and shook her husband by the shoulder, but he was dead. Tribal lore claims that Owl Friend always slept on wolf skins, had eyes that looked like a wolf, and was "always watching, and seeing everything that happened."[22]

Those who were considered lupine in spirit often adorned themselves in wolf hide, teeth, fur, or other parts of the animal's anatomy. Arikara men wove hair of the wolf and buffalo together in sacred blankets, while Nez Perce warriors pushed a canine of *hemene* through the septum of their noses. Cheyenne warriors wore wolf tails hanging from their breechclouts to denote both fleetness and endurance. Mandan warriors, on the other hand, wore the tail of *harrata* at their heels to represent their personal accomplishments in war. For one dead enemy, a warrior wore a whole wolf's tail. Killing a second enemy entitled him to another tail for the opposite foot. Counting coup on a body without actually performing the killing rated a wolf's tail with the tip cut off. The tail provided a practical benefit as well; as quickly as a warrior made tracks, it erased them.[23]

A wolf skin could save lives. Pretty Shield, a Crow medicine woman, said that as a little girl she and her mother once were pursued by a Sioux war party. As the warriors followed their horses' tracks, her mother dismounted and took a wolf skin from her saddle, brushed the ground with it, and sang to her wolf spirit. Then she remounted, telling her skeptical daughter that the Sioux would now be unable to track them. Almost immediately, remembered Pretty Shield, a huge thundercloud appeared followed by a fierce wind which blew away their tracks and allowed them to escape.[24]

Eskimos and Athabaskan Indians valued wolf fur for parka ruffs because the fur rarely collects frost, even at minus 40 degrees. Prior to 1890, the Blackfeet were policed by Black Soldiers, a group of warriors who wore wolf skin headbands with two feathers at each side, and wolf skin anklets and wristlets. They painted their bodies and limbs red, and their cheeks with two black lines representing canine teeth. The leader wore a wolf cape and carried a red staff adorned with wolf fur strips. Nearby Piegan warriors donned the cape of a large gray wolf, slit down the back so the head hung on the bearer's chest.

Others—particularly hunters or warriors who wished to imitate a wolf for hunting, war, or ceremony—might place a skinned wolf head on their own crown with the cape flowing over their shoulders and back. The full war dress of some Nez Perce warriors consisted of a wolf's head, with ears standing erect, fantastically festooned with bear claws, feathers, trinkets, and bells. A Crow warrior who had captured a horse during a raid put a wolf skin on his back with the head over his right shoulder and the tail dragging. Thus arrayed, the man rode his captured horse through the village with a short rope dangling from its neck, the object of admiration by fellow warriors.[25]

When it came to winter counts, an Indian chronology system for recording events, buffalo hides were principally used, but some tribes favored those of the wolf. Ceremonial wolf bundles consisted of sacred, spiritually charged articles wrapped in wolf skins with the fur either removed or reversed. Among the Cheyenne, women weren't allowed to tan wolf skins until they performed a purification ceremony. The man who directed this ceremony was a member of the Young Wolf Medicine Society. After offering him a small gift of food or calico, the women sat down and bared themselves to the waist. The man painted their hands and ankles with red paint. Next he drew a circle to represent the sun on each one's chest, a crescent moon over the right shoulder, and finally, their faces from nose to throat. After several additional rites, including cutting a small piece of fur from a wolf hide, the initiates formed a circle and danced, pausing at the cardinal points to howl.[26]

Some tribes disallowed women from dressing wolf hides entirely. Such was the case when Father Pierre-Jean DeSmet encountered the Assiniboin on the upper Missouri River in 1840. Unable to fathom how the wolf related to their world view or in what manner the Assiniboin might demonstrate their respect toward the animal, the Jesuit priest attributed the women's behavior to the fear "that the wolves sometimes go mad, bite those they meet and give them the hydrophobia."[27]

Although the wolf's howl remains one of the great enigmas about the animal, Native Americans explained their rich voices in a variety of ways. Howling was talking with the spirit world. More prosaically, it could mean that wolves were calling coyotes, foxes, and ravens to the remains of their kills, since both Indians and Eskimos observed that wolves were providers for a larger community of animals. Returning members of Kiowa war parties sometimes stopped outside their village and howled, signaling that they had killed some Pawnee, a tribe they called the Wolf People. Among the Blackfeet, howling took the form of a ceremony. In time of danger, when hunting, or on the war path, the young men of the tribe gathered in a circle, stretched a raw hide between them, and beat it like a drum. They said no words, but howled at regular intervals. Young women stood behind them, and joined in. This song was said to be very ancient, having been handed down for generations in the belief that the wolf would inspire the singer with his cunning.[28]

A person endowed with Wolf's spirit was sometimes known to understand the speech of wolves. Brave Wolf, a Cheyenne man, had the gift of prophecy given to him by his father, who had obtained it from wolves. It was said that Brave Wolf, by listening to wolves howl, always knew what was going to happen. Like Brave Wolf, those persons who best comprehended wolf ways were said to have gained their knowledge after living with the animals. Most often they were lost, hungry, and near death when wolves rescued them. After being returned to their people, they repaid the kindness by feeding their benefactors. A typical story was that of a Sioux woman named Marpiyawin who became lost one day while looking for a lost puppy. Tired and hungry, she crawled into a cave and when she awoke found herself surrounded by wolves. She lived with them a long time and learned their language. Eventually they guided her back to her village where she became known as "The Old Woman Who Lived with the Wolves." From then on, whenever wolves howled nearby, Marpiyawin understood what they were saying and always went out to greet and feed them.[29]

The Cheyenne tell a similar tale when a large village was attacked by Colorado militia at Sand Creek in November 1864, and over one hundred women and children were slaughtered. Two women and their children managed to escape but soon became lost. Cold and starving, they took refuge in a shallow cave under a bluff. In the middle of the night, the women said a large wolf came into the cave and lay down beside them. At first they were afraid, but in the morning the wolf continued traveling with them, stopping to rest whenever they did. One of the women finally addressed the wolf: "O Wolf, try to do something for us. We and our children are nearly starved." The wolf led them to a freshly killed buffalo, which they hungrily consumed. Over the next few weeks, the wolf never left their side, always finding food for them when they were hungry, protecting them from both animal and human enemies. Finally he led them to a Cheyenne camp on the Republican River, and after delivering his charges and receiving food in return, the wolf vanished.[30]

Sometimes the stories involved the treachery of other people, and wolves play a part in retribution. Also Native Americans didn't ignore the possibility that a person might find it difficult to give up their wolf ways and return to living with humans. Once a Cheyenne man named Black Wolf fell into a deep pit dug by two jealous women. Stoned by the women and left for dead, he was rescued by four white wolves. After living with them and learning their ways, Black Wolf began to grow the long teeth and black hair of a wolf all over his body. When he was finally captured in a snare set by fellow tribesmen, he told how the two women had tried to kill him. Then, with the tribe's permission and in a howling rage, he slayed the women, cut up their bodies, and fed them to the waiting wolves. From that time forth, Black Wolf lived part of every year with his wolf family.[31]

The story of Black Wolf's revenge implies that the wolf wasn't always viewed without trepidation by Native Americans. To one Omaha band, the wolf represented the restlessness of humans, their refusal to accept fate, and their dark destructiveness. Among the Northwest's Walla Walla, a certain wolf possessing "great medicine" was capable of changing people into rocks. To some of today's Alaska Koyukon, wolves, as well as certain other animals, possess potent spirits called *biyeega hoolaanh* which are easily provoked and may be highly vindictive. Wolves in particular are feared by some Koyukon because they foretell misfortune—if a wolf howls in a strange manner, someone may die in the village.[32]

Wolves might also capture and spiritually possess people. Well into the twentieth century, an elaborate wolf ritual was practiced by the Northwest Nootka, Kwakiutl, and Quillayute. The ritual included several variations, but was usually performed at the beginning of winter before a full moon, served as a formal tribal initiation for young people, and lasted from five to nine days. It was based on a common myth about a young man, the culture hero, who is stolen by a pack of wolves. Unable to kill him, they become his friends, eventually returning him to his village to instruct people how to become successful hunters, fierce and brave in war. Among the Nootka of Vancouver Island, the ritual took the form of an elaborate masked ceremonial dance called *tlugwana* (or *klukwana*). Initiates were cut with mussel shell knives, symbolically bleeding themselves to eliminate the human blood odor, and people dressed in giant wolf masks howled and danced around them in a wolf frenzy. By the final day, the initiates were exorcised of Wolf's spirit and reborn into the tribe, but retained the power of the wolf. So forbidding was this ceremony that when Wolf's spirit was in the performers, it was said that any uninitiated person who looked upon them would instantly die.[33]

The arctic explorer Peter Freuchen witnessed a wolf possession in Greenland in 1911 when he attended an Eskimo seance. At one point during the rite inside a large igloo, a man named Krisuk suddenly "had a seizure. He stood up howling like a wolf, and people around him had to defend themselves against his attacks." As Krisuk leaped and charged about, his fellow terrified villagers fled. When the wolfman attempted to attack Freuchen, the explorer pushed him to the ground. To his amazement, Krisuk jumped up, burst through the igloo wall, and ran howling through the village.[34]

Among the Navajo, wolf possession could be even more ominous. Their word for wolf, *ma'iitsoh,* means big trotter, but it's also a synonym for a witch. Through witchcraft, a man might transform himself into a kind of werewolf, known as a "skinwalker." Dressed in a wolf hide, the skinwalker is believed to climb on the roof of a house or hogan at night and drop the powdered bones of dead children through the smoke hole. The result is illness, bad fortune, or even death for the inhabitants. In addition, skinwalkers are associated with cannibalism, incest, and necrophilia. At night they are said to run through graveyards and have intercourse with corpses.[35]

Such stories or beliefs portraying wolves as demonic or frightful are rare. Fear simply was never a large part of wolf lore among most Native Americans. In the case of the Nootka, the wolf represents desirable qualities, dangerously obtained yet worth the risk. In most other instances, Wolf epitomizes the duality of human nature. Native Americans recognized and accepted the fact that animal and human nature are inseparable and that part of that nature is darkly portentous. But where fear did occur, it was most often vested in the power or spirit of Wolf, not in the animal itself.

Some native people seemed to genuinely enjoy the presence of wolves. In the early 1770s, Samuel Hearne observed that the Chipewyan Indians of central Canada believed wolves were "something more than common animals." They frequently located dens in order to simply "play" with the young animals, wrote the astonished explorer. "I never knew a Northern Indian [to] hurt one of them; on the contrary, they always put them carefully into the den again; and I have sometimes seen them paint the faces of the young wolves with vermillion, or red ochre."[36]

Hearne's experience depicts what most Native Americans felt about wolves: they marveled at the animal's elusiveness, loyalty, and affection, its willingness to defend its territory; its stamina and ability to travel long distances and resist hunger for many days; its acute use of odor, sight, and sound in locating prey and avoiding danger; its patience, following a sick or wounded prey for great distances; and its contentment to be away from its home for long periods of time. Working cooperatively with fellow pack mates, the wolf demonstrated time and again its power over prey by encircling it, ambushing it, or running it to exhaustion—the same methods that Native Americans themselves used. In all these manifestations, they found the wolf supremely worthy of emulation.

Blackfeet hunters were particularly fond of the animal they called *mahkwoyi,* or Big Mouth. As they prepared for a hunt, they slept on wolf skins and sang songs to encourage wolves to join them and bring good luck. While traveling and looking for prey, if a wolf howled nearby, a man in the hunting party would affably sing out, "No, I will not give you my body to eat, but I will give you the body of someone else, if you will go along with us." Some Indians claimed that wolves would lead them to game for this very purpose. Among the Skagit of the Pacific Northwest, persons assuming the spirit of *stakayu* was sure to have success in hunting, particularly if wolves accompanied them.[37]

Sometimes it worked the other way: humans scavenged wolf kills. The Koyukon believed that in the Distant Time, when wolves were still part human, a wolf-person lived among them. Because of the favors they had bestowed upon him, wolves should share their prey with people. Consequently, Koyukon hunters may take any kills made by *teekkona* that they find unspoiled. During the early 1800s in northern Canada, one English explorer, Sir John Richardson, was startled when he witnessed a lone Athapascan Indian chase wolves from a fresh caribou kill and confiscate the carcass.[38]

Hunters, in particular, possessed a level of understanding concerning nuances of wolf behavior that is wholly missing among less attentive observers. Some Nunamiut Eskimo hunters today are able to determine a wolf's sex and age at a distance by observing its pelage and behavior. They also maintain that black wolves tend to be more high-strung than wolves of other colors, and that two- and three-year-old females are the best caribou hunters. Tension in the muscles in the feet of a rabid wolf, say the Nunamiut, spread the footpads slightly to make a wider track than that possessed by wolves not suffering from the disease.[39]

Some Native Americans were particularly adept at imitating wolf methods. Like wolves in winter, the Cree of the northern Plains herded buffalo onto glazed lake or river ice where they slipped, fell, and could be more easily dispatched. Some Eskimo claimed that they imitated wolves after they saw them surround caribou in an effort to drive them close together before attacking. Before the arrival of the horse, Pueblo people ran deer to exhaustion, as did the Waswanipi Cree who hunted moose by pursuing them on snowshoes in deep snow until they collapsed. Like wolves, the Waswanipi also appear to have avoided hunting certain areas containing moose from time to time, in effect allowing their populations time to recover. According to a Tlingit man interviewed by John Muir in the 1890s, seal hunters received a lesson in the art of camouflage when they saw wolves catching seals by "swimming slyly upon them with their heads hidden in a mouthful of grass."[40]

Hunters sometimes assumed the guise of the wolf itself. In the western Plains, a Shoshoni hunter might lay in deep grass or sagebrush and slowly wave a wolf tail over his head, just as he had observed wolves do, to attract curious antelope close enough to kill. Perhaps the most artful imitation was that of actually donning the fresh skin of a wolf in order to approach game. While buffalo and other large prey frequently fled at the sight or smell of humans, they often remained largely tolerant of wolves who constantly lurked nearby. Disguised hunters deftly took advantage of this phenomenon, sometimes howling and gamboling about on all four limbs like real wolves to quiet any suspicious herd members. When the hunters came close—often almost within touch of the animals—they rose up, drew their bows, and let arrows fly with such force that they occasionally traveled completely through the animal. A Plains Cree named Jacob Bear and a companion once demonstrated a dramatic refinement of this technique to anthropologist Alanson Skinner. Jacob Bear covered himself in a white blanket simulating a wolf skin, while his cohort did the same with a hide of a buffalo calf. While Jacob Bear feigned attack, the ersatz calf bleated and cried so fearfully that nearby cows and bulls approached close enough to be shot.[41]

Because of their vast numbers and prodigious size, buffalo were the main prey of both wolves and native hunters of the Great Plains. Wolf success was markedly enhanced by the predator's ability to capitalize on buffalo wounded or disabled by hunters, in addition to scavenging discarded remains of human kills. Of course, even without human assistance, wolves were accomplished predators. Although they preyed primarily on the young and weak (while Indians preferred animals in their prime) wolves were also capable of pursuing and killing healthy animals. Beginning in the 1600s, the prosperity of both Indians and wolves dramatically improved with the dispersal of the modern horse throughout the continent, one that reached full abundance near the end of the following century. Horses revolutionized how Indians lived and hunted, allowing them greater speed and range, and thus access to more game. At the same time, more tribes moved onto the Great Plains and became buffalo hunters. The result was a far larger number of carcasses than that of the pre-horse era. Consequently, the population of wolves in the Great Plains probably reached its zenith sometime during this prey cornucopia of the late 1700s. By the early 1800s, due to increased hunting and habitat loss, buffalo had begun their fateful decline, and with them, wolves and Plains Indians.

Even in its heyday, buffalo hunting was never a sure thing. The animals' unpredictable and erratic wanderings—probably as much a result of the relentless pursuit of Indians and wolves as the availability of grass and water—all too frequently left both predators scrambling to find substitute prey. This was especially true for wolves during the late winter and early spring denning season when their hunting range was restricted. It was also the case for tribes like the Mandans and Hidatsa who were part-time agrarians and only semi-nomadic. Among the Lakota Sioux, who became nomadic hunters after moving onto the Great Plains in the mid-eighteenth century, men or women who dreamed of wolves were considered *wakan,* possessing a sacred power that among other skills, enabled them to foretell where there were buffalo.[42]

The number of buffalo determined how and where wolves and Indians hunted. In times of scarcity, the Cheyenne pursued alternative game either alone or with one other companion. When buffalo appeared in appreciable herds, hunters quickly formed a close-knit cooperative group. Wolves did likewise. Both human and wolf territories were flexible. During stable periods when game was relatively common, alien groups or individuals who were discovered trespassing on another's territory were usually subject to severe punishment or even death. In times of either extreme privation or abundance, however, these boundaries often broke down and trespassers were tolerated. As buffalo became increasingly scarce in Nebraska in the

1860s and 1870s, the Pawnee and Omaha tribes put aside their traditional enmity and allowed each other access across one another's territory as they pursued the last animals. Wolves have been known to do the same.[43]

Sometimes deep winter snow made travel difficult for the herds. It also impeded humans and wolves, at least until those times when the surface froze hard enough to support their weight but not that of their prey. Then buffalo were particular vulnerable, a time when, as Cheyenne hunters lyrically proclaimed, they fell like the snow itself. On firm ground and in the absence of snow, buffalo were fast runners, maintaining a speed of thirty to thirty-five miles per hour for a half mile, and were capable of continuing at only a slightly slower pace for ten miles or more. Like wolves, Indians usually gave up the chase if an animal was not overtaken within a relatively short distance.

Both wolves and Indians treated their kills in similar fashion. If buffalo were plentiful, they often ate only prized portions of a carcass, caching some, or entirely abandoning the remainder after eating only a small amount. Wolves weren't the only ones who found certain delicacies, particularly *au naturel* viscera, appetizing. Cree Indians relished raw fat from the udder, and the Hidatsa preferred the entire organ full of tepid milk. Once when John James Audubon observed Indians kill a buffalo and immediately split open the carcass and devour the raw stomach "with the greatest voracity," he was intrigued enough to taste it. He found the tripe "very good," although he admitted that "its appearance was rather revolting." Both Indians and wolves savored marrow found in leg bones, as well as certain muscles—particularly buffalo hump, tongue, and a two-inch-thick strip of fatty tissue along the crest of the hump, called *dépouille* by French trappers. When wolves killed a pregnant cow, they sometimes first devoured the fetus. Indians also preferred unborn calves. One white trader among the Gros Ventre in 1868 praised *in vivo* calves as "the greatest delicacy of all." Indians also drank buffalo blood, said by the Crees to make them fearless like wolves.[44]

In times of scarcity, each predator tended to utilize entire carcasses—meat, bones, hair, brains, entrails, even hooves. Both generally preferred fresh kills, although sometimes they had to settle for less. When buffalo broke through river ice, drowned in great numbers, and were carried downstream with the spring thaw, wolves and Indians alike feasted on the putrid carcasses. Some tribes were quite fond of these aged corpses, even when fresh meat was plentiful. Also, Indians might obtain water from buffalo in times of drought by chewing the gristle of a buffalo's snout or drinking the partially digested contents of its stomach. Wolves were probably no different.

If Indians who hunted felt a powerful affinity with the wolf, those who fought made even greater claims on the animal. Warriors sometimes joined wolf cults or societies composed of unrelated members. During the 1850s some Oglala Sioux warriors formed a cult originally known as the Wolf Society until whites mistranslated the name to the Dog Society. These young warriors painted their mouths and cheeks red and enjoyed the privilege of entering any lodge and taking such food as they desired, growling and otherwise behaving like their namesake. Although most of the society's songs have been lost, they were said to be quite melodious, always ending in a resounding howl.[45]

In addition to forming wolf societies, warriors sought to imitate the stealth, courage, and ferocity of wolves. Proper preparation was crucial. Before departing for war, the Hidatsa performed the *Tseshatiake* or Wolf Ceremony. The leader was known as Old Man Wolf and the warriors as Young Wolves. Participants fasted for four days and nights, practiced self-torture, and concluded with a run and an exhausting dance. Members of the Omaha Wolf Society also danced prior to battle, wearing entire wolf skins with the muzzle painted red. Those who had killed enemies in the past painted their hands and wrists red to symbolize their victim's blood. When they had been successful against an enemy, the Osage celebrated by singing this song: "It is I, the wolf, who feasts upon the fallen foe."[46]

The Wolf Soldiers were the last of the seven great Cheyenne warrior bands to form. According to oral history, a man named Owl-Man became lost in a snowstorm and was near death when he discovered an empty tipi on the prairie. Entering, he lay down and quickly fell asleep. When he awoke, he heard voices, and looking out, saw dozens of wolves. As they entered the tipi, the wolves became human, one old wolf telling Owl-Man: "We have powers of cunning such as no other animals have, and we have the whole earth for our home." The old wolf then instructed Owl-Man in the way of dressing for war by donning a wolf pelt over the head, and painting the lower half of the face, neck, arms, and ankles red, while the rest of the body was painted yellow. The wolf people then sang and danced for four days. When Owl-Man awoke he saw four real wolves running swiftly away from him. He then returned to his village and instructed his people in the ways of wolves. As they entered enemy territory, the Wolf Soldiers sang traveling songs to bolster their bravery:

> *Wolf I am*
> *In darkness*
> *in light*
> *wherever I search*
> *wherever I run*
> *wherever I stand*
> *everything will be good*
> *because Maheo {the Creator}*
> *protects us.*
> *Ea ea ea ho.*[47]

In summer 1837, most of the Wolf Soldiers were killed during a raid against a Kiowa, Apache, and Comanche encampment on the Washita River, the survivors re-forming as the Bowstring Society the following year.

War parties sought leaders with lupine qualities. Among the Osage, these leaders were simply called Wolves, men who were ever alert, active, and tireless. They also were capable of resisting homesickness, one of the great fears of young men who traveled long distances, often for months at a time, in pursuit of glory. Once it appeared, homesickness was said to quickly spread throughout members of a war party, virtually assuring its failure. Whenever an Omaha leader sensed its presence, he quickly organized a *mi'kaçi* or wolf dance, appealing to Wolf's spirit that the dancers might "partake of his predatory character, of his ability to roam and not be homesick." The dance was lively and dramatic, imitating the movements of wolves—their rapid trot, and sudden and alert stops. "Wolves have no fear as they travel over the earth," sang the dancers. "So I, like them, will go forth fearlessly, and not feel strange in any land."[48]

The Iowas believed that resolve was weakest when, after a long night of dancing and singing in preparation for the warpath, the would-be warriors retired for a few hours of rest. Thus villagers often regaled warriors with a song that consisted of endless wolf howls, complete with a barking and whining chorus that was sure to annoy them until they arose, ate a quick breakfast, and departed.[49]

Once on the war trail, the warriors' mimicry became even greater. An Omaha leader selected eight men as scouts to travel in all four compass directions some distance from the main group. These men frequently wore wolf capes, traveled by night, and otherwise imitated wolves by traveling only in ravines or on forested ridges. To call in scouts, the leader ascended a prominent rock or hill and howled. Then, before returning, a scout howled to alert the group of his approach. Among the Cheyenne, it was forbidden to point at an actual wolf with a knife lest the animal take offense and refuse to bestow its power on the war party.[50]

A scout who could understand the language of wolves was particularly valued. Ghost Head, a Sioux warrior of the nineteenth century, described a horse raiding party against the Crows: "I took a wolf skin to a nearby hill and facing the Four Winds, called and cried to the wolves, asking them the whereabouts of the enemy. When I returned from the hill, we smoked and then I told the men what I had learned—how many days away the enemy was, how large their camp was, whether we would meet an enemy war party, and how many men were in it."[51]

Oglala Sioux scouts who were members of the Wolf Cult (*ozunya cin nupa*) and said to be "very fleet of foot, like a wolf," slit the neck of a wolf hide and placed it over their heads, painted their arms from the elbows down and their legs from the knees down with red ochre, then went out in pairs until they had located the enemy. As the war party drew near, the leader smoked a special black pipe carried in a wolf hide previously prepared by a virgin in order to approach the enemy unseen. The lances carried by the warriors were wound with strips of wolf skin and bedecked with owl and crow feathers; the wolf may know everything, but the crow finds anything hidden, and the owl sees at night. A similar warpath wolf ritual was performed by the Crow, Ponca, Sauk and Fox, Menominee, and Ojibway.[52]

The Plains tribe that most personified the wolf was the largest band of Pawnee, the Skidi, who lived on the Loup River in present-day Nebraska. Neighboring tribes of Cheyenne, Wichita, and Comanche possessed enormous respect for their ability, such as traveling all day and night, living on carcasses they found, or on no food at all. Like wolves, their eyesight was said to be so good that they could see "two looks away," their hearing so sharp that they could hear a cloud pass overhead. The universal Plains Indian sign for wolf—made by spreading the first and second finger of the right hand, holding the hand palm out beside the right shoulder, and motioning forward and upward—came to mean Pawnee, or Wolf People. Similarly, the sign for scout combined the signs "wolf" and "look."[53]

At night Pawnee scouts were so adroit at approaching an enemy's camp that even when camp dogs detected their presence and barked, the "wolves" howled so convincingly that the dogs soon quieted. During daylight, a Pawnee scout who wished to ascend a nearby promontory to observe the surrounding country would dress in a white wolf skin, drop to all fours, and trot to the top of the hill. There he would smell the ground, lift his leg as if to urinate, and sit down on his haunches. Anyone at a distance who saw him, would take him for a wolf looking for buffalo. The Pawnee called their war parties *araris taka* or the Society of the White Wolf. In addition to wearing wolf skins, warriors often painted their faces and limbs with white clay and wore two white eagle feathers in their hair to resemble wolf ears. When traveling they never moved in a direct line, but, wolflike, followed an ever-changing course.[54]

Once in battle, Wolf's spirit could provide great protection to its owner. During a skirmish with the U.S. Army at Beecher's Island in Colorado in 1868, a Cheyenne warrior named Wolf Belly repeatedly charged back and forth in front of soldiers at close range without being touched in the resulting torrent of bullets. Another Cheyenne, Wolf Man, reportedly was struck in the chest by two bullets at point-blank range during a battle on Wyoming's Powder River in 1865, but merely shook them out of his vest. Even when the power failed to work, the symbolism of that power remained strong. During the Big Hole battle of the 1877 Nez Perce War, a warrior named Sarpsis Ilppilp was wearing a white wolf skin cape when he was killed close to the soldiers' line. So valued was the cape that at least eight warriors tried to recover it and several were wounded before one, himself shot in the attempt, finally succeeded. In 1838 on the Washita River, a Kiowa warrior named Sleeping Wolf almost single-handedly repulsed an attack by Cheyenne and Arapaho warriors before being killed. So respected was this man's courage that all nine Cheyenne who struck coup on him that day honored Sleeping Wolf (also known as Yellow Shirt for clothes he wore that day) by naming their children after him.[55]

Wolf's power could also heal. Once, in a battle with the Sioux, a Crow warrior named Swan's Head was shot twice through the lungs and given up for dead. After the fight, a medicine man, Bird Shirt, moved the mortally wounded warrior to a brush shelter and began singing. According to a witness named Plenty Coups, Bird Shirt took a wolf skin and began painting himself: "his legs to the knees, his arms to their elbows, his nostrils, and strips below his eyes he made red, while he sang steadily with the beating drums." Then he dabbed clay on his head, making ears so realistic "that I could not tell [them] from a real wolf's ears." As drums beat faster, Bird Shirt then trotted around Swan's Head four times. Each time he shook his rattle and dipped the nose of the wolf skin in water and sprinkled it on the warrior, whining just "as a wolf-mother whines to make her young pups do as she wishes." Suddenly, Swan's Head sat up. Bird Shirt turned his back to the warrior and howled four times. Then he lifted the wolf skin four times, and each time Swan's Head appeared better until he finally stood up. "He was bent, his body twisted, but his eyes were clear while Bird Shirt trotted around him like a wolf, whining still, like a wolf-mother coaxing her pup to follow her."

Bird Shirt led Swan's Head to a nearby stream, pawing the water and splashing it over the wounded man's head. Then, continuing to whine, he "nosed the water with the wolf skin, and made the nose of the skin move up and down over the bullet holes, like a wolf licking a wound." Black blood spurted from the wounds, followed by red blood, then Swan's Head and Bird Shirt returned to the village where they smoked together. Swan's Head eventually died from his wounds, but what remained clear in Plenty Coup's memory was the incredible manner in which the ceremony had brought Swan's Head back from death's door, as if his wounds were of no consequence.[56]

In the late nineteenth century, Kiowas told ethnologist James Mooney about a warrior who was abandoned to die after having been desperately wounded in a battle with Mexican troops in southern Texas some fifty years before. That night, while lying on the ground awaiting death and unable to move, the warrior heard a wolf howl nearby. Soon the animal approached closer and began licking the man's wounds with such soothing effect that he fell asleep. When he awoke much refreshed, the wolf suddenly spoke to him, telling him to keep up his courage, that he would not only live but would soon be rescued. A short time later some friendly Comanches discovered the wounded warrior and returned him to his village. At the next sun dance the grateful man made a public offering for his rescue, taking the name Gray Wolf. Mooney believed the story was "not impossible." A wolf could have licked the warrior's wounds much as a dog might do, and by its companionship, have enabled the man to hold out until rescue. Nonetheless, the ethnologist assured readers that the wolf's conversation was strictly the imagination of the warrior.[57]

In addition to war wounds, the wolf provided healing remedies for a multitude of injuries and sicknesses. Wolf liver was used by the Aztecs as one ingredient in a concoction for curing "black blood" (melancholia), and they believed that pricking the breast with the sharpened bone of a wolf could stave off death. Moctezuma appears to have kept wolves in his zoological gardens specifically for these and other medicinal purposes. Among the Haida, a shaman treated a sick person by wearing a wolf's tail on top of his head so that it drooped down his back. Dancing around his patient, he made scooping motions with his hands and arms as if to remove the illness and cast it away. To the Kwakiutl, the most powerful shaman or *pahala* was the one who assumed the power of Wolf. For internal pain, he prescribed four bites of hot wolf fat, while four bites of a wolf's heart, eaten raw, cured asthma and vomiting of blood. Kwakiutl people who were bewitched were said to soon recover after drinking wolf blood.[58]

To prevent frostbite, a Cherokee man would rub his feet in the ashes of the previous night's campfire and sing four verses of a short wolf song, ending with a prolonged howl. Then he would paw the ground with his feet in imitation of a wolf, whose feet it was believed were never frostbitten. Among the Hidatsa, if a woman was experiencing a difficult birth, a shaman came and smoked with her husband, then took a wolf skin cap and gently stroked the woman on her back, singing and rattling an instrument called a *schischikue* or wolf rattle.[59]

Rabies was a potentially deadly, if uncommon, threat. Most animals that acted suspiciously were easily avoided, but a rabid wolf could suddenly enter a village and bite a number of people before it could be dispatched. The Cheyenne called such a wolf *wun stah' wun ne,* meaning one who "loses his heart, sense, mind, or intelligence," and they believed that February and March were the most likely months for a rabid wolf to appear. Among the Blackfeet, a victim who showed disease symptoms was bound hand and foot with ropes, rolled in a green buffalo hide, and a fire was built on and around him until the hide dried out and began to burn. Then fellow villagers quickly put out the fire, removed the victim from the robe, and pronounced him recovered. During the late nineteenth century, when naturalist George Bird Grinnell inquired as to how this treatment cured rabies, the Blackfeet replied that there was "so much water coming out of his body that none was left in it, and with the water the disease went out, too. All the old people tell me that they have seen individuals cured in this manner of a mad wolf's bite." Other authors report that Indians realized the ineluctable consequence of this disease and seldom attempted any kind of treatment.[60]

When its power failed to heal, Wolf sometimes played a part in death. This portrayal could be numinous, such as when the Blackfeet termed the Milky Way the Wolf Road, the path worn across the heavens by traveling spirits of many generations of Blackfeet dead. Among both the Naskapi Cree and some Canadian Eskimo, wolves guarded portions of the nether world, and to the Great Lakes Menominee, the wolf was Lord of the Dead.

But Wolf's role could be also pragmatic. The Cheyenne believed that wolves and other animals would scatter the dead across the prairie in preparation for the wind to carry their remains to the four cardinal directions, wherein dwelled the Sacred Persons. This was especially true of warriors whose bodies were intentionally left on the field of battle. Other tribes or individuals believed that the scavaging of human corpses by animals was inevitable, but chose to forestall the event by tightly wrapping the dead in robes and placing them on scaffolds, in trees, or in caves or rock crevices. If bodies were buried, soil or stones were often piled on them to foil scavengers. Still others went to great lengths to keep wolves permanently away from the dead. Hernando de Soto's 1539 expedition to Florida discovered Juan Ortiz, a member of the ill-fated Pánfilo de Narváez expedition twelve years earlier, who, as a slave of the Apalachee Indians, had been put to work for over a decade chasing carrion-foraging wolves from a village burial mound.[61]

In the mid-1700s, Swedish scientist Peter Kalm traveled through Pennsylvania and described the aftermath of a smallpox outbreak that killed hundreds of Seneca Indians: "The wolves then came, attracted by the stench of so many corpses, in such great numbers that they devoured them all, and even attacked the poor sick Indians in their huts, so that the few healthy ones had enough to do to drive them away."[62]

In the late autumn of 1781, a major smallpox pandemic struck the tribes of the northern Great Plains and Upper Great Lakes. By winter, as many as 60 percent of all infected native people between the Rocky Mountains and Hudson Bay were dead. Fur trader William Walker observed huge numbers of Cree corpses lying about "like rotten sheep, their Tents left standing and the Wild Beast Devouring them." Walker and his men were so horrified to see wolves eating corpses that they attempted to cover the dead with brush and tree limbs.[63]

Smallpox struck again in the summer of 1837, this time among the Mandans, Arikaras, Hidatsa, Sioux, Assiniboin, and Blackfeet of the upper Missouri River. Six months later, an estimated 17,000 Indians were dead. The Mandans—of whom less than 100 survived from a former population of about 1,600—were particularly repulsed at the idea of being scavenged by wolves. Among the victims was the famous Mandan chief Four Bears, who couldn't conceal his hatred of whites who had introduced a disease so vile that he had "to die with my face rotten, that even the Wolves will shrink with horror at seeing Me, and say to themselves, 'That is the Four Bears, the Friend of the Whites.' "[64]

Although there are numerous instances throughout the history and lore of Native Americans that report the feeding of wolves on human dead or dying, little evidence exists to indicate that wolves preyed on otherwise healthy individuals. Nevertheless, it's difficult to believe that wolves have never, however infrequently, attacked and killed native people during the not-so-recent past. Some Eskimo, and to a lesser extent Indian, oral history supports this view, although such reports are mostly from the time before the introduction of firearms and involve lone individuals or children. Although he didn't witness the event, explorer Peter Freuchen described an Eskimo woman in Greenland whose face and shoulder were heavily scarred after being attacked by a wolf. When the woman fainted, the wolf ran away. Wolf attacks are also reflected in Eskimo lore, such as the myth of Alarana and Aligunaluk, two children who were the only survivors of a village famine. Discovered by wolves, they were killed and eaten. An old she-wolf, who was also a medicine woman, wrapped their bones in caribou skin and sung them back to life. Soon they transformed themselves into caribou and taught people how to survive using the ways of animals. For the most part, wolf attack stories occur among people who lived outside the range of buffalo, suggesting that wolves may have been less of a threat to humans where natural prey was abundant.[65]

If wolves rarely killed Native Americans, the reverse was not true. Although many tribes officially frowned on the killing of wolves, under certain circumstances and with proper respect, they could be taken for a variety of reasons: pelts, rituals, food, or because they preyed on trapped animals, meat caches, and livestock, that is, if they could be caught. According to the Iroquois, when the Creator made the animals of the earth, He shot each one in the left hind leg so that humans would be able to catch them, but He missed the wolf.[66]

Wolf predation on horses was so great for some Flathead bands of the northern Rocky Mountains that they were forced to rely on their neighbors, the Nez Perce, for a steady supply of the animals. Although the Nez Perce resided outside the range of buffalo and thus also the bulk of wolves, the predators were still a problem, both in their Idaho homeland and when they traveled to the Montana plains to hunt. Upon rising in the morning, a herald would ride through camp, singing: "I wonder if everyone is up! It is morning. We are alive, so thanks be! Rise up! Look about! Go see the horses, lest the wolf has killed one!"[67]

Killing a wolf could be a dangerous business unless it was done in a suitable manner. The Comanche believed the animal should always be killed with an arrow; often the arrow's head was a sharpened wolf's tooth. If a rifle was used, it would never again shoot straight; if a horse chased a wolf, the horse would become lame. When a wolf preyed on Cherokee livestock or raided fish traps, it had to be slain by a professional wolf hunter or the wolf's kin might seek revenge. After tracking down and killing the offender, the hunter addressed a prayer to Wolf's spirit that concluded by laying the burden of blame upon the people of another village. Then he inserted seven small sourwood twigs into the detached barrel of a gun and placed the gun in a stream. In the morning the twigs were removed, the barrel dried, and the spirit of the slain wolf entirely appeased.[68]

An Eskimo hunter might propitiate *amawk's* spirit with offerings of needles and thimbles, if the wolf was female; a knife, if it was male. Then the wolf was skinned. After first removing the head (the skull was used as a whaling charm), the hunter brandished a knife through the air in order to drive Wolf's spirit away. Food taboos followed in which the hunter was expected to eat cold, uncooked food for four days after taking a female wolf, five days for a male. Throughout this period, Wolf's spirit was asked to return and tell other wolves of the good treatment it had received. Like the Cherokee, sometimes the hunter told Wolf that he was from another village. Eskimos also occasionally took pups from a den, raised them for several months until their fur was prime, then killed them with a stone-headed arrow. As penance, the killer had to sleep in a snow hut for one full moon or chance enraging the animals' wrathful spirits.[69]

Among the Kwakiutl, if a warrior or *papaga* (merciless man) had a son whom he desired to become a stealthy warrior, he would kill a wolf and place the child's hands on the wolf's forepaws, praying, "We have come to beg the slyness of your paws, that it may be in this boy's hands." Then the child swallowed four pieces of the wolf's heart which gave him the ability to creep unheard into a house, "as a wolf creeps through a thicket." Such a killing, however, was fraught with risk, for the Kwakiutl believed every wolf carried a magic crystal, *hwela,* in its right foreshoulder that contained its life and could cause mischief if not rendered sufficient respect. When a hunter found a dead wolf in the woods, he would sit down and pretend to weep, scratching his face and praying. Then he wrapped the body in a blanket and either buried or covered it with stones.[70]

For an extended period during the 1970s, anthropologist Richard Nelson lived among the Koyukon of north central Alaska. Although an elder once told Nelson that he had taken numerous wolves in his lifetime, he did not enjoy killing them. "They're too smart," he said, "too much like people." For the Koyukon, wolf taboos abound. A hunter won't shoot a wolf caught in a trap until it looks away, and afterward the rifle must be placed in the front left corner of the house for four days. Koyukon women aren't supposed to skin a wolf, and children can't play with the hide. Once when Nelson observed a young boy pulling a wolf skin over his head and growling like the animal, his parents cried, "Hutlaanee!" (It's tabooed!), and made him stop. Sometimes a dead wolf is offered a chunk of prized body fat from a moose or caribou, a practice arising from Distant Time when Raven sent Wolf's son to hunt for him. In exchange, Wolf requested the best part of a kill always be given to his son. One day Nelson discovered a skinned wolf carcass along a trail. It had been placed on wood and cardboard to keep it off the snow and ground, and its legs had been severed at the joints, save for the tendons which were left to protect the human hunter from having his children become arthritic or crippled. The carcass had been cut open to avoid the stigma of having not "used" the animal. Pushed between its teeth was a piece of dried fish. Nelson and his Koyukon companion gave the carcass a wide berth, leaving it "to the stillness of the remote muskeg where it lay, hurrying away to the nether edge of its power."[71]

Like the Koyukon, most native people killed wolves primarily for their skins, to be used for clothing, ceremony, or disguise. A few tribes—Arikara, Mandan, Blackfeet, Cheyenne, and even the Koyukon during olden times—occasionally killed wolves for food, although most would eat young ones, resorting to older animals only if other food was scarce. Many of these same tribes relished cooked dog, so the eating of a wolf was not far afield. Among the Cree, a young wolf or *me-hin-gen,* was "esteemed good eating," according to an early European observer. Wolves yielded "a large proportion of the grease eaten by the Indians and made into the finer kind of pemmican by them." Leftover wolf fat was said to make an excellent dressing for softening leather.[72]

Before the advent of guns, native people killed wolves in a variety of ways. As in prehistoric times, wolf remains have been discovered among carcasses of buffalo that the Blackfeet stampeded over cliffs or *pishkins.* Caught up in the frenzy, the wolves probably were carried over the edge along with stampeding buffalo. The fetid odor of these sites drew great numbers of wolves, some of which were undoubtedly caught by simple snares. Sometimes hunters returned early in the morning to these kills to find the animals so gorged with meat that they were easily dispatched. Another method, popular with the Chippewa, was a sharp wooden fishhook. Baited and hung from a tree limb, it caught wolves as they leaped off the ground. When the Cree moved camp, they often would slit a dog's throat and drag it behind a travois. A hunter would drop off the trail, conceal himself, and when an unsuspecting wolf came along, shoot it with an arrow. This technique was used so frequently that some wolves became wary, hesitating to follow the blood trail. The Cree were convinced wolves could count only to seven; after the first seven people had passed by, they claimed that a hunter on the back trail usually had greater success.[73]

Eskimos used deadfalls made of ice, snares, and an ingenious device known as an *isiiviroaq.* A thin, six-inch strip of flexible baleen was sharpened on each end, folded, and then frozen inside a piece of seal blubber or fish skin about the size of a plum. Upon discovering the bait, the wolf bolted down the entire piece. After thawing, the baleen sprang back to its original shape and pierced the stomach. This device was so painful that the victim usually traveled only a short distance before lying down, and was easily found by the hunter.[74]

The most effective way for Eskimos to catch wolves was an ice trap. Permafrost precluded digging a deep hole, so during winter trappers constructed elaborate huts made of dense snow or ice with smooth sides that sloped inward, similar to an igloo without a top. Then they placed rancid seal or whale blubber inside and covered the opening with a thin crust of ice. A more elaborate version utilized a heavy sliding ice door attached to a baited trigger. In summer they built the trap with soil and covered it with brush or grass.

Wolf pits were common throughout most of the continent. On the Great Plains, a hole was dug ten-feet deep and some thirty feet in circumference, baited with buffalo bones and entrails, then covered with grass or willow wisps. Snares set around the pit often caught wolves too wary to venture across the opening. The Blackfeet built a variation of this trap, setting heavy stakes into the ground at a forty-five-degree angle pointing toward the center of a circle containing one or two dead buffalo. Wolves would jump down into the enclosure, but were unable to climb out. Occasionally, sharpened sticks were placed in the bottom to spear them as they fell into the pit. During the 1860s, one of these pits caught eighty-three wolves and coyotes during a single night. Among those trapped were several highly valued white wolves, their skins used to trim the margin of buffalo robes.

A variation of a wolf pit was sometimes used to capture eagles. A hunter would stuff a sewn wolf skin with grass, slit a hole in its side, insert a piece of buffalo meat, and, finally, dab the fur with blood and liver. Then he would excavate a shallow hole in the ground, lie down, and cover himself with willows and grass until only the wolf effigy appeared above the surface. When the eagle came and perched on the wolf, the man in one fluid motion grasped the bird by its feet, threw it to the ground, and crushed it with a knee to its breast.[75]

Pits were so prevalent in some places that they became a hazard. During an expedition to present-day Manitoba in 1800, fur trader Alexander Henry complained that the members of his party "were several times in danger of breaking our necks" in the deep pits. "These holes are covered with dry grass at the season when wolves are good, and every morning are found to contain some of those animals. In summer the grass grows strong and high about the mouths, entirely concealing them, until one arrives upon the very brink and is in danger of tumbling in headlong." When Hudson's Bay Company's Peter Skene Ogden journeyed into present-day northern California in May 1827, he was astonished to discover numerous wolf pits, some "nearly thirty feet deep" and all with sharpened stakes at the bottom. Ogden named the drainage where the pits abounded Pit River when three of his trappers fell in, resulting in their injury along with the death of a "valuable" horse. Indians feared these pits as well. During the early 1800s, on a narrow path along the upper Missouri River, a scout for a Hidatsa war party stopped and refused to travel farther, suspecting a concealed wolf pit ahead. The chief, wishing to shame the man, proceeded on and fell to his death on the sharpened sticks below.[76]

Despite occasional successes with these and other methods of taking wolves, Native Americans appear to have never killed enough to threaten their existence or affect overall wolf populations in any significant manner prior to the arrival of Euro-Americans. Their weapons and techniques were simply too crude, but more important, they had no desire to kill more animals than they required beyond their immediate needs. Nor did they possess an agenda for intensely manipulating their environment, even in periods of scarcity when they found themselves in direct competition with wolves. Although at various times and places, native people viewed the wolf with fear, respect, affection, or even indifference, never did they consider it worthy of hatred, persecution, or wanton destruction. On the contrary, a world without such animals was unthinkable. The result was a spirit of obligation toward and a sense of unity with all creatures, but particularly wolves whom they recognized were most like themselves.

Maintaining such a relationship may not have been as easy as it sounds. From the Oneida, one of the original six nations of the Iroquois Confederacy, a traditional oral poem describes an ancient time when, due to overcrowding, their people decided to move. The decision was made quickly and without regard to the fact that the place they chose was inhabited by a large number of wolves. At first they were content with the new location until wolves appeared more frequently at the edge of the village, and people began to fear for the lives of their children. Soon wolves became so bold that the men of the village spent all their time and energy driving them off, leaving no time for hunting. They knew that with great effort over a period of years they could kill the wolves, but they feared that such an endeavor would render them a changed people, more concerned with altering life to suit their purposes than regarding themselves as but another member of earth's natural order. As a result, they chose to move away and leave the land to the wolves. From that time forth, whenever a critical decision had to be made concerning the future, the Oneida considered "how much was enough and how much was too much." Someone would rise and pose the question: "Tell me now my brothers! Tell me now my sisters! Who speaks for Wolf?"[77]

Like other Native Americans, the Oneida were soon overwhelmed by an invading culture that had scant understanding of such a sense of nuance toward the earth, plants, and animals, and in particular, wolves.

Centuries would pass before anyone would venture again to speak for Wolf.

4

RAVENING RANGERS

At the conclusion of his second journey to the coast of North America, the great navigator Jacques Cartier prepared to sail home to France in the spring of 1536. Due to the hospitality of a band of Iroquois led by its chief, Donnaconna, Cartier possessed a map of the lower St. Lawrence River, the great waterway that led to the interior of the New World. Thanks also to herbal remedies of the Iroquois, Cartier and most of his men had survived a brutal attack of scurvy the winter before.

In return, on the other hand, Cartier seized Donnaconna and nine other Iroquois as gifts for King Francis I, imprisoned them, and prepared to weigh anchor. It was a journey from which they would never return. Gathering on shore the evening before the ship departed, Donnaconna's fellow villagers seemed to sense this fact. As darkness fell, hundreds of people began emitting deep, mournful wails that resonated across the water and lasted throughout the night. It was a sound, recounted Cartier, exactly like the howling of wolves.[1]

Seventy years after Cartier, Samuel de Champlain sailed to Cape Cod and landed near a large village of Massachuset Indians. Offended by the unwelcomed presence of Champlain's crew, one morning the Indians attacked, killing four men and wounding another before disappearing into the woods. Champlain and the survivors buried their dead, planted a cross, and retreated to their ship. Soon the Indians reappeared, uprooted the cross, and disinterred one of the dead men. Then, as Champlain and his crew watched, they contemptuously turned their backs and "made mock at us by taking sand in their two hands and casting it between their buttocks, yelping the while like wolves."[2]

From such inauspicious beginnings, Europeans arriving in North America invariably associated wolves with Native Americans.

Indians didn't take offense at such a notion. Like the Iroquois and Massachusets, so many tribes admired the wolf that identification with the animal came easily. "Wolf" was not only a common clan name among certain eastern tribes, but the personal name of many chiefs and warriors. Consequently, the French were only following local custom when they began referring to Indians as "loups." At first they used the word to describe the Mahican Indians of the upper Hudson River Valley, but after the mid-1600s it was increasingly used to characterize numerous northeastern tribes. By then, however, the term had come to have a wholly different meaning, describing those Indians who proved more obdurate than others in the face of expanding white settlement. Jesuits attempting to save Indian souls in French Canada readily adopted the metaphor. "Savages" who refused redemption, the clerics declared, were possessed by the devil—*ce loup infernal*.[3]

By the time English immigrants began arriving in large numbers, the synonymy was complete. A 1638 Plymouth Colony statute levied a five shilling fine from "whoever shall shoot off a gun on an unnecessary occasion, or at any game except at an Indian or a wolf." Prior to the Indian War of 1675, the Puritan clergyman Increase Mather wrote that Indians were "ravening Wolves, who lye in wait to shed blood." Before the first century of settlement had ended, Puritan Solomon Stoddard appealed to the Massachusetts governor for assistance in hunting Indians with the use of dogs. "It might be looked upon as inhuman to persue them in such a manner," wrote Stoddard, but those who "act like wolves" deserve "to be dealt with all as wolves."[4]

To European immigrants the comparison made perfect sense, for they had come from a continent with a long history of strife with the predator. More than two thousand years before, Greeks had rewarded the killing of a male wolf with a bounty equal to the value of an ox; a female wolf, that of a sheep. For centuries, Latvians of the eastern Baltic Sea sacrificed a goat each December to wolves in order that their livestock might be spared further depredations. Every St. George's Day, Russian peasants prayed that "God grant the wolf may not take our cattle," while in Scotland priests prayed for deliverance from "robbers and caterans, from wolves and all wild beasts." During the Middle Ages in France, Spain, and Russia, wolves were known to feast on the dead of plagues and wars, and were believed to attack children and lone travelers. Fear gave rise to folklore about werewolves, creatures part wolf, part human. Satan himself was said to be such a beast. About the time Europeans began coming to the New World, people accused of lycanthropy were regularly put to death. Between 1598 and 1600, one French magistrate decreed death to six hundred citizens for being werewolves.[5]

In northern Scotland, wolves so frequently dug up corpses of the newly buried that Scots were forced to transport their dead to a rocky island for burial. To counter wolf depredations, the Irish selectively bred the Irish wolfhound, a dog large enough to pursue wolves for sport as well as to protect stock. Wolfhounds proved so popular that in 1652 Oliver Cromwell banned their export, claiming Ireland needed them all. By that date, however, wolves were already scarce throughout most of the British Isles. England killed its last wolf sometime in the early 1500s. Scotland "speared" its final one in 1743, and Ireland reported the animal gone by 1776.[6]

Despite the fact that wolves had been either exterminated or reduced to only remnant populations in most of Europe by 1700, the folklore and myths surrounding wolves was deeply ingrained in the common psyche. As late as one hundred years after wolves disappeared from England, roadside refuges known as "spittals" still existed for wolf-oppressed travelers. A small spy hole in the door, used to watch for wolves before exiting a spittal, was called a "loup hole" from which the modern word "loophole" was derived.[7]

To a great degree, it was this collective memory—a mixture of fact, fantasy, and folklore about wolves—that seventeenth-century Europeans brought with them to North America. Rarely did they have any firsthand knowledge of the animal.

But it was not long before they did; wolves literally met them at the shore. At Jamestown in 1609, Captain John Smith described "Wolues," in addition to "Lions, Beares, Foxes," that inhabited the forest just beyond the coast. On the first night that the *Mayflower* lay anchored in Cape Cod Bay in 1620, the Pilgrims were awakened by howling. They wasted no time declaring war against wolves as soon as they stepped ashore, one that would soon spread throughout the entire continent and persist for over three centuries.[8]

For the most part, their reasons were economic. Wolves preyed on animals, both wild and domestic, that colonists deemed not only valuable but absolutely essential for survival in the New World. Unlike Native Americans, their relationship with animals was chiefly pragmatic; animals were regarded as instruments of enterprise, commodities to be sold or traded. Because wolves competed for these animals, they were, in effect, economic enemies. But wolves also could be foes of a more personal nature, both to body and spirit. To Puritans who settled New England, fear of wolves was so steeped in religious symbolism that it pervaded secular life. Long after both Puritanism and wolves had faded from much of the New World, these beliefs and attitudes continued to shape public opinion about the predators.

As strict biblical constructionists, Puritans found support for their views in scripture. Following the New Testament belief that Christ sent his followers "forth as sheep in the midst of wolves," John Winthrop, the first governor of Connecticut, described himself as "a poor shepherd" whose responsibility it was to secure his flock "from the wild, rapacious quadrupeds of the forest." If wilderness represented the evil waiting to consume sinful souls, then the wolf was its most visible instrument of death and destruction. One Puritan pastor described wild New England as "a waste and howling wilderness," filled with "hellish fiends, and brutish men," a place that was nothing more than a "devil's den," haunted by "grim death and eternal night." Cotton Mather, Massachusett's most prominent clergyman, was more explicit, warning of "the rabid and howling Wolves of the Wilderness [which] would make . . . Havock among you, and not leave the Bones till the morning."[9]

Mather and others may have been speaking metaphorically, but not entirely. The threat of bodily attack by wolves was real to immigrants just arrived from Europe where such tales abounded. Some of those who had been in the New World for a time attempted to calm newcomers' fears.

One colonist assured English immigrants in the early 1600s that no wolves had "ever set upon a man or woman," and another reported that the animals always flee from people and are "afraid of us." John Lawson, the surveyor general of North Carolina, admitted in 1711 that wolves "go in great Droves by night," but "they are not Man-slayers, neither is any Creature in Carolina unless wounded." This proved true not only in the colonies but throughout the continent. Samuel Hearne, the first European to extensively explore northern Canada, wrote: "All the wolves in Hudson's Bay are very shy of the human race, yet when sharp set, they frequently follow the Indians for several days, but always keep at a distance."[10]

This should have been welcome news to immigrants had they believed it. Most, however, continued to cling to the same fears and prejudices about wolves that they had possessed in Europe. In Pennsylvania people reported seeing packs of five hundred wolves, and one man claimed he was followed by a pack of two hundred. Fear of personal harm from wolves soon gave way to another of a more real nature: colonists began losing valued animals to wolves. It made no difference that in the beginning most of these animals were wild and had served as prey for wolves for millennia. Colonists resented every single killing by a wolf.

This was true of all large wild game, but particularly white-tailed deer. Because deer were the most abundant ungulate in eastern North America, numbering twenty-five million or more animals, they were the predominate prey of both wolves and humans, Indians as well as early colonists. Unlike the quasi-feudal system that immigrants had left behind in Europe, deer and other wildlife in the New World were considered public property, the game of the commons, available to anyone who desired to hunt or trap them. Settlers often subsisted almost exclusively on deer to provide meat and clothing as they moved into the country, only later introducing domestic animals to take their place. Soon deer hunting and trapping attracted commercial interests and became a hugely successful industry. In 1753 in North Carolina alone, over thirty thousand deer skins were exported to Europe, while thousands more were used for colonists' clothing. By then a "buck" was a standard of frontier trade, equal to a Spanish peso, and known by the German name of "thaler," or dollar. Any deer lost to wolves was a dollar out-of-pocket.[11]

Whether deer were abundant or scarce, colonists were quick to fault wolves. In describing New England in 1633, colonist William Hammond wrote, "Here is good store of deer; were it not for the wolves here would be abound, for the does have most two fawns at once, and some have three, but the wolves destroy them." A century later, when deer in eastern North Carolina had been decimated by overhunting, naturalist Mark Catesby blamed the "awful creature" that travels "in droves by night and hunt[s] deer like hounds with dismal, yelling cries."[12]

After deer, colonists and wolves primarily sought buffalo, elk, moose, woodland caribou, and beaver. By the mid-1700s, most of these animals had either disappeared or had been severely reduced in colonial North America. Habitat loss played a part, but excessive hunting appears to have been the main cause of their demise. Beaver began to decline as early as 1638 when King Charles II decreed their compulsory use in the manufacture of hats. Moose and caribou, restricted almost entirely to New England, were never numerous and retreated farther into Canada as settlement advanced. Buffalo also failed to occur in great numbers east of the Appalachians and were mostly gone by 1730. The last wild elk is said to have succumbed in Pennsylvania in 1867, although the species had largely disappeared there over a century before.[13]

Because deer were the primary prey of eastern wolves, early conservation efforts on their behalf might have lessened the severity of coming trouble had colonists not so quickly eliminated them. As settlers hacked away at the hardwood forest—so extensive it was said that a gray squirrel could travel from the Atlantic to the Mississippi without touching the ground— new vegetative growth sprang up, a situation beneficial to deer, provided they are protected from overharvesting. However, husbandry of deer or much of anything else wild was not foremost on colonists' minds. In 1647 citizens of Newport, Rhode Island, passed an ordinance prohibiting deer hunting for two months, but its purpose wasn't deer preservation. Wolves, attracted to the countless deer carcasses killed by hunters, had become increasingly difficult to trap. If there were fewer dead deer, reasoned towns-folk, "the wolves would more readily come to bate and so be caught." Deer had become so scarce in Massachusetts by 1694 that hunting there was permanently regulated, but in 1718 a three-year hunting ban had to be instituted to save them. By the time of the American Revolution, every colony but Georgia had an annual closed season to help protect deer from hunters. A century and a half later, deer numbers in eastern North America reached a nadir of probably less than 500,000 animals, or just 2 percent of their former abundance. Eventually, protection succeeded. Deer have re-bounded so well that they are believed to be almost as numerous today as in colonial times. But recovery came too late to benefit wolves, described by one early historian in the wake of New England's deer declines as "great gaunt masses of hunger."[14]

As wild prey became increasingly scarce, wolves turned to domestic animals, a behavior they were to repeat with each successive wave of settle-ment throughout the continent. Compared to wild game, domestic animals were easy targets. When colonists began losing livestock, the passive re-sentment they had previously demonstrated toward wolves quickly esca-lated into full-blown retaliation.

It's easy to understand why this happened. Due to the scarcity of livestock and the exorbitant cost of transporting them by ship from Eu-rope, every sheep, goat, pig, chicken, duck, horse, and cow was invaluable. Unlike wild game, these animals were not property of the commons but private property of the dearest nature on which the colonists' very survival depended, particularly in those places where wild animals had been elimi-nated. There was simply no abiding the loss of livestock to the "common devourer."[15]

In the beginning, wolves were said to have preyed more on pigs and goats than horses and cows, although it wasn't long before these latter animals were pursued as well. Red or chestnut-colored calves were particu-lar favorites. Colonists explained this phenomenon by asserting that wolves mistook them for deer. As a result, red calves were far less valued than ones of other colors.[16]

Of all domestic stock, sheep proved the most vulnerable. Thousands imported by colonists fell prey to wolves, making the raising of sheep "a very precarious business," according to one early chronicler. It wasn't un-usual in winter for wolves "to prowl through the settlements by night in large companies, destroying whole flocks in their way." By 1643 fewer than a score of sheep survived along the lower Hudson River in Dutch New Amsterdam, down from several thousand just years before. Forty years later in Virginia, sheep were still relatively uncommon. The simple reason, insisted colonist John Clayton, was that wolves have learned that a "piece of mutton is a finer treat" than any wild game.[17]

Besides livestock depredations, wolves were a nuisance in other ways. In early New England, Indians showed colonists how to fertilize corn by burying shad or herring along with the seed. The fish took about two weeks to rot, during which time they had to be guarded day and night to keep wolves from digging up the fields. Often the mere appearance of a wolf disrupted daily life when the alarm sounded and men dropped what they were doing in order to give chase. Some people weren't above "crying wolf" when it suited their purposes. In Puritan New England, the regularity of wolf attacks on sheep just prior to church services every Sabbath, and the resulting drop in attendance, led some ministers to regard certain members of their own flock with suspicion.[18]

Colonists attempted to reduce their losses to wolves in a variety of ways. The easiest method was to simply avoid those areas inhabited by wolves, primarily forests and thick brush. So much of the unsettled countryside was heavily vegetated, however, that herders were forced to seek open ground along seashores and river estuaries. It was here that colonists first observed deer swimming to offshore islands devoid of wolves. Soon they followed, until all suitable islands from New York to Virginia were filled with livestock, finally protected from what Roger Williams, the founder of Rhode Island and an early advocate of island herding, termed that "fierce, bloodsucking persecutor." The success of islands gave rise to other ideas of how to permanently secure livestock from wolves. In 1717 some desperate residents of Cape Cod proposed building an eight-mile-long, six-foot-high wooden fence completely across the penninsula. But their neighbors living on the mainland side of the proposed palisade objected that they alone would have to deal with the "ravening rangers," and the proposal was soundly defeated.[19]

Not long after early colonists arrived in the New World, they decided to reward the killing of wolves. In 1630, ten years after the Pilgrims landed at Plymouth Rock, the Massachusetts Bay Colony established the first wolf bounty. But what began as a simple system of payment to encourage hunters to reduce the number of predators soon degenerated into a grand opportunity for fraud and abuse.

Bounties began equitably enough when colonists first attempted to transfer their expense directly to those who most profited by fewer wolves. For every wolf killed, stock owners were assessed one penny for each cow or horse they possessed, and a halfpenny per goat or pig. But this meant that owners who had the most livestock paid the greater part of each bounty, even if they lost no animals themselves. It also virtually guaranteed an escalating reward for each dead wolf as herds of livestock increased. Stock owners objected, and two years later the bounty was revoked. But by 1635 wolves were again too bothersome to ignore and the bounty was resurrected, this time as a flat payment of five shillings per wolf. This proved to be a crucial change in how bounties were administered. Instead of livestock owners footing the bill, rewards were paid out of a common treasury and the entire citizenry bore the burden. Two years later the reward rose to ten shillings. By 1648, after twelve separate changes since it had first begun eighteen years earlier, the bounty was set at forty shillings per wolf—nearly an entire month's wages for a common laborer.[20]

Colonists left no doubt about what they hoped to accomplish. In New York the law authorizing bounties claimed its goal was nothing less than that "the breed of Wolves may be whooly rooted out and Extinguished." Consequently, there was little or no endeavor to eliminate the animals that were causing specific depredations; all wolves were targeted. Bounty hunters went wherever wolf populations were large enough to support their efforts. Thus bounties encouraged widespread persecution of the animal.[21]

They also encouraged deception. The 1648 Massachusetts law required that before a hunter collected a reward, he had to show "good prufe" of each wolf by presenting its ears or head to a constable. This last proviso suggests that spurious claims already had become a problem, one that was destined to plague the bounty system time and again. By mid-century, it wasn't unusual to see grinning and bloody wolf heads nailed to the outside walls of town meeting houses. When too many wolf heads adorned the meeting house in a village near Newburyport, Massachusetts, hunters were directed to nail them to the "little red oak tree" nearby the building before receiving a bounty "for their paynes." This didn't stop abuse, however. More than one fresh wolf head disappeared during the night, only to be presented for another bounty the following morning to the constable in a nearby town. When only the ears of the wolf were required, dog or fox ears were frequently substituted. Also there was no way to prove a wolf had been taken locally; animals often were submitted which had been killed many miles distant. Finally, when only male wolves began showing up, officials correctly surmised that females were being spared in order to provide unscrupulous citizens with a perpetual income.[22]

Local governments began to feel the pinch. In some New England communities wolf bounties nearly equaled expenditures for all other purposes. Here was yet another reason to resent wolves: they took money away from vital government services. At the same time colonists were afraid to eliminate bounties or else wolves would increase, making all their past efforts for naught. It was a spiraling dilemma, but few authorities (many of whom were livestock owners themselves) could refuse the temptation to pour yet more money into the politically popular reward. This was never better evidenced than when a man in upper New York in the early 1800s caught a live female wolf, which soon gave birth to six young. He kept the wolves until the next town meeting, where in "animated discourse" he expounded on the "losses and terrors of wolves." When the man suggested doubling the existing bounty, his proposal was unanimously approved by the town council. The following morning he showed up at the town hall with the heads of all seven wolves and demanded and received his payment.[23]

By 1650 one Massachusetts town reported that it finally had managed to transform "hideous Thickets" filled with "Wolfes" into "streets full of Girles and Boys sporting up and downe." This was scarcely the case in most of New England; virtually all other communities continued to portray wolves as "very common and very noxious." As fast as colonists killed wolves, other wolves took their place.[24]

"There is little hope of their utter destruction," lamented Puritan William Wood, "the Countrey being so spacious, and they so numerous, travelling in the Swamps by Kennels: sometimes ten to twelve are of a company. Late at night, and early in the morning, they set up their howlings and call their companies together, at night to hunt, at morning to sleepe; in a word, they may be the greatest inconvenience the Countrey hath, both for matter of dammage to private men in particular, and the whole Countrey in generall."[25]

Wolf eradication was failing, said Wood, but he was unable to explain why. One contemporary writer blamed the persistence of wolves on the fact that before immigrants arrived and took possession of the land, Indians had been "dilligent in destroying the Yonge." It's difficult to imagine Native Americans practicing such intense husbandry of any wildlife populations, but if true, this custom probably was not widespread.[26]

The answer was much simpler: wolves seemed difficult to eradicate because they were. Colonists had unwittingly discovered a startling fact about wolf biology. Even though wolves may be severely reduced in number, surviving animals in the presence of adequate habitat and prey possess the ability to quickly recover. Under such conditions, female wolves breed at an earlier age and have larger litters. If some wolves managed to avoid hunters and trappers and were no longer vigorously pursued, within a few years they might reappear in numbers equal to those of former times. At the edge of settled areas where wolves had been entirely eliminated, there was yet another explanation. Here, former pack boundaries no longer existed, and animals from the adjacent wilderness quickly moved in to take their place. Thus the forest just beyond cleared land proved a constant source of additional wolves. When colonists finally realized this fact, they began to concentrate their efforts beyond their immediate environs. In Scituate, Massachusetts, in the 1650s, town authorities divided up five hundred acres of public land, deemed to shelter "wolves and vermin," into two- to five-acre parcels and required citizens to clear their assigned portion. It was also in this manner that wolves came to be exclusively affiliated with unsettled land or wilderness. This association was largely a human construct since wolves, with their tolerance for a variety of habitats, would have inhabited many of the same lands occupied by settlers had they let them.[27]

Persecution eventually succeeded. Settlers learned to persevere until every predator in a particular region was gone. Then, with each additional settlement, they left less and less wilderness in between to harbor surviving wolves. Relentless pursuit followed by habitat loss ultimately resulted in extermination.

Following Massachusetts's lead, all of the colonies eventually instituted wolf bounties. Both Pennsylvania and Rhode Island hired professional bounty hunters who were paid wages, in addition to bonuses, for each dead wolf. When Virginia's 1632 bounty law failed to control wolves, the colony attempted to enlist the help of its largest Indian tribe, the Powhatans. A 1656 statute provided one live cow to any Powhatan male who produced eight dead wolves. Its purpose was to eliminate wolves while at the same time introducing Indians to the idea of private property as "a step to civilizing them and making them Christians." The Powhatans, however, didn't want English cows, civilization, or religion; they wanted the colonists to leave. By then the English population on Virginia's coastal plain had grown to 30,000, while the Powhatans—afflicted by disease, starvation, and long-time war with the invaders—had drastically declined to less than one-quarter of their previous number.[28]

Virginia tried a different tact in 1669, conducting a census of Powhatans with the sole purpose of determining how many Indians were available to help exterminate wolves. From a total of 2,900 people, some 725 men were selected and assessed a tax of 145 wolves. When this measure also failed to control wolves (or Powhatans), Virginia proposed a flat bounty payable in tobacco: Englishmen received 300 pounds per wolf, Indians 100 pounds.[29]

Other cash-poor colonies followed suit, paying bounties in hogs, sheep, wine, grain, tobacco, rum, lead, or gunpowder. Like Virginia, those who could afford cash for bounties were often particular about who they gave it to—Indians in Massachusetts received ten shillings less than whites; later they were paid in corn or wine. The 1697 law authorizing wolf bounties in New Jersey allowed ten shillings to "Negroes and Indians," and twice that sum to "Christians."[30]

During the period when Virginians were seeking a simultaneous solution to their Indian and wolf problems, other colonies took a less high-minded approach. In 1695 South Carolina passed "An Act for Destroying Beasts of Prey," requiring every Indian bowman to bring in one wolf, panther, bear skin, or two bobcat skins. Indians who failed to comply with this law were to be "severely whipped."[31]

Puritanical Rhode Islanders in 1654 imposed an annual tax of two wolf skins on each Narraganset Indian. Wolves were no strangers to the Narragansets. So frequently did they steal from their traps and food caches that tribal members possessed an adage that the English translated: "The Wolfe hath rob'd me." Now colonists were doing the same to them, said the Narragansets, and they refused to comply. Rhode Islanders had better luck taxing themselves, and in 1688 they managed to collect fifty-three pounds to reward the killing of wolves, for "these animals were still very numerous and troublesome." Wolves remained so common by 1703 that Rhode Island authorities passed yet another bounty law, paying as much as five English pounds for particularly notorious animals. About that same time one elderly resident of the village of Warwick just south of Providence, Rhode Island, was said to sit at his window on moonlit nights "to shoot the wolves when they came howling too near for quiet sleep." Some colonists

claimed to have shot enormous numbers of wolves. A Pennsylvania frontiersman named William Long was credited in 1790 with having killed
over two thousand wolves during his lifetime, many of which he claimed to
have lured close by simply howling.[32]

In addition to shooting wolves, colonists killed them in other ways.
Wolf "drives" (called *battues* in French Canada) were perhaps the most
popular method. Men armed with pitchforks, guns, and spears, surrounded
a wood, thicket, or swamp and advanced all together toward a common
center. Sometimes wolves broke through the human ring, but often they
were slain.

Drives were successfully used in New England for at least two hundred
years. In eastern New Hampshire in November 1830, according to one
account, all able-bodied males "from ten years old to eighty" were summoned to kill a pack of wolves inhabiting a nearby forested hill of about
twenty acres. Six hundred men and boys responded, and after surrounding
the hill at night armed with torches and spears, they began advancing on
the forest at daylight. When "the beleaguered animals, frenzied by the ring
of flame and noise," attempted to break through, four were killed while the
rest escaped. To celebrate their success, "the thirsty soldiers stamped to
the bar to assuage the awful thirst engendered by twenty mortal hours of
abstinence and warfare."[33]

Wolf drives were useful in training colonial militia for forest warfare
against Indians. During 1634 in Lynn, Massachusetts, the monthly training day was spent learning how to surround a small forest, drive wolves to
its center, and then kill them. One participant characterized the day as a
most "pleasant amusement."[34]

Trapping was also popular. When the first iron furnace was fired up in
Barnstable County, Massachusetts, in 1643, wolf traps were one of its first
products. Because iron of that day was impure, traps often made up in
weight what they lacked in tensile strength, making them extremely heavy
and cumbersome. By the late 1700s steelmaking had improved, but large
animal traps were still unwieldy and their handforged manufacture slow
and laborious. In 1785 David Thompson, Canada's most wide-ranging
explorer, described a primitive steel trap "with strong iron teeth, weighing
seventy pounds, and five feet in length for wolves and wolverines."[35]

Early foot or leg traps were also costly, and most wolf hunters opted for
less expensive methods such as deadfalls and snares. Near coastal fishing

villages, hunters bound four mackeral hooks inside a small wool ball and dipped the ball in melted tallow. The baits were then distributed along fences and roadsides. Although it lacked swift potency, arsenic was used in poisoned baits. Neither of these latter two methods proved popular with bounty hunters, however, since the animals frequently wandered away to die. Poisoning also often ended up killing more dogs than wolves. When Massachusetts citizens demanded that a separate fund be set aside to pay for such mistakes, wolf poisoning there soon ceased. Set guns triggered by tripwires or baited lines also had their drawbacks. In some instances wolves were said to have learned to sever the line to the gun trigger, then eat the bait in safety. Unintended victims were also a problem. When a child in Long Island, New York, was decapitated by such a gun in 1650, authorities passed an ordinance banning set guns within a half mile of town and demanding that weapons outside the town be retrieved by sunrise each day.[36]

Perhaps the simplest and most common method of capturing wolves was one that colonists adopted from Indians: wolf pits. A would-be trapper needed only a shovel and a strong back. Baited and well-camouflaged, a pit could be used repeatedly to capture unsuspecting animals. Some pit builders refined this technique by constructing an elaborate revolving platform attached to a center timber acting as fulcrum. When the wolf jumped on the baited platform, it promptly dumped the animal into the pit below. To keep a wolf from escaping, the eight- to ten-foot-deep hole was often excavated more widely at the bottom than the top. When built correctly, observed Virginia's William Byrd, a wolf "can no more scramble out again than a husband who has taken the leap can scramble out of matrimony." The same might be said for wives. On a dark winter night in 1630 in Lynn, Massachusetts, a woman accidently fell into a wolf pit. Soon a wolf tumbled in on top of her. Both wolf and woman spent a terrifying night huddled in opposite corners of the pit until rescuers arrived in the morning. The woman was pulled out, and the "ravenous cruell creature," still cowering in one corner, was bludgeoned to death.[37]

Trapped and cornered wolves weren't always so submissive, although rarely did they pose much of a threat to their captors. This fact, however, hardly meshed with public opinion about the ferocity of wolves. Men who killed them were portrayed as risking life and limb.

In 1739 Israel Putnam, who later achieved fame as a general in the

American Revolution, was a twenty-one-year-old farmer in northeastern Connecticut who had lost seventy-five sheep and goats to a female wolf with a long history of depredations. The wolf was finally caught by the toes of one foot in a steel trap, but she gnawed off her appendages and managed to escape. Putnam, leading a group of mounted men with bloodhounds, tracked the injured animal some forty miles to the Connecticut River and then back again to a cave three miles from his house. There, after several unsuccessful attempts to smoke the animal out of her hiding place, Putnam thrust a shotgun into the hands of his black servant and ordered the man into the two-foot-wide cave entrance. When the man refused, Putnam, fuming at such cowardice and armed only with a torch and a rope tied to his feet, crawled into the hole—one described by Putnam's biographer as "silent as the house of death." Deep in the cave Putnam "discovered the glaring eye-balls of the wolf." He retreated to the entrance, filled his gun with buckshot, and disappeared into the cave again. Moments later the men outside heard a muffled explosion, and began pulling on the rope until they had dragged Putnam, overcome with smoke and noise of the blast, from the cave. Upon recovering, Putnam entered the cave a third time and grasping the dead animal's ears, was pulled out to "no small exultation" from the crowd. For his troubles, Putnam gained a lifelong reputation for fearlessness.[38]

As this story suggests, dogs were an important component of wolf hunts. Both Spanish colonists in the Southwest and English colonists in the East coursed wolves from horseback with dogs, first running them to exhaustion, then, once they were cornered, roping them and allowing the dogs to dismember their victims. In Virginia, it wasn't unusual to see a young gentlemen dragging a dead wolf tied to his horse's tail through a village, pursued by a pack of baying hounds. Dogs proved so effective against wolves that in 1648 the Massachusetts General Assembly encouraged all communities to purchase dogs in order that "all meanes may be improved for the destruction of wolves." The Assembly gave selectmen of each town the authority to requisition and board dogs for wolf hunting, and to exclude from the community any dog that failed to meet with their approval.[39]

Consequently, dogs were so common that in many areas they became a worse problem than wolves, traveling in packs and attacking both domestic stock and wild game. An unknown number probably bred with wolves, producing wolf-dog hybrids. Few people acknowledged this fact, however, and wolves continued to be blamed for depredations, even long after they had disappeared.

One reason was that dogs in early colonial times looked so much like wolves. Most dogs were obtained from Indians, and time and again, chroniclers remarked that these animals appeared more wolf than dog. One observer in Virginia in 1605 noted that rarely were Indians not accompanied by their "dogges," animals that were actually "wolves which they keep tame at command." Mark Catesby endorsed this view in 1743 when he maintained that the dogs possessed by North Carolina Indians were nothing more than tamed wolves. Years later, long after colonists had imported dogs from Europe and numerous breeds were well established in North America, wolf-dog hybrids continued to be favored by Indians. In the early 1800s, botanist Benjamin Barton observed that the appearance of dogs belonging to Delaware Indians "is much more that of the wolf than of the common domesticated dog." In addition to looking like wolves, said Barton, such dogs were less docile and "much more savage" than their domestic counterparts. Eschewing imported dog breeds, the Delawares managed for many years to maintain the purity of the wolflike animal they called *lenchum,* meaning "the original beast." The nearby Mohicans and Nanticokes did the same with their dogs, as did many Iroquois.[40]

Regardless whether wolves, dogs, or hybrids were at fault, for many years stock depredations continued to plague colonists, from poor farmers to prominent landowners. It wasn't until the late 1780s that wolves ceased to be a problem for most sheep owners along the coastal plain of southern Virginia. One of the largest herds, consisting of some eight hundred head, was owned by George Washington, who was a sheep boomer. Beginning in 1788, one year before he became president, he carried on a lively correspondence with London's Arthur Young, president of the Agricultural Society of Great Britain and one of the world's leading agriculturists. Virginia is ripe for "increasing and improving" sheep, wrote Washington, for "we are sufficiently distant from the frontiers not to be troubled with wolves or other wild vermin, which prevents the inhabitants there from keeping flocks."[41]

Young refused to believe it. "Wolves are named as a motive for not raising sheep; surely they cannot be serious, who urge it. They abound all over Europe; in France and Spain, among the greatest flocks in the world, and no wolf could get into my sheep houses, or at least, I may say, nothing is so easy as to keep him out. . . . By night, if secure from wolves, they are secure from dogs; and by day shepherds may have loaded fire arms to kill all that approach."[42]

Washington remained adamant, and for good reasons. Europe was no toehold of civilization surrounded by wilderness serving as a natural sanctuary for wolves. Europeans had long ago adopted labor-intensive shepherding techniques that had struck an acceptable balance between limited numbers of wolves and a large population of humankind. North America in the late eighteenth century was still largely an unknown land. Many colonists had limited financial resources and depended upon their own labor for every task, with little time for intensive livestock husbandry. Sheep, swine, and cattle had to fend for themselves more so than livestock in Europe. To the owners of these animals, every lamb, calf, or shoat lost to a wolf was yet another reminder of how much sacrifice was required before the wilderness was subdued.

For several years Young and Washington politely sparred over the problem of wolves in North America. Even Thomas Jefferson entered the fray when he reported in a letter passed on by Washington to Young that "in the Middle and Upper parts of Virginia, [sheep] are subject to the wolf, and in all of it to dogs; these are great obstacles in their multiplication."[43]

Depredations by wolves and dogs were also a problem in nearby Pennsylvania. Richard Peters, a friend of Washington who was president of the Philadelphia Agriculture Society, reported in 1792 that "for some time hence this will not be a great sheep country; we keep too many dogs, who destroy them and our country is much intersected with mountains, inhabited by wolves, which cannot be extirpated." Even in the Allegeny foothills that were by then "thickly settled," said Peters, wolves continue to "find retreats and breed prodigiously." Despite a bounty for the past half century, their persistence was a daunting obstacle for which there appeared no "speedy remedy."[44]

As an example, Peters recounted his recent visit to a small town near Harrisburg, Pennsylvania. There he was kept awake much of the night by "the howling of wolves," an occurrence that was so common, he claimed, that only he seemed to notice. The next day, while Peters was visiting the local courthouse, a man appeared carrying two wolf pups and demanded a bounty reward. Before the money could be rendered, someone shouted that the mother wolf had been seen running after the hunter and was even then approaching the courthouse. The wolf had come "not to give bail," Peters wryly observed, but to "rescue her offspring." The wolf got within one hundred yards of the courthouse before it was shot dead.[45]

By 1800, only a few years after Peters made these remarks, dogs were officially recognized as the chief cause of decline of the sheep industry in Connecticut, Rhode Island, and Virginia. As late as 1890, dogs reportedly killed some 3 percent of all sheep in Massachusetts and 6 percent in Connecticut.[46]

By then wolves had long been gone from southern New England, most having disappeared by 1800, along with beaver, deer, bear, and turkey. Wolves in northern New England held on a little longer. In Vermont a generous state bounty of twenty dollars per adult wolf had so reduced the animals that only a handful were turned in by 1850; a few years later, no one claimed the reward. Maine eliminated its bounty in 1838, and its last official wolf was reported killed in the early 1880s, although the animal was believed to be a migrant from Canada. During that same decade, wolves disappeared from the St. Lawrence Valley, Nova Scotia, New Brunswick, and southern Ontario. Wolves, however, continued to be hunted on Ontario's northern frontier. After authorizing its first wolf bounty in 1793, the province finally discontinued bounties 180 years later for the purpose of "reducing public expense."[47]

Farther south, wolves disappeared from South Carolina about 1860. They persisted in New Jersey until 1887, Pennsylvania until 1891, and New York until about 1900, although these animals were probably migrants from Canada. North Carolina followed in 1905, and finally, the last wolf in the original colonies was killed in the Okefenokee Swamp in southern Georgia in 1908.[48]

These final dates are misleading. As healthy and viable populations of wild animals, wolves were gone from most of eastern North America long before the death of the last animals.

—— 5 ——

SHARK OF THE PLAINS

From the time Europeans first set foot in the New World until after the American Revolution, none of them or their descendants had anything good to say about the wolf.

This was particularly true of those individuals at the edge of the frontier who were attempting to wrest a livelihood directly from the land—farmers and livestock owners. To the east of the frontier, people who lived in places where wolves were mostly a memory, albeit a strong one, sided with country folk. Such empathy lessened somewhat as frontier turned into hinterland, and hinterland became increasingly urban, but even in cities, fear and prejudice ruled the day. In the first American edition of a popular natural history of mammals published at the beginning of the nineteenth century, the author asserted that "once the wolves have tasted human blood, they always give it the preference." The first authoritative American dictionary, Noah Webster's *A Compendious Dictionary of the English Language,* was similarly judgmental, labeling the wolf a "ravenous" and "rapacious" creature.[1]

But perceptions about the wolf, however deep-seated and pervasive, had already begun to change. In 1791 William Bartram, a fifty-year-old

Quaker, scholar, and accomplished naturalist, published an account of a journey he had completed over a decade before through the wilderness of the Carolinas, Georgia, and northern Florida. Bartram wrote vividly and passionately of the southern wilderness and its plants and wildlife, compiling the most exhaustive list of native birds of that era.

During his travels in Florida, Bartram was startled awake one night by the "heavy tread of some animal" as it escaped into the brush. Upon investigating, he realized that a wolf had made off with a string of fish he had hung on a nearby tree. This prompted the naturalist to consider why the predator had settled for fish when it could have had him instead. "How much easier and more eligible might it have been for him to have leaped upon my breast in the dead of sleep, and torn my throat, which would have instantly deprived me of life, and then glutted his stomach for the present with my warm blood, and dragged off my body, which would have made a feast afterwards for him and his howling associates." From the standpoint of the wolf, Bartram asked, "Would not this have been a wiser step?"[2]

Others before Bartram had determined that North American wolves rarely, if ever, preyed on humans, but he was the first writer to ponder why. The naturalist carried his reasoning no further, admitting that despite his experience, a wolf's howl would always remain a "terrifying" sound to his ears. Nonetheless, his was a significant first inquiry into wolf behavior and its relationship with humankind.[3]

Like Bartram, the individuals who harbored the least resentment toward wolves were those arriving first on the frontier—explorers, naturalists, missionaries, fur traders and trappers. This had been the case during the colonial era and was no less true now as the frontier pushed ever westward. Like Native Americans with whom they often lived, traveled, or traded, frontiersmen generally accepted wolves within the membership of New World fauna. The predators could be bothersome, but for the most part, their presence was tolerated. There were good reasons why this was so. Unlike settlers who would soon follow, frontiersmen were usually on the move, possessed few or no domestic livestock, and thus were only occasionally in conflict with wolves. But even more important, as they ventured farther west they encountered such an abundance of wild animals—buffalo, antelope, mountain sheep, elk, and deer—that most of them didn't consider the wolf a competitor. During this early era of frontier expansion, the predator even had value.

Following the end of the bloody French and Indian War in 1763, the victorious English seized control of much of the continent's lucrative fur trade from the French. Soon English traders and trappers marched west into previously uncharted territory in search of new fur sources. By 1780, their rich discoveries created a boom in the supply of New World furs destined for worldwide markets. Until now wolf pelts had created little interest, but soon they became valued for winter outer clothing (coats, ruffs, and hoods) since the fur did not mat or hold frost, as well as for being a superior leather in the manufacture of shoes. As a result, between 1780 and 1799 some 330,000 wolves were reported commercially harvested in North America. With an annual average harvest of over 16,000 animals, this was the greatest number of wolves ever killed within such a short period in the continent's history.[4]

The records fail to describe the source of these furs, but since wolves in the former colonies had largely disappeared by this time and the West beyond the Mississippi River had yet to be fully exploited, these animals probably came from central and eastern Canada, the upper Mississippi Valley, the Great Lakes region, and from trans-Appalachia. The records are disappointing in another respect, neglecting to distinguish between wolves and coyotes, which were often lumped together.

After the turn of the century the demand for most furs declined with the increased production of textile clothing. Wolf pelts fell out of fashion with coat manufacturers; the hair was coarse, long guard hairs proved brittle, and variations in color made matches difficult. Soon the value of wolf pelts plummeted. Traders of the era now reported that "a wolf's skin may be purchased for a small quantity of tobacco." Between 1800 and 1808, fur trader Alexander Henry of the North West Company reported a total of 3,661 wolf pelts from the Red River District of central Canada, a number less than half the annual harvests of the previous decade. A few years later, Canadian Ross Cox maintained that wolf skins were taken mostly to placate Indian trappers who turned them in along with more valuable furs. Wolves had become so worthless, said Cox, that "the price given for them would not defray the expense of their carriage." According to one trader's estimate, the animals then most sought after were (in descending order): beaver, otter, muskrat, marten, bear, fox, lynx, fisher, mink, wolf, and buffalo.[5]

By the time of this dramatic decline in the value of wolf furs, trappers and other frontiersmen were ranging deep into the interior of the continent, the rich grassland home to millions of hoofed animals and the greatest concentration of wolves found anywhere in the world.

The earliest account of western wolf abundance occurred when Coronado passed through present-day Kansas in 1541, the expedition chronicler reporting "very great numbers of wolves on these plains, which go around with the cows [buffalo]." Two hundred years later, near what is now the Saskatchewan-Alberta border, Anthony Henday, the first white man to explore central Alberta, recorded in his diary: "Wolves without number." Later he wrote, "I cannot say whether them [wolves] or the Buffalo are most numerous." But it was not until Lewis and Clark traveled up the Missouri River in 1805 that anyone described wolves in greater detail.[6]

Near the mouth of present-day Montana's Sun River, Lewis recorded that the expedition was serenaded by "vast assemblages" of wolves "howling around us and lolling about in the plains in view at the distance of two or three hundred yards." Along the Yellowstone River, Clark was so overwhelmed by the abundance of wolves and other animals that he refused to estimate their number, fearing that readers would dismiss his observations as simply "incredible." When the explorers left the plains and traveled west of the Rockies, they found fewer wolves. Lewis reasoned, probably correctly, that compared to the prairies, here "there is but little game on which for them to subsist."[7]

A few years later in 1810, Englishman John Bradbury visited the upper Missouri River and remarked that wolves "were almost constantly in sight." In 1831 in the same vicinity, the artist George Catlin reported seeing as many as fifty to sixty wolves at a time. Prince Maximilian followed on Catlin's heels two years later, finding wolves "abundant" from western Pennsylvania to the headwaters of the Missouri. Ten years after Maximilian, Lansford Warren Hastings, one of the early travelers on the Oregon Trail, recorded wolves "very numerous." He warned those following him that they should expect to pass "many hundreds of them" each day.[8]

When Charles Hoffman crossed the eastern plains by wagon in 1834, he avoided boredom by playing "prairie loo," a game in which two players, one on each side of a wagon, kept track of animals seen on his side. A wolf or deer counted ten points, a grouse one, and the winner was declared when a player amassed one hundred points. Hoffman's companion quickly won when a pack of eleven wolves appeared. "Some of these fellows would stand looking at us within [a] half gunshot as we rode by them," said Hoffman.[9]

In 1843 John James Audubon journeyed up the Missouri River and found wolves "extremely abundant," often seeing one or two dozen each day. At Fort Union, Audubon echoed William Clark, saying that "the number of tracks or rather paths made by the wolves from among and around the hills to that station are almost beyond credibility." Farther south in 1850, the naturalist S. W. Woodhouse reported wolves "very common throughout the Indian territory [Oklahoma], Texas, and New Mexico."[10]

As evidence of wolf abundance, these accounts must be viewed with caution. Similar to fur harvest records, few observers bothered to distinguish coyotes from wolves—all were "wolves." Also both animals often followed travelers for great distances, vanishing, then reappearing from time to time, and thus may have only seemed more plentiful. Despite these caveats, coyotes and wolves appear to have been relatively common features of the West's fauna—coyotes more so, although the dominance of wolves over coyotes is believed to have kept the latter less numerous and widespread than today. Based upon maximum wolf densities today where prey is abundant, the central continent's rich prairie grasslands may have supported as many as 200,000 wolves or half of the continent's total wolf population. Because their hoofed prey primarily inhabited prairies, foothills, and large river valleys, rather than mountainous areas, these locations also contained the most wolves.[11]

Soon frontiersmen developed their own jargon to distinguish coyotes and wolves. A coyote became known as a "prairie jackel," "brush wolf," "small prairie wolf," or "medicine wolf," after a traditional Indian name for the animal. The wolf was called "big prairie wolf," "buffalo wolf," or "loafer," so named because wolves were often seen resting after gorging on a kill. In the Southwest, the wolf was christened "lobo."[12]

Before long, observers began to distinguish between wolves themselves. Those found on the prairies were larger than eastern wolves, although not so big as those farther north in Canada, referred to as "timber" wolves. Individual animals showed so much variation in size that some observers believed color a better gauge. By most accounts black wolves were relatively rare in colonial America, while gray and, to a lesser extent, white or light-colored wolves predominated. As people traveled west to the Mississippi Valley, some claimed they saw more black wolves. In 1833 in eastern Kansas, Maximilian observed so many black and gray wolves, and so few white ones, that he became convinced they were wholly different species. Other travelers, however, reported just the opposite. This confusion was reflected in the subspecies name the naturalist Thomas Say (who came to his calling naturally, great-grandson of John Bartram and William's grandnephew) bestowed on the first scientific specimen of a plains wolf taken in 1823 in Nebraska—*nubilus,* derived from the Latin word *nubes,* meaning cloudlike, obscure, or indefinite in origin. Finally, the naturalist Elliott Coues settled this debate when he correctly proclaimed in 1867 that wolf colors were simply "remarkable variations," and had nothing to do with speciation. Gray predominates, declared the naturalist, but wolves run the gamut from coal black to snow white.[13]

Another notable characteristic of wolves recorded by frontiersmen was their fearlessness. Near the Judith River, a tributary of the Upper Missouri, Lewis and Clark came upon a "great many wolves" feasting on dead buffalo. The wolves "were fat and extreemly gentle," recorded Clark, enough for him to approach closely and kill one with a bayonet. Even in that day and age Clark's experience may have been exceptional, but it suggests how unthreatening some wolves then found humans. Native Americans who inhabited the Upper Missouri—Blackfeet, Gros Ventre, Assiniboin, and Crow—killed either no wolves or relatively few, and their most effective methods were limited to crude traps or the range of spear or bow and arrow. Wolf behavior changed after the animals learned to fear firearms, but until that time, they were often unusually bold.[14]

Having successfully scavenged behind nomadic tribes for millennia, wolves readily trailed the newcomers. They could always be counted on to clean up the remains of game that hunters shot for food, particularly once they learned that the sound of a gun often announced a meal. Sometimes a wolf appeared too quickly to please hunters, gaining the sobriquet "shark of the plains." Lewis and Clark were frequently annoyed when they returned to the site of a kill to retrieve meat and found that wolves had expropriated the remainder. At one buffalo carcass they found twenty-seven wolves had left nothing but bones. Wolves so quickly discovered dead animals that the expedition's hunters learned to shoot only those they could immediately recover. This became the general practice of most frontiersmen, although some never ceased attempting to foil wolves. Flagging carcasses with handkerchiefs or bright material was sometimes successful, but not always. One morning in 1806 in present-day Colorado, when Zebulon Pike returned to two buffalo he had killed and flagged with clothing the evening before, he discovered wolves already had consumed the animals. Thirty-odd years later, fur trapper Osborne Russell and his companions killed ten buffalo along the Greys River in western Wyoming. They took the tongues and buried the meat under three feet of snow, having "laid some stones on the snow over it and burned gun powder upon them to keep away the wolves." The next morning they returned to find "the wolves had dug it up and taken the best of it, notwithstanding our precautions."[15]

Wolves also hung about camps, occasionally attacked a party's horses and mules, and generally made a nuisance of themselves. In May 1822 near Taos, New Mexico, Jacob Fowler recorded that "the Wolves maid an atackt on our Horses the[y] Wounded one Hors and two mules We Have maid a strong Pen Close to the Camp and Still Shut up all the Horses at night While We Remain at this Place to protect them from the Wolfes." Near Edmonton, Alberta, in 1847, the artist Paul Kane reported that eight hundred horses belonging to trappers in the area never strayed far during winter because "their only safety from their great enemies, the wolves, is remaining near the habitations of man." If Kane had any doubts this was true, they were soon dispelled when one day he hobbled his horse, briefly left it alone, and returned to find "two wolves making a dead set at my poor horse, who was trembling with fear. One of them was in the act of springing at him. It was impossible for him to get away, as his forefeet were tied together. I instantly levelled my double-barrelled gun and killed both, one after the other."[16]

Most travelers were irked by wolves about their camps, but at least one man found this an admirable quality. When Englishman George Ruxton journeyed some two thousand miles through Mexico and the southwestern United States in 1846, he found wolves' constant presence indicative of "almost incredible" intelligence. "They will remain round a hunting camp and follow the hunter the whole day, in bands of three or four, at less than a hundred yards' distance, stopping when they stop, and sitting down quietly when game is killed, rushing to devour the offal when the hunter retires, and then following until another feed is offered them."[17]

Ruxton also observed an interesting relationship between wolves and coyotes. After a hunter killed a buffalo, coyotes often approached closely and sat watching while the wolves "lope hungrily around, licking their chops in hungry expectation" some distance back. Hunters would throw pieces of meat to a coyote who would attempt to run away, but "before he gets many yards with his prize, the large wolf pounces with a growl upon him, and the cayeute, dropping the meat, returns to his former position, and will continue his charitable act as long as the hunter pleases to supply him."[18]

Some wolves were so daring that they came directly into camps. During the 1840s, traveler Rufus Sage recorded that wolves "proved a constant source of annoyance," running off with kettles, pans, and other camp paraphernalia. One "piratical pest" even made off with Sage's fur hat from his head while he was asleep. In another instance a companion, using his prized leather saddle as a pillow, awoke to find a wolf had filched the saddle during the night. After "gently drawing it from beneath the head of the unconscious sleeper," said Sage, the wolf "bore off his prize to devour it at his leisure." Sage assumed that such wolves were hungry, but curiosity may have been a better explanation. Regardless, wolves gained a reputation for mischief. When Horace Greeley, famed editor of the New York *Tribune,* traveled across the West in the 1860s, he described the wolf as an opportunistic "scoundrel," possessing a brazen cunning of "imposing caliber." To anyone unfamiliar with the West, declared Greeley, it was impossible to "realize the impudence of these prairie-lawyers."[19]

Such boldness sometimes cost wolves their lives, although ammunition was in such short supply on the early frontier that most people refused to waste it on an animal they didn't consider dangerous or of little value for fur or food. No one shot them, said Lansford Warren Hastings, because their skins "are entirely worthless." When frontiersmen had nothing else to eat, however, they turned to wolves. While wintering on the Oregon coast in 1806, Lewis and Clark reported their not infrequent reliance on the flesh of dog and wolf. This may not have been as onerous as it sounds; many frontiersmen learned to eat dog from Indians and found it quite palatable. In 1832 near present-day Salmon, Idaho, several American Fur Company trappers recorded that "we killed a grey wolf which was fat, and made us a tolerable supper." When two trappers, John Day and Ramsay Crooks, found themselves stranded for several months along the Northwest's Umatilla River in the early 1800s, they survived mostly on a large wolf they managed to kill. They cut up the meat, dried it, and pounded the bones to make soup. Not only did the wolf save their lives, said the trappers, but it tasted "very good."[20]

Members of Audubon's 1843 expedition often entertained themselves by shooting wolves gathered about their camp or by chasing them down on horseback. One day from high atop the palisade at Fort Union, Audubon anxiously watched as the fort's proctor, Alexander Culbertson, ran down a white wolf on horseback, shot it, scooped it up across his saddle, returned to the fort and dumped it at the artist's feet—all in less than twenty minutes. "The beast was not quite dead when it arrived," noted Audubon, "and its jaws told of its dying agonies; it scratched one of Mr. C.'s fingers sorely; but we are assured that such things so often occur that nothing is thought of it."[21]

Twice the expedition ran out of food and each time killed a wolf to eat, but at the last minute managed to locate and kill a buffalo instead. The dead wolves ended up as fish bait, and Audubon drew and painted the specimens he caught. One night around the campfire, one of the party's members recalled that the men discussed "the quality of Wolf flesh, some averring most stoutly that a good fat Wolf was better eating than 'Dog meat.' "[22]

Not everyone had such appetizing choices. When John Fremont attempted to survey a rail route across the San Juan Mountains of Colorado in January 1849, all that the starving and destitute men of his expedition could find to eat was a single dead wolf. "All one side and entrails had been eaten away," wrote one of them, "but we divided the skin and roasted it, hair and all, for one meal, drank the meagre broth for another, and then ate the meat and even devoured the bones."[23]

Although frontiersmen ate wolves as a last resort, such was not the case when wolves turned to humans for food. As Native Americans had long known, the predators readily fed on human corpses. Maximilian traveled west during the 1830s in time to witness the results of yet another devastating smallpox pandemic among Native Americans. "The prairie all around is a vast field of death covered with unburied corpses," most of which Maximilian noted ended up as food for wolves. By the end of the great western migration across the continent in the 1860s, wolves demonstrated a penchant for non-Indian flesh as well. Of the 250,000 people who set off on the Oregon Trail, more than 30,000 perished along the way. Some died from Asiatic cholera, but most were the result of mishaps—shootings, drownings, hypothermia, and starvation. According to one trail traveler in 1850, there was "scarcely a grave that had not been robbed of its contents by wolves, and the bones of its occupant lay bleaching on the prairie."[24]

Perhaps the most famous corpse known to have nourished wolves was the missionary Narcissa Whitman, one of two white women to first travel the Oregon Trail. Narcissa died at the hands of Cayuse Indians in southern Washington in November 1847, her golden hair matted with blood, quirt welts on her face, shot twice, and hastily buried in the mission cemetery. Wolves dug up her body and ate the flesh of one leg before she was finally reinterred.[25]

Wolves were still at it some twenty years later when war broke out between the U.S. Army and Plains Indians. Soldiers assigned to Fort Kearny in central Nebraska reported that they had to bury their dead in deep holes, place heavy planks over the coffins, and then haul large stones to fill the graves. Without these precautions, they said, wolves almost invariably exhumed the dead.[26]

Although a carelessly prepared grave was often discovered by wolves, a body left unburied was a dead certainty. Westerners frequently described anyone violently killed and left on the prairie as having been "made wolf meat." During a running fight with Indians in western Kansas in July 1867 in which two soldiers were believed to have died, brevet General George Custer inexplicably refused to order the recovery of their bodies. A subordinate officer, Captain Arthur Carpenter, took it upon himself to send out a search party for the two men in order to prevent wolves from consuming them. Lucky that he did, for the searchers found one of the men wounded but very much alive. The other man was dead; his body was retrieved before wolves discovered it.[27]

Sometimes wolves could not wait to claim a victim. One August night in 1806 along the Yellowstone River, William Clark reported that the expedition rudely awoke to the screams and curses of Sergeant Nathanial Pryor. While Pryor slept, a wolf, apparently believing him a corpse, bit him in the hand. Before the animal could escape, another man shot and killed it.[28]

Wolves proved so deft at finding exposed or buried cadavers that many frontiersmen possessed a grim fatalism about the fact. In the mid-1840s, Lieutenant J. W. Abert was returning from an exploration of the Southwest when one of his men grew ill and died during a snowstorm in eastern Colorado. Unable to bury the victim, Abert simply left him, declaring it was the man's "destiny to leave his bones on the desert prairies, where wolves howl his requiem."[29]

Abert was not the first or last frontiersman to associate death with the howl of a wolf. Most listeners found the low, mournful quality of the sound unsettling. In fact, the wolf's voice appears to have contributed greatly to many people's fear and dislike of the animal.

"I know of nothing so sad as the howling of wolves," wrote Montana author James Willard Schultz, "they chillingly voice deep, hopeless despair." A howl possessed a quality "that made even the most lighthearted and careless of men pause and listen." Many persons, said Schultz, "could not bear the sound." One of those was Frances Carrington, wife of the commander of Fort Phil Kearny during the 1860s, who claimed she often went sleepless at night due to the "frightening" and "hideous" constant howling of wolves outside the fort.[30]

Others expressed ambivalency. Rufus Sage spoke for many of his day when he stated that the wolf's forlorn cries imbued the landscape with "a savage wildness," producing a sensation of both "terror and admiration." Trapper Herbert Andrus agreed. Along Wyoming's Powder River, Andrus claimed to have been kept fearfully awake one night by an assembly of nearly one hundred wolves, all of whom made "a most terrific howling— some [wolves] milling around keeping up a continuous baying, and others sitting still uttering one prolonged wolf-howl after another." Hours later the animals finally dispersed, but Andrus remained awed by the event. "We had the feeling that we had been a party to something few white men were ever fortunate enough to witness. You know, there is nothing on earth like a lone wolf call—it makes you draw a little closer to the fire, dig a little deeper into your blanket and shudder, knowing in your heart the many things you'll never know."[31]

Not everyone heard it this way. George Catlin thought that the soft and plaintive howl of a wolf was the sound of a "lonesome" animal who had become "lost in the too beautiful quiet and stillness about him." Even

James Schultz admitted that "to the true lover of nature it had a peculiar—if perhaps undefinable—charm." Some listeners actually praised the sound. Maximilian was camped one night in 1833 along the Missouri River when a dozen wolves appeared on the opposite shore and "entertained us with a concert of their sweet voices." Perhaps the most generous tribute came from Thomas Farnham, an early traveler to the Northwest. It is remarkable, said Farnham, to realize that every morning precisely at daybreak, thousands upon thousands of wolves raise their voices in a symphony of sound which "swells along the vast plains from Texas to the sources of the Mississippi and from Missouri to the depths of the Rocky Mountains."[32]

Although wolves brazenly hung around camps, closely followed travelers, swiftly attacked and killed unprotected stock, and eagerly disinterred and fed upon human corpses, most frontiersmen admitted that they stopped short of killing people.

After many years trapping in the Rocky Mountains during the early 1800s, Osborne Russell maintained that wolves "are not ferocious towards man and will run at sight of him." Russell's contemporary, Canadian trapper Ross Cox, was known for his many exaggerated tales, casting himself in death-defying escapes from venomous rattlesnakes to flesh-slashing eagles. Yet in a candid moment Cox asserted that, unlike European wolves, "an American wolf, except forced by desperation, will seldom, or ever, attack a human being." When Scotsman Issac Cowie arrived in Canada to become a fur trapper, he greatly feared attack by wolves. But he soon learned that "instead of men being afraid of wolves, the wolves were afraid of men." Even when near starvation, Cowie insisted, "wolves never plucked up courage to attack people."[33]

Here was a phenomenon that echoed time and again throughout the North American frontier: observers seemed genuinely astonished to discover that wolves did not kill humans.

John James Audubon lost his fear of wolves long before his western travels. When the artist journeyed along the Mississippi River during the winter of 1810, he and a companion passed the nights chasing wolves that ventured out on shore ice. Later in southern Kentucky, Audubon happened on a man walking along a trail with a black wolf. "On speaking with him about this animal, he assured us that it was as tame and gentle as any dog, and that he had never met with any dog that could trail a deer better. We were so much struck with this account, and with the noble appearance of the wolf, that we offered him one hundred dollars for it; but the owner would not part with it for any price."[34]

Not long afterward in western Indiana, Audubon witnessed the capture of three wolves trapped in a farmer's pit. When he inquired how the farmer proposed to retrieve the live animals, to his dismay, the man leaped into the pit armed only with an axe and a knife and proceeded to hamstring the back legs of each wolf. Hoisting the crippled animals out of the pit with a rope, the farmer then turned his dogs on them until they had "satiated their vengeance on the destroyer of their master's flock." This technique used on captured wolves, said Audubon, was the farmer's way of "paying them off in full" for their former depredations. Although the artist harbored no fear of a wolf in the wild, he was apprehensive about what the animal might do if cornered, admitting, "I was not a little surprised to see the cowardice of the Wolves."[35]

Audubon was not alone in this judgment. Others similarly interpreted the timidity of wolves in the presence of humans, and when they failed to live up to their fearsome reputation, the result was profound disappointment. Wolves are "exceedingly cowardly," declared the U.S. Army's Colonel Richard Irving Dodge, "one alone not possessing courage enough to attack even a sheep."[36]

Despite these and other steadfast disavowals of wolf attack upon humans by early western travelers, many people—particularly settlers and homesteaders who followed on frontiersmen's heels—remained unconvinced. There are several reasons why this was the case. Not long after Audubon's journey, the population of the United States exploded to over twenty million people, many of whom were either recent European emigrants or their immediate descendants. During the next decade some three million Europeans would make the journey across the Atlantic; during the 1880s, the number was over five million. These newcomers, like those of colonial times, brought along not only their Old World wolf fears and prejudices, but each successive immigrant wave served as a wellspring of these attitudes, influencing and reinforcing the opinion of yet others.[37]

Attack by wolves also seemed entirely logical. Just as William Bartram had asked, why should an animal like a wolf, powerful and capable of killing prey many times its size, not kill humans?

Fear of attack was no small matter to those persuaded of the animal's murderous intentions. During the mid-1800s in southeastern Wyoming, John Steele was traveling alone when a pack of wolves began following him. As darkness fell, the animals came ever nearer. Unnerved, Steele shot the closest ones, then heard "awful sounds" that he identified as the dead wolves being "devoured" by their brethren. When Steele observed "their glaring eyes and saw how easily they might spring upon me, I realized, that like David, there was but a step between me and death." After a sleepless night, which Steele described as nothing short of "terrible," by morning the animals had vanished.[38]

As nineteenth century wolf stories go, Steele's tale, even his conviction of being at death's door, is more believable than most. Whenever wolves followed travelers who were alone and unused to such behavior, the experience could be unsettling. Often such tales did not stop with a sleepless night, for few writers could resist the temptation to embellish the scene. The savage beasts killed and ate their companions, disemboweled their wives, and tore their children limb from limb in blood-drenched feasts of agony, gluttony, and gore. Here was yet another reason to believe that wolves killed and ate humans: such stories fulfilled people's expectations of what life on the wild frontier was like. Even if these stories weren't true, they *should* be.

So many patently false wolf attack tales circulated throughout the nineteenth century that it's difficult to sort out those that may have been authentic. George Bird Grinnell—competent naturalist and keen student of the American West—believed few stories about wolf attacks. Nonetheless, one that did seem plausible to him involved the eighteen-year-old daughter of the famous western trapper and scout Jim Baker. In 1881, Baker's family was homesteading in northwestern Colorado when his daughter went out one evening at dusk to herd some milk cows home for the night. "As she was going toward them," said Grinnell, "she saw a gray wolf sitting on the hillside, just above the trail. She shouted to frighten it away, and when it did not move, took up a stone and threw at it. The animal snarled at her call, and when she threw the stone, came jumping down the hill, caught her by the shoulder, threw her down, and tore her badly on the arms and legs. She screamed, and her brother, who happened to be near and had his gun, ran up and killed the wolf." Grinnell described the wolf as "a young animal, barely full grown." Shaken and bearing the scars of the attack for the remainder of her life, the girl survived.[39]

Another convincing chronicler was Josiah Gregg, an early trader and frequent traveler of the Sante Fe Trail during the 1840s. Once while traveling through Missouri, Gregg spotted a wolf and gave chase on horseback. After overtaking the exhausted animal, he struck it over the head with a wooden club, but the club broke in two. The wolf then attacked and bit his horse; it reared and Gregg toppled off. "I was no sooner upon my feet than my antagonist renewed the charge," said Gregg, "but, being without weapon, or any means of awakening an emotion of terror, save through his imagination, I took off my large black hat, and using it for a shield, began to thrust it towards his gaping jaws. My ruse had the desired effect, for after springing at me a few times, he wheeled about and trotted off several paces, and stopped to gaze at me." Gregg, realizing that he "had the best of the bargain," took to his heels in the opposite direction.[40]

In both these instances, the attacking animal was provoked and may be seen as defending itself. At the very least these accounts suggest that not all wolves were as meek and docile as observers like Audubon and Dodge professed. In light of his experience, Gregg doubted that wolves preyed on humans, "though they probably would if very hungry and a favorable opportunity presented itself."[41]

Alleged wolf attacks sometimes had another source: hydrophobia or rabies. Small carnivores such as skunks and raccoons are the primary carriers of this deadly viral disease that was virtually fatal until a treatment was perfected in 1885. Wolves occasionally became infected, however, and because they were large, quick, and capable of determined attack, such animals were greatly feared.

At fur trappers' rendezvous on the Green River in western Wyoming in 1833, a white rabid wolf wandered into camp during two different nights and bit numerous people and stock animals. Exactly how many victims died as a result is unclear, but one account claims at least thirteen people, along with a prized bull which was being herded west as a nucleus for one of the first Oregon cattle herds. George Holmes, who fellow trappers called "Beauty" for his handsome looks and genial disposition, was one of those victims. After the camp erupted late one night with shouts, curses, and the deep bellowing of the bitten bull, William Drummond Stewart discovered Holmes "seated on the ground, the side of his head and his ear bleeding and torn." By the time the rendezvous ended that summer, several victims had developed hydrophobia symptoms—irrational behavior, fearfulness, foaming about the mouth, and inability to consume water—and died shortly afterward. As weeks passed, Holmes began to believe he had escaped infection, until the bull became ill and died. After that he grew despondent and morose, convinced he was going mad. Soon he became a "melancholy and wasted form," said Stewart, "his blithe and sunny smile gone," a man stricken with a fatal disease. Within a few days, Holmes was dead.[42]

Thirty-odd years later at Fort Larned in central Kansas, a rabid wolf entered the post hospital one August night and attacked a corporal lying sick in bed, biting him severely in the right arm and left hand, completely severing one finger. Next the wolf ran out of the hospital and assaulted a party of officers and their wives sitting on a porch, biting one officer severely in both legs. Then he attacked and bit a sentry. According to witnesses, the wolf moved quickly through the post, snapping and tearing at everything within its reach—tents, window-curtains, even bedding on a clothesline. A guard shot at the wolf, missed, and the animal ran between the man's legs. Finally another guard shot and killed it. In early September, the corporal began showing symptoms of hydrophobia; three days later he died. The other two men survived.[43]

Although rabid wolves were uncommon, it's not difficult to imagine the absolute terror their appearance evoked. When a huge, mad wolf suddenly appeared one night in 1841 at Rufus Sage's camp, it bit nine horses and cows before finally being killed. "He proved one of the largest of his species," said Sage, "and looked fearful as his blood-red eyeballs and foaming mouth were exposed by the campfire."[44]

How much the fear of bodily harm exacerbated the dislike many people already felt for wolves is difficult to assess, but it probably played no small role in further darkening popular opinion of the animal. Opprobrious references to wolves surfaced in everyday western speech. "To cut your wolf loose" meant to go on a bender or do something outrageous, an act not infrequently associated with a "curly wolf"—a mean or tough fellow. By mid-century, wolves were often compared to those other troublesome western inhabitants whom many newcomers came to fear and loath—Native Americans. During the late 1860s and 1870s, when Indians were violently rebelling against dispossession of both their land and culture, one Colorado newspaper claimed that these "unprincipled nomads" and "treacherous vagabonds" should "be hunted to their doom like so many wolves."[45]

After the Sioux rebellion in Minnesota in 1862, in which some four hundred settlers lost their lives, citizens of St. Paul sent a petition to President Abraham Lincoln calling for the banishment of every Sioux Indian from the state. "The Indian's nature can no more be trusted than the wolf's," claimed the citizens. "Tame him, cultivate him, strive to Christianize him, as you will, and the sight of blood will in an instant call out the savage, wolfish, devilish instincts of the race."[46]

Soldiers were particularly fond of the metaphor and readily adopted the common convention used by some plains tribes in referring to valued Indian scouts as "wolves." But the word appears more often as a pejorative. When the U.S. Army attempted to extract a promise of good behavior between the Wichitas, Kiowas, and Comanches in 1833, an officer declared that such a pledge was as fruitless as attempting "to establish a truce between the howling wolf of the prairie and his prey." Those Indians who were elusive and difficult to engage in battle were often called "cowardly wolves." Speaking of warring Apaches in Arizona, Lieutenant Britton Davis said: "Exasperated, our senses blunted by Indian atrocities, we hunted them and killed them as we hunted and killed wolves."[47]

Before the great herds of hoofed wild animals began their precipitous decline, trappers, hunters, and explorers recorded much about the relationship between wolves and their prey. While many of these accounts would fail today's scientific rigor, they provide a glimpse into how wolves hunted, as well as the effects of their predation.

Wolves killed a variety of large wild ungulates, but as William Clark observed in 1806, they mainly followed "the large gangues of Buffalw," feeding "on those that are killed by accident or those that are too pore to keep up with the gangue."[48]

Accidental death resulted from blizzards, tornadoes, and fires, although drownings were the primary cause. Buffalo sometimes perished while attempting to swim rivers or lakes, but these numbers were insignificant compared to animals trapped and drowned by collapsing ice, either thin ice that formed in autumn or the melting ice of spring. One trapper on Canada's Qu'Appelle River during spring breakup in 1795 recorded 7,360 buffalo "drowned and mired along the river," in some places so numerous that "they lay from three to five files deep." During breakup on the Red River in April 1801, Alexander Henry witnessed "entire herds" of drowned buffalo floating by his trading post, creating such a "horrid stench" that the fur trader was unable to eat his supper. How much wolves relied on such carcasses is unknown, but as with human cadavers, they were quick to take advantage of death's bounty. In May 1848 near Fort Pitt on the Saskatchewan River, artist Paul Kane recorded "great numbers of wolves" devouring carcasses of drowned buffalo. Several men set off from shore in boats and shot wolves as they fed on the dead animals, altogether an "amusing" pastime, claimed Kane, "our men greatly enjoying the sport."[49]

Most frontier accounts agree with William Clark's observation that when wolves hunted buffalo they selected primarily the young, weak, sick, or disabled. How many actually fell to wolves can only be estimated. Reports of the number of buffalo during the early nineteenth century vary widely between 28 million to 100 million, although most authorities place the total at no more than 40 million animals. Plains Indians told frontiersmen that wolves took as many as one-third of each year's calves. No one knows if this figure is correct, but based on 40 million buffalo, it suggests that over 2 million of the 7 million calves produced each year were killed by wolves. Yet due to a calf's relatively small size, even this daunting number would have failed to provide enough meat to support the 200,000 wolves inhabiting the Great Plains. Given an average daily requirement of 10 pounds of meat per wolf, the predators needed the equivalent of no less than 3,000 adult buffalo each and every day.[50]

With so many wolves about, early travelers frequently witnessed the hunting and killing of prey, a relatively rare occurrence today. What astounded observers was how well the predators hunted together. They "behave with great sagacity," said Rufus Sage, and "exercise a perfect understanding and concert of action with each other on such occasions." Once from a high vantage point, Sage watched a pack approach an unsuspecting buffalo herd. Most of the wolves spread out in two long parallel lines and waited while two of their members approached the herd from the downwind side, singled out a victim, and began running it toward the rest of the pack. As they came close, the two lead wolves slowed, letting others take up the chase. Each wolf bit and tore at the flanks and hindquarters of the buffalo, then fell behind to let the next in line "take part in the grand race." The pack continued this relay technique until the exhausted and bloody victim finally fell.[51]

Two years later Sage witnessed a similar hunt, although this time the prey was antelope—an animal which he declared "rivaled the storm-wind in fleetness"—trapped in a narrow box canyon. After observing the antelope from the canyon rim, the wolves first gathered together as if to "discuss strategy," and then began to chase their prey, relieving each other from time to time as they ran the animals up and down the canyon. Finally, a few exhausted antelope became "crazed with terror" and fell victim to their "rapacious pursuers." Although he disliked wolves, Sage returned to camp with a higher regard for the "instinctive intelligence of wolves (savoring so strongly of reason and calculation) than I had previously entertained."[52]

Other observers were similarly impressed by the level of cooperation among wolves. During his travels along the Platte River in the 1840s, Father Pierre-Jean DeSmet wrote that wolves "display much boldness and sagacity in their rapacious operation, and seem to act in concert and as if by understanding." Like Sage, DeSmet claimed wolves successfully pursued prey using a relay strategy, a behavior which scientists today have not witnessed. In addition, he saw them run panic-stricken buffalo over cliffs. "Then our highwaymen also go down by the roundabout way," said the priest, "and partake together of the fruit of their industry." Twenty-five years earlier along the Columbia River, Ross Cox observed wolves form a "horseshoe line," much as Indians did, and force antelope toward the edge of a precipice. The technique, said Cox, left the antelope "no choice but that of being dashed to pieces down the steep and rocky sides of the ravine, or falling prey to the fangs of their merciless pursuers."[53]

Over millenia buffalo devised a variety of individual and group defenses to thwart their pursuers. They were large, quick animals—bulls weighed nearly a ton, cows half a ton—bearing sharp horns and hooves capable of inflicting injury or death. Calves were the most easily killed by wolves, but they were vulnerable for only a relatively short period each year. Cows birthed during spring when herds were widely dispersed and smaller in number than those of late summer and fall. This fact alone discouraged discovery by wolves. The precocious calves usually attempted to rise within twenty or thirty minutes of birth; within an hour or two they were walking; a few days later they could run.

The behavior of buffalo when wolves were about perplexed numerous observers. Catlin said that often the herds appeared to be indifferent to individual wolves, allowing them "to sneak amidst their ranks, apparently like one of their own family." Lewis and Clark also witnessed this phenomenon, dubbing wolves "shepherds" of the herds. From such accounts it appears that buffalo readily distinguished between wolves they considered threatening and those they did not. If the predators attacked, however, buffalo either bolted or stood their ground. Their choice may have been determined by their proximity to one another. When they were relatively close together, claimed Catlin, "wolves seldom attack them, as the former instantly gather for combined resistance, which they effectively make." In these instances, both cows and bulls were said to protect calves, although probably cows were more often their defenders. Audubon noted that when a cow and her calf were attacked, "the cow bellows and sometimes runs at the enemy, and not infrequently frightens him away." Some accounts describe calves being abandoned by their mothers during attack and relying strictly upon bulls for protection. Since abandonment is rare among today's surviving wild herds in Canada, these reports may have arisen when wolves were seen stalking isolated groups of young calves and older bulls that failed to keep up with a fast-moving herd.[54]

Other observers claimed that buffalo invariably formed a defensive ring or circle consisting of adults standing shoulder-to-shoulder, facing their protagonists with their young safely inside the perimeter. Although such behavior has been witnessed today, it is an infrequent defense. In the past such behavior may have been more common, particularly on the open prairies away from protective cover when wolf packs were said to be larger than those known today. In encountering so many wolves, buffalo may have formed into tight groups that resembled circles. Plainsmen didn't help their case when they found proof of such behavior in countless rings, between ten to fifty feet in diameter, of verdant vegetation on the prairies, avowing they were the result of buffalo wearing down grass as they circled to defend themselves against wolves. Standing water filled these compacted circles each spring, they said, resulting in new growth. Notwithstanding affirmations to this fact by famous western writers from John C. Fremont to Elizabeth Bacon Custer, scientists later determined such circles were formed, not by buffalo, but by a soil fungus. As the fungus expands concentrically over the years, it enriches the surrounding soil and encourages new plant growth.[55]

If a herd elected to flee rather than fight, wolves quickly chose one animal for pursuit, even leaping over the backs of other buffalo in their single-minded determination. Those who failed to run fast became victims. In spring and early summer, calves were the most vulnerable, but by late summer and autumn they were able to keep up with running adults.

An adult buffalo brought to bay could be a formidable opponent, and wolf injury and even death were probably quite common. Said George Ruxton: "No animal requires so much killing as the buffalo."[56] This truth was echoed by James Schultz who once witnessed wolves attack a bull. As the wolves circled the animal

> suddenly they leaped forward, two to feint attack upon his head, the others to run swiftly to and fro behind him, getting ever closer to his heels, their purpose to hamstring him. He seemed to know their plan—perhaps he had been attacked by wolves before—he sought to protect his rear, and to do that tried to face all ways at once. Old though he was and huge, between anger and fear he developed a surprising agility. To run from them was impossible; the battle had to be fought there on the spot. He lunged now at this wolf, again at that one, wheeling all the time; in fact, he spun round and round like a huge, erratic top. We could hear his snorts of rage.[57]

In describing how wolves actually killed victims, observers maintained that they either starved them by biting off their tongues, or hamstrung them by severing tendons in their hind legs. Like Schultz, most claimed the latter was the preferred technique. "The poor creature is first hamstrung to prevent its escape," declared Rufus Sage. Josiah Gregg concurred, saying, "I have myself seen them with the muscles of the thighs cruelly mangled." Doubtless this may have been sometimes true, particularly with antelope or buffalo calves. But larger animals are much more difficult (and hazardous) to hamstring and this technique is rarely, if ever, observed today in wolves. More likely they assaulted a victim's nose, neck, legs, flanks, and particularly the haunches until it collapsed from exhaustion, shock, and blood loss.[58]

Like Gregg and Sage, few observers failed to pass judgment on what they saw. Most sided with the victim, saying what was most disturbing about such death was that wolves often began feeding on a victim before it ceased struggling. It was shocking, exclaimed Sage, but the animal is "literally devoured alive!" Fur trader Henry Boller labeled wolves "sneaking wretches" for their depredations on "poor" buffalo. After once viewing wolves "smeared with gore" bring down a victim, Boller was so incensed that he could not resist favoring "one gentleman with a leaden pill to aid his digestion."[59]

One man who resisted finding fault with the hunting behavior of wolves was George Catlin. Unlike human hunters, wolves slayed buffalo in less numbers and "for far more laudable purpose than that of selling their skins." As early as 1832, long before most other observers, Catlin prophesized that buffalo and other wild animals would soon fall before the coming hordes of white invaders and what he termed their "insatiable avarice."[60]

The artist then posed a question that had become far more relevant than the one William Bartram had asked forty years earlier.

What will wolves do, asked Catlin, "after the buffaloes are all gone, and they are left, as they must be, with scarcely anything to eat?"[61]

6

CIVILIZATION'S ENEMY

When George Catlin packed up his paints and brushes and headed home to New York City in 1833, perhaps he knew what wolves would do when buffalo were gone. Certainly, anyone who possessed livestock at what was then the edge of the settled frontier could have told him. It was a litany that had repeated itself many times during the past two hundred years: a significant number of people moved into an area, wild game was either killed or displaced, and wolves quickly turned to domestic animals.

One of the earliest reports of depredations by wolves among western settlers came in 1763 when the Jesuit priest Juan Nentvig wrote that "wolves do damage among cattle" in Mexico's state of northern Sonora. Here, and subsequently throughout much of the American Southwest, large numbers of cattle (primarily longhorns) were introduced and allowed to roam mostly unprotected over the range, crowding out wild game. Tough and belligerent, longhorns were reported capable of defending themselves from wolves, but soon ranchers replaced them with more marketable, but less hardy, shorthorn breeds. By the early 1800s, sheep had also spread throughout much of Mexico and portions of the Southwest. Josiah Gregg reported that after many losses, most Mexican stock owners had learned to corral their herds and flocks at night and guard them with "watchful and sagacious dogs against prowling wolves and other animals of prey."[1]

About this same time, settlers in Ohio complained of wolves. One sheepman, Bezaleel Wells, required his shepherds to live in an oxcart and herd their animals around the cart every night for protection. Not far from present-day Cleveland, 600 men and boys gathered on Christmas Eve in 1818 to rid an area of what one chronicler of the event called a "superabundance of wolves." By the time the melee ended, 300 deer, 21 bears, and 17 wolves lay dead, most having been beaten or shot to death. The wolves were promptly skinned, turned in for bounty, and the resulting cash used to host a holiday celebration, complete with "honest whiskey."[2]

That same year in New Harmony, Indiana, sheep were reported heavily guarded each night after the "wolf menace" had reduced many flocks to a mere twenty head. According to one early historian, sheep were not introduced into Wisconsin before 1837 because "wolves were so numerous and destructive as to discourage it." During the early 1840s, real estate developers in eastern Iowa assured prospective buyers that they wouldn't be disturbed by the "ravenous beasts" because there were by then "very few wolves." But a dozen years later, after wild game had mostly disappeared from Iowa, some of these new landowners complained that wolves had become so numerous and brazen that they leapt onto porches to plunder smoked hams hanging from the eaves of houses. Depredations were so rampant in Louisa Country, Iowa, by 1858 that the state agricultural society complained no one raised sheep because of the "multiplicity of wolves."[3]

Oregon and California Trail emigrants received a taste of what damage wolves could cause livestock from the moment they departed Independence, Missouri. Wolves were often plentiful along the trail, readily killing many, if not all, abandoned livestock—thousands of lame or fatigued oxen, horses, and mules which were simply discarded by travelers when they no longer proved useful. In 1846 near Wyoming's Sweetwater River, emigrant Edwin Bryant wrote that discarded livestock "immediately become the victims of wolves, who give them no rest until they fall." A curious Bryant trailed one ox pursued by wolves "for ten or twenty miles," finding places along the way where "he would turn and give battle to his remorseless pursuers" before finally succumbing. Farther west along the trail, when a group of Latter-day Saints became stranded and were forced to abandon their cattle, rescuers found it almost impossible to keep "droves" of wolves from the animals. After the predators succeeded in killing twenty-five head, the rescuers gave up and opted for a less grisly death by shooting the remaining fifty cattle.[4]

Despite these notable exceptions, few of the voluminous number of overland accounts mention difficulty with wolves. The simple fact was that most trail travelers didn't consider the predators a problem. This was because they possessed few livestock, and what animals they abandoned were doomed regardless. Had travelers attempted to transport large herds across the continent, the results probably would have been quite different. The experience of one man who attempted such an endeavor may have discouraged others. In 1853 Thomas Flint drove 2,000 sheep, cattle, oxen, and horses from Iowa to California. Flint reported wolves a constant worry and the cause of several stock deaths.[5]

Upon reaching California, emigrants suffered few livestock depredations since wolves there were relatively scarce. Those traveling to Oregon Territory, however, told a different tale. Although Lewis and Clark had reported few wolves in the lower Columbia River basin at the beginning of the century, both the human and livestock population of the area vastly increased during the 1840s, and wolf depredations soon became widespread. Livestock in those days were often shipped by sea, milk cows bringing as much as $80 each, so most owners could scarcely afford a loss. As early as 1841, the U.S. Army's Charles Wilkes noted that at Fort Vancouver cattle had to be corralled at night and sometimes even in the day due to "numerous wolves that are prowling about."[6]

Depredations became so pervasive in the Willamette Valley two years later that settlers assembled and adopted a resolution providing for a three dollar bounty on wolves. Until then, Canadians and Americans living in the Northwest had been at odds over forming a government, but agreement about the wolf "menace" broke the deadlock and civil government soon followed. Losses to wolves were even more vexing farther east up the Columbia River Valley. There an army officer near Walla Walla, Washington, reported a large herd of horses run over a hundred-foot-high cliff by wolves stampeding the animals at night. "The wolves are very numerous in this country," the officer exclaimed, "and exceedingly troublesome."[7]

Like Oregon and Washington emigrants, those who settled the continent's interior appear to have suffered depredations primarily wherever wild game no longer occurred in substantial numbers. When Brigham Young led the Latter-day Saints west to Utah in the late 1840s, he urged them to conserve and protect native plants and animals, extending mercy "to the brute creation." Nevertheless, two years later Mormons had introduced so many livestock and so depleted wildlife in the Great Salt Lake Valley that they declared "a war of extermination" against the predators they termed "wasters & destroyers."[8]

Emigrants who settled farther east in the center of buffalo range before the 1870s had better luck. In central Kansas the commander of Fort Dodge, Colonel Irving Dodge, scoffed at the notion that wolves killed many livestock, insisting that they were nearly "harmless." The predators, maintained Dodge, preferred wild game and only attacked domestic animals when buffalo or other wild prey were scarce.[9]

But just as George Catlin had predicated forty years earlier, the time of buffalo was rapidly coming to an end.

Catlin's foreboding of the great herds' fate came in 1832 at Fort Pierre in South Dakota, after he watched a band of Sioux arrive with "fourteen hundred fresh buffalo tongues" for which they were traded a few gallons of watered-down whiskey. Soon both buffalo tongues and robes became a popular novelty in eastern cities. By 1840 they constituted a thriving market comprising as many as 90,000 buffalo each year, one which Indians primarily supplied until white hunters began showing up on the prairies to take over the hunting.[10]

By the end of the decade thousands of emigrants were streaming west each year along the Oregon Trail, and the herds split into a northern and southern segment. This division became permanent when the Union Pacific Railroad pushed west from Omaha, Nebraska, in 1865, reached Cheyenne, Wyoming, in 1867, and met the Central Pacific in 1869 at Promontory, Utah. Soon other railroads steamed west, the Kansas Pacific, the Atchison, Topeka & Santa Fe, and the Canadian Pacific. Towns sprang up along the rail routes, and with trains providing ready access to eastern markets, the slaughter commenced in earnest. Buffalo hunters, described by one hunter as "the saltiest goddam men on the Western frontier," took to the Plains in great numbers, some killing as many as 300 buffalo each day. During one eighteen-month period during the 1860s, William "Buffalo Bill" Cody claimed to have killed 4,280 buffalo.[11]

Although some of the animals were sought for meat, most were killed for their skins. In the beginning, the thick-furred pelts were used as blankets or robes. Cows provided the choicest pelts, and hunters often shot into the herds indiscriminately, littering the Plains with calf and bull carcasses that remained unused. By one estimate, for every marketable skin at least three buffalo died. Josiah Gregg lamented that the hide of most animals proved useless. "Were it valuable, thousands of hides might be saved that are annually left to the wolves upon the Prairies."[12]

By 1871 chemists perfected a tanning process, and soon the British army decreed that buffalo leather made the best boots for soldiers. Two years later, a severe economic depression in the United States forced 90,000 workers in New York City and 20,000 in Chicago out of work. Some of those unemployed traveled west, adding to the already one million whites residing beyond the Mississippi River, and took up buffalo hunting. Between 1871 and 1874 in parts of Nebraska, Kansas, Oklahoma, and northern Texas, there was little work to be had but buffalo killing. By 1875, the southern herd had "melted away like snow before a summer's sun," said Colonel Dodge. Where countless buffalo had once roamed, "there were now myriads of carcasses. The air was fouled with sickening stench, and the vast plain, which only a short twelve months before teemed with animal life, was a dead, solitary, putrid desert."[13]

Even as Dodge wrote these words some five thousand hunters were moving north, and what had happened on the southern Plains now occurred in Canada, Montana, Wyoming, and the Dakotas. Within a few years it was over. Theodore Roosevelt reported that a ranchman he knew traveled a thousand miles back and forth across Montana during 1884, and not once was he ever "out of sight of a dead buffalo, and never in sight of a live one." By then, from a population of perhaps forty million animals half a century earlier, no more than a few hundred plains buffalo survived anywhere in North America. Roosevelt was probably correct when he observed, "Never before in all history were so many large wild animals of one species slain in so short a time."[14]

Often ignored in accounts of the demise of buffalo is the profound effect their loss had upon other denizens of the Great Plains. Native Americans were finally compelled onto reservations, due more to the loss of their primary food source than any successful military action. Also numerous animals and plants, from grizzly bears to ravens to soil fungi, had coevolved with the herds for millennia. When buffalo disappeared so rapidly, the ecological consequences were nothing short of catastrophic.

In the beginning, wolves and other predators may have fared better than most animals. Buffalo carcasses provided an abundant food source, so much in fact that plains wolves were often reported in greater numbers from the late 1840s through the early 1860s than earlier in the century. Said Montana's James Willard Schultz of this time, "There seemed to be thousands and thousands of the great shaggy fellows."[15]

One nineteenth-century mammalogist, J. A. Allen, was convinced that next to Indian hunters during this period, wolves "were the greatest scourge of the buffaloes, and had no small degree of influence in effecting their decrease." Given what is known today about the ability of wolves to inhibit the recovery of reduced prey populations, Allen may have been correct. On the other hand, it's not at all certain that an increase in the number of wolves necessarily resulted in greater predation on buffalo. There may have been so many carcasses available that wolves simply resorted more to scavaging dead animals than hunting live ones. Regardless, by the 1870s when buffalo began to vanish over much of their former range, wolf populations began to disappear as well.[16]

The reason was not only the loss of the herds. The wild hunters themselves had become the hunted.

It's no mystery how wolf hunting began during the mid-nineteenth century. As early frontiersmen had noted, when hunters shot buffalo, wolves quickly learned what the sound portended and soon arrived on the scene. There they patiently waited for hunters to skin the animals and withdraw before attempting to feed on the carcass. In Alberta in 1865, buffalo hunter John McDougall reported: "I have never seen gray wolves so numerous as now. When we are skinning and cutting up the buffalo they form a circle around us and wait impatiently until we load the meat into the Red River carts. Then as we move away, they rush in to fight over the offal. Many wild fights are witnessed but ammunition is scarce and we refrain from shooting."[17]

Beginning about 1860, hunters realized that a profit could be made by impregnating carcasses with poison, then returning later to skin the dead wolves. Prime wolf pelts were worth only $1 during the 1840s, but rose to $2 by the mid-1860s, finally reaching $2.50 a decade later. After a decline of nearly a half century, wolf skins were again deemed valuable. The Russian army, in particular, sought the pelts for soldiers' winter coats. Soon hunters discovered that wolves were not only far easier to obtain than buffalo, but they could be more profitable. Those men who took up the pursuit were called "wolfers," and the practice itself became known as "wolfing."[18]

What made wolfing lucrative was a powerful and deadly poison—strychnine. Trappers had used arsenic and other poisons in the past, but these substances killed relatively slowly, allowing animals to wander away before dying. Strychnine, which is derived from the seeds of an East India tree *nux vomica,* has a bitter, acrid taste, and kills rapidly in relatively minute quantities. The poison was introduced to Europe during the Middle Ages, arriving in North America sometime in the mid-1600s. No one knows why it never achieved popularity in the eastern part of the continent, but settlers there may have lost too many valued dogs for it to gain wide acceptance. Also some early trappers believed that strychnine reduced the quality of furs, making them less supple and more difficult to work. The earliest written record of its use in the West was about 1849, when a United States boundary survey team reported Mexican ranchers using the poison to protect their livestock against wolves and coyotes. By 1860 strychnine was readily available throughout much of the western United States, but Canada's Hudson's Bay Company, concerned about fur quality, prohibited its trappers from using it. Canadian wolfers, however, did not work directly for the company and use of strychnine soon spread throughout much of Canada as well.[19]

A wolfer's technique was simple. A buffalo was freshly killed, its abdomen sliced open and sprinkled with a few grains of poison. Then the wolfer made several additional incisions about the carcass, dropping more strychnine into the wounds. In the morning he returned to find dead wolves scattered near the carcass. Ten or twenty wolves was not unusual. One man in Canada reported as many as 120 animals during a single night.[20]

Luther "Yellowstone" Kelly, a wolfer and U.S. Army guide, described how easily the animals were poisoned. In 1875 near Montana's Musselshell River, Kelly had just shot a wounded cow buffalo when he looked up to see about twenty wolves close by. "They formed a very pretty picture on the gray prairie," said Kelly, "that was almost wind-swept of snow. They were not the dirty, gray Buffalo-wolf, but seemed to be more of the Timber species, with tawny markings, some approaching to creamy white. What surprised me was their utter unconcern as I came into view. They were lined up in a row, as if they had been bidden to a feast, and were not particular as to the manner in which it was served." Kelly disemboweled the cow and loaded the carcass with a three-eighth-ounce dose of strychnine. "My audience took an unusual interest in the work of preparing this bait," he said, "but scarcely moved from their first position." The next day Kelly returned to find "their beautiful carcasses covered the prairie, and we secured 22 fine pelts."[21]

Because wolf skins were prime only during winter months, wolfing had great appeal. A man could work at other employment during the summer, then purchase food and a few supplies before traveling out on the prairie alone or with one or two companions for the winter. One season's work usually produced about $1,000, although a good winter might yield $3,000 (almost as much as the annual salary of a U.S. Army colonel). In 1873 in Helena, Montana, *The Daily Herald* reported a group of wolfers had arrived with 10,000 skins hauled in five or six wagons, resulting in "a very profitable winter."[22]

From a camp, wolfers often rode a circuit over several miles, first killing and then poisoning buffalo, returning the next day to skin dead wolves at each location. When fresh buffalo were scarce or wolves wouldn't approach carcasses, wolfers rendered buffalo tallow into bite-sized portions, lacing each with a few grains of strychnine. Known as "drop baits," they scattered these near old carcasses. While wolves might be wary of a poisoned buffalo, they rarely resisted tallow baits. During the 1870s in Montana, western photographer Laton A. Huffman once discovered "where a wolf father had found one of the tallow balls and carried it to its puppy, bitten it in half, and shared the deadly morsel. We found the old wolf and the young one dead side by side." When buffalo were scarce or tallow was too difficult to render, enterprising wolfers killed and poisoned song birds and discarded them along a known wolf path.[23]

By most accounts, death by strychnine poisoning was extremely painful, the animal unable to stand, writhing in agonizing and involuntary convulsions before death overtook it. Strychnine's only saving grace, when administered under proper conditions and dosage, was that it was relatively fast acting; victims remained on their feet for only one or two minutes after ingesting the poison, and were usually dead within five or six minutes.

Having killed a number of wolves using strychnine in New Mexico during the late nineteenth century, Ernest Thompson Seton called it a "horrible—horrible—hellish" death. Few wolves survived the experience, said Seton, although he once witnessed a wolf vomit a poisoned bait before the strychnine took effect. Another wolfer, Joseph Henry Taylor, claimed that an individual who managed to survive invariably lost its fur, remained sick for a long time, and that "no phantom of horror presented itself in such a ghastly way, as the reappearance of a sick and famished wolf, with a hide denude of fur or hair, staggering around in a dazed sort of way in search of food to prolong life. Such a sight will sometimes haunt a wolfer from his calling," admitted Taylor, "callious [sic] though his nature to suffering may be."[24]

Wolfing was not without its troubles. Strychnine lost potency in warm temperatures; although it might eventually kill, it was slower acting than during cool periods, and the animals often wandered away to die. According to several accounts, at least half of all poisoned animals were never recovered. But intense cold also could be a problem. If poisoned wolves froze before they could be skinned, a wolfer often had to wait until they thawed. If he waited too long, the skins spoiled. Ravens, magpies, vultures, and eagles quickly opened holes in dead wolves and ruined their skins. Consequently, wolfers had to check their poisoning sites frequently. Poison killed these birds, too, along with untold other animals—coyotes, foxes, badgers, skunks, bears—that fed both on dead wolves and poisoned baits. According to Frank North, an army guide and one-time Texas wolfer: "Many, many hundreds of ravens were killed by eating the carcasses of the poisoned wolves." Another wolfer in Kansas claimed that ravens disappeared entirely from the central Plains from eating poisoned baits. Adding to these difficulties, sometimes a wolfer miscalculated the length of winter and ran out of food. Fur trader Issac Cowie knew several Canadian wolfers who were "compelled to live on poisoned wolves, and glad to get them." The men, said Cowie, simply avoided the stomach containing the strychnine.[25]

Hostile Indians were another hazard. Native Americans deeply resented wolfers, particularly when their dogs died after feeding on poisoned carcasses. Some even claimed their horses perished after eating grass contaminated with poisoned saliva from dying wolves or leftover strychnine discarded by wolfers at the end of a winter's work. Strychnine could kill unsuspecting Indians as well according to Robert Peck, whose unpublished memoirs was discovered about the turn of the century by George Bird Grinnell. In central Kansas in 1860, said Peck, three wolfers ventured into Kiowa country. While one man was out poisoning carcasses, the other two men were overcome and killed by a band of twenty Kiowa warriors. The Kiowas followed the surviving wolfer's trail and surprised him as he was placing strychnine inside a dead buffalo. Surrounded on all sides, the man cut his horse's throat and huddled behind the dead animal for protection. With his last bullet he shot himself in the head. Before the warriors departed, they cut off part of the hind quarter of the buffalo and returned with it to their camp. Later that night, five warriors suddenly convulsed and fell dead.[26]

Occasionally, Indians managed to use whites' eagerness for wolf pelts to their advantage in their warfare against the U.S. military. At Wyoming's Fort Reno in 1867, soldiers killed a coyote less than one hundred yards from the fort and laced the carcass with strychnine in hope of killing wolves. The next morning three or four wolves lay dead around the carcass, and a private named Blair volunteered to retrieve the pelts. Blair had scarcely begun skinning the animals when six Sioux suddenly rode out of a nearby gully. Said one shocked eyewitness, the warriors "filled Blair with arrows, took his scalp and then tomahawked him right before our eyes!" At Fort Phil Kearny, Sioux warriors observed that soldiers frequently poisoned buffalo carcasses in order to secure wolf pelts in slaughter yards just outside fort walls. Wrapping themselves in wolf skins, the Sioux once crawled close enough to shoot a sentry who mistook them for scavenging wolves.[27]

In Canada, relations between wolfers and Indians finally collapsed in violence. During spring 1873, a group of wolfers from Alberta and nearby Montana, angry over some stolen horses, attacked and killed thirty Assiniboin Indians in what became known as the Cypress Hills Massacre. A decade later a group of wolfers, calling themselves the "Spitzee Cavalry" and objecting to the sale of repeating rifles to Indians, staged a protest. They resented buffalo killed by Indians, and feared that such arms would only hasten what most people then foresaw as the inevitable end of the herds. Without buffalo, the wolfers correctly concluded, wolfing was doomed. When they attempted to stop one trading post proprietor from selling the weapons, the man seized a red-hot poker from a nearby blacksmith's fire and held it over a barrel of gunpowder. Get out, he warned them, or they would all go to hell together. The men rushed for the door, said a recorder of the event, and "thus ended the career of the extremely ambitious, but singularly ineffective Spitzee Cavalry."[28]

Such times bred hard men. Wolfers in Alberta were said to have been even more disreputable than whiskey traders, then the scourge of all "civilized" westerners. Life was little valued and relationships between wolfers were fragile, attested to by one wolfer in a letter to another in Montana: "Dear Friend—My partner, Will Geary, got to putting on airs and I shot him and he is dead. The potatoes is looking well. Yours truly, Snookum Jim."[29]

By 1883 the worst fears of wolfers finally came to pass. That year only 40,000 buffalo hides were shipped from the northern Plains; the following year, a mere 300. Commercial buffalo hunting was over, and with it, wolfing. In the United States, 273 wolf pelts were reported taken in 1885, down from nearly 7,000 five years earlier. About this same time, author Francis Parkman revisited those areas of the West he had made famous years before in *The Oregon Trail*. Mingled among buffalo bones littering the prairies, Parkman found the bones of "those discordant serenaders, the wolves that howled at evening about the traveller's campfire." Poison, he observed, had "hushed their savage music."[30]

How many wolves died during the wolfers' heyday will never be known. In addition to the great number of poisoned animals that went unrecovered, many fur harvest records of that time have been lost or were simply never tabulated. One authority claims some 173,000 wolves were taken between 1860 and 1885, but this number primarily reflects Canadian records; those of the United States, where most wolfing took place, are missing for much of this period. Moreover, as in earlier times, harvest records seldom distinguished between wolves and coyotes. Like their larger cousins, coyotes readily scavenged buffalo carcasses and fell, perhaps even easier than wolves, to poison. Although their furs brought less money, they were still eagerly sought by most wolfers. Because coyotes are believed to have occurred in greater abundance than wolves, doubtless they made up the bulk of harvest totals. Robert Peck reported that three quarters of his 1861–62 winter harvest of 3,000 "wolves" were actually coyotes, a proportion probably not unlike that of other wolfers.[31]

The most we can say with assurance today is that wolfing undoubtedly took a great toll of both species. Between the loss of buffalo and twenty-five years of relentless poisoning, wolves and coyotes were greatly reduced over large portions of their former habitat, and actually may have been extirpated in certain areas. Even such out-of-the-way places as Yellowstone National Park weren't immune from enterprising wolfers. By 1880 the park superintendent, Philetus Norris, reported that although wolves and coyotes had once been "exceedingly numerous" throughout the park, "the value of their hides and their easy slaughter with strychnine-poisoned carcasses of animals have nearly led to their extermination."[32]

Although wolfing as an industry ceased in its last strongholds of Montana, Wyoming, the Dakotas, and southern Alberta and Saskatchewan by the mid-1880s, like buffalo hunting, it ended much sooner farther south and east. So many wolves had been killed in southern Kansas by 1871 that wolf hunters there paved a small road some seventy-five yards long through a swamp entirely with bones from the carcasses of skinned wolves. It comes as no wonder that three years later, mammalogist J. A. Allen reported that although wolves in Kansas had been "formerly very abundant," poisoning had so diminished their numbers that "comparatively few now remain." The same was true of those states east of Kansas where advancing settlement had already displaced most wolves long before wolfing became popular. Farther north in the Dakotas, according to Theodore Roosevelt, they were also scarce. After buffalo vanished there, "wolves diminished in number so that they seemed to disappear."[33]

Had wolves been solely dependent upon buffalo, it's likely they would have vanished entirely from the Great Plains. But they were (and are) versatile predators, capable of "switching," as biologists say today, to alternative prey. Although other large ungulates—antelope, deer, moose, bighorn sheep, woodland caribou, and elk—were also slaughtered in unprecedented numbers by commercial market hunters both during and after the demise of buffalo, they were not considered as valuable. Unlike buffalo, they often occurred in widely scattered, less concentrated, and thus less accessible populations. A reduced but significant number of these animals managed to survive hunters, serving as prey for those few wolves who had escaped poisoning. Moreover, a certain number of the predators had probably always lived outside the range of buffalo, relying on other prey. Because these wolves were never as numerous as those found on the Plains, they hadn't been targeted by wolfers. Thus surviving wolves—

possessing the ability to travel great distances and quickly recover their former numbers—provided a source for potential repopulation. The only thing missing was an ample number of suitable prey, for which they did not have long to wait.

Livestock had been increasing in the Great Plains and surrounding regions ever since emigrants first began moving into the interior of the continent. But not until the rapid decline of buffalo and other wild ungulates during the 1870s and 1880s did they arrive in great numbers. By now beef was constantly in demand to help feed the 40 percent of Americans in the Northeast, and 20 percent in the West, who lived in cities. Following the national financial panic of 1873, speculators looked to the West where a Union Pacific brochure claimed there lay "a billion acres . . . boundless, endless, gateless, and all of it furnishing winter grazing." Cattle became all the rage for investors when stockmen reported purchasing them in the spring for $5 a head and selling them for $50 in the autumn. Even with interest rates as high as 36 percent, investors reported stunning profits. As a result, cattle literally flooded into the West.[34]

In Wyoming, where cattle numbered no more than about 10,000 in 1870, the territory boasted two million by 1885. That same year Montana reported 600,000 and nearby South Dakota and Colorado some 800,000 each. Boosters in South Dakota claimed there was room for millions more. From Texas to Canada, twenty million cattle now inhabited the Plains, with more arriving each year. Not only had cattle suddenly become the continent's most common large ungulate, but they had done so at a critical time for those wolves who had managed to survive the period of wolfing.[35]

As stock owners began moving into the region, they reported little trouble from wolves, probably because wolfers had so drastically reduced their population. But this situation changed rapidly after wolfing abruptly ceased. By the time cattlemen decided they had a wolf "problem," the predator was well on its way to reestablishing itself over much of its former range.

To an overwhelming degree, cattlemen themselves were the cause of wolf recovery. After stocking the grasslands, they expected the animals to live just as buffalo had. What early ranchers called "open range" was de rigueur; cattle were simply turned loose to fend for themselves over huge ranches. The herds were rounded up twice a year, once each spring to brand calves and again in the autumn to send them to market. During the remainder of the year, including winter, cattle wandered unattended and unprotected over large tracts of mostly public domain. Often ranchers didn't even know how many thousands of animals they owned.

During the cattle industry's boom years, stock owners accepted some loss to wolves with scarcely a complaint. Granville Stuart, one of central Montana's first ranchers, matter-of-factly reported in 1881 that wolves killed 5 percent of his 5,000-head herd, but that Indians and winter storms together took as much as 8 percent. Then former wolf-hunters-turned-stock-rustlers moved in, the profit margin declined, and their treatment presaged what would soon befall their former prey. In June 1884, Stuart organized a vigilante group nicknamed "Stuart's Stranglers" and hung twelve suspected thieves. That same year wolfing ended in Montana, and Stuart's herd grew to 12,000 head.[36]

Then disaster struck in a way Stuart and other ranchers had never foreseen. The price of calves dramatically dropped in 1885, prompting Stuart to crowd his unsold cattle onto already overgrazed ranges. Drought descended upon the Plains during the next summer, and both grass and cattle were in poor condition when the first winter snowstorm commenced in November. Then, in an ominous sign, snowy owls begin showing up from northern Canada for the first time in nearly a generation. Subzero temperatures followed yet another heavy snowfall in December. After alternate thaws and frosts, the snow surface froze like concrete, making cattle grazing all but impossible. In January a storm dropped sixteen inches of snow in sixteen hours, followed by a ten-day blow. By February, cattle began dying by the thousands from Oklahoma to Saskatchewan in what western stock owners today still remember as the Great Die-up of 1887. When the snow finally melted in April, it revealed the emaciated carcasses of some 8,000 of Stuart's cattle; other ranchers lost up to 90 percent of their herds. Across Montana alone, as many as half a million cattle lay dead. The winter, observed one rancher, had been nothing less than "simple murder."[37]

Wild animals also suffered that winter; the carcasses of deer, antelope, and elk were often reported among those of cattle. What few elk and antelope still inhabited Kansas, the winter finished off. Game populations throughout much of the West already had been greatly reduced by commercial market hunters, but few ranchers regretted their loss. They viewed these animals, not as the primary prey of wolves and thus a critical buffer for minimizing livestock depredations, but as competitors for range. In northeastern Colorado the year before, a rancher slaughtered over one thousand antelope simply to stop them from eating grass he desired for livestock. Ranchers also feared that if cattle associated for long with wild ungulates, they too would turn wild. The sooner wild game was gone the better.[38]

How wolves fared during the Great Die-up, in addition to a previous devastating winter which had struck the southern Plains the year before and another that ravaged the Great Basin in 1889–90, is not difficult to gauge. Although one Kansas rancher found "wolves drifted with the cattle and piled up with them" dead in snowdrifts, others claimed the predators made short work of weakened and defenseless livestock. Ranchers who had previously experienced few or no difficulties with wolves suddenly began reporting increased depredations. In Oklahoma, a cowboy recalled that most of his ranch's surviving calves suffered wolf bites on their backs, and many cows had lost their udders and tails to wolves. Winter-killed livestock, said ranchers, proved a bonanza for wolves and resulted in a great increase in their numbers. Although incomplete, fur harvest records suggest this may have been true. During the severe winters of 1886 to 1891, the number of wolves harvested continent-wide shot up to an annual average of nearly 10,000, a number greater than most previous wolfing years. Even more significant, over two-thirds of this harvest took place in the United States.[39]

Although the ruinous winters had largely bypassed northern Mexico and the American Southwest, ranchers there were having troubles of their own. Like their countrymen to the north, profits were great enough in the early 1880s that wolf depredations were largely tolerated. By late in the decade, however, much of the area had become one huge livestock ranch and overgrazing of the perennial grama grasses abounded. Beginning in 1890, a three-year drought resulted in the deaths of half to three-quarters of all cattle in Arizona Territory, followed by another national financial panic in 1893. What had been a thriving industry all but collapsed. Although wolves were never as numerous in this part of the continent as they had been on the Great Plains, they were said to have become more abundant during and immediately after the drought than in previous years.[40]

This drawing of a nine-hundred-year-old pictograph from a cave near Billings, Montana, is the continent's earliest representation of a wolf attacking a bison. A canid similar to today's red wolf evolved in North America one million years ago. (*Based on a drawing by William Mulloy*)

Western artist George Catlin captured the ability of Plains Indians to don wolf skins in order to closely approach buffalo. (*National Gallery*)

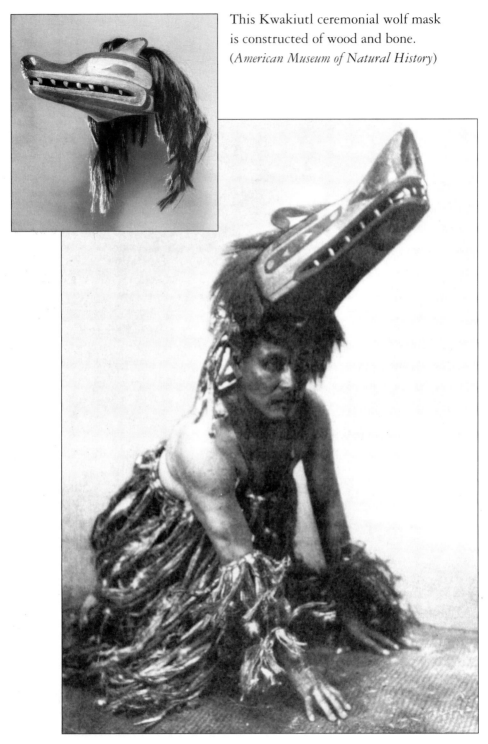

This Kwakiutl ceremonial wolf mask is constructed of wood and bone. (*American Museum of Natural History*)

Photographer Edward Curtis witnessed this Kwakiutl wolf dancer in 1914. (*Library of Congress*)

John James Audubon's son, J. W. Audubon, painted the first detailed portrait of a black North American wolf, based on his father's 1843 sketches. (*Library of Congress*)

In this nineteenth-century pencil-and-wash drawing entitled *Greedy Wolves over Dead Buffalo*, artist Peter Moran illustrated a scene that was once common to much of the Great Plains. (*Amon Carter Museum*)

Just hours after trapping and shooting the Custer Wolf near Custer, South Dakota, government hunter Harry Williams poses with an unidentified rancher, October 1920. (*National Archives*)

Pelts of coyotes and wolves comprise this government hunter's seasonal catch from Montana in 1928. (*National Archives*)

Cowboys readily pursued wolves whenever they found them, as portrayed in this painting by Charles M. Russell. (*Montana Historical Society*)

In open country a wolf seldom escapes fast horses and their riders. (*Library of Congress*)

Trappers frequently set two or more traps close together in order to completely disable a wolf and reduce its chances of escape. (*Arizona Historical Society*)

This red wolf trapped in 1929 near Gillham, Arkansas, was collared with a leather belt, tied to a wooden stake, and had its jaws wired shut. Such wolves frequently died of dehydration or were dismembered by hunters' dogs. (*National Archives*)

Most wolf trappers preferred the Newhouse #14 for its double-spring action and its spike jaws. (*National Archives*)

When artist N. C. Wyeth's *The Fight in the Peaks* appeared in *Scribner's Magazine* in 1917, most people still believed that wolves readily attacked and killed humans. (*Reprinted from* Scribner's Magazine)

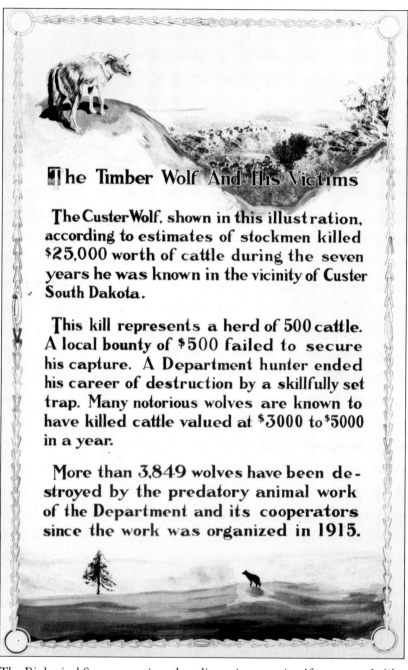

The Timber Wolf And His Victims

The Custer Wolf, shown in this illustration, according to estimates of stockmen killed $25,000 worth of cattle during the seven years he was known in the vicinity of Custer South Dakota.

This kill represents a herd of 500 cattle. A local bounty of $500 failed to secure his capture. A Department hunter ended his career of destruction by a skillfully set trap. Many notorious wolves are known to have killed cattle valued at $3000 to $5000 in a year.

More than 3,849 wolves have been destroyed by the predatory animal work of the Department and its cooperators since the work was organized in 1915.

The Biological Survey continued to disseminate antiwolf propaganda like this 1940 poster well after most wolves were extirpated from the conterminous United States. The National Park Service approved the killing of Yellowstone Park's last wolf in 1926. (*Denver Public Library*)

In Alaska's McKinley National Park during the 1940s, Adolph Murie conducted the first extensive scientific wolf studies and played a crucial role in providing the predators with their first sanctuary from human persecution. In 1978 the U.S. Fish and Wildlife Service downgraded the eastern wolf to "threatened" while all other "Lower 48" subspecies were protected as "endangered," thus allowing the killing of wolves in Minnesota. (*Louise Murie MacLoed Collection*)

FIRE

THE OUTLAW

DON'T TURN HIM LOOSE ON THE NATIONAL FORESTS

Wolves were still vilified as late as the 1970s, as evidenced by this National Forest Service fire-prevention poster. Wolf bounties, which began in the East a decade after the landing at Plymouth Rock, didn't move west until the 1880s. (*Bruce Weide*)

To capture Canadian wolves for reintroduction to the northern Rockies, biologists, using helicopters to approach the animals, first immobilized them with tranquilizer guns. (*LuRay Parker, Wyoming Game and Fish Department*)

Captured wolves were blindfolded, radio-collared, and moved to holding opens while awaiting shipment to Idaho and Yellowstone National Park. (*LuRay Parker, Wyoming Game and Fish Department*)

After anxious delays due to inclement weather and last-minute legal wrangling, twenty-nine wolves were released in Idaho and Yellowstone National Park in January 1995. (*LuRay Parker, Wyoming Game and Fish Department*)

When a Montana hunter shot and killed the father of the first litter born to one of the reintroduced wolf packs near Yellowstone National Park in spring 1995, U.S. Fish and Wildlife Service biologists rescued the survivors and transported them back to the park. (*USFWS*)

Poison was used extensively in Alaska during the 1940s and 1950s, resulting in the deaths of many hundreds of wolves. (*USFWS*)

Once hunters mastered the difficulties of airborne wolf-hunting, it became one of the most popular and effective means to kill the predators in Canada and Alaska. Though the practice is illegal today, critics charge that airborne hunting is still widespread in Alaska. (*USFWS*)

Following this boom-and-bust era, ranching throughout the West was never again the same. Stock owners who had survived were forced to adopt new techniques of smaller, more manageable herds made up of hardier animals. Many owners diversified into sheep and, to a lesser extent, horses. Year-round open range herding, as it had been practiced, ended. Ranchers kept closer watch over their animals, and began fencing land and putting up hay for winter feeding. All these changes pointed to the new reality of the western livestock business, which continues to this day: the time of spectacular profits was over and every single animal mattered.[41]

Exactly how severely wolf depredations affected the reformed livestock industry is difficult to say. No one was officially counting dead animals except their owners, and because many of those owners were often at the same time petitioning county, state or provincial, and federal governments to help combat wolves, their declarations have been viewed with much skepticism. The extent of their claims was enormous.

Thomas Kendrick, a prosperous rancher and U.S. senator from Wyoming who later played a prominent role in the federal government's effort to eradicate wolves, maintained that wolves in 1893 destroyed 50 percent of his calves. That same year ranchers in a nearby county petitioned the governor for assistance, declaring that "from one-sixth to one-fifth of all the colts and calves dropped in the state are devoured by wolves." Four years later, a rancher named R. M. Allen claimed that the value of livestock in Wyoming alone lost to wolves totaled "not far from a million dollars a year," an amount then four times the state's entire annual administrative budget.[42]

In Montana, the results of an 1894 state agricultural questionnaire reported that stock owners lost an average of over 9 percent of their animals each year to wolves. Sheep owners in Texas claimed between 10 and 25 percent, and those in Nebraska 5 percent. A few years later in South Dakota, Theodore Roosevelt declared that wolves had become "a veritable scourge" to cattle owners there. Yet during several years of operating his own ranch, Roosevelt admitted that his losses to wolves never exceeded 20 cattle. About that same time, another South Dakota rancher reported wolves each year killed 3 percent of his calves, 1 percent of his cows, and 5 percent of his young foals. Altogether, according to one rancher's estimate, wolves destroyed "not less than 500,000 animals annually" across the West.[43]

Where the truth lies is anyone's guess. Some stock growers claimed to have suffered such hardship from wolf depredations that they were forced from business. For others—probably the vast majority—depredations were no worse than before the reformation of the industry, only now they refused to tolerate such losses. The predicament of the latter was perhaps best characterized by O. W. Williams, a rancher of the period who later became a judge of Pecos County, Texas. Wolf depredations weren't usually a devastating calamity, declared Williams, but were "a constant, steady source of loss," not unlike "a grievous tax that is laid on year by year, which must be borne with patience, and is counted every year as an entry in the volumes of profit and loss."[44]

Patience soon ran out. Faced with financial losses from weather, disease, rustlers, poisonous plants, taxes, railroad transportation increases, and a fickle cattle market, wolf depredations were often the only difficulty that didn't leave stock owners feeling powerless. They could do something about wolves.

They began by placing a price on their heads. Bounties had continued to be popular ever since colonial times, despite their drawbacks. Most early western ranchers paid the rewards out of their own pockets, or later, after stock owner associations formed, from membership dues or special funds raised by per capita assessments on members' livestock. Wolf pelts still brought several dollars in the late 1880s and early 1890s, and one or two additional bounty dollars for each animal attracted men who had formerly been wolfers.

Before long, stock growers became influential members of communities and began pressuring county and provincial or state officials to bear the financial burden of bounties. They argued that, as owners of the largest amount of private property, they paid the majority of taxes. Livestock killed by wolves reduced that tax base; therefore, it was in every citizen's best interest to help pay bounties. This reasoning worked well wherever stock growers had political leverage, but it often met resistance from that portion of the public who viewed bounties as a thinly veiled subsidy for the livestock industry, even when stock owners offered to help finance the cost. Consequently, bounty laws were often hotly contested, and weren't infrequently repealed one year only to be resurrected the next. At the eastern edge of the Great Plains, Iowa enacted a wolf bounty as early as 1838.

Farther west, Colorado followed in 1869, Wyoming in 1875, the Dakotas in 1881, and Montana in 1883.[45]

Uncertainty over the future of bounties led some stock owners to exaggerate their losses in hope of convincing lawmakers of their dire need. In 1894 in Yellowstone County, Montana, ranchers lobbying the state legislature for a reinstatement of a discontinued bounty law reported that wolves killed 52 percent of their calf crop, although nearby counties reported only a fraction of that amount. A few years later Ben Corbin—a North Dakota rancher, and self-appointed "champion wolf hunter of the Northwest" who claimed to have killed more wolves than any living man—published a popular pamphlet advocating increased wolf bounties by asserting that North Dakota possessed no less than 343,000 wolves, all of whom possessed the capacity to rapidly reproduce. If nothing is done to stop them, claimed Corbin, within one year the West would be overrun by 10 million wolves! Corbin also preyed on public fear of wolf attack. There were so many wolves in North Dakota that "little children dare not go to school because of these prowling and ferocious beasts." In Texas, a rancher reported witnessing a migrating "herd" of wolves numbering several thousand animals. Such fear took a decidedly lycanthropic turn when Wyoming's *Big Horn Sentinel* reported in 1887 that wolves had killed a band of twenty-five sheep, some of which they had "sucked at the veins until satisfied" before wantonly slaughtering the rest.[46]

If hyperbole and fear didn't work, some stock owners resorted to shame. During a bounty debate at an 1892 Iowa livestock convention, one sheepman, disgusted that thirty-four years of bounties had not eliminated the animal, exclaimed that "it is a stain, a foul stigma, on the civilization and enterprise of the people of Iowa that these wolves remain." The answer, declared the man, was to raise the bounty from three dollars to twenty. "The boys will then arm themselves with the best rifles of long range, will watch and hunt for the game, and speedily exterminate the lupine race." Here was yet another solution to ridding livestock of wolves: increase the rewards. If bounties were sufficiently lucrative, reasoned supporters, hunters would kill more wolves.[47]

Eventually this clamor had its effect. Just as bounties were intended to wear down wolf populations by constant attrition, stock owners managed to erode the resistance of lawmakers. Although bounty laws continued to periodically wax and wane in relation to stock owners' political clout, by the mid-1890s, bounties on both wolves and coyotes had become a reality of most governments from Alberta to Arizona. In Wyoming, ranchers wielded so much power that for seven years they managed to convince the state legislature to appropriate more money for the destruction of wolves and coyotes than that allocated to the state university. When state bounties were deemed insufficient to keep hunters on the trail of wolves, stock owners and livestock associations dug into their own pockets and either hired full-time salaried hunters or offered additional private rewards. In 1890 one Wyoming county livestock association paid a $5 reward, in addition to the state's $2 bounty, for each dead wolf. Ten years later south of Yellowstone National Park in Jackson, Wyoming, ranchers offered $40 per animal. By 1910, some stock growers in Wyoming and Colorado were paying as much as $400 for a single dead animal. As a result, wolves were vigorously pursued by every conceivable means.[48]

Because it was both easy and effective, poisoning was preferred in the beginning. In Montana, some livestock associations actually purchased large amounts of strychnine and distributed it gratis to bounty hunters. With buffalo gone, hunters poisoned cattle carcasses, one man in eastern Montana reporting a poisoning "line" 150 miles long. Professional bounty hunters weren't the only distributors of strychnine. Most cowboys and ranch hands always carried poison with them, stopping to insert some into any dead cow found on the range in hopes of killing yet another wolf. During a single week in the 1890s in Yellowstone County, Montana, one ranch hand reported poisoning nine wolves for which he received $27 in bounties, $13 for the pelts, in addition to having "lots of fun."[49]

After decades of poisoning by wolfers, many surviving wolves weren't so easily beguiled. Strychnine still proved effective on young, inexperienced animals, but older ones were infinitely more wary and difficult to kill than those of former times. Instead of approaching close at the sound of a gun, they ran away. Compared to wolfing days, they were seldom seen, and then only at night. Although Granville Stuart continued to set out poisoned baits on his Montana ranch, he now observed that rarely would a wolf "touch a dead carcass, preferring to kill their own meat."[50]

Trapping required vastly more skill than poisoning, but it often proved more effective, particularly with cautious animals. Steel traps had come a long way since colonial times by the late nineteenth century, both in strength, design, and weight. By 1895 most trappers preferred the New-house No. 4¹/₂, an enlargement of the popular No. 4 beaver trap. This trap proved heavier than necessary for catching most wolves and was superseded shortly after the turn of the century by the No. 14. Wolf trappers favored this model for it contained toothed jaws that better held the leg or foot of an animal and weighed less than four pounds. For larger wolves, particularly those found in western Canada and Alaska, trappers later preferred a slightly heavier model, the No. 114. The jaws of this trap contained a greater arc to better hold larger paws.[51]

The device itself, however, was only one portion of the difficult craft of trapping wolves. Some trappers favored setting traps around bait, while others preferred random or "blind-sets" along often-used trails or wolf "runs." Almost all used scent for attracting the animals, often made of wolf parts, and, in particular, wolf urine. To obtain urine, trappers caught males and wrapped wire around their penises before killing them, the wire preventing the voiding of their bladders upon death. Few good trappers shared their scent secrets. One popular recipe that came to light after wolves were gone called for grinding wolf liver and kidney together, adding wolf dung and urine, then placing the mixture in a jar to rot in the warm sun. "Never let flies blow the mixture," cautioned the recipe's author, "for this always spoils it." So-called scent posts, used by wolves to mark territory boundaries, were choice locations to dab this robust mixture, one guaranteed to last five days through rain, sun, or freezing temperatures. Among other essential tools of the trade, trappers carried along a "numbing club" to dispatch trapped wolves.[52]

Eventually, like those few wolves who survived an experience with poison and thereafter refused to scavenge dead livestock, some wolves learned to avoid any metal object that remotely resembled a trap. An old horseshoe, a broken spur, or even a discarded tin can was enough to alert a cautious animal. Some hunters became convinced that these wolves, in turn, taught others. Wyoming stockmen recognized the difficulty of killing trap-wise animals, and in 1913 state lawmakers passed a statute making it a misdemeanor punishable by a fine of up to $300 for anyone to release a live wolf from a trap.

If trapping failed, some hunters turned to dogs. Individual dogs were seldom a match for a wolf, but a fight with a pack of ten or more usually resulted in the wolf's death. Dogs who caught wolves sometimes had reason to wish they hadn't. Theodore Roosevelt, who was quite fond of pursuing wolves with dogs and wrote extensively about the "sport," described a wolf brought to bay as "a terrible fighter, with jaws like that of a steel trap and teeth that cut like knives, so that the dogs are continually disabled and sometimes killed." The feat, claimed Roosevelt, "can only be performed by big dogs of the highest courage, who all act together, rush in at top speed, and seize by the throat; for the strength of the quarry is such that otherwise he will shake off the dogs, and then speedily kill them by rabid snaps with his terribly armed jaws." Despite such formidable defenses, Roosevelt told of one Montana stock owner in 1886 who managed to kill 146 wolves using dogs.[53]

Greyhounds were ideal, capable of such speed that if a wolf delayed for more than a moment when a chase began, it was often overtaken. If dogs failed to catch a wolf within the first mile, however, it generally possessed the stamina to outrun them. Some wolves became adept at foiling dogs by swimming across lakes or rivers in order to disguise their scent, or running along railroad tracks where the strong odor of metal and creosote bewildered pursuers long enough for them to escape. Others were said to circle behind a dog pack to ambush and kill slower ones who could not keep up. Desperate wolves could be quite resourceful. During the late 1890s in Oklahoma, a pack of dogs followed by their mounted owner, A. J. Brasier, were chasing a wolf when the exhausted animal suddenly ran toward a nearby farmer's house, burst through the screen door, and took shelter under the dining room table just as the farmer and his family were sitting down to supper. When the breathless Brasier rode up and demanded the wolf, the family felt such pity for the animal that they let it escape, much to "the great disgust of Mr. Brasier and the dogs," recalled a chronicler of the event.[54]

Wolf hunters also resorted to killing young wolves, a procedure known as "denning." Wolf dens were usually well hidden, but hunters devised a simple and deadly method to find them. During March or April when wolves were birthing, a mounted hunter rode in a large circle several miles wide, noting wherever wolf tracks crossed the perimeter. By the time the hunter had completed the circle, often he had detected a number of trails leading into and out of an area. He then determined the point where these trails converged, like the spokes of a wheel, and there he concentrated his search. Sometimes he brought along a dog. In its zeal to protect its young, a wolf would often pursue the dog, running back to the hunter who then shot the wolf. Once a den was located, the hunter dug out the young wolves, speared them, or extracted them with a grappling hook. One renown Colorado wolf hunter, Bill Caywood, even enlisted his young son to crawl into dens to retrieve wolf pups. Sometimes the boy discovered the mother wolf inside the den with its young, but Caywood always managed to pull out the boy unharmed. When the bodies of wolf pups weren't necessary for bounty proof, or if they proved irrecoverable, a hunter either collapsed the den with dynamite, or built a fire at the entrance and asphyxiated them. Sometimes he would save one live pup, chain it to a tree or stake, then lie in wait, hoping its cries would lure other pack members close enough to shoot. Although denning could be time-consuming, of all the methods used to destroy wolves, it ultimately proved the most deadly for it severely hampered the ability of wolves to successively replenish their numbers.[55]

For some hunters the experience of killing young pups was unsettling. Elbert Bowman of eastern Montana reported that it "goes against the grain" to kill the "fat, chubby little rascals" that "will snuggle up to you as friendly as any puppy you ever saw." Although they may be potential murderers, said Bowman, and would soon become "as cruel as man himself after they are grown," at this stage in their lives "they were just plump, friendly, little things that nuzzle you and whine little, pleased whines." Years later, after wolves had disappeared from Montana, Bowman expressed regret that "never again will I hear the strange savage music of their howling. I miss them," he said, "yet I would not wish them back."[56]

With bounties stimulating such a variety of killing methods, stock owners and lawmakers alike were perplexed when, after several years, they didn't seem to be working. "Immense numbers" of both wolves and coyotes had been turned in for bounties, observed the author of an 1896 federal report, but the animals appeared to be as numerous as ever. The only encouragement the report's author offered was a single sentence portending an aroused interest in predators by the federal government: "The necessity of exterminating wolves and coyotes has become more apparent."[57]

Fraud, more prevalent than in colonial times, was one reason why predators continued to be reported in great numbers. Hunters killed wolves in one state, collected a bounty, then traveled to an adjacent state to collect additional, sometimes greater, rewards. States encouraged deception by requiring vastly different standards of proof. Wyoming, for instance, canceled pelts by punching a hole in one foot, while Utah required only the wolf's head for evidence. Pelts were also faked. Wyoming wolf hunters turned in so many coyote, dog, badger, and even stretched jack rabbit pelts, that in 1905 the bounty law was amended to require wolf skins be examined exclusively by a county clerk or notary public. In addition, the pelt had to include all four paws, skin of the head, with both ears, upper and lower lips, and upper jaw bone, or the entire head. Finally, the claimant had to produce an affidavit attesting to when and where the animal was killed, signed by "at least one responsible citizen and taxpayer" residing in the county. Perjury penalties as steep as $500 did not halt abuse. Fraudulent claims became so commonplace in British Columbia that the curator of the provincial museum was required to examine wolf skulls before a bounty could be paid.[58]

Another reason wolves and coyotes didn't appear to be responding to bounties was the nature of the reward system itself. In the beginning, bounties failed to target individual animals responsible for depredations, and instead cast a wide net, resulting in the deaths of innocent and guilty alike. Stock growers were well aware that not all wolves killed livestock. Wallis Huidekoper, vice president of the National Live Stock Association, once remarked, "It is a well-known fact that stock-killing individuals among wolves are only a small proportion of their kind inhabiting a given area." Those wolves responsible for depredations, however, having survived repeated attempts on their lives, often proved the most difficult to kill. Bounty hunters, on the other hand, pursued the most vulnerable animals, usually younger, immature wolves unfamiliar with poison or traps, and then moved on to hunt more promising areas, allowing stock killers to continue their depredations. To ranchers and farmers who estimated wolf numbers by livestock losses, wolves seemed as common as ever. In other instances, hunters intentionally avoided eliminating all wolves in an area in order to guarantee a supply the following year, in effect, "cropping" the annual increase while leaving enough animals to reproduce. In eastern Montana, some hunters went a step further by capturing wolf pups, confining and feeding them for several months, then collecting the higher bounty paid for adults.[59]

Even when hunters managed to substantially reduce the number of wolves of a particular area, seldom did they kill them all. Local officials often compounded this predicament when, in their belief that the predators were no longer a problem, they reduced or abolished bounties altogether. After hunting pressure eased, surviving wolves, with their potentially high reproductive rate, soon replenished former numbers. Or wolves simply moved in from adjacent areas where bounty laws had either lapsed or never existed in the first place.

Despite these inherent difficulties, given enough time, perseverance, and economic incentive, bounties eventually worked. As colonists had demonstrated, the effort could take decades. In Montana, where over 80,000 wolves were reported bountied between 1883 and 1918, hunters turned in 5,866 adult wolves in 1896, but that number steadily dropped until five years later they produced only 1,403 animals. In Wyoming, nearly 30,000 wolves were turned in for bounty between 1895 and 1917, often averaging 3,000 to 4,000 biennially, yet in the final years the number fell precipitously.[60]

Although the problem of widespread fraud and uneven inspection and reporting standards renders these figures not entirely reliable, they imply a downward population trend. Like Montana and Wyoming, most state records indicate that, despite the incentive of increased bounty rewards, less wolves were being reported by the beginning of the twentieth century than during the final decades of the nineteenth. About this same time William Hornaday, the country's preeminent zoologist and director of the New York Zoological Park, visited the northern Plains and found that although the wolf was "far from extinct," it had been "greatly diminished" and was even "scarce" in places. Theodore Roosevelt agreed. Wolves in Texas and Oklahoma are "rare," he said, and throughout other western states they "are now decreasing in numbers, and in most places are decreasing rapidly."[61]

Stock owners, however, were far from satisfied. They had been at this crossroads before. Wolves had been brought to heel during the period of wolfing, then again through years of vacillating bounty laws, only to rebound once persecution ceased. With their hands now firmly about the predator's throat, they weren't about to let go.

In January 1899 at the National Live Stock Association's annual convention in Denver, Colorado, members attempted to authorize a uniform western bounty plan, but the effort failed due to disagreement over bounty price and how the system should be funded. Ranchers returned home and pressed their legislatures for yet higher bounties with rhetoric that had become so commonplace that even they had begun to believe it. Declared one Montana cattleman, "The cattle business would be immensely profitable were it not for the wolves."[62]

In North Dakota, Ben Corbin summed up what was now the pervasive view of stock owners throughout the West. "The wolf is the enemy of civilization," he declared, "and I want to exterminate him."[63]

7

KILLING FOR BLOOD LUST

By the end of the nineteenth century, wolves weren't the only wild animals whose survival prospects had dimmed throughout much of North America.

Less than one hundred years had passed since William Clark had stood at the edge of the Great Plains, and described the number of wolves and other large mammals as beyond mortal belief. During that brief span the human population of the United States had increased fifteenfold, from five million to seventy-five million. In the wake of this aftermath, most large wild animals were now gone, victims of the greatest ecological holocaust to strike the continent since the glacial age ended ten millennia before. Of the sixty-odd million hoofed mammals that had once roamed the mid-continent's grasslands and served as sustenance for wolves and a variety of other creatures, unbridled hunting and loss of habitat had reduced their number until perhaps no more than one or two million survived. Filled with a collective remorse about the loss of so many animals and alarmed at the thought of their possible extirpation, early conservationists—sport hunters, humanitarians, and so-called nature lovers—began organizing to save remnant populations of deer, moose, buffalo, wild sheep, elk, and antelope.[1]

127

Wolves and other large predators were not so fortunate. Those wolves that still survived in central North America by 1900 had become largely dependent upon domestic animals. If they were killing livestock, reasoned sport hunters, they must be also killing what little wild game remained. Nature lovers agreed, tending to side with "good" animals—the innocent or defenseless prey—while wolves were "bad." After visiting Yellowstone National Park in 1906, naturalist John Burroughs summed up the view of most conservationists of the day when he observed that predators like wolves "certainly needed killing." The "fewer of these there are," said Burroughs, "the better for the useful and beautiful game."[2]

Others were more emphatic. Perhaps the most famous anti-predator spokesperson was Theodore Roosevelt, a man who wore many hats during his life, including that of conservationist, sport hunter, and rancher. As a deft and energetic politician, Roosevelt is largely credited with bringing the fledgling conservation movement and government together for the first time during his presidency from 1901 to 1909. But like most early sportsmen-conservationists, his ideology was strictly utilitarian, emphasizing more efficient management of natural resources and manipulation of natural order to suit human purpose. In Roosevelt's view, wolves and other predators didn't fit into that scheme, and he said so unequivocally: wolves were "the archetype of ravin, the beast of waste and desolation." Another prominent conservationist, zoologist William Hornaday, who probably did more than any other person to save buffalo and other large ungulates from extinction, could scarcely find words loathsome enough for wolves. "Of all the wild animals of North America, none are more despicable than wolves." Every one is "deadly dangerous to man" and "a black-hearted murderer and criminal," claimed Hornaday. "There is no depth of meanness, treachery, or cruelty to which they do not cheerfully descend. They are the only animals on earth which make a regular practice of killing and devouring their wounded companions, and eating their own dead."[3]

The final partner in early conservation efforts, the humanitarians, objected to all killing of animals on moral grounds, but they made an exception for those that preyed on others. Henry Salt, an early radical animal rights champion, believed his advocacy did not accrue to "wolves and other dangerous species" because they so plainly caused the suffering of other animals.[4]

128

There would be no room in conservationists' ark for wolves.

Public disapproval of the animals was further encouraged by other voices, although with less conviction than that of Roosevelt, Hornaday, and Salt. As the continent's population became increasingly urbanized, books and magazines began reaching more readers. At the same time, public interest in and nostalgia for wildlife began to grow, and nature writing became more influential than it had ever been before. Wolves were favorite subjects of popular early twentieth century authors such as William Long, Jack London, and Ernest Thompson Seton. Although these writers anthropomorphized and sentimentalized wolves while still pandering to readers' fear of them as vicious creatures, they also exhibited a certain ambivalency about them, one that reflected as well as influenced the attitudes of readers. In many ways, these writers helped set the stage for the eventual rehabilitation of the wolf's image.

William Long wrote extensively about wolves slaughtering defenseless prey, but he claimed to be revolted by the "persistent slandering of honest wolves." In Long's view, the predators never killed "weaker creatures indiscriminately," nor did they feed like sharks, but ate their prey "as peaceable as a breakfast table." Jack London's *The Call of the Wild* (1903) and *White Fang* (1905) sympathetically portrayed wolves as savage creatures, endowed with near-human intelligence but forced to do nature's brutal bidding. He signed his letters "Wolf," named his dog "Brown Wolf," and built "Wolf House" in California.[5]

Ernest Thompson Seton, who often drew a wolf print on letters and used the moniker "Wolf Thompson," wrote with more authority than Long or London because during his youth he had trapped and killed wolves in New Mexico. His short story, "Lobo, King of the Currumpaw," was immensely popular when it first appeared in 1894, and was periodically republished for the next fifty years, eventually reaching millions of readers. In this sentimental but sympathetic story (which Seton claimed was "mostly" true), ranchers are foiled time and again in their attempts to trap and kill the "outlaw king." Seton finally captures the animal and its mate, maintaining that their death, like that of all wolves, was inevitable given their incompatibility with civilization. "It cannot be otherwise," stated Seton. Nonetheless, he mourned the loss of the animal he believed best defined the spirit of wilderness. Wolves may be vicious killers, he said, but they also possess qualities that humans could well admire. They care for each other's young, mate for life, fight to protect one another, and live together in harmony.[6]

Still, Seton could not resist poetic license when it came to a good tale. He thought nothing of imparting human traits to wolves in his stories, having them commit suicide, demonstrate remorse over killing another wolf, and even converse with one another. In one particularly gruesome story in which wolves attack humans, he described a wolf lapping up pools of blood as it "feasted on the warm and quivering human meat." Later in his life, Seton admitted that "we have been fed for so many generations on tales of the Wolf's ferocity, treachery, rapacity, cowardice, and strength" that most people have a "wholly wrong picture of this most interesting animal." Yet, more than most other nature writers, Seton himself helped create that very image.[7]

Perhaps today's most revered conservationist from the era, John Muir, had little to say about wolves. Muir generally ignored predators, preferring to devote his attention to animals whom he considered "dainty-feeders." In his early years, he appears to have greatly feared wolves. During an 1864 outing in Canada, he wrote that he had stayed awake one night in front of a roaring fire "to keep them at bay." After visiting Alaska in 1890, he became convinced that wolves would attack humans and "were much more danger- ous than bears." Once when Muir heard wolves howling nearby, he beat a hasty retreat to the top of a large boulder. There he prepared to defend himself with his ice ax, but the wolves never appeared. Nevertheless, Muir later spoke favorably of such creatures as rattlesnakes, lizards, grasshoppers, even flies, and he appears to have held an equally favorable view of predators, at least in principle. "It is right" that creatures "make use of one another," he once stated. "Wild lambs eat as many flowers as they can find or desire, and men and wolves eat the lambs to just the same extent."[8]

One of the early century's most perceptive writers about wolves was Fred A. Hunt, a man whose name has been virtually forgotten today. In an obscure 1901 literary magazine article entitled "The Wake of the Wolves," Hunt made a startling prophecy: "It is quite probable that, as the years pass, the people will be just as zealous for the protection and preservation of our wild animals as they now are, and have been, for their extinction." Wolves, said Hunt, and other "such 'varmints' may be subject to careful conservation and even be the object of anxious solicitude, for rarity induces value."[9]

Another uncelebrated writer, Henry Shoemaker, a Pennsylvania newspaper editor, took up Hunt's argument in 1914 when he published a short book entitled *Wolf Days in Pennsylvania.* Wolves, like all living things, had been created by God with "a purpose," declared Shoemaker, and thus have "an inherent right to live, to be protected by mankind." Before they were eradicated in Pennsylvania, they trimmed deer herds and kept them from over-populating their habitat. "Nothing had been gained by their extirpation," he said, and reintroducing them to the state "would prove a great benefit" to sportsmen and animals alike.[10]

Had turn-of-the-century stock owners encountered Shoemaker's and Hunt's words, doubtless they would have considered them prattle from an alien world. As it was, they paid little attention to the utterances of nature writers or conservationists, particularly since most of them voiced a negative view of wolves not unlike their own. Stock owners were the ones wresting a living from the land, and wolves were a curse upon their enterprise. The question in their minds was not should wolves be eradicated, but how soon.

Even without advocates, wolves may have survived in remote, unsettled areas had stock owners not taken their oppression of the predators to those places also. This was particularly true in the western United States where millions of acres of federal forest reserves, mostly in mountainous areas, served as public grazing range for both livestock and wild game. Beginning in the early 1900s, stock owners complained to federal officials that these lands served as sanctuaries and "breeding grounds" for "hundreds of thousands" of wolves and other predators. If government was going to lease these lands for grazing, demanded stock owners, it had an obligation to provide safe pasturage. Pressure grew until 1906 when the newly formed U.S. Forest Service requested help from its sister agency in the Department of Agriculture, the Bureau of the Biological Survey, in "ridding the forest reserves and cattle range of gray wolves."[11]

That same year, bureau biologist Vernon Bailey traveled to Wyoming and New Mexico to investigate the extent of wolf and coyote depredations. Upon Bailey's return to Washington, D.C., President Roosevelt invited him to the White House to see what he had learned. Although there is no record of their conversation, immediately following Bailey's meeting with the President, the Biological Survey recommended that the government begin "devising methods for the destruction of the animals." Roosevelt's

131

role in this directive is unclear, but his earlier pronouncements leave no doubt of how he or his administration felt about wolves. Two years after meeting with Bailey, Roosevelt welcomed his Oklahoma hunting companion and famed wolf hunter, Jack Abernathy, to the White House. Abernathy was renowned for his ability to chase wolves on horseback, corner the exhausted animals, grasp their jaws with his bare hands, and wire them shut before turning his dogs loose to dismember the animals. When Abernathy arrived with a film of his latest wolf hunt, Roosevelt quickly stripped portraits from the East Room wall and called for a projector. Roosevelt found the film so delightful that he asked Abernathy to repeat the showing for guests the following week.[12]

Not long after his trip west, Bailey authored a bulletin instructing hunters, stock owners, and forest rangers how to efficiently kill wolves and other harmful predators. Then the Biological Survey sent him to the upper Midwest. There he reported that wolves had become so numerous in Michigan's Upper Penninsula, northern Minnesota, and Wisconsin that they threatened the "extermination of deer." Bailey doubted that wolves could ever be entirely eradicated, but he called for "persistent efforts" to bring about "a permanent reduction of the numbers of these destructive animals, if not their practical extermination in the cattle country."[13]

These efforts began to pay off as early as 1907 when a record kill of 1,723 wolves was reported by forest rangers in 39 western national forests, then estimated to be about one-tenth the total area still inhabited by wolves in the United States. Although Bailey went on to serve thirty more years as the Biological Survey's chief field naturalist, and never publicly wavered in his support for destruction of wolves and other predators, privately he became increasingly uncomfortable with the program he had helped initiate. His concerns, however, stemmed more from the perceived pain and suffering of individual trapped animals than any sympathy for wolves as a species or misgivings about their loss. Bailey even designed a snare wire trap, said to be more humane than the popular Newhouse steel trap. Wolves may be "cruel killers," he later admitted, but they were "not half as cruel as we have been. The more we see of some wolves, the less we think of some men." All in all, "they are an enemy we can well admire." Among Bailey's scant notes and mementos residing today in the Smithsonian Institution is a faded photograph of a large gray wolf held in two steel traps. The caption reads: "Feet Frozen but no less Painful. Yes, he killed Cattle to Eat. But, Did he Deserve This?"[14]

About the same time that rangers began killing wolves in national forests, wolf attack hysteria gripped the continent. In Wisconsin, three loggers were said to have lost their lives to wolves "after a terrible battle," but not before axing seven of the animals to death. One of the victims' skeletons, attested the *Chicago Tribune,* was found choking that of a wolf. In Manitoba, all that was found of two mail carriers killed by wolves were their bloody hands and feet; wolves had eaten everything else, even the mail bags and most of the mail. Near Cokeville, Wyoming, two men were treed by seventeen wolves for a day and a half. The men finally saved themselves by cutting limbs from the tree and "braining" the wolves as they leaped with slavering jaws beneath them. When a wolf suddenly appeared in downtown Keokuk, Iowa, men and boys with clubs cornered the animal in an alley and bludgeoned it to death. Attack tales became so frequent in Ontario that a newspaper editor finally offered a $100 prize to anyone who could prove he or she had been attacked. Fourteen years later the paper reported that "the prize is still safe in the editor's cash box."[15]

Encouraged by the government's response on federal lands, stock owners turned up the volume at their 1908 National Live Stock Association meeting in Denver. Rancher after rancher took the floor to denounce wolves. "Every family of wolves" destroys $3,000 worth of livestock, said one man. Another unnamed but "prominent" Colorado rancher claimed that 15 to 20 percent of all young livestock in the state were killed each year by wolves; another from New Mexico accused wolves of causing losses in excess of $500 million across the West. The public continued to side strongly with stock owners' plight. Even as unlikely a publication as the *The Woman's National Daily* lent support by declaring that those readers who think this campaign is "cruel" must remember that "these animals also are cruel." Wolves were like bad sportsmen, said the newspaper, killing wantonly and maliciously.[16]

Momentum began to build for the federal government to assume responsibility for the control of wolves and other predators. Resisting that pressure was an unlikely man, C. Hart Merriam, chief of the Biological Survey. Merriam had trained as a physician, but his avocation had always been natural history. In 1885 he was appointed head of the Division of Economic Ornithology and Mammalogy, which later was elevated to bureau status and renamed the Biological Survey. From the start Merriam ran afoul of Congress, which had originally created the agency to help rid the country of "noxious" bird and mammal pests for the economic benefit of agriculture. Merriam's interests, however, were geared more toward taxonomy and pure science. At 1908 congressional hearings, he testified that the "great bulk of mammals are pests," but he cautioned that "the first step in fighting them is to find out what they are and what their life habits are." Merriam wasn't opposed to predator control, having earlier directed a massive national poisoning campaign against prairie dogs, but he had come to believe that the agency first should do its homework. Some congressmen disagreed, and two years later Merriam found himself out of a job.[17]

With Merriam gone, the Biological Survey came under control of a series of directors more amenable to returning the agency to "practical" endeavors. In 1912 the survey began field testing predator control projects, but congressional support for large-scale federal involvement remained elusive. Finally, during 1914 and 1915, two events occurred that persuaded Congress and the reform-minded administration of President Woodrow Wilson that wolves and other predators were a threat that required federal action. First, war broke out in Europe, making food production for the Allied cause a top national priority. Second, a rabies pandemic in the West resulted in the destruction of over $5 million worth of livestock, for which stock owners exclusively blamed wolves and coyotes.[18]

At its annual convention in March 1915, the National Live Stock Association, citing the importance of cattle and sheep to the war effort, adopted a resolution urging federal assistance in combating wolves and other predators. By now wolves had been eradicated from eighteen states, but they were proving tenacious elsewhere, despite decades of bounty laws. Stock owners claimed they were losing $15 million each year to predators. What they wanted was a comprehensive program that only the federal government could provide. Despite opposition to federal involvement in what some congressmen deemed solely a private or state responsibility, Congress finally acted in July 1915, appropriating $125,000 to the Biological Survey (one-third of its entire budget) specifically for the destruction of "wolves, coyotes, and other animals injurious to agriculture and animal husbandry."[19]

Although it had been slow to enter the fray, the federal government now embarked on an official program of wildlife destruction unparalleled either before or since that time by any nation in the world.

The Biological Survey was both eager and ready. It soon formed a subsidary division to begin "control" work. Although the name changed several times over the years, it was best known as Predator Animal and Rodent Control (PARC). Eight districts were established throughout the West, and some 300 experienced hunters and trappers were hired to trap, poison, shoot, or otherwise annihilate wolves and other predators. Unlike bounty hunters, these federal employees wouldn't quit when predators became scarce or bounties unprofitable. By the end of the 1915 fiscal year, PARC agents had killed 424 wolves, 11,890 coyotes, 9 mountain lions, and some 3,000 other predators—mostly skunks, black-footed ferrets, bob-cats, badgers, and foxes.[20]

Despite their success in enlisting federal help, stock owners did not give up on their own efforts to eradicate wolves. Foremost, they continued to press for an increase in funding. At the 1916 National Live Stock Associa-tion annual convention, members passed a resolution calling for a federal appropriation of $500,000.[21]

By then wolf bounties still could be found in twenty-seven states, some paying as much as $25 per animal, and had become such an entrenched feature of state and local governments that they attracted little opposition and even less scrutiny. Unequivocal proof of rampant fraud failed to quell their popularity. When Vernon Bailey's bulletin entitled "Key to the Ani-mals on Which Wolf and Coyote Bounties are Paid" was published in 1909, most western states ignored its admonishments exposing deceptive bounty claims. In 1915, Wyoming, once praised by Bailey as having the best bounty records of any state, paid bounties on nearly 1,600 wolves taken during the previous eighteen-month period. Yet one year later, one dozen expert federal hunters working diligently throughout the state could find only 113 wolves. The following year they reported even less. Regard-less, in 1917 the Wyoming legislature increased the bounty appropriation from $60,000 to $75,000, and tripled the reward for adult wolves to $15 each. Montana was no different. Wolf bounty claims there totaled nearly 1,100 animals in 1915. That same year, the state's 16 federal hunters reported finding 70 wolves; the next year, only 52.[22]

Wyoming and Montana were not unusual. By the time of federal predator control takeover, western states were paying nearly $1 million each year in bounty rewards, much of it for "wolves" that never existed except on paper. In light of the low federal kill, eventually most states began to scrutinize bounty claims more closely, and payments declined or ceased altogether. Some states, however, continued to pay claims long after wolves were gone, often by openly allowing bounty hunters to substitute coyote for wolf skins. Between 1913 and 1932, Iowa rewarded nearly $300,000 in "wolf" bounties, although not a single wolf was reported killed in the state during that period by federal hunters. As late as 1958, one Iowa county reported paying $2,072 in wolf bounties. By one estimate, three-plus centuries of wolf bounties throughout North America cost governments, stock associations, and private individuals as much as $100 million.[23]

Although Montana wasn't able to divest itself of bounties until 1933, it did manage to eliminate one dubious anti-wolf measure championed by stock growers. In 1905, the state legislature had authorized the state veterinarian to inoculate captured wolves and coyotes with sarcoptic mange and release them to spread the disease to others. When the victim's hair fell out, it soon died of exposure. Eleven years later, after numerous releases of infected animals with no reports of success, the legislature, fearing that the disease might spread to livestock, finally abandoned the program.[24]

Another popular endeavor among stock growers was a "wolf roundup." In August 1917, some 700 mounted and armed men assembled in central Wyoming, formed a circle 140 miles in circumference, and to the cheers of 2,300 spectators and beating drums, began advancing toward the circle's center. On hand to film the largest wolf roundup in history were four Hollywood camera crews. Organizers were confident that "hundreds" of wolves would be killed, but when the riders converged later that day, not a single wolf had been seen.[25]

By 1918, it was undeniable that wolves were far less numerous than stock owners had claimed. Federal hunters and trappers simply were not finding that many animals, only about 500 or 600 each year, a number that fell to fewer than 100 by the mid-1920s. Bounties, coupled with decades of oppression, had nearly eliminated the animals, and the federal effort would prove only the denouement to what stock owners themselves had nearly accomplished.[26]

On the other hand, despite stepped-up control efforts, hunters were killing ever greater numbers of coyotes. Moreover, coyotes were turning up in places they had never been seen before. Neither the Biological Survey nor stock owners understood that in eliminating wolves, they had simply allowed coyotes to expand into the vacant ecological niche wolves had left behind. Once an animal primarily of the Great Plains, by the mid-1920s coyotes had spread to New England, Florida, the Pacific Northwest, and as far north as Alaska and Hudson Bay. Yet even as the coyote increasingly became the target of eradication efforts, the agency continued to portray the wolf as its principal "enemy," claiming that although it no longer occurred in great numbers, individual wolves were killing as much as $5,000 worth of livestock each year, often "for no apparent reason other than amusement or sheer lust of killing." Posters depicting long-fanged, snarling beasts standing over slain cattle, along with a "most wanted" wolf list, were disseminated to agency offices throughout the West. One regional supervisor adopted the slogan, "Bring Them in Regardless of How." Nor did the agency fail to make a connection between wolves and the ongoing world war. Just as the allies were trouncing Germans "inspired with the ideals of wild beasts," asserted a 1918 Department of Agriculture newsletter, the agency was winning "the war in the West" against wolves.[27]

That same year, due to growing administrative expense, despite a doubling of funding by Congress, most predator control work began to be shared under cooperative agreements between states, counties, other federal agencies, and, to a much lesser degree, private stock owner associations. PARC provided trappers and equipment, while the "cooperators" contributed one-quarter of the program's cost, primarily paid by an assessment on livestock. This co-dependency had far-reaching consequences, making the agency increasingly linked to the livestock industry for both political and financial support.

By 1920, the number of federal hunters grew to over four hundred (soon to reach a peak of five hundred) while the number of predator control districts expanded from eight to fourteen, incorporating additional states. At the same time, more than half of the Biological Survey's $500,000 budget for agency field projects had become dedicated exclusively to predator control work. During these early years, most wolves were taken by trapping. Soon after the Biological Survey's inception, the agency became the Oneida Company's (maker of the Newhouse trap) largest single customer. Anticipating this demand, the company developed a new double-spring wolf trap, the No. 44, strictly for government use, shipping it to western states in "carload lots." Government hunters were no longer restricted to public lands, but were now free to pursue wolves on private lands also. Whenever reports were received of wolf depredations, federal hunters were immediately dispatched to the area. "In this way," claimed the agency's 1920 report, "the careers of many of the most notorious stock killers of the western ranges have been ended." That autumn, the Custer wolf—perhaps the most notorious wolf of all—was slain in South Dakota.[28]

But the agency had not yet won its war with the wolf. By 1921, its operations covered most western states and extended eastward to western Missouri and northern Michigan. It also began targeting the gray wolf's smaller cousin, the red wolf, primarily in Texas, Oklahoma, Louisiana, and Arkansas. In their last refugia, wolves proved remarkably difficult to eradicate. Particularly vexing were those states that shared a common border with Mexico or Canada.

After several hundred wolves had been killed during the first few years of federal control in Arizona and New Mexico, district supervisor J. Stokley Ligon, reported less than seventy wolves existed in each state. Ligon was sure eradication was on the horizon, stating in 1918 that "the gray wolf will be exterminated throughout the West within reasonable time." One year later, he claimed no more than a dozen adult wolves remained in New Mexico, causing so little damage that "little complaint is heard." But in 1921, seventy-nine wolves were killed in New Mexico and thirty-seven in Arizona. As fast as wolves were eliminated, new ones wandered into the states from across the border. Since Mexico had no government wolf control effort, federal officials offered their services. Mexico, however, was still smarting from illegal American raids across the border in search of Poncho Villa and refused. For awhile the bureau seriously considered building a wolf-proof fence along the entire border, but this improbable plan was squelched when the expense proved prohibitive. Finally, the agency commenced an intensive poisoning campaign along the border, and far fewer migrant wolves were the result. Although Ligon reported by 1924 that wolves in New Mexico "are no longer a real menace," ranchers continued to complain of depredations, a minor problem Ligon largely attributed to dogs or coyotes, not wolves.[29]

During this period, poison proved successful in other areas of the country as well. It hadn't been used extensively against wolves since early bounty days, but now trappers and hunters found it effective wherever the predators had grown unfamiliar with its use. Consequently, the Biological Survey decided to begin mass production of strychnine baits. In 1921, it set aside money to fund a research center to develop new and better poisons. One year later, with the help of thousands of stockmen, the agency had distributed over one million poison baits across the West. The estimated result was over eighty thousand dead coyotes and nearly seven hundred wolves, most of which were never recovered. The Biological Survey was pleased with the kill, reporting by 1924 that "gratifying results have been obtained in the destruction" of these "animal criminals." The number of surviving gray wolves, claimed the agency, probably did not now exceed ten to fifty animals in any single state.[30]

Not everyone supported the massive poisoning campaign. By 1924, some scientists outside the agency—particularly members of the American Society of Mammalogists, a professional society formed in 1919 with strong ties to many of the nation's leading universities—had begun to question whether the Biological Survey was more interested in exterminating predators than controlling them. By now populations of large wildlife species like deer, elk, and antelope that had appeared on the verge of extinction only two decades before were beginning to show signs of recovery. The science of ecology was only in its infancy, but some scientists had begun to suspect that predation had its place in the scheme of things, although they lacked credible data to support this view. One of those scientists, Joseph Grinnell from the University of California at Berkeley, published one of the earliest pleas for predator protection in 1916 stating that in national parks, "predacious animals should be left unmolested and allowed to retain their primitive relation to the rest of the fauna." Fearing that whole species might be lost through the agency's indiscriminate use of poison, the mammalogists, led by Grinnell, expressed particular concern about non-target species such as song birds and small mammals. They also cited the controlling effect coyotes were thought to have on rodents. In a prescient mood, some even remarked that these animals may have other, as yet undiscovered, values.[31]

Responding to these criticisms, the Survey's chief scientist and spokesman, Edward Goldman, admitted that some "local" populations of predators and other animals might disappear, but he labeled the mammalogists concerns as "emotional," saying that the agency was only carrying forth control efforts originally begun by stock owners. Coyotes were in no danger of eradication, said Goldman, but wolves "no longer have a place in our advancing civilization."[32]

Goldman's remarks were coldly received. Soon the break between non-government scientists and those who worked for the Biological Survey, many of whom like Goldman were also members of the society, erupted into a major rift. Some mammalogists accused the agency of exclusively serving the livestock industry. Agency scientists had little rejoinder, for by now the Biological Survey was firmly wed to stock owners who, through cooperative agreements with the federal government, provided half the cost of predator control—a number that in the decade since the program had begun totaled over $5 million. Survey hunters and scientists both worked in concert with ranchers and shared many of the same attitudes about predators. Still, the mammalogists had little proof that predators provided any beneficial effect. Eventually the society formed a committee to look into the allegations, but its members split in their appraisal of what should be done and produced separate reports. One group said predators had "value" and suggested that they be preserved in certain national parks or areas of the public domain, although the report's authors failed to identify the areas or the specific animals they would protect. The other report charged both the Biological Survey and the livestock industry with blatantly attempting to exterminate certain wildlife, an act it asserted was unjustifiable on either economic or scientific grounds.[33]

But there were limits even for the most ardent mammalogists—wolves and mountain lions were purposefully excluded from both reports. Whether committee members genuinely believed they shouldn't include them in their argument against predator control, or that these predators should be sacrificed in the name of compromise, isn't entirely clear. One of the most vociferous opponents of the agency's eradication efforts, A. Brazier Howell of Johns Hopkins University, admitted in a letter to the new chief of the Biological Survey, Paul Redington, that predator control was sometimes "advisable" and the society didn't wish to end it completely. "Also we make no mention of wolves and mountain lions which, whatever their values from an aesthetic viewpoint, are truly killers and are destructive."[34]

Despite Howell's concession, the agency refused to compromise. In January 1927, a representative of the Biological Survey attended the National Live Stock Association's annual convention in Salt Lake City, Utah, and assured stock growers that the agency deplored the "radical utterances

of fool conservationists" with whom it didn't agree. A year later Redington, a former U.S. Forest Service administrator more interested in building
a bureaucratic empire than tearing one down, left no doubt where he stood
when he addressed an assembly of agency personnel. As unbelievable as it
may be, he said, there were those "who want to see the mountain lion, the
wolf, the coyote, and the bobcat perpetuated as part of the wildlife of the
country." Several months after Redington's speech, a book about the Biological Survey appeared in which the author, after extensive interviews
with agency personnel, asserted that the wolf was "under control" throughout the western United States, and the complete extermination of these
animals of "truly satanic cunning" was now "only a matter of time."[35]

Even before Redington revealed his position, additional critics of the
agency's predator policies had begun to surface. Naturalist George Bird
Grinnell, who had helped found the first Audubon Society and the New
York Zoological Society, declared that all species are "a tangible value to
the community and so are worth saving," one that the present generation
must preserve "for those who are to come after us." As to the future of
predators, Grinnell echoed Fred Hunt's earlier pronouncement by saying
that "experience has shown that if these wild things are utterly destroyed, a
later generation will feel that it must replace them. This replacement is
often impossible, but even if it can be accomplished, the task is one of
time, difficulty and great expense. It is far more economical to spend today
a little money to keep these living things in existence than to replace them
at a later time—or to try to replace them and fail to do so."[36]

Another critic was Edmund Heller, a prominent naturalist who had
once coauthored a book with Theodore Roosevelt on African wildlife. In
writing about Yellowstone National Park's wildlife in 1925, Heller proposed that "a few" wolves be allowed to survive in national parks to "add
fire and alertness" to game animals that otherwise would "become like
cattle" in the absence of predators. "I hope some day to see a pack of wolves
in full cry after their hoofed quarry and see with my own eyes how they
pull down their game."[37]

Dissension also appeared within the National Park Service. In April
1924 at the annual convention of the American Society of Mammalogists,
Milton Skinner, a former Yellowstone Park naturalist, accused the agency
of complicity in exterminating predators. Parks should protect "all wild
life," said Skinner, including wolves and coyotes. "To many persons, a wolf

or a coyote is as important as a deer," and he called the effort to eliminate them in national parks "indefensible."[38]

Two years later the service's director, Stephen Mather, finally responded to these criticisms by announcing that, while wolves and other large predators would continue to be killed in parks to protect "weaker" species, it had never been park service policy to wholly exterminate them. Mather's lukewarm support for predators, however, came too late; the eradication of the wolf in all national parks (or park designees) outside of Alaska was a fait accompli—they were gone from Crater Lake, Grand Teton, Mount Rainier, Olympic, Rocky Mountain, Great Smoky Mountains, Sequoia, Glacier, Yosemite, Yellowstone, and Grand Canyon. Neither did it reflect the director's personal feelings about predators, nor what really had been going on behind park boundaries. Since its inception in 1916 the service, under Mather's direction and in close cooperation with the Biological Survey, had quietly waged an intensive effort to eradicate wolves and other predators from national parks in order to protect deer, moose, buffalo, and elk—the "beautiful" creatures that Mather believed visitors wanted to see.

Yellowstone National Park, the flagship of the national park system and one of the last to lose its wolves, was a special target. In 1886, following the period when wolfers had nearly extinguished wolves in the park, the U.S. Army took over its administration until the park service officially assumed civilian control in 1918. Although the army's park duty was to protect wildlife, soldiers shot wolves whenever they saw them and poisoned others, killing several dozen during their thirty-year tenure. Nonetheless, by 1915 a report claimed that wolves were so common that they had become "a decided menace" to the park's game herds. That same year, the Biological Survey sent Vernon Bailey to Yellowstone to investigate. Bailey found the population of wolves "abundant" and causing "great havoc among the game animals." Predator control commenced the following winter, resulting in the deaths of 180 coyotes, 12 wolves, and 4 mountain lions. By 1922, the park superintendent reported that killing wolves had become "one of the most important duties of the park protective force." Wolf control should be "vigorously prosecuted," he claimed, "whether or not this meets with the approval of certain game conservationists."[39]

Wolf control ended in Yellowstone by 1926, not because of Mather's pronouncement, but because there were no more wolves. After a dozen years of eradication, federal hunters had killed at least 136 animals (including about 80 pups), although likely many others fell to poison. Wolves were seen occasionally in the park in subsequent years, but no breeding pairs were found and soon sightings became extremely rare. What few wolves may have survived appear to have succumbed to poison, which wasn't officially banned from national parks until 1930 by Mather's successor, Horace Albright. The following year, in describing his new park policy toward predators, Albright, who had been superintendent of Yellowstone during the park's intensive period of wolf eradication, declared that henceforth all animals, including predators, "should be kept inviolate within the parks." No longer would there be "widespread campaigns of destruction," particularly of those "disappearing species" that might be making their "last stands." Albright then hedged by authorizing the use of poison "in case of emergency," and allowing other measures if predators "are actually found making serious inroad upon herds of game or other animals needing special protection."[40]

Like Mather, Albright privately remained opposed to predators, fearing that a stand in favor of them might preclude western support for additional national parks. Consequently, poison continued to be used in Yellowstone for the next two years (and outside park boundaries for the next forty years). A subsequent 1933 National Park Service wildlife report, which became official policy three years later, declared that each park species was "a priceless creation." Large predators like wolves and coyotes were particularly important, for in parks they "find their only sure haven" and "are given opportunity to forget that man is the implacable enemy of their kind." Despite such ringing rhetoric, Yellowstone rangers continued to kill well over a hundred coyotes each year through 1935, a fate that doubtless would have befallen wolves had any survived.[41]

By the late 1920s, the Biological Survey found itself under increasing fire and began to feel vulnerable. Until now the agency had successfully sought congressional appropriations each year, but as criticism mounted, it began lobbying Congress for an extended mandate. The agency wanted to more than double its annual predator and rodent control funding to nearly $1.4 million, and extend the program for at least another ten years. Paul Redington began to tone down agency pronouncements. Employees should cease talking about "extermination" of predators, he said, and substitute a softer word: "control." Even wolves were given a new spin. Extermination of the animal had never been the agency's goal, claimed Redington at the

1930 National Wool Growers Association convention. The wolf may have "largely disappeared from the West," he granted, but it was alive and well in Canada and Alaska, and thus will never "cease to be numbered in the fauna of the North American continent." Soon afterward, however, the agency appealed to sport hunters to increase their support of predator control. Of the 150,000 deer, elk, moose, and other large wild game killed nationwide each year, claimed a report, fully 60 percent were the "victims of predatory animals," game that had been "stolen" from sportsmen.[42]

In December 1929 a bill was introduced in the U.S. House of Representatives authorizing a ten-year predator control program for the "eradication, suppression, or bringing under control" of predatory animals on public and private land. There was virtually no opposition. When Montana congressman Scott Leavitt, a former U.S. Forest Service supervisor and the bill's sponsor, brought a wolf skin to the House floor, a Minnesota congressman shouted out sarcastically, "Does the gentleman mean to state that the federal government was a party to the dastardly murder of that animal?" The House erupted in laughter.[43]

Then Leavitt read a stirring speech, saying that after years of "unrelenting warfare" in which predators had caused stock owners damage in excess of $20 million annually, wolves had finally had been brought "under control." This bill, maintained the congressman, provided the necessary "vigilance" to ensure that they never returned.[44]

Leavitt's speech had been written by Stanley Young, a PARC biologist and administrator, Redington's hand-picked choice to help usher the legislation through Congress. Young had joined the agency in 1917 and continued for the next twenty-two years to serve in a variety of positions, eventually becoming chief of PARC and the agency's foremost public defender. Later in his life, he professed a fascination, even "affection," for wolves and wrote numerous books and articles about them, culminating in his 1944 magnum opus *The Wolves of North America,* coauthored with Edward Goldman. But at the time that this critical legislation was being considered by Congress, Young confided to Arthur Carhart, his conservationist friend and coauthor of a book the two men had just written about wolves, that "the grey wolf has no place in modern civilization. In my opinion, this animal is one hundred percent criminal, killing for sheer blood lust."[45]

When the bill reached the U.S. Senate Agriculture and Forestry Committee, it no longer needed Young's guidance. Senators from Idaho, Wyoming, Arizona, Montana, and other western states seized control and railroaded the bill through the hearings. Virtually every western state's cattle and sheep association, and many sportsmen groups, sent resolutions supporting the bill's passage.[46]

Wyoming senator John Kendrick, who had previously owned and managed one of the largest ranches in the West, served as the state's governor, and possessed undying animosity toward predators. Although the seventy-three-year-old Kendrick had received "quite a few letters from university people insisting on moderate action in connection with the extermination of predatory animals," he was unable to conceive of anyone making such a plea had they had personal experience with the "terrific disaster wrought on herds and flocks by wolves and coyotes," or their behavior, one that was "the most barbarous thing imaginable." There is nothing "so vicious in its cruelty as the method employed by the gray wolf in destroying his prey," he told fellow senators. "His prey is literally eaten alive, its bowels torn out while it is still on its feet in many cases." Kendrick claimed that he and his ranch hands had killed hundreds of wolves during the 1890s. Wyoming still had "too many gray wolves," he said, even though a Biological Survey report only two years before had determined the state then contained probably no more than five wolves.[47]

Two representatives of the American Society of Mammalogists, Harold Anthony and A. Brazier Howell, attempted to speak against the bill, but Kendrick and other senators interrupted, badgered, and did all they could to embarrass the two scientists.

When Kendrick learned that Anthony, the curator of mammals at the American Museum of Natural History, resided in New York City, he demanded, "I wonder if you, in the Eastern States where the most of these protests come from, conserve your wolves and coyotes, and if so, how you would like to have some of ours distributed in your country so as to breed them?" Anthony admitted that mammalogists weren't interested in conserving "especially destructive predatory animals" like wolves, but instead were concerned primarily about indiscriminate poisoning of non-targeted wildlife. But Kendrick either ignored or disbelieved him. Wolves were a scourge to stockmen, he ranted, and a rancher "must fight in any way he can!"[48]

When A. Brazier Howell testified after Anthony, he became so incensed at Kendrick and the other senators that he could scarcely hide his contempt for either them or what he believed was the federal government's schizophrenic attitude toward wildlife. "It is utterly ridiculous," he fumed, for Biological Survey employees "to expect for long to get away with posing as both the country's greatest conservationists and its greatest destroyers of wildlife!"[49]

The senators, however, had the last word. The bill was favorably reported out of committee, passed both Houses by over a two-thirds margin, and was signed into law by President Herbert Hoover as the Animal Damage Control Act of March 2, 1931. Although Congress failed to appropriate all of the funding the agency had requested, the Predatory Animal and Rodent Control division had achieved its ten-year mandate. But more important, it had officially established its statutory authority, thereby assuring its bureaucratic perpetuity far beyond a mere ten-year term, one that continues even to this day. The war against predators was now the official law of the land.

As far as gray wolves were concerned, the new law didn't result in the deaths of a great many more; almost all were gone from the conterminous United States by 1931. Since its inception sixteen years earlier, PARC reported having killed about 3,500 gray wolves, although the actual number was probably a good deal greater due to poisoned animals that were never recovered. A few wolves would continue to show up from time to time, particularly in those border states like Montana and Arizona where nearby populations still occurred in Canada and Mexico. Also some states may have harbored small, remnant gray wolf populations for another decade or two, although most authorities believe Minnesota was the only state where they did not disappear entirely.[50]

In the span of three hundred years nationwide, but only seventy years in the West, hunters in the United States had managed to kill off the wild prey of gray wolves; settlers, farmers, and ranchers had occupied most of the wolves' former habitat; wolfers had poisoned them; bounty hunters had dynamited their dens and pursued them with dogs, traps, and more poison; and finally, the government had stepped in and, primarily at the livestock industry's behest, quite literally finished them off.

Now that wolves were gone, it was time for Fred Hunt's prophecy to come true.

8

TURNING THE TIDE

By every apparent yardstick, both the livestock industry and the Biological Survey emerged in 1931 as the clear victors in the public debate over predator and rodent control. Stock owners, in particular, had been hard hit by the worsening economy, and any government assistance to help reduce their losses was welcomed. But it wasn't enough. Three years later they were back before Congress demanding a $525 million bailout to save them from "ruin and starvation" caused by rock-bottom livestock prices. Predators, it seems, were a minor problem compared to the jaws of world-wide depression.[1]

Following passage of the control bill, the Biological Survey began gearing up to help stock owners combat predators to a far greater degree than it had done during the previous sixteen years. By 1932, more than half the agency's annual budget was dedicated exclusively to eradication of "noxious animal pests." Those scientists who believed that the primary mission of the agency was to preserve wildlife rather than destroy it had lost, and the "gopher-chokers," as PARC employees were nicknamed within the agency, had won.

The agency's detractors weren't so easily dismissed, however, and the seeds of discord they had sown began to multiply as accusations raged back and forth at subsequent annual meetings of the American Society of Mammalogists. Still chafing over the drubbing he had received from western congressmen, Harold Anthony wrote an open letter published in the journal *Science,* charging the Biological Survey with "organized slaughter" in its effort "to make the West a sheep man's paradise," and causing the country's wildlife nothing less than "the most serious crisis in its history."[2]

Soon the Biological Survey's Edward Goldman fired back. Decrying the "captious and dictatorial attitude" of the naysayers, Goldman accused Anthony of "misleading halftruths and irresponsible criticisms." But his deepest contempt was for A. Brazier Howell, "whose widespread propaganda and narrow viewpoint" Goldman believed had deceived both the scientific community and a gullible public. The row became so devisive that some prominent individuals who had helped found the professional organization, but who were also Biological Survey employees, resigned their membership.[3]

Not all scientists in the Biological Survey agreed with Edward Goldman, but few possessed the courage to challenge the agency's course. One who did was an outspoken biologist named Olaus Murie. During the early 1920s, the thirty-year-old Murie was sent by the agency to Alaska to investigate complaints that great numbers of wolves were killing wildlife, and to determine whether PARC should begin an eradication program there. After completing a dogsled journey around Mount McKinley (now Denali) National Park, Murie reported that he had observed "very little evidence of wolves," concluding that demands for their control had come from hunters and trappers "anxious to have an increase in bounty laws." The outcry against wolves, said Murie, was inversely proportional to game numbers: when game was abundant, stories of predator atrocities were few; when game was scarce, wolves became scapegoats. In 1922, Olaus's younger brother, Adolph—who two decades later would complete a landmark study of wolves in the park—joined him and the two brothers investigated other areas of Alaska, arriving at the same conclusion. Olaus admitted that it was difficult to separate fact from fiction, so entwined were wolves in mythology and backwoods folklore, but he came away convinced that they weren't the villains they had been made out to be.[4]

Not long after he returned from Alaska, Murie found himself embroiled in the dispute over predator control in the West. When mammalogists raised their complaints during the mid-1920s against the Biological Survey, the agency appointed Murie to investigate. After inspecting hundreds of poison bait stations throughout the West, he concluded that poisoning was killing many non-targeted species. But what Murie found even more unsettling was the fraud and misinformation regarding predators. Ranchers were selling sheep and then reporting them killed by wolves or coyotes, a practice condoned by agency administrators. Moreover, PARC officials spent much of their time and money cultivating public hatred against predators. Upon entering PARC field offices, Murie reported being greeted with posters displaying "grinning visages" of wolves or coyotes "cruelly murdering" lambs or calves. Control may be necessary at certain times and places, admitted Murie, but much less often than was being advocated. PARC employees were exclusively serving the interests of stock growers at the expense of true wildlife conservation. They "are not conservationists at heart," he charged.[5]

When PARC officials read Murie's report, they were outraged. Stanley Young accused him of favoring predators "on every possible occasion," and setting a poor example for other agency biologists. From Vernon Bailey, Murie received a "cussing out" along with the accusation that his study was nothing but "a pack of lies." The criticism became so venomous that Murie feared for his job, writing his supervisor to rather naively ask, "Am I a black sheep in the Bureau fold now?" But he refused to back down. Writing to A. Brazier Howell, Murie admitted that he had grown "very fond of native mammals, amounting almost to a passion," and thought of the wolf as a "noble animal, with admirable cunning and strength."[6]

Murie didn't lose his job with the Biological Survey, although he continued to speak out against predator control when he later studied coyote predation at the National Elk Refuge in northwest Wyoming. Finally, disillusioned with the agency's policies, he quit in 1945 to became president of the Wilderness Society, an organization he had helped found. Later in life Murie reflected on the predator control controversy during the late 1920s, and concluded that scientists shouldn't have so readily abandoned wolves and mountain lions. "The mammalogists had not approached the matter on the fundamental issue. The point we have all had in mind is really that we want to preserve the 'injurious' species. They are the ones that are really threatened." There was still "a fine lot of enthusiasm for the preservation" of desirable animals, but why was there none for wolves and other large predators? Meanwhile, these animals "are quietly, unobtrusively slipping out of our fauna." The problem now facing conservationists, said Murie, "is to find places where animals such as the wolf can exist in moderate numbers and prevent their complete extermination."[7]

Other scientists, both inside and outside government, eventually came around to Murie's point of view, but their apostasy was slow and sometimes tortuous—a fact that makes their eventual repudiation of wolf persecution all the more remarkable. Sigurd Olson was a biologist, Murie's contemporary, and a popular natural history writer from the upper Midwest. In 1930 Olson wrote a story for *Sports Afield,* calling wolves "savage-looking brutes" and "grey marauders" who had been out "murdering" deer. Eight years later, after completing the first scientific study of wolves in northern Minnesota, Olson reversed his view, admitting that his earlier opinion had been swayed by unfounded prejudice and bias against the animal. The wolf, he concluded, "is an integral part of the wilderness community, the destruction of which would destroy the fine balance between related forms." But Olson had learned that being a wolf advocate wasn't easy, for "the politics of wolf preservation and the science of studying wolves is more vicious and complicated than any wolf pack I've had the pleasure of studying."[8]

Like Olson, the biologist and writer who is remembered today as one of the most eloquent early defenders of wolves didn't come by his opinions quickly or painlessly. Aldo Leopold studied forestry at Yale University, and firmly believed the utilitarian ethic that the only animals worth preserving were those beneficial to humankind. After graduating in 1909, Leopold became a U.S. Forest Service ranger in New Mexico and Arizona, where, until 1918, he worked with PARC's J. Stokley Ligon to eradicate wolves. "Stockmen and the game protectionists are mutually and vitally interested in a common problem," wrote Leopold in 1915. "This problem is the reduction of predatory animals." A few years later, he was more emphatic. Sportsmen and stockmen "demand the eradication of lions, wolves, coyotes, and bobcats." In 1920, Leopold told members of the American Game Protective Association that New Mexico's wolf population had been reduced from three hundred to thirty animals in only three years, and called for continued perseverance "until this job is finished."[9]

But in the years that followed, Leopold's resolve weakened. Toward the end of his life, he wrote about the experience that altered his view of wolves. One day during his time in the Southwest, Leopold and several companions chanced upon a female wolf and shot her. "We reached the old wolf in time to watch a fierce green fire dying in her eyes. I realized then and have known ever since, that there was something new to me in those eyes—something known only to her and to the mountain. I was young then, and full of trigger itch; I thought that because fewer wolves meant more deer, that no wolves would mean hunters' paradise. But after seeing the green fire die, I sensed that neither the wolf nor the mountain agreed with such a view."[10]

Reflecting about the relationship between deer and wolves, Leopold concluded that it was one of much greater complexity than he or others had presumed. Deer needed predators to trim their numbers and keep them from destroying their environment, he said. To do away with predators such as wolves was tantamount to "ecological murder," with far-reaching consequences both to deer and their habitat. "I now suspect that just as a deer herd lives in mortal fear of its wolves, so does a mountain live in mortal fear of its deer."[11]

Leopold may have reached this personal epiphany during his years in Arizona, but it was fully fifteen years later that he ventured to publicly challenge the conventional view with his seminal book *Game Management*. By now wildlife management was rapidly changing. Ecology and the study of interrelationships between plants, animals, and their environment was growing, although little data was then available to support Leopold's notion of predator-prey relationships. Nonetheless, science should prove the necessity, he said, before automatically advocating predator eradication. The best wildlife management was that which restored or preserved natural mechanisms of control, and he chided those scientists who sanctimoniously dismissed predator advocates as "chicken-hearted." At the same time, Leopold refused to join those scientists who discounted economic concerns of predation and demanded a complete cessation of predator control. With one foot in the camp of ecologists and the other in that of "practical" conservationists, Leopold addressed the broad question of human interaction with the environment, articulating his view in simple, common-sense words that have become his hallmark: "A thing is right when it tends to preserve the integrity, the stability, and beauty of the biotic community. It is wrong when it tends otherwise." Wolves and other predators, declared

Leopold, belong to the biotic community as much as any other species. In a 1944 book review critical of Young and Goldman's *The Wolves of North America,* he admitted that it may have been necessary to eradicate wolves in those places where they intensely competed with livestock. But why had the government insisted on extirpating them virtually everywhere in the continental United States? Then he proposed the unthinkable: Should not some of the animals have been saved "to restock Yellowstone?"[12]

Despite his efforts on behalf of predators, Leopold didn't live to see either a majority of scientists or the public embrace his view. A few years before he died fighting a brush fire in Wisconsin in 1948, members of a Wisconsin hunting club rebuffed his support of wolves, stating that "the wolf is the Nazi of the forest." If a man killed as many deer as wolves, they said, he would be thrown in jail. Then the hunters demanded that Leopold answer a simple question: "Do you like the wolf better than the man?" There is no record that Leopold ever answered the hunters, but his frustration with human attitudes about wolves was evident in his 1944 essay "Thinking Like a Mountain," in which he offered what may be the most-quoted passage ever written about the wolf: "Only the mountain has lived long enough to listen objectively to the howl of the wolf."[13]

The evidence that Leopold and other predator advocates so desperately needed to advance their position was a long time coming. Paul Errington, one of Leopold's students, investigated bobwhite quail during the early 1930s and eventually concluded, contrary to popular belief, that predation had a minimal effect on overall quail numbers. Predators primarily took individuals that could be considered "surplus" members of a prey population, and thus didn't constitute a threat to the long-term well-being of their prey. Errington went on to study many more predator-prey relationships, further defining the mechanisms of predation to show that previous notions concerning predators were largely untrue.[14]

By far the most useful argument in favor of predators showed up in the West. The Kaibab Plateau, a 1,200-square-mile area along the North Rim of the Grand Canyon, supported one of the continent's largest surviving mule deer herds at the beginning of the century. In 1906, the government declared the area a game reserve and two years later incorporated it into the Kaibab National Forest. To protect deer, the forest service ended hunting, reduced livestock grazing, and asked the Biological Survey to control predators. Between 1906 and 1931 the agency, by its own count, killed

4,849 coyotes, 554 bobcats, 781 mountain lions, and 30 wolves. Deer had grown to such alarming numbers by 1920 that their habitat was suffering. When Leopold visited the area as part of an investigative committee in 1924, he described the forest as looking as if "someone had given God a new pruning shears and forbidden Him all other exercise." Recommendations to drastically reduce the number of deer met with bitter opposition from both sport hunters and the National Park Service. No one in the Biological Survey, other than Olaus Murie and a few other scientists, was willing to suggest that perhaps it had been a mistake to eliminate predators. As late as 1928, Vernon Bailey was calling for yet more predator control for Kaibab. Two years later, possibly as many as 70,000 deer starved to death.[15]

After the Kaibab crash, Leopold and other scientists effectively used it as an example of what could go wrong when predators are eradicated from an ecosystem, and what they called the "balance of nature" is disrupted. Drawing on the work of Errington and others, they claimed that predators kept prey populations healthy by culling the sick, weak, and old—animals Errington deemed surplus. If predators were eliminated, prey numbers could quickly reach dangerous proportions. Since that time, this simplistic explanation has fallen into disrepute. Instead of the relatively steady-state that "balance" implies, predator-prey numbers may fluctuate dramatically, at least in the short term. Likewise, predators like wolves may kill more than just excess animals and, in certain cases, may inhibit the full potential growth of a prey population. In the case of the Kaibab, a host of factors—including predator-prey cycles, weather, past livestock grazing, political ineptitude, as well as a lack of predators—contributed to the decline. But during the 1930s and for many decades afterward, the Kaibab became the rallying cry of predator advocates.

By the late 1930s and early 1940s, scientists' concern about the eradication of wolves and other predators began spilling over into the public arena. Other professional organizations—most notably the New York Zoological Society, no longer led by William Hornaday—condemned federal predator control. In 1939, Gideon Graham, a self-educated, Oklahoma state senator, former rancher, and one-time wolf-hunter-turned-conservationist, wrote a popular book called *Animal Outlaws*. Graham had become galvanized against the killing of wolves after observing a hunt sponsored by the Isaak Walton League in which he watched a wounded wolf torn limb from limb by a pack of dogs. Graham despised the Biological Survey, labeling it a "B. S. outfit," a "colossal bureau" full of "political parasites" bent on continuing their poisoning and trapping campaign until they had exterminated the wolf from the entire continent. Not long after Graham's book appeared, Canadian author and naturalist John Stanwell-Fletcher published an article in *Natural History* magazine, declaring that after spending three years in the Canadian wilderness, he believed more than any other creature the wolf represented "the spirit of wilderness itself." If the wolf is exterminated, said Stanwell-Fletcher, "we shall have lost one of the most virile, wise, and beautiful of all wild creatures."[16]

At the same time that this nascent reformation of the wolf's public image was taking place, the Biological Survey was also getting a face-lift. In 1939, Franklin Roosevelt's New Deal administration transferred the bureau to the Department of the Interior where, after several name changes, it eventually became the U.S. Fish and Wildlife Service (USFWS). The Division of Predatory Animal and Rodent Control was transferred also. Although PARC underwent reorganization, changing its name to the Branch of Predator and Rodent Control (BPRC), its role remained undiminished. With gray wolves virtually gone from the continental United States, predator eradication largely focused on coyotes and, to a far less degree, red wolves.

In Alaska, however, gray wolves were still relatively abundant, with an estimated population of 5,000 animals, and it was here that the agency now turned its attention. The Biological Survey had maintained a presence on and off in the territory ever since Olaus Murie had traveled there in the early 1920s, but due to lack of funding, its efforts consisted primarily of a handful of employees who instructed private trappers how to trap and poison wolves and coyotes. Despite Murie's findings that wolves were relatively scarce, hunters and fur trappers continued to complain about wolf depredations of caribou, Dall sheep, moose, and deer. In 1929, Alaska's PARC director appealed to superiors to begin a large-scale wolf eradication program to protect Alaskan big game "before the thief gets them." Although Paul Redington had visited Alaska the year before and expressed alarm at the number of wolves there, he was preoccupied with seeing the agency's ten-year authorization bill through Congress, and Alaska continued to take a back seat.[17]

The territory, however, was soon thrust to the forefront of national attention following several harsh winters, first in 1928–29, then again in 1931–32. At Mount McKinley National Park, Alaska's premier park designated in 1917 primarily as a game refuge, the population of Dall sheep fell drastically from previous estimates as high as 25,000 animals to less than 1,500. In 1931 park service director Horace Albright acted quickly, authorizing McKinley's rangers to "kill wolves on sight," resulting in the deaths of some 23 animals. During the next few years, public outcry for additional wolf control grew throughout Alaska. The territory's principal outdoor magazine, *The Alaska Sportsman,* frequently published articles condemning depredations. "The wolves' fangs account for countless thousands of harmless denizens of the woods each year," read one photograph caption describing a hunter with a dead wolf. "A dead wolf is a good wolf."[18]

By the mid-1930s, PARC began to kill wolves outside McKinley and offered to expand its efforts inside the park's boundaries. The National Park Service, however, was not so anxious. A growing number of park officials had begun to recognize the importance of a permanent wolf sanctuary somewhere in North America. Chagrined that such efforts had failed in the lower 48, they now urged that "every effort" be made to preserve McKinley's wolf population. Their position was further strengthened by the agency's new policy toward predators, which had been adopted since Albright had retired in 1933, one that disallowed their destruction unless depredations threatened other park animals with "immediate danger of extermination, and then only if the predator is not itself a vanishing form."[19]

The result was vacillation—wolf control in McKinley was halted in 1935, then, following a public outcry that sheep faced extinction in the park, was reinstated on a limited basis a year later. Finally park officials attempted to settle the controversy once and for all by ordering a study to determine the severity of wolf depredations. The scientist they tapped for the job was Adolph Murie, Olaus's younger brother. Like Olaus, Adolph was a heretic to those traditional officials who opposed predators. His previous work in Yellowstone National Park had exonerated coyotes and quelled efforts to restore a control program there, despite a determined campaign by park administrators to halt publication of his findings. But he was one of the service's top predator scientists, and conservationists supported his appointment to handle what one of them labeled the "general hysteria about wolves" in Alaska. Murie began his three-year study in

McKinley, a place he once described as "just like being in heaven," in 1939. Five years later the park service published his *The Wolves of Mount McKinley*, regarded today as the first comprehensive natural history of wolves, a graceful blending of both the animal's behavior and ecology.[20]

Murie's study shook many myths. In the words of one contemporary wolf scientist, Murie "broke the spell of Little Red Riding Hood." He learned that wolf families did not consist of simply a mother, father, and pups, but included extended family members who weren't necessarily related. Wolves weren't savage and quarrelsome, but had a "friendliness" about their interactions that reflected a remarkably complex social behavior. Moreover, Murie surmised that deep snowfall—not wolves—had caused the decline in the park's sheep population, and that sheep and wolf numbers had probably reached "an equilibrium." Wolves appeared to prey mostly on weak or debilitated sheep, a condition that he believed would benefit sheep over time by eliminating less fit animals from the breeding population. Although Murie noted that the park's wolves, estimated in 1941 between forty and sixty animals, might inhibit a rapid recovery in sheep numbers, park officials decided against any further wolf eradication.[21]

World war soon took the spotlight off Alaska's wolves for several years, but as the conflagration wound down those critics who opposed the park service's position once again demanded wolf control, not only within McKinley but throughout Alaska. In 1945 Alaska's territorial legislature increased the wolf bounty to $30, a move supported by Frank Dufresne, the federal Alaska Game Commission Director who oversaw the territory's hunting and trapping and was staunchly anti-wolf. The wolf, declared Dufresne, was the "master killer of all wildlife," the "villain in Alaska's pageant of wildlife," and the "worst natural enemy" of large game.[22]

On April 12, 1945, the day that President Franklin Roosevelt suddenly died, the Senate received a memorial from Alaska's legislature endorsed by the territorial governor, Ernest Gruening. These "destructive creatures" were breeding in Alaska's national parks and spreading into the surrounding countryside, wreaking havoc and killing caribou, reindeer, deer, moose, and wild sheep. Unless the government promptly mounted a "full-scale attack" in parks, these animals were "doomed to extinction." Gruening told McKinley Park Acting Superintendent Grant Pearson that he had "positive proof" that at least one twelve-year-old child had recently been killed by wolves. "I would recommend they be exterminated," Gruening flatly told Pearson, and Pearson did not disagree.[23]

Murie again censused McKinley's sheep in autumn 1945, and estimated they had declined to five hundred animals. Now even Murie became alarmed. Although there was no evidence that wolves had caused this decrease, he recommended as a "precautionary measure" eliminating ten to fifteen wolves from the park, with additional but limited control measures in subsequent years. Murie wasn't insensitive to the political implications of this move. He hoped a reduced level of control would satisfy critics, fearing that if he advocated complete protection, a public backlash might result that would end in total eradication of the predators from the park. Murie was convinced that wolf control outside of McKinley would probably increase in the future as Alaska's human population grew, and that ultimately the park might provide a crucial sanctuary for wolves. "This is not the critical time for the wolves," he wrote. "That time is coming, when wolves become scarce. Now is the time to build up a generous attitude toward the wolf and the park service." His report was passed to other scientists, and few questioned his conclusions. Aldo Leopold understood Murie's difficult position. "There are not many people from whom I would accept without question a recommendation for wolf control, but in his case I do accept it."[24]

During the following winter, rangers were handed a surprise when they began looking for wolves to kill—there were few to be found. Finally by summer, they managed to trap and kill five wolves, and shortly afterward Murie reported that probably no more than fifteen animals remained in McKinley. Critics, however, continued to demand nothing less than their wholesale extirpation. Primarily at the insistence of the Camp Fire Club of America, a sportsman group that had been influential in originally setting aside McKinley as a national park, a bill was introduced into Congress to force the park service to provide "rigid control" of McKinley's wolves as a protective measure for sheep and other large ungulates. Federal officials regarded this legislative action as a dangerous precedent since until now Congress had not attempted to meddle in the actual management of parks.

At committee hearings during spring 1946, a host of prominent anti-wolf foes testified in support of the bill, including former parks director Horace Albright, and spokesmen for the U.S. Army and the U.S. Geological Survey. James R. Clark, a chief scientist for the American Museum of

Natural History, declared that wolves are "bad killers" and that the government should "wipe them all out in the park." The famous mountaineer Bradford Washburn agreed, testifying that wolves kill for "fun." Opposing the legislation were Aldo Leopold and representatives from the National Parks Association, the Izaak Walton League, and the National Park Service. Ultimately the bill died a quiet death in committee, but not before the Secretary of the Interior was compelled to speak against its passage.[25]

Despite the bill's demise, political pressure remained strong to expand wolf control—pressure that Murie and other park personnel continued to resist, believing that once sheep populations recovered, the clamor to kill wolves would disappear. But sheep were not cooperating; their numbers remained low. In 1948, the park service ordered an independent review headed by Harold Anthony, the mammalogist who some twenty years before had played such a prominent role opposing the Animal Damage Control Act. Anthony surprised everyone by advocating increased wolf control. As a result, McKinley Park rangers stepped up their efforts, but one year later wolves had become so scarce that none could be found. Murie now became concerned about the park's low number of wolves and complained to Superintendent Pearson about how the control effort was being conducted. Then he asked to take over the trapping, arguing that he could best administer the program. Pearson consented, and Murie recorded in his diary that "the wolf trapping seems to be now under control." From that time forth, wolf eradication in McKinley Park became only a token effort, partly due to Murie's direction, but also because wolf numbers had declined so steeply that the animals were rarely seen.[26]

By 1953, McKinley's Dall sheep finally began to recover. Although many people both inside and outside the park service attributed their recovery to wolf control, Murie believed their increase had more to do with natural cyclic phenomena little understood by scientists. Regardless, wolves were no longer deemed a threat to sheep and the control program permanently ceased, with the park's wolf population eventually recovering as sheep continued to increase in subsequent years. Conservationists claimed victory, but no one was denying that it had been a Pyrrhic victory at best. Altogether in the twenty-three years since wolves had first been targeted in McKinley Park, at least seventy-six animals had been killed, a number less than control proponents desired but more than wolf advocates had wanted. The important point, conservationists said, was that the battle to exterminate wolves from McKinley Park had ultimately failed, and as a result the world had its first success in providing wolves a sanctuary from human persecution.[27]

No one gauged the truth of this assertion more strongly than sport hunters who continued to vilify the park service and, in particular, Adolph Murie. Jack O'Connor, an avid big game hunter and widely read outdoor columnist, accused Murie of "mysticism," saying that the public should not "believe anything that any Park Service biologist" said. Wolves should be trapped, poisoned, and killed everywhere, declared O'Connor, including most national parks. Other hunters tended to agree. An article appearing in a 1948 issue of *Outdoor Life* entitled "America's Longest War: The Battle with the Wolves" praised eradication, expressing the belief that "many sportsmen hail this as a good thing." Even Frank Dufresne, now chief of the USFWS's Division of Information, joined the chorus by declaring, "In man's scheme of things, at least, the wolf has no place."[28]

Officials at the Bureau of Predator and Rodent Control were also deeply disturbed, and with good reason. They perceived not only a roadblock to their intended expansion of predator control throughout Alaska, but a rehashing of the eradication battle that they had fought and won more than a decade before. Also with the agency no longer comfortably tucked away in the Department of Agriculture, but now under the same aegis as national parks, bureaucratic turf was at stake. When Albert Williams, assistant BPRC agent for Alaska, read Murie's report and wrote a memo in 1946 agreeing that wolf predation "was not a very serious problem" in Alaska and probably never would be, his supervisor attached a note saying that Williams was obviously "a poor choice for such an assignment" due to his "lack of ability as a promoter." Another agent more savvy than Williams concerning the politics of predator control prepared the official Alaska report for the bureau that year. If something isn't done soon to curb wolf depredations, concluded the report's author, wolves would continue to "decimate" Alaska's sheep, caribou, and moose herds.[29]

Although they had been dealt a blow by the park service's opposition to wolf control, BPRC officials decided to ignore national parks (then amounting to less than one percent of Alaska) and expand their operation in other parts of the territory. Beginning in the 1890s, reindeer had been brought to Alaska from Siberia to give Eskimos an opportunity to raise the animals for market and "make these useless and barren wastes conducive to wealth and prosperity." Reindeer, claimed boosters, could become the livestock of the North, the answer to Alaska's need for economic diversification. Commercial reindeer herds had steadily increased until by 1932 over 640,000 animals existed in western and northern Alaska. No one, however, reckoned on a host of problems that accompanied introduction of this non-native animal—inbreeding with wild caribou, overgrazing and habitat depletion resulting in starvation of both reindeer and caribou, Eskimo disinterest and poor herding techniques, as well as wolf predation. But when reindeer began dying, wolves caught the brunt of the blame. "If there is any hope of making a stock country out of interior Alaska," declared Frank Dufresne, "there must first be a lot of wolf killing done."[30]

Throughout the 1930s and 1940s, Alaska's federal predator control agents demanded more funding to protect reindeer from wolves. In 1939, as Adolph Murie began studying McKinley's wolves, a trapper named Jim Allen in Wainwright, Alaska, believed he had discovered a way "to get rid of these gangsters." After careful deliberation, Allen submitted to the Alaska Game Commission a method that was sure to kill "a pile of wolves":

> My plan is this, if it were possible to get a couple of planes, I would suggest army planes, from what I read the Govt. has plenty of them, with a machine gun or a gun of that type in each of them, with a man who knew how to handle and shoot, it would not take long to knock over a lot of them and the ones not killed would leave in a hurry.[31]

Although Allen's proposal to kill wolves from aircraft was not new, having been first suggested by a PARC agent several years before, the use of machine guns mounted on military airplanes proved an imaginative twist. Allen's idea was filed away, but it wasn't forgotten.

By 1943 fewer than 200,000 of Alaska's reindeer survived. That year the Washington D.C. *Daily News* reported that wolves had created "a bloody carnival" among Alaska's reindeer, having slaughtered no less than 30,000 animals the winter before. Unless "drastic and immediate steps" were taken to kill these "marauding packs," warned the newspaper, Alaska's reindeer industry was doomed. Soon afterward the U.S. Army Air

Corps offered to assist Alaska's predator control, and military personnel conducted several forays by helicopter and airplane to shoot wolves in reindeer areas.[32]

In 1948, after several futile efforts to convince Congress to greatly expand wolf control in Alaska, BPRC officials finally succeeded. That year a $104,000 appropriation allowed the hiring of nine additional field agents. Alaska's territorial legislature was so encouraged by this action that it raised the wolf bounty to $50, thereby encouraging private citizens to pursue the predator as well. A few years after the federal program began, officials were able to claim that several hundred wolves had been destroyed, and the work of saving reindeer "for proper use by humans rather than for wasteful slaughter by predators is being accomplished." By now the Korean War had commenced and the bureau couldn't resist an opportunity to promote predator control as essential to the war effort. If wolves and "other destructive animals were neglected during the present emergency," claimed a report, "the nation could lose up to one-fifth of its productive potential of essential food items." Despite such lofty pronouncements, the bureau's efforts appear to have had little salutary effect on Alaska's reindeer industry, one that was failing for many reasons other than wolf depredation. When federal wolf control finally got fully underway in Alaska in 1950, less than 25,000 reindeer survived anywhere in the territory. In later years the industry never did recover its former numbers, even in those places where wolf populations had been severely reduced.[33]

Although protection of reindeer provided the initial justification for expanded federal wolf control in Alaska, the BPRC easily switched its emphasis to protecting wild game once the industry collapsed. With Alaskan tourism then undeveloped, providing annual revenues of only $1.5 million compared to $12 million produced by sport hunting and fishing, more harvestable game meant more money to Alaska's economy. Caribou—the most numerous and sought-after wild prey in Alaska by both humans and wolves—was particularly touted as an animal that required protection from wolves.[34]

Because the territory was huge and the bureau's resources were limited, it devised new and innovative ways to kill wolves. Adapting an ancient Eskimo method, agents coiled six-inch steel springs, tied them with cat gut, and wrapped them in seal blubber in hope that wolves would bolt down the morsel. In southeast Alaska, a BPRC field agent during the

1940s devised a method of concealing poison inside seal blubber, then covering the bait with fetid seal oil. He claimed that rancid oil was particularly attractive to wolves, while not drawing other predators like marten, mink, eagles, or bears (as long as it was used during winter when bears were hibernating). To further guarantee wolves were the primary victims, he placed the baits on frozen lakes far from shore where few predators other than wolves roamed; come spring the ice melted and any leftover poison quickly disappeared. Out of one such set of 500 hundred baits in 1946, the agent reported finding 131 dead wolves and estimated that 400 more had died. This method proved so successful that fur trappers in southeast Alaska began to complain when wolves grew scarce, and as a result, the agency was forced to reduce its poisoning campaign.[35]

The bureau now had at its disposal two new potent poisons. The best known was sodium monofluoroacetate, or as it was commonly dubbed, "Compound 1080." The U.S. Army had originally developed the poison to use against rats in the Far East during World War II. After the war, when the Fish and Wildlife Service attempted to readapt the original formula as a predicide, it finally succeeded in 1948 with the one-thousand-eightieth formula. Unlike strychnine, this tasteless, odorless poison wasn't particularly quick-acting, taking between four and ten hours to kill an animal. But it lasted a long time, continuing to kill again and again as non-target animals fed on previously poisoned ones. In an early experiment with bait laced with Compound 1080, these animals died: 673 coyotes, 24 dogs, 3 badgers, 8 ground squirrels, 4 weasels, 1 cat, 4 eagles, 4 hawks, and 9 magpies. By 1950 the agency had placed some 16,000 baits throughout the western United States and Canada. Although thousands of wolves, mostly in Canada, are suspected of having died as a result, many were never found.[36]

Another promising poison was sodium cyanide. In 1953, the agency managed to adapt what was known as a "coyote getter" to kill wolves in Alaska. This mechanical device originally contained a .38 caliber cartridge filled with cyanide (today's wolf version fires a .50 caliber cartridge and is known as an M-50). Fetid blood was spread on this device, and when the wolf tried to pick it up or pull on it, the shell exploded, blowing cyanide into the animal's mouth. A coma-induced death usually followed within twelve to fifteen seconds.[37]

These poisons vastly increased the ability to wage war against predators throughout the continent. There is little question that had wolves managed to survive in any appreciable numbers in the contiguous United States until the 1950s, they would have been swept away in the poisoning passion that consumed the nation. In Alaska, however, the territory was so vast that another method was needed to locate and kill wolves, one that had been recommended over a decade earlier: the airplane.

Federal agents were hesitant at first; shooting wolves from a moving aircraft could be highly perilous. Once a wolf was located the animal usually began running, forcing the pilot already flying close to the ground to slow the airplane almost to a stall in order for the gunner, using a shotgun and leaning out of the opposite side, to kill the animal. Since the airplane traveled faster than the wolf, the shooter was forced to use a "negative" lead, actually aiming behind the running animal in order to hit it. Previously hunted wolves learned to dart under the plane or dodge erratically to escape, the pursuit requiring keen reflexes and continuing as much as twenty miles before the exhausted animal was finally overtaken and killed. A careless shot from an over-excited shooter might bring the aircraft itself down. Near Point Barrow, Alaska, in 1952, Maurice Kelly, the federal agent in charge of the arctic program, accidently shot off the tip of his airplane's propeller during a wolf hunt. The pilot managed to land, hacksaw off the other side of the propeller for balance, and fly the crippled aircraft back to an airfield. Kelly never did live down his embarrassment, forever after dubbed by cohorts as "Prop-shot Kelly, the Terror of the Tundra."[38]

Once hunters mastered the killing of wolves from airplanes, the technique proved devastatingly effective. During a six-week period in spring 1952 in northern Alaska, three two-man airborne hunting teams managed to kill 259 wolves in an endeavor known as "Operation Umiat." Jay Hammond, one of the federal hunters who participated in the hunt and who later became Alaska's governor, wrote an article for *Field & Stream* entitled "Strafing Arctic Killers." Hammond estimated that if poison and other methods were included, over 500 wolves were killed that spring. So effective was this hunt that wolves for many years afterward became quite rare in northern Alaska, so scarce in fact that Inupiat Eskimos strongly objected. Caribou were not any more plentiful as a result of wolf control, they said. Before control, wolf furs, then valued at $4 or $5 each, had provided many native people with their only source of income. Now with wolves nearly gone, complained the Anaktuvuk Pass Council, the government had forced the village to turn to welfare to survive.[39]

These supplications were buried under the self-congratulatory praise the Fish and Wildlife Service heaped on the program, and the agency immediately planned similar wolf hunts in other parts of Alaska. Inspired by these results, private aerial bounty hunters took up the chase, killing some 600 wolves across Alaska during the next several years. By the conclusion of federal wolf control in 1958, when Alaska began preparing for statehood and most predator control projects shifted from the federal government to the Alaska Department of Fish and Game, 1,338 wolves had been officially killed by the BPRC. If wolves killed by private bounty hunters are included, some 2,000 animals died during this period alone in Alaska, although the number is believed to have been greater due to widespread poisoning. About this same time biologists discovered the calving grounds of the western Arctic caribou herd, demonstrating how little was really known about the animals, much less the relationship between caribou and wolves. After statehood the BPRC continued to kill wolves, but the agency was reduced to only three permanent employees, and its efforts were largely confined to reindeer range located on the far-western Seward Penninsula, a vastly shrunken area since collapse of the industry.[40]

The twentieth century was also a turbulent time for wolves in Canada. Here is where most of the continent's wolves survived (as they do today), in vast roadless areas away from human settlement that tends to concentrate primarily along the Canada-U.S. border. By the early 1900s wolves had disappeared entirely from the Island of Newfoundland, Nova Scotia, and New Brunswick, and by 1920 they were gone from the southern portions of most provinces adjacent to the United States. This was particularly true of the western provinces where wolf range receded as the livestock industry expanded into formerly unsettled country and wild prey declined in number. Beginning about 1930 the number of ranches began to level off, wolf persecution eased, and wild game, primarily moose, deer, caribou, and elk, staged a comeback. Wolves responded by also increasing and beginning to reclaim much of their former range. By the 1940s, however, as the predators became more common, persecution began to intensify, not only from ranchers and farmers who claimed the animals were depredating livestock, but also from provincial and federal authorities bent on protecting more desirable wildlife from wolf predation and preventing the spread of rabies. Throughout the country, from arctic tundra to both Pacific and Atlantic shores, wolves were intensely pursued by Canadians with a passion and aptitude only surpassed by their neighbors in the United States.

Ontario, which along with the Northwest Territories supports Canada's largest wolf population today, retains the distinction of having the continent's longest history of continuous persecution. As early as 1793 the province awarded a wolf bounty, one which didn't cease until 1972, and then only after bitter public debate when some 20,000 citizens petitioned the government to end the reward that alone cost taxpayers over $1 million during the twentieth century. (A few years earlier, Ontario's parliament nearly passed a proposal to quadruple the bounty.) Beginning in 1947 persecution increased, so that by the time bounties ended twenty-five years later some 33,000 wolves had been killed. Many more wolves are believed to have died as the result of extensive poisoning with Compound 1080.[41]

Farther west in Alberta, hunters and stock owners had largely eliminated wolves and other wild game from the southern portion of the province during the early 1900s. Wolf populations fared poorly in the remainder of Alberta due to low game numbers, and wolves probably numbered no more than 500 animals by the late 1920s. As game began to recover during the 1930s and 1940s, wolves rebounded spectacularly. By 1951 Alberta supported some 5,000 wolves. Then rabies began spreading throughout the province and wolves and coyotes were blamed, although only a single case of an infected wolf was actually verified. Beginning in 1952 and continuing for the next four years, Alberta waged a massive poisoning campaign against the predators, distributing throughout the province 40,000 cyanide "getters," 100,000 cyanide cartridges, 628,000 strychnine baits, and an unknown number of Compound 1080 baits. The result was some 246,000 dead coyotes and 5,500 dead wolves; less than 500 wolves remained in Alberta by 1956.[42]

In British Columbia, wolves were similarly subjected to a massive poisoning campaign, although here the poison of choice was primarily Compound 1080. By 1955 British Columbia's wolves, probably numbering 6,000 animals before the campaign, were virtually wiped out throughout most of the province's interior and reduced to only one-quarter of their previous number province-wide. On nearby Vancouver Island, wolves were first believed to have been entirely extirpated, although a few survivors were eventually discovered.[43]

The most intensive wolf control ever to take place anywhere in Canada occurred in the Northwest Territories. Beginning in the 1940s, and due primarily to overexploitation by native subsistence hunters, the territory's barren-ground caribou population fell from a previous population high of some 2 million animals to less than 300,000. In order to halt the decline and aid caribou recovery, the Canadian Wildlife Service from 1952 to 1962 poisoned and aerially shot some 16,000 wolves. By the time the control program officially ended in 1967, wolves across northern Canada were reduced to one-quarter of their original number. Afterward the territory commenced a $40 wolf bounty that continued until 1975, producing an additional 5,000 carcasses.[44]

As a result of both Alaska's and Canada's control programs, North America's wolf population probably reached its nadir during the 1950s. By the end of the decade, possibly no more than 20,000 wolves survived— about 5 percent of the continent's original number prior to the arrival of Europeans. The predator's future appeared so dismal by 1961 that Canada's foremost wolf biologist, Douglas H. Pimlott, questioned whether wolves would exist anywhere in North America by the end of the century. "Or will man have exterminated the wolf as a final demonstration of his 'conquest' of the wilderness and of wild things that dare compete or conflict with him?" The plight of the wolf, said Pimlott, "poses one of the most important conservation questions of our time."[45]

Were the continent's wolves really in danger of wholesale extirpation? Probably not, although they may have ceased to exist in greater portions of Alaska and Canada than they do today had governments persisted in their efforts. (Today, wolves are believed to number between 50,000 to 60,000 animals in Canada and 6,000 to 8,000 in Alaska.) Even in the Northwest Territories, with an average annual kill during the 1950s of some 1,400 wolves, the predators were never at the point of extinction.[46]

As it was, just as North America's wolves reached their all-time population low, Canadian wolf eradication began to decline due to several reasons, not the least of which was the widespread recovery of ungulates throughout much of the country, resulting in less pressure on authorities to limit the number of wolves. How much wolf control measures encouraged this increase of game populations is impossible to say, but most scientists agree that the killing of wolves probably hastened game recovery. Regardless, many officials were glad to be rid of the expense and controversy of the extensive program. (A reduced level of wolf control continued in certain provinces and territories until relatively recently, and periodically still occurs today in the Yukon.) In the Northwest Territories each dead wolf had cost $73 per animal; in British Columbia wolf control exceeded $1 million, slightly more than had been expended during nearly thirty-five years of bounties.[47]

No less important than game recovery in the demise of wolf control during the 1960s were two other reasons: conservationists' growing interest in and concern about wolves, and new discoveries by scientists about wolf ecology. Soon these two groups would join forces to form a powerful political advocacy for wolves, fulfilling the legacy first begun decades earlier.

Popular books played a major role in changing the public's traditional views about the predators. During the mid-1950s, Lois Crisler and her husband, Herb, journeyed to Alaska's Brooks Range to film caribou migrations for Walt Disney, and from this experience Lois wrote *Arctic Wild* (1958). During their two seasons in the north, the Crislers acquired and raised several wolf pups and observed wild wolves hunting caribou. Their repeated observations that wolves often killed injured, weak, or sick animals and that healthy ones frequently escaped offered readers a new and generous view of predation. Wolves were creatures of the wilderness, they said, and thus celebrated and symbolized the freedom and independence to be found in wild country. By portraying wolves as intelligent, graceful, and affectionate animals, they challenged the conventional wisdom of killing wolves simply to protect caribou and other large game animals.

Soon after Crisler's work came the most popular and influential book ever written about wolves, Farley Mowat's *Never Cry Wolf* (1963). As a student in the summer of 1948, Mowat accompanied a scientific project studying wolves and caribou in northern Manitoba for the Dominion Wildlife Service, the precursor of the Canadian Wildlife Service. Rebelling against the then-prevalent idea that wolves should be destroyed to protect caribou herds, Mowat refused to assist the study and traipsed off to make his own observations. He saw few, if any, of the predators, but the summer's experience convinced him that wolves weren't the demons most people believed them to be and that their persecution should cease. When *Never Cry Wolf,* a fictional and largely fanciful account of a biologist studying wolves in the far north, appeared years later, the book was presented as Mowat's actual experiences, a fact that led to his sound condemnation within scientific circles. Mowat came in for additional criticism when he portrayed wolves as feeding as much on field mice as caribou. These distinctions, however, were lost on most readers, and the story proved immensely successful, selling over one million copies since publication, as well as appearing twenty years later as a popular Walt Disney film.

Despite its misrepresentations, Mowat's book shattered many myths and untruths that had hung about the wolf's neck for centuries. Mowat's wolves weren't savage brutes, but instead were playful and social creatures, good and protective parents—animals entirely ill-deserving of the treatment they had received. After firmly aligning readers' sympathies with wolves, Mowat wrote at the book's conclusion a one-paragraph epilogue briefly describing the poisoning campaign during the late 1950s by the Canadian Wildlife Service. Canada's massive wolf-killing effort was nearly at an end by the time *Never Cry Wolf* appeared, but Mowat's powerful conclusion guaranteed wolf control would never again go unopposed anywhere on the continent.

Three years after Mowat's book, author Roger Caras published *The Custer Wolf,* a fictitious account of the famous wolf killed in 1920 in South Dakota. In this sentimental but poignant tale, Caras described the death of prey animals by wolves as proof that "nature was in harmony," and that "there was nothing savage, harmful, or tragic in all this." After enduring humankind's unrelenting persecution, the wolf had become something nature had never intended, "the curse of a generation of ranchers and the symbol of destruction across a wide and fertile land." It wasn't the wolf who was the villain, claimed Caras, but man, "eternally guilty of crimes beyond counting—man the killer, the slayer, the luster-for-blood—[who] has sought to expurgate himself of his sin and guilt by condemning the predatory animals."[48]

These three books prompted hundreds of letters protesting wolf control to both the U.S. Fish and Wildlife Service and the Canadian Wildlife Service. That the wolf was no longer an outcast in some of the public's mind was never more evident than when Douglas Pimlott offered to present public lectures about wolves at Ontario's Algonquin Park. The response was overwhelming. In summer 1963, the park began offering an "evening of wolf listening," surpassing all previous attendance records when over 600 people arrived to engage in performing a group howl, which was answered by wild wolves. Pimlott quickly grasped the significance of such an event. "Almost inevitably the silence that follows the end of the howling of the pack is suddenly broken by an intense babble of the voices of the people all talking together, excitedly sharing the thrill of a superb wilderness experience," wrote Pimlott. "Almost inevitably, too, disinterest fades and people begin to understand why man should always be prepared to share his environment with creatures of nature." Since that time, over 65,000 people have attended wolf howls in Algonquin.[49]

At the same time that much of the public began to demonstrate a new attitude toward wolves, science began finding answers to questions that early wolf proponents—Leopold, Olsen, and the Murie brothers—had sensed but could not provide thirty years before.

In 1957 the National Park Service asked Durward Allen, a wildlife biologist at Purdue University, to conduct a study of wolves and moose of Lake Superior's Isle Royal National Park. During the late 1940s, wolves had crossed fifteen miles of lake ice from Canada and reinhabited the island, becoming the only population of the predators within the country outside of Alaska living under relatively natural conditions. The Isle Royale study eventually became one of the world's longest continuous investigations of wolves and their prey, and served as a training ground for numerous wolf scientists. Allen's student, L. David Mech, who subsequently became one of the world's foremost wolf authorities, produced *The Wolves of Isle Royale* in 1966, the first park service publication concerning wolves since Adolph Murie's work some twenty years before. Mech's study concluded that wolves had kept the park's moose population from overbrowsing its food supply, culled primarily weak and unhealthy individuals, and actually stimulated moose reproduction. The two animals—predator and prey—had reached a "dynamic equilibrium," Mech suggested, a relationship that, if left undisturbed, probably would continue indefinitely. (It did not. The number of wolves on Isle Royale declined in subsequent years, although the precise reasons—inbreeding, infertility, disease, or prey availability—remain unclear.) Both Allen and Mech soon followed this report with a host of popular and scientific publications that contributed to keeping the predator foremost in the public eye. Mech, in particular, became an advocate for wolves, his strong leadership bringing him praise and adulation from supporters, but criticism from some colleagues who claim his opinions have come to dominate wolf science.

Allen's and Mech's research in the United States and Pimlott's in Canada fueled the growing public perception that wolf persecution should end. Pimlott, in particular, recognized that science alone couldn't accomplish this goal and, having identified human misunderstanding as the greatest threat to wolves, he became an outspoken proponent of building public advocacy for the predators through education. Conservationists probably could never change the view of true wolf haters, he argued, but they could appeal to the "masses of people who are interested in nature but who have never thought that the preservation of an animal like the wolf really mattered." Pimlott foresaw a time when wolves would be reintroduced to national parks in both Canada and the United States, and people would begin to see wolves "as they are—one of the most interesting and intelligent animals that has ever lived on our globe." Such thoughts, Pimlott assured readers, "are not mere fanciful daydreams."[50]

In 1960 Michigan lifted its longtime bounty on wolves, although any breeding populations of the animal probably had disappeared from both Michigan and neighboring Wisconsin by then. In Minnesota, the wolf bounty law lapsed in 1965. The state legislature voted to continue paying wolf bounties, but the governor, Karl F. Rolvaag, vetoed the bill, earning the lasting enmity of many of the state's sport hunters. Some hunters actually dragged a dead deer to the steps of the state capitol in protest, but despite strong support, the legislature was unable to revive the measure. By then Minnesota had perhaps fewer than five hundred wolves, and had become the only state outside of Alaska with a known population of the predators.[51]

By the mid-1960s, the staunchest holdout (besides stock owners) against rehabilitating the public image of the wolf in the United States was the bloated government bureaucracy that had fed for so long at the antipredator trough: the Branch of Predator and Rodent Control. Although BPRC had largely turned its attention to coyotes since the near extirpation of wolves throughout the conterminous states, it refused to acknowledge that wolves were gone. By 1964, following a half century of predator control, the bureau claimed to have killed a total of 70,000 wolves. Yet only some 5,000 of that number had been gray wolves. What were the other 65,000 animals?[52]

The agency claimed they were red wolves, a rather small, often reddish, cinnamon or, more rarely, dark-colored canid whose size and appearance resembles an animal midway between a wolf and a coyote. The red wolf once inhabited the southeastern one-quarter of the United States, but due to persecution, its range had shrunk by the beginning of the twentieth century until it occurred primarily in the south-central states. Indeed, Texas and Oklahoma alone accounted for 55,000 "wolves" that the agency reported killed between 1915 and 1965.[53]

But the BPRC knew that few of these animals were red wolves. The species had never been populous and its range had declined steadily as settlement advanced. By the 1930s, biologists suspected that the coyote was invading the former range of the red wolf, and in some places where the animals overlapped, normal behavioral mechanisms that keep species apart had broken down and the two animals had interbred. In appearance the resulting offspring most often resembled large coyotes. Although these hybrids were never common, the bureau seized on the fact that they occurred at all, and promptly declared that the coyotes federal hunters were killing by the thousands each year in the south-central states were really wolves.

The first sign that the species wasn't doing well surfaced in 1962 when a Texas biologist, Howard McCarley, investigated wolf skull specimens killed by government hunters and found that most of them were coyotes. The following year, graduate student Ron Nowak, who is now a scientist with the Fish and Wildlife Service and the country's leading wolf taxonomist, wrote the service's acting director, Lansing Parker, expressing concern about the survival of the red wolf in light of the agency's continued persecution of the species. Parker replied that the high number of red wolves killed each year was ample proof that the predator was "maintaining itself satisfactorily," with a population between 4,000 to 8,000 individuals, and was in absolutely no danger of disappearing. Five years later, Stanley Young (now retired from the agency but still an influential and stalwart defender of eradication) wrote an article for *American Forests* concurring with Parker that the red wolf was not only alive and well, but that "much of its habitat remains little disturbed." Young assured readers that there was no reason to believe that red wolves wouldn't continue "to be a part of our southern fauna for all time."[54]

Even as Young wrote these words, two Canadian biologists, Douglas Pimlott and Paul Joslin, were completing a preliminary study of red wolves, having determined that the only surviving animals consisted of a few remnant and isolated populations that were fast disappearing. By 1970 only about one hundred red wolves were believed to exist in the wild, making the animal then the rarest large mammal species in North America.

Why did the BPRC tenaciously insist, despite certain knowledge to the contrary, that thousands of coyotes, and a much lesser number of coyote-red wolf hybrids, killed each year were red wolves? The most obvious answer is that had officials admitted that the red wolf was facing extinction, they would have been forced to curtail all predator control efforts over a significant portion of the country. Used to relying on public acceptance or indifference toward predator control for so long, with little or no oversight as a scion of the powerful livestock industry, the agency believed it could twist the facts any way it desired. But the real reason goes deeper. Having so successfully waged war on the wolf of the past, federal predator control officials were simply unwilling to surrender the symbol that had served them so well.

It wasn't long, however, before the BPRC came under increasing attack from a growing environmental movement displeased with the federal government's predator control policies. In 1964 Secretary of the Interior Stewart Udall asked the newly created Special Advisory Board on Wildlife Management to review and assess the agency. The board consisted of several scientists including, among others, fierce critics of predator control: its chairman, zoologist A. Starker Leopold, Aldo Leopold's eldest son; Stanley Cain, a plant ecologist; and Ira Gabrielson, the past chief of the Biological Survey. Gabrielson, in particular, had come a long way in his thinking about predators. In 1931, he had been one of several agency employees to resign his membership in the American Society of Mammalogists in protest of the society's opposition to predator control. Later he reversed his opinions of predators, even going so far as to defend them as a necessary and critical component in the country's fauna, and championing Adolph Murie's work with wolves.[55]

Known as the Leopold report, this review was highly critical of BPRC policies. In many respects, it echoed Olaus Murie's complaint about the agency nearly forty years earlier. Poisoning had not proven effective in protecting livestock from predators, claimed the report, and probably had cost more than it provided in benefits. Furthermore, contrary to bureau dogma, wildlife probably didn't require protection from predators at all. Predator control had become "an end in itself," and no longer should be considered "a balanced component" of wildlife management. The bureau had become a "semi-autonomous bureaucracy whose function in many localities bears scant relationship to real need and less still to scientific management."[56]

A shake-up of BPRC followed the Leopold report, but in the field, where federal agents continued to maintain a close and friendly relationship with stock owners, little changed. As the agency dragged its bureaucratic feet, conservationists stepped up their attack. Organizations like Defenders of Wildlife, the Audubon Society, and the National Wildlife Federation continued to protest widespread poisoning and trapping of predators. They were joined by mainstream national publications in 1970 when an article decrying the government's complicity in the extermination of the black-footed ferret appeared in *The New Yorker*. That same year, *Sports Illustrated* published a three-part inflammatory series entitled "Poisoning the West." Secretary of the Interior Rogers Morton ordered yet another advisory committee of scientists and others to review the agency's predator control policies in 1971. Both Starker Leopold and Stanley Cain, its chairman, were members of the new review committee.

The result, called the Cain report, was yet another stinging indictment of the nation's predator control policies, assigning blame not only to the agency but also the livestock industry. Since 1950, said the committee, the federal government, in cooperation with states and the livestock industry, had spent over $110 million to further the "private interests" of stock owners. There was little scientific justification for predator control as it had been practiced, particularly the widespread use of poisoning that had resulted in the deaths of so many animals. It was clear that the agency and stock owners had fostered a mutually beneficial relationship, one the committee called an "old boy" arrangement, that had "flourished over the decades without the objective information to warrant it, even in the face of public criticism." In short, predator control was a program "in which there is substantial public cost and very little if any public benefit." The committee's report prompted yet another agency reshuffle, one that finally reached down to the level of field personnel. Among other changes, the agency adopted the more ambiguous, but less controversial, name that it continues to be known by today: Animal Damage Control.[57]

Shortly after the Cain report appeared in early 1972, President Richard Nixon, in an address proclaimed as "an environmental State-of-the-Union," banned the use of the most common predicides—strychnine, cyanide, and Compound 1080 on both public and private lands. At first glance, Nixon's action was largely symbolic with regard to wolves, but in terms of the future it removed what may have proved a major hurdle to eventual wolf recovery. Cracks, however, began appearing in Nixon's poison ban in 1975 when President Gerald Ford modified the order to allow the use of "coyote getters." Then in 1981, President Ronald Reagan revoked the ban on Compound 1080, although its use was greatly restricted compared to former times. Five years later, Reagan shifted Animal Damage Control from the Department of Interior back to the Department of Agriculture, where it had originated over seventy years before and where it resides today.

In recent years, the agency has weathered frequent demands from both inside and outside government for its dissolution. But it has always managed to survive—due largely to the influence of the livestock industry among western congressmen—demonstrating that it is as resilient as the predators it once pursued. Although its present role regarding wolves is greatly diminished, as recently as 1994 its work cost some $38 million, over half of which was funded by federal tax dollars, resulting in the deaths of, among other creatures, some 100,000 predators primarily for the benefit of private agriculture. At the same time, defenders of the agency maintain that predator killing is bound to continue with or without federal participation. They warn that states, heavily influenced by stock owners and generally possessing much less stringent regulations, will kill even more predators in the absence of federal oversight.[58]

In the words of historian Thomas Dunlap, predator control has become "one of those programs that is opposed by many and held in place by the determination of a few. Its existence is an outrage to its enemies, the limitations on it irritating to its supporters."[59]

9

RETURN OF THE NATIVE

If the future of wolves in North America never looked more bleak than during the 1940s and 1950s, it had brightened considerably a mere decade later. By no means did wolf persecution come to a halt, but it had slowed, enough to state undeniably that it would never again wield the absolute power it once held over the fate of the animal. In addition to science, literature, and film, simple demographics had as much as anything to do with this dramatic reversal of anti-wolf attitudes. While one in every three families lived on farms at the beginning of the century, less than one in twenty-two did so fifty years later. Many citizens no longer saw nature only as an obstacle, a force to be subdued and brought under exclusive human control. With increasing urbanization and rising educational levels, a significant number of citizens possessed nostalgia for wildlife and the natural world, even going so far as to demand protection for those animals that their forebears had dismissed as nothing but "varmints." In the case of the wolf, there was also a large dose of remorse over how the predator had been treated in the past and its continuing, albeit diminished, role as victim in a human-dominated universe.

Studies of public attitudes toward wolves and other predators seemed to bear this out. Compared to perceptions of other animal life, wolves (and coyotes) generally continued to receive low marks. But this judgment varied considerably depending upon the demographic group, with wildlife enthusiasts, persons of higher socioeconomic status, non–livestock producing westerners, and those under thirty-five years of age often demonstrating outright affection for wolves. The actual nature of the animal was probably little better understood by most constituents of these groups than it was centuries before, but now the wolf and its past had become *the* symbol of what was wrong with human attitudes toward wildlife. For this vocal and growing segment of society, wolves had been transposed from beast to beauty, and it was time to set things right.[1]

The mid-1960s to mid-1970s was a period of terrific social upheaval, and environmentalists lost no time making the most of it. The United States led the way when Congress passed the Wilderness Act (1964), the Marine Mammal Protection Act (1972), and created both the Environmental Protection Agency and the President's Council on Environmental Quality (1970). But of all wildlife conservation efforts that most affected the survival of wolves, two stand above the rest.

One was international in scope. In 1970 Canada's Douglas Pimlott proposed creating a committee of scientists dedicated to promoting the preservation of wolves worldwide. Three years later, wolf experts from Bulgaria, Hungary, Italy, Norway, Finland, Spain, Switzerland, Russia, Canada, and the United States formed the Wolf Specialist Group of the International Union for the Conservation of Nature. One of the group's first functions was to develop a Wolf Manifesto, or blueprint for global wolf conservation. Wolves, declared the document, like all other wildlife "have a right to exist in a wild state," one that "derives from the right of all living creatures to co-exist with man as part of natural ecosystems." At the same time, the committee adopted specific guidelines that encouraged governments to protect wolves, while still allowing for their control where they conflicted with human interests. This last proviso (which some conservationists still steadfastly oppose) amounted to a practical admission that, in some instances, strife between wolves and humans was inevitable, and the best hope for the species lay in reaching a practical accommodation to this fact. Should this not happen, some scientists feared that the resulting backlash might reawaken old fears and hatreds against the predator even worse than before. Says one contemporary wolf researcher, "It's better to sacrifice a few to save many."[2]

The other conservation effort that greatly benefited wolves took place in the United States. In 1973 Congress passed, by an overwhelming majority, the Endangered Species Act (ESA). Aptly termed a veritable "bill of rights for nonhumans," this single act remains, despite powerful attacks over the years from both states and Congress itself, the world's most comprehensive wildlife protection legislation. For the first time, private enterprise—timber, mining, agriculture, and other industries—was forced to demonstrate that its actions would not adversely effect species considered precariously close to extinction. And, contrary to traditional law that vests states with responsibility for most wildlife, the act gave the federal government control over those species considered most at risk. After nearly four centuries in North America and some twenty centuries worldwide, the wolf finally had won its first comprehensive legal protection from human oppression.[3]

The act was a long time in coming. Nine years earlier—even as its predator control branch was publicly proclaiming that the red wolf was "thriving," and hanging onto the premise that though the gray wolf was mostly gone in the continental United States, it was alive and well in Canada and Alaska—the U.S. Fish and Wildlife Service had taken the lead in identifying species that were facing extirpation and deciding what it could do to save them. Among the first sixty-six species it listed at risk of extinction in 1964 were the red wolf and the gray wolf outside of Alaska. Nominal protection was provided by Congress in 1966, then again in 1969, but neither of these actions brought substantive changes in the predator's status. Ignoring lawmakers, the Department of Defense in 1972 placed an order for nearly 300,000 military parkas, specifying that they be trimmed with wolf fur. Only after conservationists and some congressmen strongly objected did the department reluctantly drop the wolf fur requirement.[4]

Convinced that endangered species needed additional safeguards, Congress passed the much more comprehensive act the following year. The new law established stiff penalties for anyone harming such species, set aside "critical habitat" for their maintenance, and allowed the government to acquire land in order to protect ecosystems that endangered species depended upon. Finally, it established separate lists for both "endangered" and "threatened" species, the latter category for those considered vulnerable but not in immediate danger, thus requiring somewhat less strict protective measures.[5]

Then Congress went a crucial step further. Wherever possible, endangered species should be returned to become viable and integral parts of what remained of their former ecosystems. In short, endangered species were to become recovered species. Furthermore, once they recovered, they were to be "de-listed" or removed from the protection afforded by the act. To reach this goal, Congress directed the Secretary of the Interior to appoint a recovery team for each threatened or endangered species and begin the arduous task of restoration. Naturalist George Bird Grinnell's fifty-year-old prediction had finally come true. After having spent hundreds of thousands of dollars over the years to "control" the wolf, now the government would expend millions to bring it back.[6]

That goal was not easily accomplished. First, each species had to be selected for inclusion and a protection and recovery plan developed, approved, and implemented. In the case of wolves, protecting what few animals survived was one thing, but recovery was quite another. For the most part, the obstacles were more political than biological. Both suitable habitat and wild prey existed in extensive portions of the country, and the predators had shown themselves time and again to be capable of survival in less than optimum conditions once human oppression ended. The problem was the same one wolves had faced all along. No matter how public opinion had shifted favorably toward them in recent years, prejudice, fear, and outright hatred still consumed a significant and vocal segment of society. Nowhere was this fact more evident than among state governments, particularly those in the West. Although the wolf had been gone for almost fifty years when the Endangered Species Act became law in 1973, twenty states still had bounties on the animal. The new federal legislation superseded these laws and most states soon amended their out-of-date statutes, but some defiantly vowed to fight federal wolf recovery.[7]

Restoring the wolf would prove an uphill battle all the way.

One year before the ESA became law, Fish and Wildlife Service biologists agreed that there was no mammal in greater need than the red wolf, and it was targeted for the first recovery effort. Early estimates of its numbers had proven too optimistic; the animal was in much worse trouble than previously believed. Although scientists were unsure how many wolves actually survived in the wild, they feared coyotes would soon swamp what little genetic purity the species still possessed. They also believed that the humid, swampy, bottomland forests just east of Galveston Bay, Texas, which held the largest concentration of remaining wolves, was poor wolf habitat and infested with parasites that took a great toll on surviving animals. Moreover, much of the land was privately owned by cattle ranchers who were not overjoyed at efforts to save the animal. The area was increasingly threatened by development schemes, which included swamp drainage and burning of coastal marshes. Finally, there was little enthusiasm from state wildlife departments in either Louisiana or Texas for saving the red wolf. Some biologists believed it was already too late.[8]

The Fish and Wildlife Service quickly decided on a radical and unproven plan. It would remove all red wolves from the wild and commence a captive breeding program to save the species from extinction. Beginning in 1973, the service began live trapping of wolves in Texas and Louisiana and moving them to the Point Defiance Zoo and Aquarium in Tacoma, Washington. Over the next six years, forty-three wolflike canids were captured, but only seventeen were deemed to be true red wolves. Of these, fourteen successfully reproduced when scientists began a rigorous breeding program aimed at building up the animal's numbers. By 1980, the living canid that most closely resembles the million-year-old progenitor of modern wolves existed only in captivity.

To a great degree, it was Fish and Wildlife Service biologists who championed saving the red wolf. Unlike the gray wolf, when both species were first declared endangered during the mid-1960s, few people knew of its existence, and it had little public following. Consequently, when scientists began casting about for a likely site for red wolf recovery, they also believed it lacked the controversy surrounding its more famous cousin. They considered reintroducing wolves to eastern Texas, the Florida Everglades, and several islands off the South Carolina coast, but eventually they settled on the Land Between the Lakes region of Tennessee and Kentucky, a remote mountainous area administered primarily by the federal Tennessee Valley Authority. There they quietly negotiated with state and federal agencies. But private landowners and sport hunters got wind of the proposal and harshly objected to the government's less than open method. They also complained that deer hunting and public access would suffer if wolves returned. Both Tennessee and Kentucky withdrew their support. Even several environmental groups opposed recovery when they learned that existing coyotes in the area were to be destroyed. As a result, the service canceled its proposal.

The red wolf's break came in 1984 with the opening of a new federal wildlife refuge, the 120,000-acre Alligator River National Wildlife Refuge in northeastern North Carolina. Federal officials believed the refuge posed the best chance for recovery: it contained few, if any, coyotes, was sparsely inhabited by farmers with little domestic livestock, and had an ample supply of deer and racoon suitable for wolf prey. The area was also freighted with its share of symbolic wolf and Euro-American history. It was only a short distance away in Jamestown, Virginia, that Captain John Smith nearly four hundred years before had provided the first English written record of North American "wolues."

The Fish and Wildlife Service also had a new card up its sleeve. Two years earlier the agency had devised a powerful new tool to aid recovery plans calling for reintroduction. Under the 1982 "nonessential-experimental population" amendment to the Environmental Species Act, either captive-reared or captured specimens of an endangered species could be reintroduced to an area where the species formerly existed, as long as loss of those animals didn't jeopardize the species' continued survival. This new category provided for much more flexible management than that of the original ESA. Land-use restrictions were far less stringent and plans could be customed-tailored to specific areas—all changes that meant recovery efforts would probably meet with less local opposition.

This time the agency eschewed secrecy; its representatives visited schools and civic groups, assuring the public that deer populations wouldn't suffer significant loss, and that biologists would capture and relocate any wolves that strayed from the refuge. The program proved so successful and public acceptance so great that additional private and public land was obtained for wolf recovery that today totals nearly 500,000 acres. The nearby community of Manteo, North Carolina, even adopted the animal as its symbol.

Four pairs of captive-born wolves were released on the refuge in 1987, and the following year the first red wolf was born in the wild. Mortality was high in the beginning, but eventually biologists refined their methods until, by 1995, the refuge and surrounding private lands supported some sixty free-ranging red wolves that were successfully reproducing wild-born litters. Coupled with a reintroduction program begun in the Great Smoky Mountains National Park in 1992, the service's eventual recovery goal calls for at least 220 wild red wolves in the southeastern United States.[9]

Most biologists today point to this first experiment in conservation history designed to restore a species that had been declared extinct in the wild as an unequivocal success. But the survival of red wolves is still uncertain, from both legal and scientific standpoints. In 1991, molecular biologists using preliminary DNA analysis discovered that the red wolf primarily possesses genetic characteristics of both coyotes and gray wolves, suggesting that it may not be a true species after all, but a hybrid. If this assessment ultimately proves correct, it may explain why the coyote was able to so successfully interbreed with the red wolf after human persecution had reduced red wolf numbers. What remains unclear (and may never be resolved) is whether hybridization first took place in the recent past or, as some taxonomists suggest, countless millennia ago. Regardless, the legal consequences of being classified a hybrid may spell life or death for red wolves since protection is presently afforded only to true species or geo-graphically isolated populations of those species. Most biologists believe that, whatever its ultimate taxonomic fate, the red wolf is worthy of restoration based upon its record of longtime survival as a unique member of North American fauna. On the other hand, its shaky evolutionary history has caused a number of private landowners in North Carolina and Tennessee, as well as some biologists, to demand that the animal be denied protection and removed from the endangered species list.[10]

Threats to red wolf recovery have surfaced elsewhere as well. In response to an anti-federalist Zeitgeist that swept across the United States in 1994, two counties in northeastern North Carolina passed resolutions demanding immediate eviction of wolves. In January of the following year, the North Carolina legislature, which until now had remained neutral over wolf re-covery, enacted a state law permitting the killing of wolves on private property. Within several months four wolves had been shot. Although this action was widely deemed as a blatant attempt to circumvent federal law, the Fish and Wildlife Service declined to prosecute the landowners respon-sible for the deaths, and instead attempted to relax some of the regulations concerning the killing of wolves in defense of property. Opponents, how-ever, weren't satisfied. In August 1995, North Carolina's Senator Jesse

Helms introduced federal legislation to bar further appropriations for red wolf recovery in the state. Though the measure failed, it did so only by the narrowest of margins. According to most scientists, the best hope for recovery of small but healthy wild populations of the animal is to be found presently only in North Carolina. Should the government be forced to abandon recovery efforts there, the future of the red wolf in the wild may be imperiled.[11]

Not long after federal biologists commenced their efforts to save the red wolf, they began deciding what to do about the gray wolf, particularly the eastern subspecies (*C. lupus lycaon*) which once ranged throughout southeastern Canada and the eastern United States. The animal still occurred in southern Ontario and Quebec, but other than a small number living in Isle Royale National Park, it could be found in the United States only in the northern one-third of Minnesota. Like the red wolf, the eastern gray wolf had been officially listed as an endangered species by the Fish and Wildlife Service several years before Congress passed the ESA. But unlike the red wolf, there was strident disagreement whether it was truly at risk.[12]

The state of Minnesota was particularly unhappy about the wolf's listing. Citing preemption of states' traditional authority to manage wildlife, officials there didn't want to surrender management of wolves (or any other species) to federal authorities. They suggested wolf numbers were as high as 750 animals, up some 250 since bounties had ended a decade earlier, and that the population appeared to be relatively stable and self-sustaining. The animals had ample protection, they claimed, since an extensive amount of Minnesota's wolf habitat occurred on the Superior National Forest, land that the forest supervisor had closed to the hunting of wolves in 1970. To further placate concerns, Minnesota proposed a plan in 1972 to create a permanent wolf sanctuary adjacent to Canada, declare the wolf a game animal, and establish strictly enforced statewide hunting and trapping regulations along with closed seasons—all efforts that provided substantially more protection than the predator had enjoyed in the past.

But plan opponents countered that little was really known about Minnesota's wolves. They pointed to a recent study which concluded that wolves were declining in one area due to a diminished deer population. The two hundred or so wolves killed each year by private hunters, trappers, and a new state predator control program aimed at depredating wolves, they said, would only further jeopardize the animal's tenuous status. Moreover, some scientists feared that, like the red wolf, survivors might begin hybridizing with coyotes, then rapidly spreading into eastern North America. (Although this subsequently proved true, investigations revealed the amount of gene mixing probably was small and didn't compromise the animal's taxonomic integrity.) Summing up this view, Lewis Regenstein, a spokesman for the Fund for Animals, called the state plan "merely a slower road to extinction."[13]

At first the Fish and Wildlife Service sided with Minnesota, endorsing the plan. Then in December 1972, the Department of the Interior stepped in and suddenly announced the government was withdrawing support. Although Minnesota's plan raised the wolf's status from that of an unprotected predator to a managed game animal, said a department spokesman, the government couldn't sanction public hunting of an endangered species. With passage of the ESA the following year, wolves came under full protection and responsibility of federal law. Minnesota, however, was reluctant to comply, and continued to kill wolves until the Fish and Wildlife Service finally warned state officials that their actions were now illegal. Soon afterward, an eight-person recovery team—made up of representatives from Michigan, Minnesota, Wisconsin, and the National Park, National Forest, and Fish and Wildlife Service—was appointed to develop a sound plan "for maintenance, enhancement and recovery of this subspecies throughout as much of its present and former range as feasible."[14]

The decision to reject Minnesota's plan was hardly surprising. There may have been legitimate scientific disagreement over the animal's status, but there was little when it came to national politics. By now the country was largely sympathetic to the wolf's plight. This was particularly evident when a television documentary about the killing of wolves entitled *The Wolf Men* was broadcast in November 1969. As twenty-four million viewers (then over 20 percent of the viewing public) looked on, the film showed wolves being trapped, hunted, and gunned down using airplanes in Alaska. One wolf hunter even ate raw wolf meat from an animal he had slain, although he later said he had done so as a joke. The film's veracity was later challenged, but the immediate result was a flood of 16,000 anguished letters, 6,000 of which ended up on the Secretary of the Interior's desk. Accused one writer: "The federal government lacks concern for wildlife and is bent on killing rather than saving wildlife." Another demanded to know, "How can the government condone this killing?" According to a random sample of the letters, as many as 87 percent of writers believed wolves were endangered and demanded that the federal government protect them.[15]

Just months after the film appeared, David Mech followed up his work on Isle Royale with the most comprehensive book ever written about wolf biology, *The Wolf: The Ecology and Behavior of an Endangered Species.* Mech's popular treatment left no doubt in what category the country's top wolf biologist, who was a member of the recovery team, felt the predator belonged. After nearly a decade of media coverage in favor of the wolf, widespread knowledge of the federal government's complicity in its demise, and, according to some authorities, concern about its future, the Department of the Interior had little choice but to deny Minnesota's plan.

In the beginning, the recovery team attempted to produce a plan that concentrated strictly on the ecological concerns of the animal and ignored the political and social considerations that recovery poised. This proved not only naive but impossible; politics simply couldn't be divorced from any wolf recovery effort.

This fact became painfully obvious shortly after the team had been appointed. In March 1974, the Fish and Wildlife Service experimentally released four radio-collared wolves in the Upper Peninsula of Michigan. The action was taken with virtually no prior effort to garner local public support. Deer hunters, in particular, opposed wolves. One prominent group, the Northern Michigan Sportsman's Association, passed a resolution condemning the action. Eight months later, amid much local controversy about the release, all four animals had been killed at the hands of humans. Within the next two years, three additional wild wolves, believed to have been migrants from Canada, were found either trapped or shot.

Not long after the killing of these wolves, a public survey in Michigan posed the question: "Should wolves be restored to the Upper Peninsula?" The response was strongly in support—54 percent in favor versus 12 percent against. Herein lay an important lesson that would prove true wherever wolf recovery was attempted: support by a majority of citizenry did not guarantee success. The mostly urban public might enthusiastically embrace recovery, but wolves didn't live in metropolitan backyards; they inhabited wilderness and semi-wilderness areas. Rural residents who lived near those places often weren't eager to see the predator return, enough to risk criminal penalties of as much as $20,000 (later increased to $100,000) in fines and one-year imprisonment for killing an endangered species. For several years after wolves were officially protected in Minnesota, as many as two hundred to three hundred animals were killed illegally each year.[16]

An even more disturbing problem was the depth of enmity some people continued to demonstrate toward wolves. One Minnesota farmer, who claimed to have been forced out of business when wolves allegedly killed eighty-one of his cattle, was particularly bitter. "We're going to kill the wolf whenever we can, wherever we can," he vowed. "The only thing that's going to stop us is a bullet between the eyes!" In Michigan, one of the dead wolves had been defiantly deposited on a game warden's doorstep. Some sportsmen there formed a new organization, the Baraga County Wolf Hunters Association, adopting the creed: "Preserve our Deer—Shoot a Wolf." The group offered a $100 reward for any wolf shot in the county. In another incident the summer before, two representatives of the North American Association for the Preservation of Predatory Animals had just returned to New York at the conclusion of a promotional tour with two tame wolves. The men left the animals overnight in their van. In the morning they found the vehicle's door pried open and the wolves dead, poisoned with strychnine.[17]

Clearly, wolf hatred would prove no small obstacle to recovery.

Chief among recovery opponents were livestock producers. This was particularly true where forested land in northern Minnesota gave way to an increasing number of farms and ranches in the southern two-thirds of the state. The team finally agreed on a zonal approach. Wolves would be wholly protected in a "primary" zone, or wolf sanctuary, located in the best wolf habitat in the northeastern part of the state. In additional zones extending west and south, they would be allowed to extend their range into habitat less optimal, but still potentially capable of supporting the predators. The difficulty came in deciding how to deal with wolves that depredated livestock in these latter zones.

The Fish and Wildlife Service began by capturing and relocating depredating wolves, but the process not only proved difficult and expensive, it often failed when the predators quickly returned to former haunts and killed yet again. Finally, the agency concluded that "problem" animals had to be permanently removed to allow those wolves that didn't prey on stock the best chance of recovery. But because wolves were an endangered species, there was disagreement over whether any of the animals could be legally killed. When the draft plan was released in 1975, the agency proposed that Minnesota wolves be downgraded to "threatened," a status which still offered protection but allowed the elimination of depredating wolves. At the same time, the agency sought to establish a wolf population of about one hundred animals outside of Minnesota, possibly in Wisconsin or Michigan. It also proposed safeguarding any other gray wolf populations in the country (although none were then known) by recommending that wolves outside of the Minnesota recovery area continue to receive full protection as endangered species. By the time the reclassification became official in 1978, Minnesota wolves had rebounded dramatically during four years of federal protection. Biologists estimated the state now supported some 1,250 animals. Some environmentalists became so encouraged that they began to speak of officially declaring the wolf the national mammal.[18]

Not all conservationists were pleased, however. Some argued that the government had no business killing wolves at the same time it was encouraging recovery. A lawsuit by these groups failed to stop the plan, but a federal judge did place tough constraints on the control program. Meanwhile, Minnesota wildlife officials complained that reclassification didn't go far enough, saying they had been correct all along, that wolves should never have been listed, and they vigorously lobbied to take over greater management of the animal. By 1982 the government finally acceded to the state's demand to allow a limited sport harvest of wolves, hoping that this action would defuse anti-wolf sentiment while also reducing depredation problems. Environmentalists cried foul and immediately sued again, this time with success. In February 1985, after several rounds of legal wrangling, the Eighth Circuit Court of Appeals rejected Minnesota's proposed sport harvest, but allowed the government to continue wolf control. The following year the service turned over its control program to Animal Damage Control, the successor of the same federal agency that decades earlier had so successfully eliminated wolves. Once again federal predator control officials were in the wolf-killing business, only this time they exclusively targeted wolves that depredated livestock.[19]

Throughout Minnesota's wolf control controversy, this question begged an answer: How serious were wolf depredations? Little was known about livestock losses when the species was first declared endangered, but this eventually changed. After an exhaustive twenty-year study, biologists learned that of the 7,200 farms throughout the predator's range in northern Minnesota, wolves played a relatively small role in livestock deaths.

During any single year, less than 30 of the farms suffered depredations, for which the state compensated owners an annual average of $32,000. In terms of overall livestock lost to wolves during the highest depredation years, the predators killed only about 1 out of every 2,000 cattle and 27 out of every 2,000 sheep, even though they had ample opportunity to kill many more. Other studies bore similar results. In British Columbia, wolves accounted for one-tenth of one percent of all livestock deaths.[20]

These results ultimately have had great implications for wolf recovery programs elsewhere. Whenever the predators have access to wild prey, scientists conclude, they seem to prefer to hunt those animals, usually failing to recognize and select domestic livestock as potential prey. At the same time, some livestock depredations are a fact of life. There is no prospect that they will disappear entirely wherever wolves and domestic animals live in close proximity to one another. By 1996 Minnesota harbored about 2,000 wolves, of which 120 to 160 depredating animals are killed each year as part of the government's control program. As wolves continue to expand across the state into areas of greater human habitation, however, depredations are likely to increase, resulting in demand for additional control.

Whether or not Minnesota wolves ever warranted endangered species status may still be debated, but the results of that protection are undeniable. Wolves have spread from Minnesota (and possibly Canada) to neighboring states. Wisconsin and Michigan today each support about 60 or 70 animals, while dispersing wolves have increasingly shown up in both North and South Dakota. Provided wolves in Minnesota continue to do well, and once populations in Michigan and Wisconsin remain at 100 or more for five consecutive years, they will be removed from the endangered species list, and the states will take over full management of the species within their borders.[21]

A less obvious feature of both eastern gray wolf and red wolf recovery was how these successes eventually paved the way for the establishment of other wolf populations. At the same time that the Fish and Wildlife Service was ironing out a plethora of problems—from the genetics of captive breeding to control of depredating animals—it tackled a much greater challenge: reintroducing wolves to the West. Here resided perhaps the country's best available wolf habitat, some of it little changed from a century before,

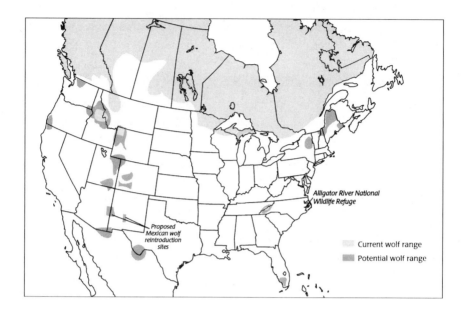

consisting of large tracts of mostly undeveloped federal land with a generous supply of suitable wild prey. In the northern Rocky Mountains, prey
numbers were at their highest levels in nearly one hundred years. But the
West also hadn't changed in another respect. It was still home to a vast and
virulent anti-wolf sentiment, making the recovery of wolves there the most
difficult task of all.

Fish and Wildlife Service biologists identified two prime recovery areas:
the southern and northern Rocky Mountains. Of these locations, the subspecies considered most at risk was the Mexican wolf (*C. lupus baileyi*),
named for Vernon Bailey, the Biological Survey biologist who had played a
foremost role in the effort to eradicate this smallest, possibly oldest, and
southernmost wolf from the Southwest.[22]

Once the Mexican wolf had ranged in high mountainous regions, called
"sky islands" in the arid Southwest, from deep in Mexico, north to western
Texas and southern Arizona and New Mexico. Here, cooler temperatures
and adequate rainfall provide better prey habitat than surrounding desert
lowlands. Following eradication in the United States, few, if any, breeding
wolves survived north of the border by the late 1920s. But in the sparsely
settled woodlands of Mexico's Sierra Madre mountains, a number of the
animals persisted until the 1950s, enough so that dispersing lone wolves

not infrequently turned up in the United States. By then, however, major agrarian land reform in Mexico had brought a great increase in the human population of this mountainous region. Along with people came a growing number of wolf-human conflicts. By 1958, Compound 1080 had been widely distributed throughout much of northern Mexico, leading one predator control official to observe that while the Sierra Madres had once had "abundant" wolves, the animals were now under "complete control."[23]

When the Mexican wolf was finally listed as an endangered species in 1976, no one knew how many of the animals survived, but biologists suspected the worst. A wolf had been killed in New Mexico in 1970. In December of that same year, two wolves were killed in west Texas. Another dead wolf had shown up in Arizona several years later, believed to have been taken by a private trapper working for a $500 bounty placed on its head by local stock owners. Mexico looked like the only possibility.[24]

In 1977 the Fish and Wildlife Service, with permission of the Mexican government, sent an experienced trapper, Roy McBride, to Mexico to live-capture several wolves for a captive breeding program. Trained as a wildlife biologist but a professional trapper by trade, McBride knew Mexican wolves perhaps better than any living person, having once worked for Mexican ranchers to eradicate depredating wolves. But by 1980, McBride had managed to capture only five animals—four males (one of which soon died) and a pregnant female. Worse yet, he estimated that despite official legal protection of wolves by the Mexican government, the use of poison was widespread and ranchers killed the animals at will. Probably no more than fifty wolves survived throughout the country. Given the present intensity of persecution, concluded McBride, the wolf "faces imminent extinction" in Mexico.[25]

Based on McBride's dismal outlook, a recovery team was appointed in 1979 and began developing a plan to eventually reestablish a self-sustaining population of at least one hundred wolves within the species' historic range. Like red wolves, Mexican wolves would have to be bred in captivity until their numbers recovered sufficiently to be released into the wild. But to give the breeding program the best chance of success, more wolves were needed. McBride returned to Mexico in 1981 to capture additional animals but, after an extensive search, he found none. The number of Mexican wolves remaining in the wild was officially estimated to be between ten to thirty animals, although some biologists began to doubt if there were any at all.[26]

By the time the recovery plan appeared in 1982, the five captive animals had grown to ten; three of the original males had died, but the female had given birth to two litters. Now the recovery effort hit a major snag, and the Fish and Wildlife Service began to question whether or not Mexican wolves could ever be restored to the wild. The problem was where to put the animals, provided enough captive-reared wolves could eventually be produced. Mexico lacked the will and resources to protect the wolves it had, and when the agency began assessing likely recovery sites in the United States, it failed to identify one sufficiently distant from human habitation. Despite the fact that forty million acres of public land resided in Arizona and New Mexico, public grazing of livestock was common on much of this federal land, and anti-wolf sentiment among ranchers remained strong. The service admitted that it would have to build a broad base of public support before recovery could proceed, and that opposition would have to be overcome by public outreach and education. Yet it failed to take any meaningful steps in that direction.[27]

The agency also became convinced that state cooperation was essential in any reintroduction plan, since ultimate responsibility for the animals would revert to states once populations had recovered. New Mexico had participated in the plan from the start, but Arizona had shown little interest and refused to appoint a representative to the recovery team. Texas, whose state wildlife agency had long sided with agricultural interests opposed to recovery, was completely out of the picture since a state law there banned any live wolves within its boundaries. Like Minnesota, each of these states openly resisted federal control of what they deemed was their traditional management role. With state wildlife agencies largely funded by sport hunters pursuing the same prey as wolves, reintroduction seemed nothing short of economic and political suicide.

Unless an acceptable recovery site could be found, concluded the Fish and Wildlife Service, there seemed little reason to continue the expensive captive wolf breeding program. That program was already in jeopardy. Mexico was balking about captured wolves from within its borders being used for reintroduction in the United States. The political climate in Washington, D.C., had changed as well. The conservative administration of Ronald Reagan was now in charge, and the new director of the Fish and

Wildlife Service, Frank Dunkle, was decidedly unsympathetic to wolf reintroduction. Future funding for new endangered species programs like that
of the Mexican wolf had never looked more unpromising.

Under this pall, wolf recovery limped along until 1986. Twenty-eight
wolves were now in the captive breeding program, all progeny of the
original female wolf Roy McBride had captured nearly a decade earlier.
Although there were (and still are) sporadic reports of wolf sightings in
Mexico, for all practical purposes the species appeared to be extinct in the
wild. In March the government announced that it wanted to resolve the
question of Mexican wolf recovery once and for all, and it requested recommendations of potential recovery sites from Arizona, New Mexico, and
Texas. Arizona and Texas remained reluctant to commit themselves. Arizona, in particular, had never been happy about the priorities outlined in
the federal recovery plan, claiming that public education and support
should precede site selection. Arizona Game and Fish Director Temple
Reynolds wrote a letter to Frank Dunkle, saying that the state's site recommendations are "on the back burner," as far as he was concerned, and that
the federal government should postpone wolf recovery indefinitely. The
only recommendation for a recovery site came from New Mexico: the
White Sands Missile Range, a 3,700-square-mile area administered by
the U.S. Army.[28]

White Sands had all the right characteristics. It was closed to the public
for most of each year and had no livestock grazing, with an ample number
of deer capable of supporting a small population of about twenty or thirty
wolves. Another reason the Fish and Wildlife Service was hopeful about
White Sands was that the Mexican wolf plan had been newly reclassified
under the 1982 experimental population rule, allowing greater versatility
in how the wolves would be managed.

Given assurances that any wolves would be granted this new designa-
tion, in early 1987 the commanding general, Joseph Owens, gave the go-
ahead for a preliminary reintroduction study of the missile range. But five
months later, Owens bowed to pressure from the nearby ranching community and suddenly withdrew his support for the project, citing that wolves
were not in "the best interest" of the range. Without White Sands, the
entire recovery effort verged on collapse. "We have no sites," admitted a
dejected Michael Spear, the regional director of the Fish and Wildlife
Service. "The wolf reintroduction program, as of now, is terminated."

Spear tried again the following year to convince Owens to change his mind, but the general refused.[29]

Conservation groups—both national and regional—that had up to now kept in the background, along with some recovery team members critical of the Fish and Wildlife Service, began to complain about the agency's foot-dragging. Predicating the entire program on state cooperation, they said, was dooming recovery. Finally in April 1990 they sued, contending that the government had failed to implement the plan released eight years before. Meanwhile, as lawyers from both sides haggled over what was being done or not being done to restore Mexican wolves, events were beginning to favor recovery.[30]

That same month, a new army general took over administration of White Sands, and quickly approved reevaluation of the missile range as a reintroduction site. Then in August, the Arizona Game and Fish Department announced the results of a statewide public opinion poll. An overwhelming number of respondents—77 percent—favored wild wolves in the state, while only 13 percent opposed the notion. Public meetings that followed showed similar support, prompting Arizona to begin evaluating possible recovery sites and developing its own proposal. Reintroduction received another nudge in May 1991 when the International Union for the Conservation of Nature announced that it considered Mexican wolf recovery the highest priority of wolf conservation programs anywhere in the world.[31]

In addition to these favorable events, the coalition of environmental groups kept up pressure on the federal government, tenaciously refusing to give up their lawsuit. In summer 1991, the Fish and Wildlife Service appointed a new recovery team, including representatives from the U.S. Forest Service, Mexico, Arizona, and New Mexico. The new team began revising the original plan and developing an environmental impact statement (EIS) regarding recovery. A final and unexpected boost came from the Arizona Cattle Growers Association and the Wool Producers Association, which until now had steadfastly opposed wolf recovery. Both organizations announced their tentative support, provided certain criteria were met. Encouraged by this move, Defenders of Wildlife announced its intention to initiate a $100,000 compensation program similar to one begun in Montana several years before. Money from this private fund was earmarked to remunerate stock owners for any economic loss due to wolf depredations, thereby easing the financial burden that might otherwise fall upon state governments.[32]

The following year, Arizona finally released its recommendation for possible recovery sites, the most promising being the Blue Range in eastern Arizona, a 7,000-square-mile area capable of supporting about 100 wolves. Together with White Sands, room finally had been found to provide an eventual home for some 120 wild Mexican wolves. More may follow later in Texas's Big Bend National Park and limited portions of southern Arizona and New Mexico.

With recovery back on track, and given assurances that it would continue, environmental groups withdrew their lawsuit. Soon the Fish and Wildlife Service began a widespread public education and outreach program, maintaining that it had enough captive wolves to begin reintroduction—more than 100 animals, all descendants of the pregnant female wolf Roy McBride had captured seventeen years before. Although there had been much doubt in the beginning about the deleterious effects of inbreeding, no negative characteristics were apparent. Currently, this population possesses nearly 80 percent of its original gene diversity. In 1995 two additional captive-reared lineages, previously uncertified because of uncertainties about their origins, were approved for the breeding program, bringing the total captive population of Mexican wolves to 139 individuals.[33]

In summer 1995, after nearly twenty years of rancorous and what had seemed to many hopeless debate, the Fish and Wildlife Service completed a draft environmental impact statement calling for the release of the first Mexican wolves in the Southwest beginning in 1996.[34]

Since that announcement, both opponents and proponents have struggled to win public opinion. At one meeting to gather comments on the EIS, environmentalists came dressed as Little Red Riding Hood, the Big Bad Wolf, and the Three Little Pigs in an attempt to demonstrate that the time of wolf myths was over. Arizona ranchers angrily retaliated by threatening to kill any released wolves. At the same time, both Arizona and New Mexico state game and fish departments refused to endorse the plan, even though a majority of some 10,000 written public comments supported recovery. Siding with public opinion the following spring, Secretary of the Interior Bruce Babbit issued his final decision approving the release of Mexican wolves in the Southwest.[35]

10

SYMBOL OF THE WEST

During the dark hours before dawn on the morning of May 22, 1988, an automobile carrying three teenagers failed to yield the right-of-way at an intersection in Livingston, Montana. Two city policemen pursued the vehicle and pulled it over. As the officers got out of their patrol car, they saw fresh blood smeared on the vehicle's rear bumper. When questioned, the driver, Jeff Newman, told the men a story they did not believe. A few hours earlier Newman had been driving near Chico, a town near the southern border of the state just outside of Yellowstone National Park, when he struck a wolf running across the road. He placed the animal in his trunk, drove to Livingston, and dumped it in an alley. Newman then led the officers to the alley.

There lay the first dead wolf officially found in the Yellowstone National Park region in sixty-two years.

Where had the animal come from? The closest wild wolves were 240 air miles away in Glacier National Park near the Canadian border. Having closely monitored the wolves as they moved into the park from the Canadian Rockies since the late 1970s, scientists doubted the wolf could have traveled so far without detection. Near Chico, a man named Jack Lynch was known to keep captive wolves, but when contacted, he vigorously denied losing any animals. All captive wolves were required by Montana law to be tattooed inside the gum, and the dead wolf had no tattoo. Still, the wolf's feet were suspect. Its pads were soft and lacked calluses, its claws long—signs suggestive of a captive-reared animal.[1]

The final possibility quickened speculation among biologists. Wolf sightings in and around Yellowstone Park had been reported ever since the last wolves had been killed there in 1926. Many residents of the region believed that the original Rocky Mountain subspecies, *Canis lupus irremotus,* had never been entirely eradicated. Its rediscovery could have profound effects. After many years of advocating wolf recovery for Yellowstone Park, the federal government was proposing reintroduction with another wolf subspecies, since no wild or pure captive Rocky Mountain specimens were known. The Endangered Species Act specifically forbade such action if *irremotus* still lived.

Several weeks later, the Fish and Wildlife Service's Ron Nowak rendered an ambiguous verdict: measurements of the wolf's skull fell squarely within the range of *irremotus.* But Nowak couldn't determine whether the animal was a true specimen or just an unusually small Canadian wolf, or if it was captive-reared or wild. The only certainty was that wherever the animal had come from, it had been living up to the subspecies' name, loosely translated from Latin as "the wolf that is always showing up."[2]

Given the wanderlust of wolves, scientists probably shouldn't have so quickly discounted the animal's possible migration from Canada. Ever since Alberta and British Columbia ceased their wolf control programs by the 1960s, the predators had been increasing in number and moving down the Canadian Rockies toward the United States. Alberta now harbored some four thousand wolves, with six thousand in British Columbia. As early as 1941, an uncommonly large wolf typical of western Canadian wolves—*Canis lupis occidentalis*—had been killed near Three Forks, Montana, only sixty miles from Yellowstone Park. Then in 1964 and 1968, two more were killed south of Glacier National Park. Ten years later, another large wolf was killed in central Idaho. Finally in April 1979, an eighty-pound female wolf was captured, radio-collared, and released near Glacier Park, where she continued to track back and forth across the border for over a year.[3]

By the time this live specimen appeared in Montana, Bob Ream, a wildlife biology professor at the University of Montana, had gathered credible reports of some four hundred recent wolf sightings in Montana, Idaho, and northwest Wyoming. Several years earlier, Ream had correctly surmised that wolves were returning to the Rocky Mountains from Canada. Now with a live specimen in hand, he began scrambling to find additional money to fund wolf research. But neither Montana's wildlife agency nor the Fish and Wildlife Service were particularly interested. Officials of both organizations simply had not made up their minds what to do about wolves.[4]

As early as 1973, Montana passed its own Endangered Species Act. The state law, however, failed to provide as much protection as the federal statute, and with wolves not yet officially present, Montana had taken a wait-and-see attitude. One year later, the Fish and Wildlife Service appointed an interagency recovery team for the Rocky Mountain wolf. But while designing a plan, the team bickered over state versus federal management, the size of desirable wolf populations, natural recovery versus reintroduction, and how to deal with livestock depredations. By 1977 Idaho had also extended legal protection to wolves, but it joined Montana in demanding more influence over how recovery should be implemented. Finally in 1980, five years after it had begun, the team produced a plan. No one then realized that restoring wolves to the West would become one of the most bitterly fought wildlife recovery efforts of all time.[5]

Due to the high degree of posturing by state team members, the fact that any agreement had been reached at all was surprising. The plan was pragmatic, recognizing the need to minimize conflicts with humans and to control livestock depredations if recovery was to gain public approval, but it offered no specific management guidelines. It called for recovery of at least two viable wolf populations in the Rockies, but neglected to identify suitable locations. Natural recovery was favored, but reintroduction could be considered in places where self-sustaining populations were not likely. Although Yellowstone Park wasn't specifically identified as such an area, it was clearly on team members' minds.[6]

No sooner was the plan completed than it drew intense fire. Joe Helle of the National Wool Growers Association condemned recovery as "a ridiculous idea—like trying to get the dinosaurs reinstated," and vowed "to fight this to the bitter end." For less implacable critics, the issue wasn't whether there should be wolves, but how to manage them once they returned. The great fear of most opponents was that large tracts of both public and private land would be designated "critical habitat," land set aside and rendered off limits to human use should the wolf return as a fully protected endangered species. Land restrictions involving another recently listed species, the grizzly bear, had been immensely unpopular with state wildlife agencies and certain public land users. Years after being listed, bears still hadn't recovered sufficiently to be removed from federal protection and have their management turned over to the states. Thus, opposition centered less on wolves themselves and more on federal intervention in what many western residents considered was yet another excuse to lock them out of their own backyard.[7]

The plan also had the inauspiciousness to be released just as Ronald Reagan's administration was taking over the reins of government. Consequently, in 1981 the original wolf recovery plan was scrapped, several new members were appointed (including anti-wolf activist Joe Helle), and a revision was ordered. That the incumbent leadership of Fish and Wildlife wanted no part in wolf recovery was plainly evident when a lone Canadian wolf moved into northern Montana and began depredating livestock that same year. After several failed attempts to capture the animal, the central Montana Animal Damage Control District Supervisor, Jim Hoover, was told by a Fish and Wildlife official to "kill the animal and claim it died from being over-tranquilized." When Hoover balked, the animal was officially declared a wolf-dog hybrid, and the order was given to destroy it. Later it proved to be a pure-bred wolf.[8]

To an overwhelming degree, recovery in Yellowstone National Park was the bottleneck. The park borders three states—Idaho, Montana, and Wyoming—making negotiations more complex than had the issue involved a single state. Opposition may not have been so great had the government been able to guarantee wolves would stay within the 3,500-square-mile park. But the park itself makes up only the core of a massive aggregate of surrounding lands known as the Greater Yellowstone Ecosystem (GYE), an area spreading into surrounding states, totaling some 25,000 square miles, and considered by many scientists to be the world's largest remaining natural temperate ecosystem. Three-quarters of the GYE is federal land— two national parks, six national forests, and two wildlife refuges—over half the area is roadless, and nearly one-third is designated wilderness. Nevertheless, private livestock graze much of these lands in summer, and ranches and farms surround the area. The GYE also supports nearly 100,000 large wild ungulates including elk, mule deer, moose, bighorn sheep, mountain goats, antelope, and bison, making it prime wolf habitat. Many of these animals seasonally wander outside the park onto state and private lands where they support a multimillion-dollar sport hunting industry.

Opponents argued that wolves would never stay in the park, but would quickly move into adjoining lands. In their eyes, releasing wolves into Yellowstone was the same as turning the predators loose in all three states, then being told by the federal government that they had no control over the consequences. Besides, some critics charged, had not wolf reintroduction in Yellowstone been attempted before and failed? Park officials found this last accusation difficult to refute.

During the late 1960s, Glen Cole, then the park's supervisory biologist, had begun accumulating reports of possible wolf sightings. In the thirty-five years since park wolf control had ceased, rumors had repeatedly surfaced that some wolves survived. What Cole discovered was that a "fairly consistent" number of wolf sightings had been reported ever since 1932. Cole and other park officials wanted to determine if wolves still existed. If not, they were quietly entertaining the idea of releasing wolves to help control burgeoning elk populations. Attitudes had changed considerably since the days when officials espoused managing the park intensely; now it was deemed important to keep human intervention to a minimum and let nature take its course. As much as possible, national parks such as Yellowstone were to be managed as if they were a slice of primitive America, representative of the time before Euro-Americans had arrived. After decades of unpopular elk reduction hunts by rangers, and a growing perception that aspen and other vegetation was suffering from overgrazing, park officials found themselves wishing the predator had never been eradicated. The wolf, Cole noted, was the only large faunal species missing from the park.[9]

Not long after Cole began documenting wolf sightings, the number of reports suddenly soared. A large dark canid that appeared to be a wolf was photographed in the Lamar Valley by a seasonal ranger in December 1967. Tracks indicated more than one animal. A few weeks later, a wolf was reported shot and killed (but never recovered) just east of the park in the Shoshone National Forest. Then a pack of four or five wolves was reported just south of park headquarters. In August 1970, two adults with pups were seen near Slough Creek in the northeast part of the park. Finally, in 1971, a park biologist on a routine game survey flight saw what appeared to be a lone wolf in Hayden Valley, a major big game area in the center of the park.[10]

These and other sightings convinced Cole that wolves existed in Yellowstone. Cole himself claimed to have seen two wolves between 1967 and 1969. He estimated that wolves were "rare" in the park, that their population probably didn't exceed "a dozen animals," and he fretted that lack of protection outside the park, where poisoning was still widespread and predators were often killed to protect livestock, "is an uncomfortable situation." After a few years, wolf sightings began to decline, and Cole decided reintroduction was the best course. In 1975, he wrote a report recommending the release of between fifteen and twenty wolves, but the report languished on the desk of the park service's regional director. That same year, Cole moved to Voyageurs National Park in Minnesota.[11]

By then another biologist, John Weaver, began conducting an intensive two-year study in Yellowstone. Weaver reviewed the 500-odd sightings in the park since the 1930s, and determined that only about 116 of the reports should be considered "probable" wolf sightings. After looking extensively but vainly throughout the park for wolves, he finally found evidence—tracks and howlings—of what appeared to be a lone wolf just east of the park boundary in spring 1977. But when no additional evidence was forthcoming, he concluded that a viable wolf population no longer existed in or near the park. Still, in examining the records, Weaver failed to satisfactorily explain why over half of the total "probable" sightings collected over the past forty-five years had occurred during the three-year interval 1968 to 1971. He attributed the surge to Cole's better record keeping during this period, a fact that Cole himself had recognized at the time. But Cole believed that this only "partially" explained the increased sightings. Had wolves survived the eradication period, had they moved down from Canada, or had they been introduced sub rosa?[12]

If wolves had been released, who had done it? A wolf owner disposing of unruly pets or the park service? Corroborating evidence for the latter is strictly anecdotal, but nagging, nonetheless. Dick Randall, a past Animal Damage Control hunter who later became a fierce but highly respected critic of federal predator control, claimed that a top-ranking Fish and Wildlife Service official in 1987 admitted to him that the park had released wolves during the late 1960s. A park employee later showed Randall four or five wooden crates said to have served as shipping containers for the animals. Stamped on the boxes in faded letters was the word: "Canada." In another instance, a park employee claimed to have seen caged wolves awaiting transport in a park service garage. Perhaps the most damning evidence, however, came from former Wyoming governor and U.S. Secretary of the Interior Stanley Hathaway. While snowmobiling near Yellowstone Lake one winter with then-park superintendent Jack Anderson, Hathaway was startled to see a wolf chasing a lame goose. According to Hathaway, Anderson admitted that the park had imported "five or six" wolves "to see what would happen."[13]

In rebutting these charges, Yellowstone officials, including Glen Cole, adamantly denied any knowledge of such an endeavor. When two nationally renown biologists with knowledge of wolves, A. Starker Leopold and Durward Allen, heard that the animals had suddenly shown up in Yellowstone, they refused to believe that park officials were culpable. In a 1976 letter to Allen, Leopold admitted that Jack Anderson had long considered reintroducing wolves to the park and that he, Leopold, had been "very much involved in the plan to try an introduction." But he refused to believe that Anderson would attempt the project without his knowledge. Leopold suggested that wolves had been there all along and blamed John and Frank Craighead, two biologist brothers who had a long-standing feud with the park service over grizzly bear management, for spreading the rumor "in an apparent effort to embarass the Park." Allen agreed, saying the rumor was nothing but "a big smear." Still, Leopold arranged a meeting of the park service's science advisory committee to develop a wolf protection plan. Soon afterward the number of sightings declined. The late 1970s and early 1980s were particularly poor years, with only a fraction of the total number of reports that had occurred the decade before. If wolves had ever been released in Yellowstone, the effort appears to have failed. Likewise, if wolves had traveled from Canada on their own or had managed to survive the early decades of eradication until the 1960s, they either moved out of the park or soon disappeared.[14]

Not long after the new team began working in 1981 to revise the Rocky Mountain wolf recovery plan, opposition spread from Montana, Idaho, and Wyoming to Washington, D.C. All three states possessed powerful conservative congressional delegations, inexorably and unanimously opposed to bringing back the wolf. Confident their views were in ascendency with Reagan's election, they made their disapproval known to administration officials even before the revised plan was completed. During a February 1983 House Interior and Insular Affairs Committee hearing, Idaho's Representative Larry Craig challenged Assistant Secretary of the Interior G. Ray Arnett about introduction. Arnett could not have been more obliging. "I think we have made that policy very clear that there was going to be no introduction of the wolf into Yellowstone at this time." Russell Dickenson, director of the National Park Service, concurred, telling Craig the problems regarding reintroduction appeared "insurmountable." But Craig wasn't satisfied. Soon he conducted public wolf hearings in Idaho that routinely and vehemently condemned wolf recovery.[15]

By 1985, the debate over wolves became so acrimonious that it threatened to scuttle the entire Endangered Species Act, due that year for reauthorization by Congress. For the following three years, Wyoming's Senator Alan Simpson, upset over a court decision prohibiting public sport hunting of Minnesota wolves (protected by law as a threatened species), refused to allow the bill to reach the Senate floor. Like many critics, Simpson objected to what the court ruling portended for Yellowstone. Both stock owners and private citizens, said Simpson, had to be able to protect livestock and big game from wolves.[16]

Meanwhile, wolf advocates continued to press for recovery. Given the level of political opposition, they recognized that wide public support was necessary before recovery could proceed, and that support could best be achieved through education. During the same summer that Simpson mounted his attack, Defenders of Wildlife brought a wolf exhibit to Yellowstone Park that was viewed by over 200,000 visitors. Some 74 percent of those questioned believed that "having wolves in the park would improve the Yellowstone experience."[17]

That summer the newly appointed park service director, William Penn Mott, Jr., toured Yellowstone and shocked everyone by taking a stance at odds with other administration officials. When asked about wolf reintroduction, Mott replied, "Where there are no predators and no normal natural balance, we may have to restore it." Mott also took Defenders of Wildlife's regional representative Hank Fischer aside and gave him some advice that turned out to be crucial. Set up a private compensation fund, he suggested, to pay livestock owners for depredations, thereby shifting economic loss from ranchers to wolf supporters and easing one of the opponents' chief objections.[18]

A few months later in October 1985, the recovery team released its revised plan. The new version called for three separate populations, consisting of about one hundred wolves each in northwestern Montana, central Idaho, and the Greater Yellowstone area. It encouraged natural recovery in Montana and Idaho, but identified Yellowstone's chances as "extremely remote." There the team advocated an experimental reintroduction, thus allowing versatility in how depredating wolves outside the park would be managed. Finally, the plan recommended that the government retain authority over the project until the animals had achieved full recovery.[19]

The pivotal debate among the team occurred over how wolves should be restored to Yellowstone—natural recovery or reintroduction. Team members like Bob Ream believed the political barriers to reintroduction were simply too great. Wolves should be allowed to return on their own, maintained Ream, eventually making their way down the Rockies from Canada, through Montana and Idaho, to the park. But others, led by John Weaver and supported by some environmentalists, believed natural recovery could take decades. In the end, reintroduction passed by a single vote. One year later, however, under pressure from both western congressmen and stock growers, the plan had yet to be approved by Fish and Wildlife officials. Balking over who would manage the wolves once they were reintroduced, Montana withdrew its representative from the recovery team, declaring it would no longer participate in the project. The wolf, said Montana's chief of wildlife, was the federal government's species.[20]

Conservationists began to see conspiratorial roadblocks at every level of government, heaping blame even on the National Park Service, which, with Mott at the helm, was the agency most strongly in favor of reintroduction. Criticism reached a ludicrously shrill level when Montana author and longtime park service critic Alston Chase, in his book *Playing God in Yellowstone,* accused the agency of sabotaging reintroduction because wolves no longer fit into the park's big game management scheme.[21]

Meanwhile, nature was following its own agenda in Montana. Bob Ream's belief that wolves would eventually reinhabit the state from Canada was finally coming true. Since first showing up in 1979, the lone female wolf in Glacier Park had moved back into Canada. But by 1985, other wolves—believed to be the original female's offspring—took up residence near the border and produced a large litter of pups. The following winter, the entire pack of over a dozen animals moved into Glacier and produced another litter, the first documented wolf reproduction in the Rocky Mountains in over half a century. Ream and his graduate students called the wolves the Magic Pack for their uncanny ability to seemingly vanish, then reappear later in an entirely different location. Soon other Canadian wolves migrated south and established pack territories in and around Glacier Park. By mid-1987, three packs totaling nearly thirty animals roamed the area. Not long afterward, a female wolf from one of these packs showed up in Peace River, Alberta, five hundred miles north of Glacier Park. "If she had turned around and gone south," observed Ream, "she could have gone all the way to Yellowstone and beyond that."[22]

Under pressure from both environmentalists and nature herself, the Fish and Wildlife Service could delay no longer. In August 1987—the same year that the original recovery team had targeted for having accomplished wolf recovery—the agency finally approved the revised plan.

Bill Mott couldn't have been more enthusiastic. "In my mind," he said in a newspaper interview, wolves "would add a great deal to the natural values and balance the ecosystem" of Yellowstone. The wolf "is not only a marvelous animal, but it is a symbol of the West. For people to be able to hear a wolf howl is going to be a very exciting opportunity." Mott suggested that the government immediately proceed with an environmental impact statement, the last requirement before reintroduction could occur and a final opportunity for public comment. From a biological standpoint, observed Mott, reintroduction would be a simple task. Biologist David Mech agreed. The park, he said, "is a place that literally begs to have wolves." Recovery there would be "a piece of cake." Mech also believed that livestock depredations would be less than those in Minnesota. There, farms and ranches are interspersed throughout wolf range, but in western states, wolf habitat is mostly confined to federal lands occupied by a large ungulate prey base with limited numbers of domestic animals. With so many wild prey, said Mech, "there should be little reason for wolves to turn to livestock."[23]

Western legislators seethed at what they deemed was Mott's betrayal. Wyoming's Representative Dick Cheney, who was soon to become Secretary of Defense, dashed off a letter to Secretary of the Interior Donald

Hodel. "I just want you to know that I am every bit as committed to preventing government introduction of wolves in Yellowstone as Bill Mott is determined to put them there," declared Cheney. "If he wants to fight, I'm ready." Cheney disbelieved conservationists or the government would ever allow depredating wolves to be killed once the recovery plan was implemented. "I don't know how to make myself any clearer on wolf recovery. I am strongly opposed to it. I do not believe it to be in the best interest of the State of Wyoming. And I would like to see some evidence that officials in your department get the message."[24]

Hodel did. The day following Cheney's letter, Mott announced that Yellowstone wolf reintroduction was "on hold" pending approval of Wyoming's congressional delegation.

Even had Cheney not pressured Hodel and Mott, wolf recovery appeared doomed from within the Fish and Wildlife Service. In 1986 Reagan appointed a new director, Frank Dunkle, who had formerly headed Montana's wildlife department and was fervently hostile to federal participation in wolf recovery. "The states are the people who have to decide how to handle these animals," declared Dunkle. Although his agency had approved the plan only a month before, Dunkle continued to publicly lambaste reintroduction. At a meeting of timber industry officials in September 1987, Dunkle assured the audience that he would not allow his agency to fund wolf recovery work. "The wolf stops at my desk," he purportedly told the loggers, declaring that restoring wolves to Yellowstone was nothing short of "foolhardy." Earlier Dunkle had told members of the Wyoming Wool Growers Association that he would subject the plan to every obstacle he could think of. "If you've seen bureaucracy in action, you know that the Glacier wolves are likely to reach Yellowstone before the paperwork is done." Dunkle's animosity toward reintroduction was so great, and his anxiousness to please anti-wolf opponents so obvious, that it prompted a disgruntled journalist covering the story to remark that "if Dunkle were a wolf, he would have licked the woolgrowers' noses, rolled over onto his back, and peed on himself."[25]

Now it was wolf advocates' turn to take the offensive. Howie Wolke, cofounder of Earth First!, warned that regardless of the government's reluctance to implement the plan, that "one way or another it's going to get done." Enough people wanted to see wolf recovery in Yellowstone, said Wolke, that "eventually, private citizens will implement it." A spinoff organization named the Wolf Action Group formed, their behavior and pronouncements so extreme that at times it was difficult to determine who they disliked more—ranchers or the Fish and Wildlife Service. Although Wolke stopped short of threatening to release wolves, he did correctly appraise public opinion. Various polls conducted during the late 1980s showed residents of all three states favored recovery, albeit not by an overwhelming margin. One poll reported 56 percent of Idaho residents favored recovery, followed by Wyoming with 48 percent and Montana with 44 percent, while the remaining citizenry were either undecided or against recovery. At the same time, both die-hard opponents and proponents demonstrated strong opinions. In another poll, 92 percent of Wyoming stock growers opposed recovery, while 89 percent of conservationists favored it. Several years later, in a straw vote sponsored by *Outdoor Life* and specifically addressing wolf reintroduction to Yellowstone Park, sport hunters were divided, with 42 percent opposed versus 29 percent in favor. Another 29 percent, however, voiced the belief that wolves moving down on their own from Canada should be allowed to reinhabit the park.[26]

In late August 1987, recovery received a near deathblow. The newly established wolves just east of Glacier Park killed several head of livestock. An Animal Damage Control trapper caught two wolves and turned them over to the Fish and Wildlife Service. The agency relocated one of them; the other it sent to a research facility in Minnesota. But when depredations continued, the agency directed ADC to break up the pack. Four wolves were killed, two were placed in captivity, and a lone male escaped.[27]

Both stock owners and congressmen quickly seized on this incident to reinforce claims that wolves were livestock killers. Before Congress, Montana's Representative Ron Marlenee described wolves tearing the bellies from farm animals, replete with the "final screams" of colts and "the throaty death-moans of lambs." Then Marlenee produced a picture of a live cow whose hindquarters had been partially eaten by wolves. Accounts of other wolf depredations began pouring into the ADC office, although later, Carter Niemeyer, the agency wolf control specialist who investigated depredations, announced that only one in twenty reports actually could be attributed to wolves.[28]

Some environmentalists were angered that the Fish and Wildlife Service had killed rather than relocated the offending animals. The entire operation had cost $41,000, causing one observer to suggest that the government would be better off paying ranchers to grow livestock to feed wolves than attempt wolf control. Defenders of Wildlife's Hank Fischer took a more moderate view, seeing this as the opportunity that Bill Mott had earlier suggested. He quickly raised $3,000 from members to pay ranchers the market value of their lost livestock. Donations continued to pour in, until by 1992, Defenders had accumulated over $100,000 to pay for future depredations. The program was so successful that Fischer later extended it to pay ranchers $5,000 each to allow wolves to den on their property.[29]

As a result of this incident, Fish and Wildlife officials—citing an obscure provision in the ESA that a "taking" could occur if it was deemed necessary "to enhance propagation or survival of the species"—began developing an interim wolf control plan to better deal with depredations until the recovery plan could be approved. Recovery, argued officials, didn't stand a chance if depredating wolves couldn't be controlled. Hank Fischer agreed, but he was also critical of the agency, saying that it had failed to anticipate a situation that it had known was bound to occur once wolves moved out of Glacier Park and into Montana's surrounding livestock country. "You don't wait for the first snowstorm to buy a snowplow," said Fischer.[30]

The killing of both livestock and wolves in Montana had a far-reaching effect: it thrust the recovery debate directly onto the floor of Congress. In September 1987, Utah's Representative Wayne Owens, complaining that "the wolf has had a bum rap in this country," introduced a bill that mandated an EIS (environmental impact statement) for wolf reintroduction in Yellowstone Park. Political grandstanding quickly followed. Ron Marlenee declared that having wolves in national parks was like having "cockroaches in your attic." If wolves returned to Yellowstone, warned Montana's Senator Conrad Burns, "there'll be a dead child within a year." In the same vein, Alan Simpson asserted that "wolves eat things human and alive." When Boise, Idaho, students wrote Idaho's Senator Steve Symms in favor of reintroduction, Symms informed them that "wolves are not only a threat to livestock, but pose a real danger to humans." Upon learning of Owen's bill, Dick Cheney interjected a moment of levity when he remarked that he would get even with Owens by proposing a bill to introduce sharks into Utah's Great Salt Lake. Owens wasn't intimidated. "Yellowstone Park does not belong to Wyoming," he stated. "It belongs to all of us."[31]

Owen's bill died in committee; he tried one more time in June 1989, but failed again. In an attempt to make certain that recovery would not occur by administrative fiat, Idaho's Senator James McClure managed to amend the Department of the Interior appropriations bill in both 1988 and 1989 to prohibit money being spent on an EIS. The park service also came in for its share of congressional strong-arming. When James Ridenour, the new National Park Service director, was summoned not long after taking office to see Ron Marlenee, Ridenour discovered a wolf pelt stretched out in front of the congressman's desk. "Ridenour," glowered Marlenee, "the only way I want to see a wolf in Yellowstone is dead." Not long afterward Wyoming's Senator Malcolm Wallop demanded that Yellowstone Park cease disseminating educational packets—primarily natural history information about wolves—to visitors, charging that the packets were an ill-disguised "lobbying effort" favoring reintroduction. Although public education about endangered species was mandated by the ESA, the park service stopped distributing the packets. It also halted any reference to wolf reintroduction in the park newspaper, terminated a popular wolf restoration slide show, and prohibited the sale of wolf restoration posters at park visitor centers.[32]

Despite Owen's failure, his efforts moved Congress off its impasse. In order to determine what would be the biological consequences of reintroducing wolves to Yellowstone and how they should be managed, Congress ordered a co-study by the National Park Service and the Fish and Wildlife Service. In May 1990, the two agencies produced the first part of a massive four-volume, 1,300-page report costing over $200,000 and befittingly titled *Wolves for Yellowstone?* Once recovered, claimed the exhaustively comprehensive report, wolves would likely kill some 1,200 wild ungulates each year—about one percent of all ungulates in the Yellowstone ecosystem—possibly reducing park elk populations by as much as 10 to 20 percent, but less for deer, moose, and bison. Bighorn sheep and pronghorn antelope would experience little loss, as would grizzly bears, while coyotes would probably decline in abundance. Livestock outside the park would occasionally fall prey to wolves, but the annual number would be small—less than twenty cattle and seventy sheep. Finally, the report recommended that wolves be reintroduced as an experimental population, allowing ranchers to kill wolves caught in the act of depredating livestock under certain circumstances outside of park boundaries.[33]

Not good enough, objected western congressmen, who claimed that the experimental provision had yet to be legally tested. They feared courts might refuse to allow the killing of wolves by private individuals—exactly what had happened in Minnesota in 1985. Some conservationists fueled these apprehensions by endorsing the idea that only designated federal authorities should control depredating animals. In May 1990, Senator McClure introduced legislation that he hoped would resolve the standoff. McClure's bill authorized reintroduction in "core" areas in both central Idaho and Yellowstone Park, but gave states exclusive control over wolves outside those boundaries before full recovery had been achieved.[34]

There was no denying that McClure's bill had taken on a sense of urgency; time was running out. By now the Chico wolf had appeared outside of Yellowstone Park, and wolf sightings were on the increase in Idaho. Just east of Yellowstone, near Meeteetse, Wyoming, a game warden reported seeing a wolf, and in northwest Montana, four new litters brought the number of wolves there to nearly two dozen. If wolves moved into Idaho and Yellowstone on their own, McClure warned fellow congressmen and members of the livestock industry reluctant to endorse his bill, they would receive full federal protection as an endangered species, and all hope of state or private control of depredating wolves would evaporate.

McClure's bill failed when he was unable to win sufficient votes from either anti-wolf or pro-wolf factions. Clearly frustrated over the issue, Congress appointed a ten-member committee. Blandly but aptly termed the Wolf Management Committee, it was composed of representatives from the federal government, Idaho, Montana, and Wyoming state wildlife agencies, livestock and sport hunting industries, and environmental groups. Their task was to hammer out an agreement, endorsed by at least six committee members, and report back to Congress by May 1991. After several meetings, it was clear that old battle lines were as rigid as ever. Led by Montana's representative, the wildlife agencies joined the stock owner and sport hunter members in demanding immediate and exclusive state control of wolf management.[35]

Conservationists countered with a declaration that turning over management to states before the animal had fully recovered not only violated federal law, but set a dangerous precedent for other endangered species. In addition, they distrusted state intentions, fearing states would fail to protect wolves once they wandered outside core areas. They pointed out that all three states had so far displayed an unwillingness to cooperate with the recovery effort. This last accusation hit home. When the Fish and Wildlife Service had asked Montana's permission to utilize road-killed deer to feed orphaned wolf pups after the pack's adults had been killed, the state refused, forcing the agency to shoot live deer on a national wildlife refuge to provide the necessary food. In Idaho, the state legislature passed a law prohibiting the state's wildlife agency from participating in surveys, research, or management pertaining to wolves without special legislative permission. And in Wyoming, the wolf was still listed as a predator, subject to killing at any time, the Wyoming Game and Fish Department barred by state law from enacting any research or protective regulations regarding the animal. Wyoming also had a dubious track record when it came to protecting other federally endangered species, nearly losing the last wild population of the black-footed ferret a decade earlier, largely through inept management.

One year later, their time almost up, the committee was hopelessly deadlocked. Finally, just days before their report was due, the new Fish and Wildlife Service director, John Turner, formerly a Wyoming state senator and a hunting guide and outfitter near Yellowstone Park, stepped in and crafted a compromise, one espoused by the agency as a "roadmap" to wolf recovery. Turner acknowledged what James McClure had stated earlier: wolves were returning to the Rocky Mountains, and now was the time to adopt a flexible management scheme. "The basic point is, wolves are coming," said a Fish and Wildlife spokesman. "Do you want to get out ahead of it?" Although Turner's solution resolved some issues, it handed over wolf management to the states before full recovery had been achieved.[36]

A majority of eight committee members endorsed the proposal, but the two conservationists, Defenders' Hank Fischer and Tom Dougherty of the National Wildlife Federation, balked. Turner's plan was not a roadmap but a "roadblock," claimed spokespersons for both organizations, and they accused the government of "caving in" to state and rancher demands. The proposal to turn over management to states before wolves had fully recovered not only violated the Endangered Species Act, they charged, but it eliminated public participation in an environmental impact statement. Although an EIS is supposed to dispassionately review sound scientific evidence for or against an action, they believed that in the case of wolves, the process would turn into a public voting contest, one the wolf would win hands-down. Soon after the proposal appeared, Defenders announced its intention to sue the federal government for failure to implement the recovery plan, now fully sixteen years and over one million dollars in the making.[37]

Neither the lawsuit nor the Wolf Management Committee's proposal ever got off the ground. When the House Interior Appropriations Committee met in June 1991, it implied that it agreed with environmentalists' objections by simply ignoring the wolf committee's recommendations. Then it set aside $348,000 for an environmental impact statement—a rare move since an EIS is usually left up to the responsible federal agency's discretion. In this case, however, western congressmen had repeatedly blocked any hope for an agency-initiated EIS. Then Congress went a step further. Despite strenuous objections from certain congressmen (and some unhappy wolf committee members), it specifically directed the Fish and Wildlife Service to prepare the EIS by 1994 and to present a recommendation consistent with existing federal law.

Now that Congress had made its pleasure known and a timetable was in effect, the agency began gearing up for wolf recovery. To head the EIS, it hired Ed Bangs, an energetic and capable biologist with over a decade of field experience in Alaska and who had been the wolf recovery coordinator for Montana since 1988. Although in order to comply with Congress's directive, the EIS would cover a gamut of options, from no wolves to full endangered status, there was little doubt from the outset that the agency would advocate the reintroduction of wolves as an experimental population for Yellowstone National Park. But for such a release to occur, the provision emphatically stated that such a population must be "wholly separate geographically" from nonexperimental populations of the same species. In other words, the law protected preexisting wolf populations—wolves could not be released where other ones already existed.

No sooner had Bangs assembled a team of interagency representatives and commenced preparing the preliminary EIS draft, than wolves began showing up again in both Idaho and Yellowstone. During 1991, one wolf (and possible others) was poisoned in central Idaho and sightings there were on the increase. That same summer a forest service wilderness ranger reported hearing possible wolf howling southeast of Yellowstone Park near Dubois, Wyoming. Although an investigation by both state and federal biologists uncovered no solid evidence, one search party reported finding tracks and hearing howling suspiciously similar to that of a wolf.[38]

In January 1992, two snowmobilers videotaped a dark wolflike canid in Yellowstone Park, although biologists who viewed the recording were reluctant to positively identify the animal as a wolf. Then in February and March, following a number of reported sightings on Wyoming's Shoshone National Forest, two Bureau of Land Management scientists (one of them familiar with wolves after having worked in Alaska) spotted a pair of large wolves east of Yellowstone Park near the Montana-Wyoming state line. Also, over 130 sightings that year in Idaho, along with the poisoned animal discovered the year before, indicated to some biologists that the state harbored as many as a dozen wolves.[39]

By now Montana's wolves had grown to four packs of forty animals, and the outlook was bright for a steady increase in their population. But they were also suspected of being the primary source of dispersing wolves showing up in Yellowstone and Idaho. If these wandering wolves kept up their present rate, suggested Fish and Wildlife's regional director Galen Buterbaugh to a newspaper reporter, natural recovery might supersede reintroduction. Breeding pairs were the key. Should they be discovered, said Buterbaugh, wolves would fall under strict protection as endangered species, and the entire reintroduction effort would have to be scrapped.[40]

Expectations quickened even more in August when a wildlife cinematographer, Ray Paunovich, recorded eleven minutes of what the park service termed "stunning, superlative footage" of a wolf feeding on a bison carcass in central Yellowstone's Hayden Valley. The quality of the film was so good that the animal's gold-yellow eyes and long legs were clearly visible. But when David Mech viewed the film, he noted that certain characteristics—the animal's dark pelage with a white blaze on its chest and a steepness in the profile of its head—were suspiciously unwolflike.[41]

One month later biologists were still debating the pedigree of the filmed animal, when a Wyoming moose hunter named Jerry Kysar shot and killed a large wolf in the Teton Wilderness, a short distance south of Yellowstone Park. Kysar claimed he mistook the ninety-two-pound coal-black animal for a coyote (which is never black), and that it had been accompanied by four other smaller gray canids. Later he said that since wolves weren't supposed to be in the area, the experience had been "like shooting a dinosaur," and he adamantly denied knowing that the animal was a wolf before he shot it. Sensitive to the political capital to be made by wolf opponents should Kysar be prosecuted, the government did not press charges. Kysar, on the other hand, quickly cashed in on his notoriety, publishing a poster of himself holding a wolf pelt and a rifle with the caption: "The government says there are no wolves in Wyoming. Clinton won't raise your taxes. Elvis lives in Jackson Hole."[42]

When scientists first viewed the animal, Kysar's description appeared prophetic—it *was* a kind of dinosaur. Ron Nowak examined the specimen and concluded that its skull measurements fell within the range of a wolf, but a number of abnormalities disallowed positive identification. Like the Chico wolf four years earlier, the skull was unusually small for a wolf of Canadian origin. Nowak proposed several tantalizing possibilities, including that the animal may have been a wolf-dog hybrid, or "a member (somewhat inbred) of a population that had survived in the wild in the Yellowstone area."[43]

More evidence was needed, so the service shipped off the carcass to its forensic laboratory in Ashland, Oregon. Six months later, following a battery of frustratingly inconclusive DNA tests to determine the animal's origin—each delay followed by assaults on the agency's integrity by both the media and politicians—the agency finally announced that it believed the specimen most closely resembled one of Montana's wolf packs, nearly three hundred miles distant. Galen Buterbaugh's prophecy seemed on the verge of coming true.

The appearance of the Teton wolf, following on the heels of so many recent wolf sightings both in Yellowstone and Idaho, clearly rattled the Fish and Wildlife Service. Western newspapers gave the story top billing; one banner headline read: "Wolf Beats Bureaucrats To Wyoming." By now Ed Bang's team was deeply involved in putting the finishing touches on a draft EIS that would advocate reintroduction over natural recovery. Although the agency had dutifully monitored wolf reports, Bangs downplayed them, maintaining that coyotes were often misidentified as wolves and thus sightings offered no sure evidence of the animals' presence. But, as journalists wryly noted, dead animals couldn't be ignored. The Teton wolf was particularly galling since it seemed to confirm what witnesses had been saying all along: wolves were returning on their own to Yellowstone. Several days after the wolf had been killed, a ranger reported seeing other wolflike canids in the same area. Yet it was a week before biologist Steve Fritts, Bang's chief wolf scientist and technical adviser, and Wayne Brewster, Yellowstone Park's head wolf biologist, visited the area. When Fritts and Brewster discovered no further evidence, they concluded that the wolf probably had been a lone dispersing animal similar to the one that had shown up the year before in Idaho.[44]

Based on these findings, Ed Bangs continued to refute that a single animal proved the existence of a wolf population in Yellowstone, or that natural recovery was poised to reach the park from Montana. Wolves might eventually repopulate Idaho and Yellowstone, he admitted, but that could take as long as thirty years. Still, Bangs and other agency biologists were uneasy. What if an entire pack or a breeding pair was found? Would that be enough to call off reintroduction?

Several weeks after the Teton wolf had been killed, Steve Fritts surveyed two dozen wolf biologists in an attempt to determine how many animals constituted a bona fide wolf population. The scientists could not agree. Although most said that reproduction was a minimal requirement, some biologists (most of them associates of Bob Ream at the University of Montana who continued to favor natural recovery) believed that any definition begged the real question concerning the legality of experimentally releasing wolves in the northern Rockies. Wolves in Yellowstone, Idaho, or Montana could never be considered *"wholly* separate geographically" from one another as defined in the experimental population rule. "That wording is unfortunate," observed biologist Daniel Pletscher. Given the great distances that wolves are known to disperse, "there are few areas in the intermountain West that would seem to qualify."[45]

Had Fritts and Bangs agreed, reintroduction might have ended then and there, but they continued to maintain that a population should be defined by reproducing individuals. Until breeding animals showed up in Idaho and Yellowstone, wolves there shouldn't be considered true populations. How many breeding wolves? At least two pairs, Fritts finally concluded. Moreover, each pair had to successfully raise two young for two consecutive years. Under this rigorous definition, Fritts observed that Montana with its several breeding wolf packs clearly qualified, but neither Yellowstone Park nor Idaho were "even close" to having authentic populations. This decree had a twofold result. Not only did it deny that reintroduction had been knocked off track by the appearance of a few confirmed wolves, but it also excluded future wolf discoveries, short of the unlikely possibility of soon discovering two well-established breeding pairs in the areas targeted for reintroduction.[46]

Wolves were not beating the bureaucrats after all.

Skeptics didn't buy Fritt's argument. Convinced that additional wolves—including breeding pairs—might already be present in both Idaho and Yellowstone, Bob Ream urged more extensive followup on wolf sightings. "What the hell is the big rush?" he asked. The public had readily accepted wolves moving into northwestern Montana on their own from Canada, proving that natural recovery had "huge political advantages." "With reintroduction, the attitude is, 'Those damn federal bureaucrats are shoving this down our throats.'" Wolves were reinhabiting the Rockies much faster than anyone had dreamed ten years before, said Ream, making the agency's estimate of three decades to natural recovery too pessimistic. A more likely period was two to ten years.[47]

Ream had other reasons to oppose reintroduction. Once wolves were released, federal funding for his study of Montana's wolves would likely dry up, as the agency poured money into wolf management, not research. But he wasn't alone in his criticism. Douglas Honnold of the Sierra Club Legal Defense Fund believed that the discovery of the Teton wolf rendered the proposed experimental release illegal. "I think you can have a population of one," said Honnold. But John Turner stood by his agency biologists. "In my interpretation, a population is one that can sustain itself," declared Turner. The EIS should proceed.[48]

Opposition arose from other conservationists as well, although for somewhat different reasons. Beginning in 1990, a Wyoming husband and wife team, Jim and Cat Urbigkit, objected to reintroduction because, in their view, wolves had never been entirely eradicated from the Rocky Mountains. Lone wolves had been killed in the state since the eradication period—in 1940, 1943, and again in 1949—but more recent evidence centered on sightings and hearsay, until the appearance of the Teton wolf. Rejecting the government's conclusion about the animal's origin and painstakingly piecing together hundreds of wolf reports in Wyoming and Yellowstone Park since the 1930s, the Urbigkits argued that *irremotus* still lived, having taken up a secretive existence, discreetly avoiding human contact. "Our government is spending up to half a million dollars on an

EIS to decide whether or not to reintroduce a different non-native sub-species of an animal that is already here," declared Jim Urbigkit.[49]

Most biologists dismissed the Urbigkits' argument that *irremotus* had survived undetected for so many decades, since wolves usually make their presence readily known in tracks, howling, and evidence of kills. This had been the case after a number of wolves moved into Glacier Park and other areas in Montana; the animals had been quickly detected. Although Bangs termed survival as "one in a million," and "highly, highly unlikely," he didn't discount the couple's threatened legal action. Steve Fritts and Wayne Brewster went to some length to convince the scientific community that the heretofore twenty-four subspecies of North American wolves were too many. Work pioneered by Ron Nowak and other scientists, they argued, showed that wolf populations in North America weren't as isolated as was previously thought, and thus didn't vary enough genetically to warrant so many separate divisions. Five subspecies or "supergroups" was a more appropriate number. Moreover, had *irremotus* survived in some unknown place, "it would probably be suffering some loss of genetic variability due to small population size." Wolves were coming from Canada whether humans liked it or not, spreading their genes to the area. Therefore, said the biologists, reintroduction using Canadian wolves "would only accelerate an ongoing process."[50]

But the Fish and Wildlife Service did not stop there. After the Teton wolf's appearance, when the Urbigkits requested more information concerning the sources of recent wolf sightings then in the agency's possession, it refused. Finally, at the Urbigkits' petition, a court ordered the agency to release the information. Wolf reports in Yellowstone had increased nearly threefold between 1991 and 1992, from 24 to 60 reports, with a tenfold increase in the number claiming to have seen more than one wolf. A year later that number jumped to 160 reports, of which all but two indicated more than a single animal. Sightings, repeated Bangs, weren't adequate proof of the animal's presence, yet he failed to explain why the agency had fought tooth-and-claw to avoid disclosure.[51]

As conservationists squabbled among themselves about how recovery should proceed, opponents continued to rage at the thought of any wolves at all. A public EIS meeting was briefly derailed by a false bomb threat, and at another meeting Ed Bangs requested six police officers and two Fish and Wildlife special agents to help keep order. Much of opponents' anger was personally directed at Bangs and other biologists. At one meeting, Wayne Brewster was threatened by an anti-wolf foe with being "shot-gunned in the back." Additional hate-charged rhetoric came from Dick Mader of Wyoming's Common Man Institute, when he asserted in a pamphlet entitled "Twelve Wolf Facts" that the wolf was the "most cruel and destructive animal on the North American continent," and likened the predator to a mass murderer. People who supported wolf recovery, he declared, are "vegetarians" who "don't believe in God." Not only were wolves killers, said Mader, but Westerners should never forget that they "desecrated the graves of early settlers."[52]

Others raised more temperate, but no less vigorous, objections. Jim Magagna, then head of the American Sheep Industry Association, questioned why the government was proposing to reintroduce a predator "that our forefathers took extraordinary steps to remove." Although Magagna admitted that only a handful of livestock so far had fallen prey to Montana wolves—all of which had been paid for by Defenders of Wildlife—he worried about what would happen once wolves became numerous and Defenders ended their compensation fund. Who would pay for depredations then?[53]

After conducting 130 hearings and meetings throughout the country to gather public input in early July 1993, the Fish and Wildlife Service revealed the long-awaited draft EIS. Wolves would be encouraged to continue their natural recovery in Montana. Provided no naturally occurring "populations" were discovered, an experimental release of some fifteen wolves would take place the following year in Yellowstone Park. Then came a surprise. The agency announced it was also planning to release an additional fifteen wolves in Idaho. Although Idaho long had been deemed a likely candidate for natural recovery from nearby Canada and Montana, the state had yet to produce a breeding pair of wolves, prompting the agency to include it in the reintroduction program.

More releases would follow in subsequent years, resulting in a recovered wolf population (a minimum of ten breeding pairs consisting of about one hundred wolves in each of the three recovery areas for at least three years) by the year 2002. The total projected expense of recovery, about $12 million, claimed the agency, would actually cost less than natural recovery because it wouldn't be dragged out over decades. Sport hunters would experience somewhat reduced hunting success, and livestock owners would lose sheep and cattle to wolves, although the number probably wouldn't exceed one hundred fifty livestock per year. Losses to both groups were estimated at $3 million, although sport hunters would incur almost the entire amount. On the positive side, an increased number of visitors coming to the Rockies to see wolves would spend over $23 million. When all the profits and losses were tabulated, claimed the study, the bottom line or "existence value" of wolves totaled over $16 million. Not a bad return on an investment, noted Molly Beattie, the new Fish and Wildlife Service director.[54]

The plan was barely out of the gate when it was assaulted from all sides. Ed Bangs wasn't surprised. Because the plan had taken "a moderate approach," he said, "that was bound to upset everyone."[55]

Terming an experimental release illegal, given the documented presence of wolves in both Yellowstone and Idaho, five national conservation groups—the Sierra Club, National Audubon Society, Greater Yellowstone Coalition, Wilderness Society, and the National Parks and Conservation Association—charged that the plan offered no protection of wolf habitat and little to wolves themselves. "It's not a wolf-saving plan, it's a wolf-killing plan," said the Sierra Club Legal Defense Fund's Doug Honnold. The groups were particularly vexed that any natural occurring or dispersing wolves in the experimental zones (which included the southern half of Montana, most of Idaho, and all of Wyoming) would lose their endangered species status under the experimental provision. It was "outrageous," said a group spokesperson, that an endangered species like wolves could be killed simply to appease ranchers.[56]

Ranchers did not feel appeased at all. Despite the fact that the plan allowed them to harry wolves on public lands and kill them on private lands if they were caught in the act of depredating livestock, they continued to voice opposition, although less strenuously than before. They objected to having to prove they had lost livestock to wolves and railed against what they deemed was yet another intrusion of federal bureacracy into their lives. Speaking for agricultural interests, Wyoming Farm Bureau president Dave Flitner labeled the plan "madness," and "the epitome of ignorance and self-inflicted economic suicide." Many ranchers faulted the huge expense of recovery, overlooking the fact that it was their own decades-long opposition that had driven the cost skyward. Fully 60 percent of expenditures called for in the plan were targeted for the intensive wolf management that opponents had demanded.[57]

Sport hunters were also worried, and perhaps with better reason. Charles Kay, a Utah wildlife ecologist and frequent dissident of conventional biological wisdom, charged that no one was looking ahead to the time when wolves became reestablished throughout the Rockies. Kay estimated that they would increase far beyond a few hundred animals—possibly to as many as 1,500 to 2,000—and create havoc with wild game herds. When the hunting public finally wises up and demands more wolf control, said Kay, it will be too late. The resulting war with environmentalists will be like that being fought in Alaska over wolves, one that Kay characterized as "a political bloodbath."[58]

Not all conservationists were at odds with the proposal. Among others, Defenders of Wildlife and the National Wildlife Federation firmly supported it. Both Hank Fischer and Tom Dougherty were particularly pragmatic, maintaining that control of depredations was essential "before the public will accept these predators." The plan wasn't perfect, said Dougherty, but it would have to do.[59]

Armed with a plan, the Fish and Wildlife Service began the immense job of assimilating public comment and preparing the final EIS. After yet another round of public hearings, by December 1993 nearly 80 percent of all people who had spoken at the hearings had voiced support for recovery. Over 160,000 comments, most of them also supportive, had been received from all 50 states and 40 foreign countries—many times more than any other endangered species had ever generated, making wolf recovery the most exhaustive ever in terms of public involvement.[60]

In June 1994, Secretary of the Interior Bruce Babbitt officially approved the plan. Reaction was surprisingly muted. After fifteen years of fighting recovery, many former wolf foes appeared simply worn out, having become resigned to the idea that some control was better than none. "If we're going to get them sent to us," said Wyoming's Alan Simpson, "we just as well have them sent to us as an experimental population." Wyoming's other senator, Malcolm Wallop, reluctantly agreed. Reintroducing wolves was "idiotic," maintained Wallop, but they appeared to be returning, one way or the other.[61]

Some opponents, however, had not lessened their resolve. A Wyoming

Farm Bureau spokesperson termed the experimental release nothing more than "a sales gimmick," and threatened legal action. By that summer, wolves were fast becoming a political issue in the upcoming national congressional election, one that would upset decades of a Democrat-controlled Congress. Soon an advertisement sponsored by an anti-federalist public action committee, Stop the War on the West, appeared in regional newspapers. A map of the United States revealed the entire western half of the country blocked off as a national park and labeled "Where the wolves & coyotes roam." There was other evidence that the wolf debate had struck deep throughout the Rocky Mountains, even dividing small communities of the region. In April 1994, when Wild Sentry—a traveling wolf education program featuring a tame one-hundred-pound wolf—visited Lander, Wyoming, the public school district superintendent suddenly canceled the program, citing objections from anti-wolf school board and county officials. Despite accusations from angry parents and students condemning the action as akin to "book burning," the program was turned away from the schools.[62]

Meanwhile, despite the unlikely event that two breeding wolf pairs would be discovered in either of the proposed release areas before the plan could be implemented, reports of sightings continued to flood in. A Wyoming Game and Fish employee claimed to have seen four wolves near Jackson, Wyoming. Then in August 1994, a two-year-old lone wolf was trapped in south-central Montana, well inside the designated Yellowstone experimental release zone. Fish and Wildlife biologists discounted its presence, suggesting that the animal was likely someone's pet wolf, but they radio collared the animal in an attempt to learn if it belonged to an unknown pack in the area. Soon they lost contact; six months later it mysteriously turned up dead in Texas, the victim of a vehicular accident.[63]

By autumn the Fish and Wildlife Service had switched from talking about reintroduction to actually preparing for it. The agency's plan was to capture some thirty wolves in Alberta, transport fifteen each to Idaho and Yellowstone Park, attach them with radio collars, and release them. Because such an endeavor had never before been attempted, biologists proposed a comparison of two methods. After capture, wolves bound for Idaho would be immediately released into the wild—a "hard" release; Yellowstone wolves would be temporarily sequestered in several one-acre pens, fed road-killed deer and elk, and released after a six-week period—a "soft" release. By now the entire reintroduction effort had attracted national attention, and reporters were scrambling to cover the story. The media response was so overwhelming that Ed Bangs refused to release the location of the capture sites in Canada until he was sure that his recovery team could reserve hotel accommodations in a nearby town.

Wolf capture was barely underway in November 1994 when the Wyoming, Montana, and Idaho Farm Bureau Federations, American Farm Bureau, and the Mountain States Legal Foundation (once the law firm of Ronald Reagan's former Secretary of the Interior, James Watt) filed a complaint in federal district court requesting a preliminary injunction to halt reintroduction. When the three-day hearing commenced in December, the plaintiffs' argument against wolves consisted of a shotgun blast of reasons, everything from the ESA's geographic separation clause to the belief that ranchers would suffer severe economic loss should wolves be returned to the West. This last charge proved the most critical. If the plaintiffs could show that they would suffer "irreparable harm" should reintroduction proceed, then the court could stop the plan.

One by one, ranchers took the stand to recount the economic hardship wolves had caused their forebears. In contrast, government witnesses— particularly Ed Bangs and David Mech—testified about the science of wolf recovery, emphasizing how conditions had changed since ranchers had battled wolves at the turn of the century. Given the abundant wild prey now available throughout much of the Rocky Mountains, said the biologists, livestock depredations should be minimal. Since 1987 Montana's wolves had killed an annual average of about two cows and three sheep, an even lower figure than that forecasted by the plan. Partway through the proceedings, District Judge William Downes took the government to task over the lack of a federal compensation program to pay for depredations. But Defenders' Hank Fischer testified that his organization's program had already paid in excess of $17,000 to less than twenty Montana ranchers suffering losses to wolves. The Defenders' program was actually better than one run by the government, said Fischer, because there was little red tape and funding wasn't subject to a whimsical Congress. Nevertheless, Defenders made no promise to maintain the compensation fund after recovery was accomplished.[64]

On January 3, 1995, Judge Downes rendered his decision. The livestock industry's "expressions of fear and trepidation, however genuine," said

Downes, "cannot be accepted as proof of immediate and irreparable harm." Reintroduction could proceed.[65]

The plaintiffs quickly announced they would appeal. Said Mountain States Legal Foundation attorney Steve Lechner, "When I'm done, they're going to have to pick up everyone of those wolves and take them back to Canada."[66]

Downes's decision came none too soon for biologists attempting to conclude the capture program in Canada and transport wolves to Idaho and Yellowstone Park. With breeding season fast approaching, they were anxious to release the animals in time for reproduction to occur. On January 11, 1995, one week following the court decision (and coincidentally, Aldo Leopold's 108th birthday), a cargo plane carrying the first group of wolves housed in individual aluminum kennels took off from Alberta for Great Falls, Montana.

But the high drama was not yet over. While the plane was in transit, Wyoming Farm Bureau filed a last-minute appeal with the U.S. Tenth Circuit Court of Appeals. As a result, the court issued a forty-eight-hour delay of the release until it could review Downes's decision. This news did not deter hundreds of wolf advocates from gathering the following wintry morning at the massive stone northern entrance, known as Roosevelt Arch, to Yellowstone National Park, which was dedicated in 1903 by Theodore Roosevelt. Most onlookers were deeply aware how far wolves had come both in time, distance, and human imagination since the former president had denounced the predators as the archetype of rapaciousness. As television camera crews jockeyed for position, a long, white trailer carrying the wolves slowly passed under the historic arch, and the crowd began cheering.

Later that afternoon, following a sobering statement by Bruce Babbitt that if the wolves were not soon released, their kennels would become their coffins, the Court of Appeals lifted its stay and the wolves were released into three one-acre pens in the park's Lamar River Valley. Armed guards took up positions nearby in case wolf opponents attempted to back up previous death threats to the animals. Inclement weather conspired to keep wolves destined for Idaho in their kennels for two more days. But by the third week in January, fifteen wolves had been released in Idaho, and fourteen others were penned and awaiting release within Yellowstone Park. When a gadfly newspaper reporter badgered Wyoming Farm Bureau's

Larry Bourett as to why the bureau had waited until the wolves were in transit before filing its appeal, Bourett responded that the government should have anticipated the result. "We didn't bring them down there," snapped an angry Bourett.[67]

Bourett's organization wasn't the only group that threatened further legal action. Still certain that the pending release in Yellowstone doomed the last *irremotus* survivors, Jim and Cat Urbigkit filed a lawsuit against the government. So did Doug Honnold on behalf of the Sierra Club, the National Audubon Society, and three other environmental groups. Honnold's argument was not with the release in Yellowstone Park, but Idaho, and he continued to protest the lack of protection the recovery plan offered existing wolves that weren't part of the experimental release. Unlike the other litigants, however, Honnold stopped short of attempting to halt reintroduction. Instead his lawsuit demanded that the government extend full endangered status to all Idaho wolves, excluding those just released.

The lawsuit so angered David Mech that he wrote Honnold, "I simply do not understand your motivation for trying to stop what otherwise will be a national success story." Honnold responded that the government had "cut a deal with ranchers" that amounted to "dumping wolves on the ground" without adequate protection. Honnold's action came as a blow to conservationist Hank Fischer who had fought for nearly two decades to negotiate a workable compromise between wolf foes and advocates. "I'd always expected that someone would file a lawsuit over wolf restoration," said Fischer, "but I never thought my friends would do it." Eventually, a federal judge joined all three lawsuits together and postponed the court hearing until a later date. It was bitter irony, observed Fischer, that "the legal system accomplished what the political system couldn't."[68]

Although no states initiated legal action, their officials continued to protest reintroduction. When the federal government failed to heed Idaho Governor Phillip Batt's request to halt the release, Batt threatened to call out the National Guard and force the wolves from the state. Unable to garner Idaho's cooperation, the Fish and Wildlife Service asked Idaho's Nez Perce tribe to help monitor the wolves, and tribal officials agreed. Nez Perce schoolchildren named one of the wolves "Chat Chaht," meaning "Older Brother," and the tribe prepared to welcome the animals back. In Montana, however, the state legislature passed a resolution demanding that wolves be introduced "into every other ecosystem and region of the United

States, including Central Park in New York City, the Presidio in San Francisco, and Washington, D.C.''[69]

By far the loudest objections came from Wyoming, where some one-third of the state's legislators are either farmers or ranchers, or have family or business ties to agriculture. Led by Roger Huckfeldt, whose chair in Wyoming's House of Representatives was adorned with an Alaskan wolf pelt, legislators approved a $500 wolf bounty bill. Wyoming's audacity embarrassed many conservationists within the state and angered those outside. Friends of Animals posted a $500 bounty for information leading to the conviction of anyone killing a wolf in Wyoming. "Two can play this bounty game," said Friends president Priscilla Feral. Then Feral doubled the reward if the killer turned out to be a member of the Wyoming House Agriculture Committee, where the bill had originated. The committee chairperson, Silvia Gams, cooly responded that it was nice to know that the value of legislators was higher than that of wolves. When the bill reached the state senate, legislators upped the reward to $1,000 and it passed by a wide margin. In February 1995, after much public hand-ringing, Republican Governor Jim Geringer reluctantly vetoed the bill, stating that he was in sympathy with its intent but questioned its legality. Legislators attempted to override Geringer's veto, but failed.[70]

With a conservative majority now in power, Congress was in no mood to tolerate reintroduction either, demonstrating just how close the entire effort had come to failing by a matter of days. During a House Resources Committee hearing, Alaska's Don Young, the committee chairman, promised to gut future appropriations for wolf recovery, even though such an action threatened to produce the undesired effect for wolf opponents of delaying recovery, and thus subsequent delisting of the animal as an endangered species. While browbeating Bruce Babbitt during the hearing, Wyoming's Representative Barbara Cubin—ignoring the fact that Congress itself had established the recovery timetable—demanded to know if Babbitt had rushed the reintroduction effort merely to avoid the displeasure of the new Republican Congress. Since Babbitt was bringing back wolves to Yellowstone Park, suggested Idaho's Representative Helen Chenoweth, then he should also open the park to hunters. Wolf reintroduction also came in for its share of bashing when Congress debated welfare reform later that spring. In March, when biologists opened the Yellowstone pens and the wolves at first proved too fearful to venture outside, legislators labeled their predicament "wolfare." The animals had become addicted to being on the federal dole, they said, having joined the ranks of "government co-dependents."[71]

As Congress blustered and Wyoming wrestled with the bounty issue, wolf killing had already become a reality. Less than two weeks after being released, a dead wolf was discovered shot by an unknown assailant near Salmon, Idaho. The predator was found lying next to a newborn calf, and evidence indicated it had fed on the animal. At first investigators believed the wolf had killed the calf, but tests later revealed that it had died of natural causes, then was scavanged by the wolf. Although the calf's owner was not a suspect, relations between investigating federal law enforcement officers and the owner broke down and nearly came to blows, each side accusing the other of bullying. Recovery in Idaho was off to a rocky start, but soon the wolves ceased their wide-ranging travels and settled down, with few additional livestock conflicts.[72]

By the beginning of April 1995, all wolves had left the pens in Yellow-stone Park, having divided into three packs. Soon they made their first wild kill since being released, a winter-weakened elk. Several days later, a pack of two wolves—a large, gray, 122-pound male, nicknamed "The Big Guy" by biologists, and a 98-pound pregnant black female—showed up just outside the northeast park entrance near Red Lodge, Montana. A few days later, the male's radio collar began beeping a rapid signal, indicating that the animal had been motionless for over four hours. The next day biologists visited the area on foot and discovered the wolf's carcass, its head and hide missing, the radio collar cut and discarded nearby.

Defenders of Wildlife immediately offered a $5,000 reward for informa-tion leading to the arrest and conviction of the person or persons responsi-ble for the wolf's death. Soon the reward grew to $13,000, and shortly thereafter, Chad McKittrick, a forty-two-year-old unemployed carpenter from Red Lodge was turned into authorities by a hunting companion and charged with killing the wolf. In October 1995, McKittrick was found guilty of taking, transporting, and possessing a protected species under the Endangered Species Act and was later sentenced to six months in prison. Meanwhile, the dead wolf's mate produced eight pups not far from where the male had been discovered. When biologists realized that she had given birth under a tree, having prepared no den site, they surmised that she had been waiting for her lost mate to return. Fearing for the wolves' safety, biologists moved them back to one of the pens in the park. These pups, along with one other birthed by another pack, they divined, were particularly vital to the recovery effort since by then it appeared that Congress might sever future funding for additional wolves.[73]

Had reintroduction been worth the effort? Hank Fischer believed it was, but it had been much more painful than necessary. The process had taken too long, had been too expensive, was entirely too divisive, and had diverted attention away from other endangered species. "When something takes that long and costs that much," said Fischer, "it's hard to call it a victory." Bob Ream and others had said as much from the beginning.[74]

But wolves were back in the northern Rockies, perhaps many years earlier than if natural recovery had been allowed to run its course. During spring 1995, thousands of Yellowstone Park visitors watched spellbound as one of the released wolf packs took up residence in the park's Lamar River Valley, and its pack members were frequently observed hunting and killing elk, howling, and exploring their new home.

In Idaho, the Nez Perce tribe began preparing to monitor the state's fourteen wolves that had survived thus far. At a ceremony honoring their return, Horace Axtell, a tribal elder and leader of the ancient Seven Drum religion, offered this blessing:

> We ask the Creator that wolves may be allowed to run free again, that they be able to live, to be a part of us, to be a part of our land, to be a part of the creation for which they were intended.[75]

—— 11 ——

HUNTING THE HUNTERS

By 1981 much had changed in Alaska during the forty-odd years since trapper Jim Allen had recommended the use of machine gun–mounted airplanes to kill "a pile of wolves."

During those four decades, Alaska's human population had increased sevenfold to half a million people. At the same time, moose and caribou populations had soared to near century-record numbers; then during the early 1970s, due to a combination of overhunting, deep winter snows, and natural predation, these figures fell precipitously. Wolves, on the other hand, had increased in the years since the federal government had ceased predator control and turned over the management of resident wildlife to the new Alaska Department of Fish and Game (ADF&G). Wolf depredations, claimed hunters, were reducing moose and caribou to "emergency" levels in certain areas, and they demanded that the wolf population be reduced. In Tok, near the state's eastern border with Canada, a brash and eager Fish and Game biologist named David Kelleyhouse believed he had the answer. He filled out the requisition order: one American 180, a .22 caliber machine gun holding up to 177 rounds, capable of firing 30 rounds per second.[1]

The order passed through channels, gaining approval of Kelleyhouse's supervisor. Then the statewide daily, the *Anchorage Daily News,* got wind of the story and the reaction was practically instantaneous. "Cancelled!" declared Bob Hinman, deputy director of the ADF&G's Game Division. "The reaction to wolf control is adverse enough," said Hinman. "We don't want to ask for more trouble."[2]

"Trouble" does faint justice to the difficulties Alaska had suffered over wolves in the twenty-odd years between statehood and Kelleyhouse's requisition. Nowhere in North America during the recent past had the predators been more controversial, and at no time had a government shown more determination to kill them. During this brief period, Alaska had demonstrated to the rest of the world that the age-old conflict between wolves and humans was far from over. Bob Hinman and other higher-ups may have squelched the killing of wolves with machine guns, but they had not silenced David Kelleyhouse (thereafter dubbed by the press "Machine Gun Kelleyhouse") or others who fervently believed in wolf control. In fact, Alaska's wolf trouble was only just beginning.

When Alaska became a state in 1959 there was little hint of the chaos that lay ahead. After assuming authority over resident wildlife, the ADF&G had proven itself in the forefront of progressive wildlife agencies. Ungulate numbers were high, attributed by some biologists to the intensive wolf control waged during the 1950s by the federal government, but probably also due to several years of favorable winters and prime range conditions. Liberal hunting seasons and bag limits followed, and with its wolf population then estimated at some 5,000 animals, Alaska halted predator poisoning. The wolf should be considered both a furbearer and a big game animal, proposed biologists, thereby elevating it to the rank of a desirable game species, making it eligible for increased state and federal funding for research and management. The Alaska Big Game Trophy Club endorsed this measure in 1961, and it became law two years later. Then the ADF&G, alarmed by the fact that wolves had not yet recovered in arctic Alaska following their persecution during the 1950s, reduced the bag limit of wolves there to two animals. Finally in 1968, the state legislature authorized the Board of Fish and Game—the body of citizens appointed by the governor, and which set state wildlife regulations and was strongly tied to the fishing and hunting community—to end wolf bounties. On the advice of a department biologist, who termed the rewards a needless state-supported subsidy, the board abolished bounties with the exception of three game management areas in southeast Alaska; by 1972, bounties had ended there as well.[3]

When the anti–wolf hunting film *The Wolf Men* was telecast throughout the country in 1969, state officials congratulated themselves on their foresight—wolves were still being killed, but at least the state no longer paid hunters to kill them. A barrage of mail followed the broadcast, mostly from viewers in the lower 48 states. The governor alone received some 4,500 angry letters and telegrams. Although later the film was largely debunked for its sensationalized and staged portrayal of wolf hunting, it had exposed the fact that wolves were killed mostly with the aid of aircraft in Alaska. Either hunters shot them from airplanes as predator control agents had done in the early 1950s, or they pursued them to exhaustion in snow-covered terrain, then landed and shot them. During the decade prior to the end of Alaska's wolf bounty, fully 60 percent of all bountied wolves were killed using one of these methods.[4]

Wolf bounties themselves had proved immensely popular since the first $10 reward had been established in Alaska in 1915. Beginning in 1949, each wolf had brought $50. By the time bounties ended, nearly 40,000 wolves had been turned in for reward, costing Alaska over $1.3 million, two-thirds of which was expended during the final twenty years. This number of wolves killed may seem remarkable, but usually less than 800 animals were bountied during any single year. Even if poisoned animals which were never recorded doubled this number, the overall effect appears to have been one of limiting increases in Alaska's wolf population but never threatening its survival. Also bounties alone were not responsible for these deaths since wolves were primarily taken for their fur value and, since the 1950s when hunting with aircraft became popular, for "sport." This fact is made abundantly clear by comparing the harvest totals for several years both before and after bounties ended, the average annual number of wolves killed prior to 1968 being only slightly greater than that of the same period afterward. Bounties, it appears, were only icing on the cake, and when they finally ended, the cake was still deemed palatable to wolf hunters.[5]

By contrast, most of the non-hunting public found wolf hunting with aircraft distasteful. Not long after *The Wolf Men* appeared, the nation was shocked to learn of eagle hunting using aircraft in western states. As a result, in 1971 Congress enacted the Airborne Hunting Act, mandating that wildlife could no longer be shot from an airplane. There was an exception, however. States could issue aerial hunting permits to "manage wildlife, or protect domesticated animals or human life." In short, Alaska could circumvent the act should the state deem it necessary.[6]

Based on this premise after passage of the act, Alaska attempted to issue permits to allow a continuation of aerial wolf hunting. But in early 1972, following an outcry from conservationists, the Fish and Game Commissioner, James W. Brooks, banned the method entirely. Brooks declared that it was time "to bring conservation practices out of the pioneer era and into accord with conditions and attitudes that generally prevail today." Nonetheless, he admitted that the issue was far from dead. "No one knows better than I do that the last word has not been heard." Brooks couldn't have been more correct. His move infuriated many Alaskan hunters who, convinced that wolves were responsible for recent declines in moose and caribou populations, demanded increased wolf control. Some hunters continued to ignore the law, and because of Alaska's immense size and limited law enforcement capability, the state could do little to halt illegal aerial wolf hunting. During the winter following Brook's decree, over 1,000 wolves were reported killed, down from the year before but about the same number taken during each of the previous two years, suggesting that the ban had little, if any, effect.[7]

Even as Brooks officially halted aerial wolf hunting, biologists were having second thoughts. Hunters were correct in one respect—moose and caribou numbers in certain areas were decreasing, and decreasing rapidly. In central Alaska, one caribou herd had fallen from 40,000 animals in the 1960s to 5,000 during the early 1970s. The Nelchina Basin, a favorite hunting area in southcentral Alaska between Anchorage and Fairbanks, had crashed from 70,000 caribou in 1962 to less than 8,000 ten years later. The area also was popular with moose hunters, accounting for nearly 20 percent of Alaska's harvest, but moose numbers had declined there in addition to other areas in the state. Near Fairbanks, they had dropped to only 3,000 animals out of some 10,000 a decade before.[8]

Biologists cast about for the reason. The evidence pointed to a combination of overharvesting, severe winters, and natural predation. The Nelchina moose population particularly worried wildlife managers. A healthy number of calves was born each spring, but failed to survive until winter. At the same time, wolf numbers were higher than they had been in decades. Reduced to only a dozen or so animals during the federal predator control era, wolves had rebounded spectacularly and now numbered some 450. Biologists were aware that moose and caribou had a long history of such cyclic population swings, and eventually they would recover. But in the meantime, high wolf and low prey numbers meant a long period before moose and caribou climbed out of their decline—a predicament popularly but trenchantly termed a "predator pit." Neither hunters nor state biologists (whose raison d'être was intimately linked with hunters' economical and political support) wanted to wait. In describing this situation that now faced Alaska's wildlife managers, Bob Hinman admitted that he and other biologists may have "deluded ourselves" in so quickly removing controls on the wolf during the past decade. "Perhaps in this effort we forgot or overlooked that the wolf *can*, in certain situations, be detrimental to the welfare of ungulate populations, and therefore inimical to human welfare."[9]

In February 1975, state biologists submitted a plan to the Board of Fish and Game to hire private pilot-gunner teams to shoot some 145 wolves in central Alaska near Fairbanks. This number, consisting of some 70 to 80 percent of the area's existing wolf population, was deemed necessary to allow moose to recover before wolves, with their high reproductive rate, could catch up. But the plan was barely approved before both the board and department biologists found themselves in a predator pit of their own.[10]

Conservationists immediately denounced the department and sued to stop the plan. With the Endangered Species Act having passed Congress only two years earlier, supporters refused to accept the killing of wolves in Alaska solely to benefit hunters, particularly when the future then appeared so bleak for the species throughout the lower 48. Alaska is "threatening the last stronghold of wolves in our nation," declared a Defenders of Wildlife spokesperson. Others feared that the state wolf hunt was just the beginning. A *New York Times* editorial summed up the feeling of most conservationists, saying that if Alaska was allowed to kill wolves in one area, "it will become a 'management tool' elsewhere in the state." Such a plan, said the *Times,* is "preposterous," "disastrous," and "it must be stopped." Although Alaska's wolves weren't officially endangered and the plan involved less than two percent of its wolf population, the state was reaping the results of what over three centuries of oppression had done to the nation's conscience regarding wolves.[11]

In March 1975, environmentalists won a preliminary injunction that halted the wolf hunt, but on a technicality, not the merits of the case. That spring the Alaska legislature split the Board of Fish and Game into the present system of two separate seven-member units, the Board of Fisheries and the Board of Game (BOG). Board members are appointed by the governor for three-year terms, and appointments are staggered in order to provide continuity when administrations change.

By December the moose and caribou situation throughout much of Alaska looked worse than ever, and the department presented the BOG with a newly modified control plan. Biologists recommended killing some 300 wolves—as many as 175 near Fairbanks, 80 in southeast Alaska, and 45 in the Nelchina Basin. This last proposal was particularly bold. In their desire to learn more about the effects of wolf predation, biologists recommended the complete eradication of all wolves in a 2,800-square-mile area within the basin, an area more than double the size of Rhode Island. Nelchina would serve as a "control" experiment to learn how soon moose recovered in the absence of wolves. As Commissioner Brooks explained, it was a proposal simply "to see what happens." Using primarily federal funding from the sale of guns and hunting equipment, the project received approval of the U.S. Fish and Wildlife Service.[12]

Environmentalists hit the ceiling. As one prominent state wolf biologist, Bob Stephenson, described the confrontation, the wolf situation in Alaska now "went to hell in a handbasket." Invoking the new National Environmental Policy Act, which required the preparation of an Environmental Impact Statement on major public projects, Defenders of Wildlife demanded an EIS be conducted since most of the land designated for wolf control was federally owned. As a result, the Fish and Wildlife Service temporarily suspended funding for the Nelchina project. Hoping to settle the issue once and for all, Defenders, joined by several environmental groups (the Natural Resources Defense Council, Fund for Animals, the Humane Society, Friends of the Earth, and other organizations and private individuals), sued both the federal government and Alaska to force an EIS.[13]

Suddenly the legal stake had moved far beyond wolves, one that Alaska deemed critical to its right as a state to manage resident wildlife. Commissioner Brooks summed up the state's position: "If we lose on the wolf, then who has the jurisdiction?"[14]

After several rounds of litigation and appeal, the courts handed down their decision: an EIS wasn't necessary for Alaska's wolf control program; the state had jurisdiction. Department biologists were relieved, but the victory had brought public rancor and bitterness down on Alaska. Between January and March 1976, while lawyers were still litigating, some two thousand anti-hunt letters poured into the ADF&G office in Juneau, while another one thousand landed on Governor Jay Hammond's desk. After years spent piloting federal wolf hunters during the 1950s, Hammond, although elected as a conservation governor on a platform of environmental protection and planned growth, was in no mood to accommodate those who would end Alaska's wolf control. But he wasn't insensitive to how the issue had tarnished the state's image. Through "propaganda" presented by the media, "we have projected to the nation an image of bloodthirsty Alaskans intent upon exterminating the last of an endangered species." If he hadn't known better, Hammond admitted, "I'd bombard Juneau with hate mail, too." Then he appealed to critics: "Surely there is room enough in Alaska for both hunter and wolf lover, but probably not on each and every acre."[15]

Alaska's legislature took a tongue-in-cheek approach to what it considered "outside meddling." Members passed a resolution calling for the relocation of Alaska's wolves to the lower 48 so that all Americans may be "benefited by a substantial wolf population," and be given an "opportunity to enjoy this interesting and valuable natural resource."[16]

Despite the fact that Alaska had won its legal battle, the Fish and Wildlife Service refused to reinstate federal funding for the Nelchina wolf eradication project. Alaska objected, but decided to go ahead on its own. During winter 1976 the ADF&G killed 112 wolves, while private trappers and hunters took another 66 animals in the Fairbanks and Nelchina areas. Environmentalists appealed to Congress to stop further hunting until the Secretary of the Interior could study the issue. But the effort went nowhere when the director of the Fish and Wildlife Service admitted in congressional committee hearings that wolf control was really a state matter, and any effort by the federal government to curtail the program infringed on the right of Alaska to manage its wildlife.[17]

Unwilling to concede, environmentalists continued to seek relief through legal action. When Alaska proposed yet another control program in western Alaska the following year to aid the western Arctic cairbou herd, having fallen in only six years from 240,000 animals to 50,000, environmentalists dragged the state and the federal government back into court. This action briefly halted the program, but by the time appeals were exhausted three years later, the courts upheld the previous decision in favor of the state. In the meantime, biologists continued to study the Nelchina moose situation. To their surprise, moose calf survival showed no improvement, even after most wolves had been exterminated from the study area. Upon closer examination, they learned that grizzly bears were the prime cause of the decline. Wolves, said project biologist Warren Ballard, had proved only "slightly guilty." Near Fairbanks, however, where bears were less numerous, wolf reduction programs appeared to be working. Four years after control began, the department had managed to reduce between 30 and 60 percent of all wolves in the area, and moose and caribou numbers were growing. In 1980, both hunters and the ADF&G recommended additional wolf reductions in other portions of the state, and the BOG responded by approving five areas, eventually resulting in the deaths of 168 wolves.[18]

This action generated some 500 letters opposing control. "Wolves are just as important as moose," wrote a nine-year-old Oregon boy. From Connecticut, a woman declared, "For hundreds of thousands of years nature has balanced her own species one against the other. I am sure our feeble efforts are not needed."[19]

The state believed otherwise. Bob Hinman characterized such public opposition as "a diarrhea of emotion and constipation of fact." By 1981, Alaska had won its legal battle to conduct wolf reduction programs. Nonetheless, the ADF&G was still cautious when David Kelleyhouse proposed purchasing an automatic weapon to more efficiently kill wolves. Having lost in court, Defenders of Wildlife and other national environmental groups had quietly withdrawn from the fray, but Hinman and others in the department refused to risk another confrontation. The Board of Game, however, proved less circumspect.[20]

In December 1982, when the board held a hearing to discuss the department's new wolf reduction plan, the chairman allowed less than twenty-four hours for written public comments. The following day, the board quickly approved the plan. Protesting this hasty procedure was a new organization, the Alaska Wildlife Alliance, a successor of Greenpeace Alaska, which was closing its doors in the state. Joined by the Audubon Society, the Alliance appealed to the state ombudsman, accusing the board of railroading the control program through without sufficient public review.

The ombudsman sided with the Alliance, ruling that the Board of Game had to follow state procedures and hold a full public review before approving new wolf control regulations. The Alliance asked the board to suspend control until the review was completed, but its chairman refused. Then the Alliance, citing the ombudsman's decision, successfully sued and stopped the control plan for that year. Finally, in March 1984, the BOG complied with the court ruling and agreed to hold public hearings on wolf control. In addition, it promised to base all future control plans wholly on scientific evidence, to consider both consumptive and nonconsumptive wildlife users in making its decisions, and to subject all plans to three-year revision and reauthorization. The Alliance, feeling that it had achieved its goal of forcing public review before control plans could be implemented, dropped its lawsuit.

Environmentalists, however, weren't completely satisfied. So far the state had killed some 1,300 wolves since first commencing control in 1976, at a total cost of about $824,000, or $633 for each dead wolf. The Alliance's Wayne Hall feared that "wolf control will continue until wolf populations are so depressed as to qualify for endangered species status in Alaska." While some conservationists were adamantly opposed to state-sponsored wolf control in any fashion, others desired to see such programs limited to "emergency" situations where caribou and moose numbers were proven to be severely depressed. To proponents of either view, killing wolves to bolster reduced, but otherwise healthy, game populations for hunters wasn't adequate justification. As one journalist perceived the attitude of Alaska hunters and state biologists: "It's as if taiga and tundra were the Stop & Shop."[21]

When the BOG decided to authorize an additional killing of some 125 wolves near Fairbanks in December 1984, environmentalists were ready. For some time, biologists had been capturing and radio collaring wolves as an efficient method of control. Using telemetry, they had learned that if collared wolves were spared, they would soon lead them to other wolves as packs reformed. It was then a simple matter to return and shoot the additional animals. The problem for the ADF&G was that the Federal Communications Commission regulated radio frequencies, and it had authorized the department's license for "research." When environmentalists complained that wolf control was not research, the FCC agreed and demanded that the department cease using radio telemetry for wolf eradication. State biologists soon worked around this ban by applying for and receiving a license for "conservation and management," but not before the event caused a hailstorm of adverse publicity.[22]

The *New York Times* declared that "radio collars were developed with the special scientific purpose of preserving threatened species, learning their habits and life histories." To use them to kill wolves was "perverted technology." Some Alaskans had a different view. Fed up with environmentalists' efforts to halt control, state legislators proposed several bills, one of which called for imposing a $250 bounty on wolves. When the bills failed, airborne poachers took things into their own hands and killed eight wolves in Denali National Park.[23]

By 1985 both the ADF&G and the Board of Game appeared exhausted. The years of tendentious debate and endless litigation had taken their toll. State biologist Warren Ballard characterized the previous decade as "bloody" and "disasterous" when it came to public embarrassment the department had suffered. Consequently, the board decided to halt control plans and investigate "more socially acceptable ways" to reduce wolf numbers other than state-sponsored aerial hunting. One suggestion was to encourage the public to kill wolves, thus removing the onus of direct state involvement. The problem was the use of aircraft. The Airborne Hunting Act prohibited public shooting of wildlife from an airplane. Yet no method in the past had proven as efficient or as popular, and to prohibit airplanes would eliminate the primary tool most hunters demanded for pursuing wolves.[24]

What state officials finally settled on was a compromise proposal termed "land-and-shoot," a popular method used by wolf hunters ever since aerial shooting had been banned in 1972. To comply with the law, once wolves had been spotted, hunters had to land and exit the airplane before shooting. To further defuse the controversy, the ADF&G then proposed that wolf hunters obtain a $10 trapping license, thus reclassifying "hunting" with the circumlocutory but less opprobrious word—"trapping."

Federal officials, who oversee some two-thirds of the state designated as public land, weren't happy with this interpretation of the Airborne Hunting Act. In addition to not shooting wildlife from aircraft, the act also prohibited the use of aircraft to "harass" wildlife, a word further defined as "disturb, worry, molest, rally, concentrate, harry, chase, herd, or torment." A wolf, argued these officials, doesn't patiently stand by and wait until an airplane lands and deposits would-be hunters, but almost invariably runs away at the first sound of an engine overhead, necessitating pursuit. Under this definition of harassment, using an airplane to pursue a wolf who is trying to escape is clearly unlawful. The reality, said one federal agent, is that this situation describes virtually all land-and-shoot incidents.[25]

Environmentalists, led by the Alaska Wildlife Alliance, went a step further, charging that most land-and-shoot hunters would not land their aircraft at all, but simply use the regulation as an excuse to carry on aerial hunting. The proposal, they charged, was nothing but a "hidden" way of enlarging the state's wolf control program. In November 1985, the BOG ignored these objections and authorized statewide land-and-shoot trapping of wolves. The Alliance filed a lawsuit attempting to overturn this decision, but eventually lost when a court upheld the state's right to establish such a regulation.

By 1987 land-and-shoot trapping was gaining in popularity, amounting to two-thirds of all methods used to kill wolves. Part of this success was due to the ADF&G's encouragement. In Tok, Alaska, David Kelleyhouse tacked up posters reading: "We encourage you to legally take a bear or a wolf. You'll also be taking an active part in management of Alaskan wildlife. Do your part." Despite the growing number of private hunters, the ADF&G maintained that some state-sponsored control was still necessary. But Governor Steve Cowper decided against funding any additional proposals, declaring that his administration was fed up with fighting lawsuits over wolf control. "It's not worth fooling with," said Cowper plainly. The governor, however, was not entirely indifferent to control proponents. When Cowper appointed to the board Victor Van Ballenberghe, formerly a state wolf biologist who had quit after a falling-out with department officials over its wolf control policy in the Nelchina Basin, hunter groups successfully blocked his reappointment.[26]

At its regular November meeting, the BOG was deluged with requests 3-to-1 in favor of halting land-and-shoot wolf trapping. As a result, the board prohibited further aerial trapping but authorized aerial hunting under the same conditions. Conservationists supported this move since trapping had occurred virtually statewide, but wolf hunting was now restricted to only one-quarter of Alaska's game management areas. Still, they continued to oppose land-and-shoot trapping or hunting on principle, claiming that whatever the ADF&G might choose to call it, it was only the department's way of sanctioning wolf control with a nod-and-a-wink to hunters who had no intention of obeying regulations.[27]

The truth of this accusation struck home in early March 1989. That month a group of well-to-do aerial wolf hunters were caught pursuing wolves illegally in Kanuti National Wildlife Refuge, some two hundred miles northwest of Fairbanks. When two rangers from nearby Gates of the Arctic National Park overheard the hunters' radio conversation, they turned on their tape recorder:

> We had five of them on the run, shot two.
>
> Jimmie got one.
>
> He wasn't completely dead. We'll go back later. The damned thing jumped up and bit my wing. . . .
>
> I wasn't paying attention too much, except for tree-tops and trying to move him back onto the lake. . . .
>
> Jimmie stuck three arrows in him. He was still blinking his eyes at us, so I don't want to take a chance on getting bit, so we'll go back a little later.
>
> He had an arrow up his ass, and he didn't like that one bit.[28]

Neither did Al Crane, a USFWS Special Agent and twenty-year veteran law enforcement officer, when he heard the recording. Crane quickly flew into the area and saw the struggle written in the snow. As the wolves had attempted to escape, they had been pursued by a plane after it had landed, its ski tracks snaking back and forth across the wolf trails. One of the skinned carcasses was inspected and found to have a broken arrow shaft in its anal area. Crane narrowed the case down to primarily two Anchorage men, Dr. John D. "Jack" Frost, an orthopedic surgeon, and Charles J. "Chuck" Wirschem, a big-game guide. After obtaining a search warrant, Crane discovered the matching half of the broken arrow belonging to one of the hunters in the party. Both Frost and Wirschem eventually pled guilty to illegally using an airplane to harass and kill wolves, and each was fined $10,000. In addition, Wirschem served fifteen days in jail, Frost received two years' probation, and both men had to forfeit their airplanes (which they later repurchased) and were banned from hunting wolves for several years.[29]

When asked by the presiding judge to explain the illegality of what he had done, Frost was unrepentant. "I think that different people would view the same acts, and one person would say that was obviously a criminal act and another person would say that's the way wolves are hunted in the state of Alaska." Several years later in an interview, Frost admitted that under federal interpretation of the Airborne Hunting Act, Alaska's land-and-shoot regulations were virtually impossible to follow when hunting wolves. For the state to attempt to control wolves using this method, he said, was "practically asking people to walk on the wrong side of the line."[30]

Following this and other incidents of illegal wolf hunting, the National Park Service began pressuring the state to ban land-and-shoot hunting in national preserves and new national parks. (Older parks designated prior to 1980 remained off-limits to hunters, but these lands represented only about 8 million acres or 14 percent of Alaska's total national park lands.) At first the state fought this move, but in March 1990, when it looked as if the park service might initiate action on its own, the Board of Game reluctantly complied. But even with these exceptions, land-and-shoot hunting was still legal over much of the state and conservationists began to despair that they would ever alter the practice. Their only hope seemed to be a proposal put forth by the ADF&G the year before suggesting that the board appoint a twelve-member citizen advisory committee of hunters, trappers, biologists, conservationists, and others and ask them to recommend how Alaska should manage its wolves. There was no denying that seventeen years of conflict had brought untold misery and public embarrassment to both the state and its wildlife agency. All sides agreed, there had to be a better way.

The animals themselves, declared biologist Bob Stephenson, were not in trouble. Alaska's wolf population was estimated to be higher than at any time since the beginning of the century, between 6,000 and 7,000 animals. During the past decade, the combination of state control programs and private hunting and trapping had resulted in the deaths of less than 1,000 wolves each year. Never had this annual harvest exceeded 16 percent of the estimated total population, a number that Stephenson asserted was "well below the levels that would be required to control or reduce the overall wolf population." Although critics countered that no one knew the precise number of wolves in Alaska, and that illegal wolf hunting accounted for many more animals, Stephenson's ballpark estimate was generally accepted. Wolf hunting hadn't decimated Alaska's wolves as environmentalists had once feared. But the matter was no longer simply one of numbers, if indeed it ever had been. Conservationists liked neither state-sponsored aerial wolf control nor land-and-shoot hunting or trapping, and they were extremely wary of what they considered were the state's past strong-arm tactics to shut them out of decision-making about Alaska's wolves. The battle lines had been drawn for so long that few people had much hope for an acceptable compromise.[31]

Over a period of six months during late 1990 and early 1991, the citizen advisory committee heard from a variety of specialists. Most state biologists agreed with the ADF&G's position on wolf control. Eminent wolf experts beyond the reach of the department, however, continued to shoot holes in the science of control.

Longtime Canadian wolf researcher John Theberge, a former protégé of Douglas Pimlott, said humankind had too poor an understanding of ungulate distribution and predator-prey population cycles to kill wolves simply to increase numbers of caribou and moose, an approach Theberge characterized as "cowboy wildlife management." What most hunters and state officials fail to comprehend, said Theberge, is that wolf control has ceased to be a matter of biology and has become one of public ethics. There was widespread revulsion over the slaughter of wolves simply to provide greater hunting opportunity. For Alaska to manage its wildlife on such a basis was "a tragic mistake," maintained Theberge, and demonstrated nothing less than "an extreme level of human ecological arrogance."[32]

Others questioned Fish and Game's assurance that Alaska's wolf population was at an all-time high. Citing extrapolations of data based on hearsay testimony of trappers, Paul Joslin, who had pioneered red wolf research during the 1970s and now was director of research and education at Wolf Haven International, believed that the state's estimate "is a classic example of arriving at a conclusion based on poor science." Finally, Gordon Haber, an independent scientist in Denali National Park who was also a hunter and a member of the Alliance and had rigorously opposed the state's wolf control programs for many years, claimed that most game populations targeted for wolf control were near or even above their habitat's present carrying capacity. The state spends too much time and energy attempting to manage local moose and caribou populations, said Haber, and fails to encourage hunters to simply hunt in those areas where game are cyclically more abundant. He also proposed that severe reduction in wolf numbers may play havoc with pack social behavior by eliminating older and more experienced pack members. Wolves have much more complex societies than previously believed, maintained Haber, and it takes generations for a pack to reach its "societal cruising speed."[33]

In the end, the citizen committee surprised everyone by hammering out a proposal that the BOG chairman, Douglas Pope, termed "an historical breakthrough." Alaska environmentalists conceded that wolf control was sometimes appropriate as a temporary measure in order to avoid a drastic imbalance between wolves and their prey. Pope called this a "courageous concession," one that "put their credibility on the line," yet allowed the committee to render an acceptable recommendation to the Department of Fish and Game.[34]

In October the department submitted its strategic wolf management plan to the board, based partly, but not entirely, on the committee's recommendations. The plan established seven management zones, ranging from a total ban on wolf hunting to intensive control. Public land-and-shoot hunting or trapping was abolished except under special permit. If wolf control was necessary, the state would manage the program, one that would be used in those zones where "sustained high harvests" of prey animals were desired.[35]

Conservationists began to fidget; they had agreed to limited and temporary wolf control only in cases where prey numbers were far below population goals, not for the purpose of indefinitely sustaining high hunting harvests. Areas designated for wolf control were to be "no larger than absolutely essential," stated the committee's report, and control was "not intended to be a common practice." They were also nervous for another reason. In 1990 Walter Hickel (previously Alaska's governor but who had vacated office to serve as Richard Nixon's Secretary of Interior in 1969) had been reelected governor. In April 1991, while the citizens' committee was completing their recommendations, Hickel appointed David Kelleyhouse as the ADF&G's new director of the Division of Wildlife Conservation (formerly the Division of Game). Kelleyhouse's reputation preceded him, a Greenpeace spokesperson calling his appointment "our worst nightmare come true."[36]

These fears were realized the following year when Kelleyhouse proposed, and the BOG approved, the department's first area-specific plan under the new wolf management scheme. The plan called for killing some 300 to 400 wolves in three of interior Alaska's game management areas in 1993, and 100 to 300 wolves annually in these areas during the following five-year period. Altogether Alaska's wolf population would be reduced by 5 to 7 percent. In defending the plan, Kelleyhouse emphasized how much wolf management had improved in the three decades since statehood: bounties had been repealed; aerial public hunting and poisoning was now prohibited; hundreds of thousands of acres of wolf habitat had been protected, and the animals still inhabited most of their original range in Alaska, amounting to some 85 percent of the state. Finally, he emphasized that the areas targeted by the plan represented under 4 percent of the state, leaving nearly 20 percent of Alaska permanently free of any wolf control.[37]

Kelleyhouse further attempted to frame the issue in terms of increased wildlife, including wolves, once predation had been brought under "control" and moose and caribou numbers had rebounded. "We feel we are going to create a wildlife spectacle on a par with the major migrations in East Africa," an expansive Kelleyhouse said in an interview with the *New York Times*. "Mom and pop from Syracuse can come up here and see something that they can't see anywhere else on earth."[38]

Alaska's conservationists erupted. In their eyes, the department's proposal grossly violated the limited wolf control they had envisaged. The National Audubon Society's Alaska representative, David Cline, who had served on the citizen's committee, labeled the plan "a mockery of the public process," accusing "department extremists" of having "betrayed" the committee's recommendations. Another organization, the Northern Alaska Environmental Center, called it a "good faith process" that had become "a wildlife management catastrophe." "In short, the Department and Board fell over backwards to maximize consumptive use of wildlife at the expense of wolves." The citizen advisory committee, charged a spokesperson, unwittingly had proved to be nothing but a "rubberstamp" for the state's wolf control agenda.[39]

The Alaska Wildlife Alliance's then-director, Nicole Whittington-Evans, agreed, categorizing the state's action as "business-as-usual." To Whittington-Evans, Kelleyhouse's reasoning sounded like alchemy. "Kill a few wolves and abracadabra! Alaska magically ends up with more moose, more caribou, and more wolves." On inspection, she said, much of Kelleyhouse's proposed noncontrol area lay within the boundaries of federally protected national parks and preserves where control earlier had been prohibited. In addition, the plan addressed only about one-quarter of the state. No one knew exactly what the department had in mind for the remaining portion.[40]

Conservationists throughout the country lined up behind Alaska's conservation community, and public opposition began to snowball.

Douglas Pope, his term on the BOG having expired, agreed with David Cline by calling the board's action a betrayal of a sensible and hard-won consensus that he and others had spent years bringing to fruition. The plan had become something it was never intended to be, declared Pope, a "hunter subsidy" demonstrating a "raw and misdirected use of political power." Anti-Alaska protests and "howl-ins" in the lower 48 and Europe sprang up almost overnight, and organizers began planning a boycott of Alaska's huge tourist industry. Even Congress was roused to action when Oregon's Representative Peter DeFazio introduced legislation to prohibit all aerial wolf killing. The bill ultimately failed, but not before extensive media coverage of what DeFazio called Alaska's "voodoo biology" plan.[41]

At first Governor Hickel defended the board's decision, accusing boycotters of meddling in state affairs, and proposing Alaska provide wolves to any lower 48 state that wanted them. In an NBC television interview with Tom Brokaw, the governor brought further condemnation down on himself and Alaska when he blurted out, "You can't just let nature run wild!"[42]

During the weeks that followed, the boycott gained momentum and the governor's office drowned in a flood of some 45,000 calls and letters opposing the killing (eventually, the number reached 180,000). Hickel even received death threats, one writer promising to kill one member of his family for each wolf that died. Kelleyhouse's Juneau office logged some 5,000 phone calls and letters. "How I hate you all," wrote one person from Wisconsin to the department. "You're crazy and sadistic. You're not hunters. You're barbarians. I will never visit Alaska." Another writer from New

York: "You are making fools of yourselves in front of the whole world! Is that what you want?" Kelleyhouse's plan was not supported by most of the state's senior wildlife managers and regional supervisors, but anyone who chose to publicly dispute management policies risked administrative reprisals. Morale suffered. "Things got really bad," said Karl Schneider, a supervisor with the Division of Wildlife Conservation since the mid-1960s, "the worst they've ever been."[43]

In October 1992, a survey paid for by conservationists but conducted by a reputable independent pollster indicated Alaskans overwhelmingly opposed wolf control as proposed by the state. Seventy-four percent of those polled believed state personnel had no business shooting wolves from aircraft, and 66 percent opposed public land-and-shoot wolf hunting. In addition, a clear majority believed the number of wolves killed in Alaska each year should be substantially reduced. Another poll sponsored by the ADF&G, however, claimed 47.5 percent of Alaskans supported killing wolves in "some areas of Alaska" in order to increase game populations. By one count, the boycott had already cost the state's tourist industry, valued in 1992 at approximately $1.1 billion, between $100 to $150 million. By comparison, Alaska hunters, both nonresidents and residents, who comprised about 14 percent of state's population, generated only about $67 million annually. Just before Christmas, the president of Seattle-based Holland America Line-Westours, which had brought 109,000 visitors to Alaska that year, chided Governor Hickel for putting its "billion dollar industry at risk, together with hundreds, if not thousands, of jobs in the state." In a large *USA Today* advertisement purchased by the New York-based Friends of Animals, a photo of a wolf was superimposed on a target. The caption read: "They call it 'management.' We call it MURDER."[44]

Finding himself in an increasingly untenable position, Hickel called for a "wolf summit" to discuss the issue, inviting international, national, and state environmental, sportsmen, scientific, and Native groups to participate. But conservationists refused to attend unless the governor first called off the control plan for 1993. To everyone's surprise, he agreed to their demand. Members of the Board of Game groused about attending the meeting and announced that nothing would change their original decision. In a more conciliatory mood, Carl Rosier, Alaska's Fish and Game Commissioner, admitted that "you can't formulate public policy independent of political perception." But Rosier refused to give up wolf control. The debate, he observed, "includes matters that don't have much to do with wildlife management." On the contrary, said the Alliance's Whittington-Evans, "it has everything to do with wildlife management as Alaska practices it."[45]

In January 1993, some 1,500 people representing opposing sides met in Fairbanks, a city whose inhabitants are generally pro-hunting and favor wolf control. Hunting advocates donning wolf fur hats and coats carried signs: "Environmentalists—Kiss My Alaskan Ass," "I Love Caribou Meat," "Wolf Management, not Wolf Worship!" and "Eco-Nazis Go Home!" Far fewer signs read: "Don't Kill Wolves on My Public Land!" and "Respect the Wolf!" Several anti-wolf demonstrators attempted to drag the still-warm carcass of a freshly snared wolf into the meeting, but they were stopped by security guards. Speakers stated pro and con positions, but in the end, no one capitulated. "The summit," said Whittington-Evans, "was basically a standoff."[46]

Several weeks later, with no letup in public opposition, Commissioner Rosier declared that the state was calling off its wolf control plans for the remainder of the year. Soon afterward, the Board of Game pronounced the strategic plan dead and postponed any further discussion of wolf control until summer. Nevertheless, some board members angrily denounced conservationists for holding Alaskans "economic hostage," and threatened to retaliate by again opening up the entire state to land-and-shoot wolf hunting. Soon after this announcement, the *Anchorage Daily News* published a column accusing the board of acting like spoiled children, serving the "narrow interests" of a minority of Alaskans, and chided them to "grow up."[47]

By summer, conservationists had their answer. At its June meeting the BOG fulfilled its threat and again opened up the state—including previously closed national parks and preserves—to land-and-shoot wolf trapping, although they renamed the practice an even more abstruse term, calling it "same-day airborne" trapping. The board increased the distance "trappers" had to be away from their airplanes before shooting a wolf to one hundred yards, but it also extended the open season to nine months and removed all bag limits on wolves. At the same time, the board reluctantly decided against initiating any state-sponsored aerial shooting programs. Instead, acting on a Kelleyhouse recommendation, it proposed actually trapping wolves. Using this method, biologists would fly helicopters into a likely area, bait the surrounding land with road-killed moose carcasses, then set traps and snares in an attempt to catch wolves. Death comes either from strangulation, exposure, dehydration, or starvation—a method noted by observers on both sides as far less humane than shooting. Although the plan had been unanimously opposed by all of the senior program managers within Kelleyhouse's department, the BOG gave the go-ahead to trap some two hundred wolves south of Fairbanks.[48]

The reaction was immediate and severe. Board member Anne Ruggles, who had voted against the measure, claimed that what the department had touted as a "biological emergency" was nothing more than a "human-use emergency." Defenders of Wildlife's Al Manville called it "irresponsible" and "a backdoor way to do wolf control," and Defenders joined the Alliance, Wolf Haven, and the Sierra Club Legal Defense Fund in a lawsuit aimed at halting same-day airborne wolf trapping. Even state officials outside of the ADF&G expressed doubts. By making trapping the state's de facto method of predator control, said Connell Murray, director of Alaska's Division of Tourism, the public will "feel that the state has been less than forthcoming."[49]

Animal rights groups quickly called for a new boycott, but this time Governor Hickel was ready. When the national group Friends of Animals published an advertisement in *USA Today* and the *New York Times* claiming that Alaska planned to allow private hunters to use radio collars to track and shoot hundreds of wolves from the air and to locate dens to kill adults with pups, Hickel sued the group, declaring the ads were lies. The governor eventually lost his lawsuit when a state superior court judge ruled that Hickel was only attempting to quell criticism of Alaska's wolf control plan, but his legal action effectively took the wind out of the planned boycott. Consequently, the effort never made headway, although some pundits attributed its failure chiefly to the widespread belief by the public that, after the wolf summit in January, the state had called off all future wolf control.[50]

Even David Mech was drawn into the controversy when, as chairman of the international Wolf Specialist Group, he wrote to Kelleyhouse saying that the proposal complied with standards outlined in the group's Wolf Manifesto. Caribou in the area were "at a low level," noted Mech, and human hunting of them had been prohibited for several years. Later a majority of Specialist Group members refused to approve Alaska's control plan, thus implying that Mech had acted on his own. Nevertheless, Kelleyhouse considered Mech's letter an endorsement of Alaska's proposed control program and forwarded copies to members of Congress and the Secretary of the Interior. Anti-hunt proponents quickly turned their wrath on Mech, one letter accusing him of being a "pimp" for wolf control supporters. Mech was philosophical: "I've lived with it for thirty-five years. Sometimes the vilification comes from anti-wolf people. Now, it's pro-wolf people." Wolf advocates, said Mech, would be better off turning their attention to areas in the world where wolves were truly endangered.[51]

During winter 1994, about one hundred wolves in the management unit south of Fairbanks were killed by ADF&G personnel using traps and snares. In addition, they also managed to trap or snare 13 foxes, 23 moose, 6 coyotes, 2 brown bears, 8 caribou, 2 wolverines, and 4 golden eagles. The trapping program, declared the Alaska Wildlife Alliance, had become a "curtain of death" for unintended victims. For each dead wolf, claimed an official state audit, taxpayers paid nearly $3,000. When the final kill was reported that year, state-sponsored trapping, coupled with the resurrection of land-and-shoot trapping, had resulted in the deaths of some 1,600 wolves—a 65 percent increase over the previous year's harvest, and the highest number of wolves killed during any year since wolf bounties had been eliminated over twenty-five years earlier. The department blamed the deaths of wildlife other than wolves on anti-hunt protestors, claiming that aerial hunting would have avoided such losses. As for the increased harvest, a department spokesperson said that late-winter snows coupled with good flying weather had created an unusually favorable condition for killing wolves, one unlikely to occur again soon.[52]

Not long after the department began its new trapping program, Alaska's legislature moved to give the destruction of wolves the weight of law. Dubbed the "wolf-kill" bill, this measure authorized "intensive management" of game populations to provide greater hunting opportunity. The "highest" use of wildlife, claimed the bill's sponsors, was to benefit humankind. Implicit in this bill was the demand that predators be killed to boost the number of game animals for human hunters, a method to be used *before* wildlife managers restricted hunting licenses or seasons to limit game harvests. Wolf control would no longer be subject to political whim or public debate. Now both the BOG and the ADF&G were mandated to kill wolves. In July 1994, Governor Hickel signed the measure into law.

Federal reaction was swift. With so much of Alaska under federal ownership and most of this acreage subject to state hunting regulations, federal managers began moving to exclude wolf hunting from certain portions of the public domain. During summer 1994, Mollie Beattie, Director of the U.S. Fish and Wildlife Service, prohibited same-day airborne wolf trapping on National Wildlife Refuges land, amounting to about 20 percent of Alaska. Agency officials cited the difficulty of enforcing the Airborne Hunting Act, and said the state regulation invited abuse. Not long afterward, the National Park Service also instituted a ban on wolf hunting in all lands falling under its administration, the two agencies' domains together making up about one-third of Alaska.[53]

Although most anti-hunt advocates welcomed this move, they had little hope that federal action would permanently protect more than a fraction of Alaska from wolf hunting. Many had begun to believe that the 1993 boycott, which then had appeared so successful, had actually backfired. Public opinion had temporarily halted Alaska's wolf control, but there had been no permanent solution. Now with public attention waning, wolf control proponents had returned with a vengeance. More wolves than ever were being killed, and predator control had become the law of the land. Somehow conservationists had to refocus attention on what had always been their greatest weapon—public revulsion at the actual killing of wolves.

Their break came on a cold, snowy day in late November 1994, and it exceeded anyone's expectations. That day biologist Gordon Haber, longtime opponent of wolf control and now employed by a group of environmental organizations to investigate the state's trapping program, discovered four wolves caught in state snares in a remote area south of Fairbanks. Three of the animals were still alive, and one of them had chewed off its leg in an unsuccessful attempt to escape. Along with Haber was a reporter from the *Anchorage Daily News.* As the two men watched, a helicopter landed and an ADF&G employee attempted to shoot one of the snared wolves. Four times the man shot the animal, but each time failed to kill it. As the wolf lay bleeding, the man trudged back to the helicopter, retrieved more powerful ammunition, and returned to finally kill it as well as the other snared wolves. Then he loaded the carcasses on the helicopter and flew away. Given the difficulty of quickly killing animals with the use of snares, the event was probably not all that unusual. What was unusual was that both Haber and the reporter filmed the entire debacle. As Haber pointed his video camera at one of the injured wolves, he spoke the words that would soon become the sentiment of most viewers: "That's just the most disgusting goddamn thing I have ever seen."[54]

Haber returned to Anchorage, made copies of the film, and the footage soon appeared on several major news networks. Viewers throughout the nation watched the state of Alaska bungle what it had earlier advertised as a humane and necessary program to enhance caribou numbers for hunters.

The Department of Fish and Game braced for the worst. Said Ken Taylor, one the state's wolf experts, "I know this will be ugly. I think everything that could go wrong went wrong." A department spokesperson then lamely tried to blame Haber for not killing the wolves when he had discovered them, saying his inactions had prolonged their misery. But Haber responded that he had been warned by the department in the past not to interfere with the program.[55]

One of those watching the television broadcast was Tony Knowles, Alaska's Democratic governor-elect who was to take office in several days. When interviewed, Knowles echoed Haber by claiming the incident had left him "disgusted," that "no animal should be treated this way," and he demanded an investigation and review of wolf control. The next day Commissioner Rosier temporarily suspended the state's program. The *Anchorage Daily News* columnist Mike Doogan called for Kelleyhouse's dismissal, saying: "The lesson is simple: If your public policy is so ugly it can't be carried out in public, it's the wrong policy." Two months later, Knowles cancelled state wolf trapping, claiming that the program had been "professionally mismanaged," but the new governor left the door open for future programs, including aerial shooting. He would support predator control provided it fulfilled three criteria: it had public support, it was cost-effective, and it was scientifically justified. To determine this last category, Knowles promised a rigorous, nonpartisan review of the program by the National Academy of Sciences. Then he called for another citizens' panel of "stakeholders" to make recommendations on how the state should proceed. Soon afterward, David Kelleyhouse resigned as head of Wildlife Conservation, taking a department position promoting Alaska's fur and trapping industry.[56]

Knowles's action wasn't well received in Alaska's Republican-dominated legislature. A few days after the governor's announcement, legislators introduced a wolf bounty bill, authorizing up to $400 (later changed to $200) for each dead wolf. One of the bill's cosponsors, Senator Robin Taylor, summed up his view of the predators: "Wolves are like rats in a dump." Former BOG chairman Doug Pope denounced the bill as "pure and simple demagoguery," but the present board chairman, Dick Burley, blamed environmentalists and the media for killing the wolf control program and agreed to review the measure. Although the bounty bill failed to be considered by the Alaska House of Representatives before the legislature adjourned during spring 1995, it is scheduled to be reconsidered during the 1996 legislative session. That action, however, may not prove as momentous as the confrontation shaping up between Governor Knowles and the state legislature over the "intensive management" bill mandating predator control. At its October 1995 meeting, the BOG, following the legislative directive, voted to reauthorize killing wolves once again south of Fairbanks beginning in July 1997, and to extend the control program through the year 2002. Governor Knowles, in turn, promised the new program must first pass his set of criteria, a process that Chairman Burley characterized as "the greatest method of stalling the public process that I have ever seen in my life."[57]

The year proved portentous for conservationists in another respect. In early May, Gordon Haber discovered the last survivor of one of the continent's most viewed and studied wolf packs strangled to death in a wire snare less than one hundred yards from the eastern boundary of Denali National Park. Known as the "Headquarters" pack because it frequented the Denali road and park headquarters area, and once numbering over twenty-five animals, the pack had steadily declined after straying into nearby areas opened to wolf hunting, despite requests by both the park service and conservationists to the Board of Game to create a no-hunting buffer zone around park lands. Other wolf packs still survived elsewhere in the park, but nowhere in North America, and perhaps the world, had wolves been so photographed or observed by so many park visitors.[58]

Nearly a quarter of a century has passed since Alaska's former Fish and Game Commissioner James Brooks observed that the last word has yet to be heard about wolf control. Brooks' prophecy appears to be even more true today because of the extreme polarization fostered by so many years of rancorous and entrenched debate.

Alaska's most senior wolf biologist, Bob Stephenson, is convinced that the wolf issue is here to stay because so many environmental groups have become financially dependent upon the controversy. "Without periodic media events and revitalization of the message that wolves may be threatened with extinction if contributions aren't forthcoming," charges Stephenson, some conservation organizations "could suffer financial setbacks." Wolf politics, he says, "are increasingly filled with ironies and are driven, in part, by the goals and financial imperatives" of these organizations.[59]

The Alaska Wildlife Alliance's Wayne Hall denies Stephenson's accusations, saying that he is merely repeating "the time-honored ADF&G practice of dismissing the opposition as less than honorable, misled, or just plain uninformed." It has been the state's actions that have prolonged the wolf controversy, says Hall, not conservationists' desire to build a constituency. Had both the BOG and the ADF&G not attempted early on to ignore their objections over wolf control, it wouldn't have been necessary to arouse such a high level of public indignation. Hall and other conservationists now insist that the issue won't be settled by anything less than a fundamental change in the state's attitude toward its wildlife, one that caters less to hunters and more to nonconsumptive users. To that end, during 1995 several Alaskan conservationists announced a statewide ballot initiative aimed at prohibiting same-day airborne hunting of wolves by the public, and restricting state wolf control programs only to cases of true biological emergency. A preliminary poll indicated that nearly two out of every three Alaskans support such a measure. Should the petition drive succeed, Alaskans may finally decide the future of wolf control in the general election slated for November 1996.[60]

But given the emotional debate that wolf control has elicited during the past forty-odd years, even a public vote may not permanently resolve the controversy between hunters and environmentalists. In one respect, Alaska's conflict represents only another instance in the troubled history between humans and wolves that has plagued the continent for centuries. In a more ominous regard, it may portend the fate that awaits other areas where wolf recovery is only just beginning.

Reflecting on the decades of strife that Alaska has suffered over wolves, biologist Victor Van Ballenberghe ventured an observation of the past as well as a warning for the future. "History indicates," says Van Ballenberghe, "that wolf control is sometimes poor biology, often poor economics, and almost always poor public relations."[61]

EPILOGUE

F. Scott Fitzgerald once wrote that there are no second acts in American lives, but wolves have proved him wrong.

Extirpated from over half of their original range in North America, their population reduced to a mere fraction of former numbers, wolves have become one of the greatest conservation success stories of the twentieth century—all during a time when many other species throughout the world have suffered severe declines due to the cascading effects of an ever-expanding human population. Continent-wide, wolves now number some sixty thousand to seventy thousand animals, a threefold increase since their all-time population low of the 1950s. They inhabit some 86 percent of their former range in Canada, and are expanding in Minnesota, Wisconsin, Michigan, Montana, and possibly Alaska. Small but potentially viable populations exist in Wyoming, Idaho, North Carolina, and the predators recently have been reported in North Dakota and the northern mountains of Washington. Reintroduction will soon occur in the Southwest, and grass-roots efforts have begun with the goal of returning wolves to upper New England, and both Big Bend and Olympic national parks.[1]

Despite these successes, the past four hundred years of wolf history has left its mark on the continent, one that still governs human attitudes and emotions toward the predators. Not everyone welcomes their return. A relatively small but influential segment of society continues to resist any increase in wolf numbers and range, and that opposition has greatly fueled the debate over recovery. While dread of personal harm from the predator has declined dramatically during recent decades, fear of economic loss has not. Wolf foes may no longer champion wholesale extirpation, but they demand that wolf populations be limited in size and space. Sometimes this means not allowing the animals to reoccupy former range, but more often it means reducing or controlling existing populations.

Wolf advocates, on the other hand, see the animal as deeply symbolic of a long-overdue conservation ethic, one that Aldo Leopold decades ago succinctly identified as "saving all the parts." The wolf, with its protracted history of oppression, was one of those parts of which humanity once desperately attempted to rid itself. Many conservationists remain haunted by this spectre of past persecution, a desire, as it were, for the blood of wolves. To them it represents a dark and altogether domineering side of human nature, one that is the antithesis of a more respectful view of the natural world and the life that shares this planet, a view not greatly dissimilar from that once embraced by many Native American cultures.

Where these opposing forces meet there is often strident discord. Although wolves have long been considered a wilderness species, that characterization is only partly correct. The animals have proved that they survive wherever suitable prey exists and humans tolerate their presence. As their numbers continue to expand and wolves increasingly come into contact with people, conflict is inevitable. The irrefutable fact remains: wolves kill to live, and sometimes they kill those animals valued by humans. Some conservationists today demand that wolves be allowed to reinhabit all available wolf range without restriction, even when the animal's depredations cause economic hardship. Anti-wolf forces emphatically reject such a notion, regarding wolf restoration as an intrusion of big government and meddling by outsiders.

Meanwhile, biologists no longer worry about the survival of the wolf as a species, but they warn that the animal's future is not yet secure. In particular, they fret about long-term genetic viability where wolves exist in small, isolated populations in close proximity to humans. Altogether, less than 5 percent of wolves in the continental United States live within national parks, which afford them the most protection.

Such fears were nearly realized in late 1995 when Congress attempted to gut future appropriations for wolf reintroduction in Idaho and Yellowstone National Park, leaving what scientists believed was an insufficient number of wolves to guarantee recovery. By drastically restructuring the program, and with the aid of generous private donations, eventually enough money was found to procure the capture and release of an additional thirty-seven wolves during winter 1996. To date, over one dozen of the total number of wolves have died (either killed for depredating livestock, run over in a vehicle accident, shot illegally, or having died from natural injuries), but this number has been far less than was originally anticipated. With reproduction of the remaining wolves exceeding expectations, federal biologists now say they may have enough animals to assure wolf recovery within the northern Rockies without further reintroductions.

Less certain is the outcome of legal challenges there. In February 1996, the original litigants opposing wolf reintroduction appeared before District Court Judge William Downes, who termed the hearing "one of the most important things I [will] ever lay my hands on as a federal judge." As this book goes to press, Judge Downes has yet to render an opinion. Meanwhile, Montana stock growers filed an additional lawsuit. Although this challenge initially failed, the likelihood of appeal by all the litigants promises to keep western wolf recovery in legal limbo for the indefinite future.[2]

In Canada, where some 90 percent of the country is largely unsettled, hunting, trapping, and wolf control remove between 3 and 8 percent of the wolf population each year, a loss easily overcome by the species' high reproductive rate. At the same time, while Canada's thirty-six national parks support some eighteen wolf packs, few of these packs are entirely protected as wolves seasonally move beyond park boundaries. As recently as 1993 in Algonquin National Park, where Douglas Pimlott conducted Canada's first intensive wolf studies, residents outside the park, angry over depredations of deer by the predators, staged a wolf drive using some thirty snowmobiles. Over half of the park's radio-collared wolves died as a result; one wolf's decapitated head was defiantly impaled on a post as a warning to wolf researchers.[3]

As this confrontation suggests, perhaps the greatest concern is how humanity will accommodate the growing recovery of wolves, with or without human intervention. Based upon present wild prey availability in the remaining roadless areas throughout the conterminous United States, it's possible the nation outside of Alaska could eventually support as many as seven thousand or more wolves. But such an increase may never happen, at least not with federal assistance. In November 1995, the Fish and Wildlife Service revealed that it has no plans to aid the species' recovery in Colorado, Utah, Nevada, California, Washington, or Oregon. Furthermore, once the wolf has reached recovery goals in Wyoming, Idaho, and Montana, the animal will no longer receive federal protection in any of these nine states. Such a move would leave future recovery entirely up to state governments, which under the present political climate doubtlessly means no wolves at all. In Colorado, where studies suggest a majority of residents favor reintroduction and that the state could support some one thousand wolves, the state legislature has repeatedly refused to rescind Colorado's original 1869 wolf bounty law.[4]

In Minnesota, where wolf recovery has been so successful that the animals will probably soon be removed from the endangered species list, a growing number of livestock depredations has resulted in a demand for greater wolf control. In July 1995, the national animal protection group, Friends of Animals, sued the federal government to stop killing depredating wolves and to begin emphasizing nonlethal methods. Soon the state of Minnesota will inherit the problem, one that is only expected to grow as sport hunters also demand a limit to wolf depredations. If Alaska's history of passionate conflict between those who would kill wolves and those who would not is any indication, Minnesota, as well as other states where recovery is succeeding, will soon face growing debate over wolf control.[5]

Yet even with all the potential difficulties confronting the future of wolves, there is no denying that a new public attitude has arrived, one in which many people are allowing and even encouraging wolves to live in closer proximity to them than at any time in recent history. In that respect, the fate of wolves is inextricably woven with that of humanity.

In the words of Yellowstone Park's wolf biologist Michael Phillips, wolf conservation has become "a dramatic expression of the goodness of the human spirit. It shows that we respect the rights of other life-forms, even when they may cause problems. It shows that we are capable and committed to correcting the mistakes of the past. Wolf restoration is a touchstone for measuring our reverence for what we have inherited and for the legacy we leave our children."[6]

Perhaps this then is the greatest achievement of the wolf's return—the rehabilitation of human attitudes toward an animal that the foremost conservation president of the United States once decreed "the beast of waste and desolation." For centuries the wolf *was* North America's beast, an animal transmogrified into a mythic and blood-lustful killer, pursued by every conceivable means, reviled with such savage vehemence that nothing short of wholesale extirpation was imaginable. Today, the symbolic power of the wolf remains while our perception of the animal, as well as ourselves, has vastly changed.

That such a transformation was ever possible at all is the ultimate triumph of wolf recovery.

SOURCE NOTES

Sources provided in the notes are in shortened form; see the bibliography for full citations. Abbreviations are as follows:

ADF&G	Alaska Department of Fish and Game
AMC	Adolph Murie Collection
AMNH	American Museum of Natural History
NARA	National Archives and Records Administration
NPS	National Park Service
OMC	Olaus J. Murie Collection
PARC	Predator Animal and Rodent Control
SYC	Stanley P. Young Collection
USDA	United States Department of Agriculture
USFWS	United States Fish and Wildlife Service
YNPRL	Yellowstone National Park Research Library

1: THE LAST WOLVES (pages 1–14)

1. The story of the Custer wolf is derived from: Bell, "Hunting Down Stock Killers" [gov't. doc.], 297; USDA, *Weekly News Letter* (27 October 1920): 4; USDA, *Weekly News Letter* (26 January 1921): 1, 16; Merritt, "The Custer Wolf," 44; Williams, "The Custer Wolf," 10–11. All quotations attributed to Williams are from his article.

2. Walter, "Wolf Wars," 25; USDA, *Weekly News Letter* (26 January 1921): 1, 16.
3. For a colorful but highly biased account of individual wolves see Stanley Young's *The Last of the Loners*.
4. Mech, *The Wolf*, 43–44.
5. Hall, *Wolf and Man*, 68; Savage, *Wolves*, 109.
6. Bell, "Hunting Down Stock Killers" [gov't. doc.], 295.
7. Gipson, "Wolves and Wolf Literature," 345–53.
8. Lopez, *Of Wolves and Men*, 94–95.
9. Carhart, *The Last Stand of the Pack*, xx, Young, *The Last of the Loners*, 11.
10. USDA, *Weekly News Letter* (26 October 1921): 2.
11. Walter, "Wolf Wars," 25–26.
12. Young, *The Last of the Loners*, 137, 196.
13. Graham, *Animal Outlaws*, 212.
14. Young, *Wolves of North America*, 106.
15. Seton, *Lives of Game Animals*, 1:305.
16. Taylor, "Buffalo Wolves," 150.
17. Shiras, "Wild Life of Lake Superior," 165.
18. Taylor, "Buffalo Wolves," 150; Young, *The Last of the Loners*, 250–74.
19. Seton, *Lives of Game Animals*, 1:307.
20. Carhart, *The Last Stand of the Pack*, 292.

2: EARLY ENCOUNTERS *(pages 15–29)*

1. Tedford, "Key to the Carnivores," 74–76.
2. Hall, "Variability and Speciation in Canids and Hominids," 155; Mech, *The Wolf*, 20.
3. Brewster, "Taxonomy, Genetics, and Status" [gov't. doc.], 3–43; Nowak, *North American Quaternary Canis*, 119, 120; Nowak, "Another Look at Wolf Taxonomy" [manuscript], 2.
4. Stevenson, "Dire Wolf Systematics and Behavior," 179.
5. Ibid., 186; Nowak, "Wolves: The Great Travelers of Evolution," 5–6; Nowak, *Another Look at Wolf Taxonomy*, 29–30.
6. Bower, "Extinctions on Ice," 284–85.
7. Ibid.; Pielou, *After the Ice Age*, 111–12.
8. Stevenson, "Dire Wolf Systematics," 189–90; Van Valkenburgh, "Tough Times in the Tar Pits," 84–85.
9. U.S. Forest Service, *Assessment of the Forest and Range Land Situation in the United States* [gov't. doc.], 168. For a more conservative estimate of buffalo numbers see Flores, "Bison Ecology and Bison Diplomacy," and White, "Animals and Enterprise."
10. Nowak, "A Perspective on the Taxonomy of Wolves in North America," 10–19 passim.
11. Nowak, "Another Look at Wolf Taxonomy" [manuscript], 2.
12. Seton, *Lives of Game Animals*, 1:260–61.

13. All prehistoric wolf population estimates are at best speculative, but present-day wolf densities seem to offer the best method. The author's estimate is derived from James Bednarz's *The Mexican Wolf* [gov't. doc.], 6–8. Of the continent's 9.4 million square miles (msm), approximately 90 percent, or 8.45 msm, was originally inhabited by wolves. This figure was further separated into three general areas: (1) land above U.S.–Canada border [4.23 msm at 1 wolf/61 square miles = approximately 70,000 wolves]; (2) land below U.S.–Canada border, excluding the Great Plains [2.98 msm at 1 wolf/24 square miles = 124,000 wolves]; and (3) the central Great Plains [1.25 msm at 1 wolf/6 square miles = 208,000 wolves]. These three areas total approximately 400,000 wolves. USFWS Wolf Recovery Coordinator Steven Fritts believes the area below the U.S.–Canada border excluding the Great Plains may have harbored as many as 1 wolf/20 square miles. If true, the total number of wolves may have been closer to 425,000. (S. Fritts to author, 17 August 1995.) Notwithstanding this estimate, a preliminary study based on the relatively new science of mitochondrial DNA variability suggests the population of North American wolves may have been as high as one million animals. (Wayne, "Mitochondrial DNA Variability of the Gray Wolf," 565–66.)

14. Peters, "Communication, Cognitive Mapping, and Strategy in Wolves and Hominids," 95–107 passim.

15. Hall, *Wolf and Man,* 68.

16. Peters, "Communication, Cognitive Mapping, and Strategy," 98–99; Canetti, *Crowds and Power,* 96.

17. Crosby, *Ecological Imperialism,* 21; Olsen, *Origins of the Domestic Dog,* 31.

18. Barclay, *Into the Wilderness Dream,* 75.

19. Walker, "Studies on Amerindian Dogs," 126; Harper, *Paul Kane's Frontier,* 272; Young, *Wolves of North America,* 176.

20. *International Wolf,* (Fall 1994): 2.

21. Budiansky, "The Ancient Contract," 76.

22. Ibid.

23. *International Wolf,* (Summer 1994): 10.

24. Schlesier, *The Wolves of Heaven,* 32.

3: SPEAKING FOR WOLF *(pages 30–61)*

1. Clark, *Indian Legends,* 310–12.

2. Schoolcraft, *History of the Indian Tribes,* 1:15–16.

3. Ibid., 5:683.

4. Jonaitis, *Chiefly Feasts,* 77.

5. Schlesier, *The Wolves of Heaven,* 82.

6. Hassrick, *The Sioux,* 92–93.

7. Mooney, *Ghost-Dance Religion* [gov't. doc.], 1093.

8. Lévi-Strauss, *The Naked Man,* 459–60.

9. Curtis, *The North American Indian,* 9:159–61.

10. Weltfish, *The Lost Universe,* 328–29.

11. *Bureau of American Ethnology Bulletin no. 88,* 88.

12. *Bureau of American Ethnology Bulletin no. 27,* 83–85.

13. Lopez, *Of Wolves and Men,* 92.

14. Heckewelder, *History, Manners, and Customs,* 253; Lopez, *Of Wolves and Men,* 105.

15. Jonaitis, *Art of the Northern Tlingit,* 84–85; Garfield, *The Wolf and the Raven,* 5.

16. Peck, *Land of the Eagle,* 106; McIlwraith, *The Bella Coola Indians,* 707–8; Emmons, *Tlingit Indians,* 346.

17. Ray, *Eskimo Masks,* 189–90.

18. McHugh, *The Time of the Buffalo,* 118.

19. Wherry, *The Totem Pole Indians,* 87; Thwaites, *Early American Travels,* 7:305.

20. Grinnell, *When Buffalo Ran,* 82.

21. Utley, *The Lance and the Shield,* 30.

22. Grinnell, *Blackfoot Lodge Tales,* 74–78.

23. Lopez, *Of Wolves and Men,* 105; Thomas, *People of the First Man,* 251.

24. Linderman, *Pretty Shield,* 170–72.

25. Curtis, *The North American Indian,* 18:189; Ross, *The Fur Hunters of the Far West,* 201; Curtis, *The North American Indian,* 4:13.

26. Grinnell, *Blackfoot Lodge Tales,* 198.

27. Chittenden, *Life, Letters and Travels,* 3:940.

28. *Bureau of American Ethnology Annual Report no. 17,* 291; McClintock, *The Old North Trail,* 243.

29. Grinnell, *The Cheyenne Indians,* 2:112; Standing Bear, *Stories of the Sioux,* 3–9 passim.

30. Grinnell, *By Cheyenne Campfires,* 149–53.

31. Ibid., 104–15.

32. *Bureau of American Ethnology Annual Report no. 27,* 171; Theberge, *Wolves and Wilderness,* 74; Nelson, *Make Prayers to the Raven,* 22.

33. Curtis, *The North American Indian,* 11: 68; Ernst, *The Wolf Ritual,* 63–81.

34. Freuchen, *Book of the Eskimos,* 169.

35. Burbank, *Vanishing Lobos,* 46–53.

36. Curtis, *The North American Indian,* 18:51.

37. Grinnell, *Blackfoot Lodge Tales,* 260–61; Schultz, *Blackfeet and Buffalo,* 136.

38. Nelson, *Make Prayers to the Raven,* 159–64; "Wolves." (1851):268.

39. Lopez, *Of Wolves and Men,* 83.

40. Martin, *Keepers of the Game,* 125–27; Muir, *The Writings of John Muir,* 3:138.

41. McHugh, *The Time of the Buffalo,* 82.

42. Walker, *Lakota Belief and Ritual,* 160.

43. Lopez, *Of Wolves and Men,* 65.

44. McHugh, *The Time of the Buffalo,* 85, 93.

45. *Bureau of American Ethnology Annual Report no. 11,* 478.

46. Curtis, *The North American Indian,* 4:185; *Bureau of American Ethnology Annual Report no. 39,* 127.

47. Mails, *Plains Indians,* 334–35; Schlesier, *The Wolves of Heaven,* 3.

48. *Bureau of American Ethnology Annual Report no. 27,* 416–17.

49. Wissler, *Societies of the Plains Indians,* 687.

50. Grinnell, *The Cheyenne Indians,* 2:125.

51. Hassrick, *The Sioux,* 92–93.

52. Wissler, *Societies of the Plains Indians,* 91.

53. *Bureau of American Ethnology Annual Report no. 17,* 291.

54. Wissler, *Societies of the Plains Indians,* 595–96.

55. Lopez, *Of Wolves and Men,* 119; Hampton, *Children of Grace,* 172.

56. Linderman, *Plenty-Coups,* 260–65.

57. *Bureau of American Ethnology Annual Report no. 19,* 489.

58. Emmart, *The Badianus Manuscript,* 54, 281; Curtis, *The North American Indian,* 10:91.

59. *Bureau of American Ethnology Annual Report no. 19,* 266; Thwaites, *Early American Travels,* 23:382.

60. Grinnell, *Blackfoot Lodge Tales,* 283; Grinnell, *By Cheyenne Campfires,* 106.

61. Morgan, *Wilderness at Dawn,* 73.

62. Kalm, *Peter Kalm's Travels,* 150.

63. Martin, *Keepers of the Game,* 131–32.

64. DeVoto, *Across the Wide Missouri,* 283.

65. Jenkinson, *Beasts Beyond the Fire,* 216; Gill, *Dictionary of Native American Mythology,* 9.

66. Novak, *Wild Furbearer Management* [gov't. doc.], 6.

67. Astrov, *American Indian Prose and Poetry,* 88.

68. *Bureau of American Ethnology Annual Report no. 19,* 265.

69. *Bureau of American Ethnology Annual Report no. 9,* 263–64.

70. Curtis, *The North American Indian,* 10:91, 99.

71. Nelson, *Make Prayers to the Raven,* 159–64.

72. Cowie, *The Company of Adventurers,* 250–52.

73. *Bureau of American Ethnology Bulletin no. 146,* 124; Cowie, *The Company of Adventurers,* 250–52.

74. *Bureau of American Ethnology Bulletin no. 171,* 268–69.

75. Schultz, *Recently Discovered Tales,* 38–40.

76. Seton, *Lives of Game Animals,* 309–10; Davies, *Peter Skene Ogden's Snake Country Journal,* 113; Thwaites, *Early American Travels,* 24:21.

77. Spencer, *Who Speaks for Wolf?,* 36–37.

4: RAVENING RANGERS *(pages 62–79)*

1. Cook, *The Voyages of Jacques Cartier,* 85.

2. Biggar, *The Works of Samuel De Champlain,* 1:423.

3. Ibid., 5:308; Theberge, *Wolves and Wilderness,* 74.

4. Freeman, *The History of Cape Cod,* 2:132; Carroll, *Puritanism,* 208–9; Demos, *The Unredeemed Captive,* 12.

5. Matheson, "The Grey Wolf" (1943): 11–18 passim; Leopold, "Predator and Rodent Control" [gov't. doc.], 1; Fogleman, "American Attitudes Toward Wolves" (1989): 76–77.

6. DiSilvestro, *Fight for Survival,* 18; Fogleman, "American Attitudes Toward Wolves," (1989): 76–77; Matheson, "The Grey Wolf" (1943): 13.

7. Matheson, "The Grey Wolf" (1943): 13.

8. Hillaby, "Wolf" (October 1967): 143; Trefethen, "Another Vanishing American," (January 1959): 17.

9. Matt. 10:6; Fogleman, "American Attitudes Toward Wolves" (1989): 6; Nash, *Wilderness and the American Mind,* 29.

10. Fogleman, "American Attitudes Toward Wolves" (1989): 65; Matthiessen, *Wildlife in America,* 58; Theberge, *Wolves and Wilderness,* 73.

11. Faragher, *Daniel Boone,* 131–32.

12. Cronon, *Changes in the Land,* 24; Matthiessen, *Wildlife in America,* 57.

13. Matthiessen, *Wildlife in America,* 63.

14. Arnold, *History of the State of Rhode Island,* 1:161; Wentworth, *America's Sheep Trails,* 470.

15. Fogleman, "American Attitudes Toward Wolves" (1989): 65.

16. Wood, *New England's Prospect,* 18.

17. Thompson, *Natural History of Vermont,* 34; Clayton, *Clayton's Virginia,* 3:35.

18. Wentworth, *America's Sheep Trails,* 471.

19. Young, *Wolves of North America,* 38; Matthiessen, *Wildlife in America,* 57–58.

20. Matthiessen, *Wildlife in America,* 57; Trefethen, *An American Crusade for Wildlife,* 35.

21. Young, *Wolves of North America,* 351.

22. Wentworth, *America's Sheep Trails,* 471; Earle, *Home Life In Colonial Days,* 366–67.

23. Cooper, *A Guide in the Wilderness,* 23.

24. Nash, *Wilderness and the American Mind,* 37; Cronon, *Changes in the Land,* 199.

25. Matthiessen, *Wildlife in America,* 57.

26. Cronon, *Changes in the Land,* 199–200.

27. Ibid., 133.

28. Goble, "Of Wolves and Welfare Ranching" (1992): 103.

29. Rountree, *Pocahontas's People,* 96.

30. Matthiessen, *Wildlife in America,* 58.

31. Nowak, "The Mysterious Wolf of the South" (January 1972): 53.

32. Young, *Wolves of North America,* 39; Arnold, *History of the State of Rhode Island,* 1:154; Rider, *The Lands of Rhode Island,* 34.

33. Beals, *Passaconaway in the White Mountains,* 269.

34. Trefethen, *An American Crusade for Wildlife,* 37.

35. Tyrell, *David Thompson's Narrative,* 42–43.

36. Dutcher, "Old-time Natural History" (March 1887): 105–6.

37. Byrd, *The Writings of Colonel William Byrd,* 78; Trefethen, *An American Crusade for Wildlife,* 36.

38. Humphreys, *An Essay on . . . Major General Putnam,* 19–23.

39. Cronon, *Changes in the Land,* 133.

40. Young, *Wolves of North America,* 174; Barton, "On Indian Dogs" (1803): 6.
41. Washington, *Letters . . . to Arthur Young,* 39.
42. Ibid., 41.
43. Ibid., 82.
44. Ibid., 129.
45. Ibid.
46. Fogleman, "American Attitudes Toward Wolves" (1989): 68.
47. Aulerich, "The Wolf" (November 1966): 10–13; Theberge, *Wolves and Wilderness,* 33.
48. Matthiessen, *Wildlife in America,* 58.

5: SHARK OF THE PLAINS *(pages 80–101)*

1. Young, *Wolves of North America,* 210; Webster, *A Compendious Dictionary,* 352.
2. Bartram, *Travels,* 157.
3. Ibid.
4. Novak, *Furbearer Harvests in North America* [gov't. doc.], 245–46.
5. Thomas, *People of the First Man,* 243; Burroughs, *The Natural History,* 87; Cox, *The Columbia River,* 239.
6. Barclay, *Into the Wilderness Dream,* 75; Gunson, "Status and Management of Wolves in Alberta" [gov't. doc.], 25.
7. Burroughs, *The Natural History,* 85, 86, 89.
8. DiSilvestro, *Fight for Survival,* 24; Thwaites, *Early American Travels,* 22:36; Hastings, *The Emigrant Guide,* 98.
9. Hoffman, *Winter in the West,* 1:18–19.
10. Audubon, *The Quadrupeds of North America,* 2:159, 160; Brown, *The Wolf in the Southwest,* 15.
11. Fritts, "The Relationship of Wolf Recovery to Habitat Conservation" (1994): 24.
12. Russell, *Journal of a Trapper,* 129–30; Brown, *The Wolf in the Southwest,* 15–16.
13. Thwaites, *Early American Travels,* 24:120; McKechnie, *Webster's . . . Dictionary,* 1226; Coues, "The Quadrupeds of Arizona" (1867): 288.
14. Burroughs, *The Natural History,* 86.
15. Chittenden, *The American Fur Trade,* 2: 830; Burroughs, *The Natural History,* 86; Roe, *The North American Buffalo,* 158; Russell, *Journal,* 110.
16. Coues, *The Journal of Jacob Fowler,* 141; Harper, *Paul Kane's Frontier,* 80.
17. Merritt, *Baronets and Buffalo,* 62.
18. Ibid., 66–67.
19. Sage, *Scenes in the Rocky Mountains,* 197; Greeley, *An Overland Journey,* 93–94.
20. Hastings, *The Emigrant Guide,* 98; Ferris, *Life in the Rocky Mountains,* 162; Thwaites, *Early American Travels,* 7:190.
21. McDermott, *Up the Missouri,* 137; Peattie, *Audubon's America,* 301–2.
22. McDermott, *Up the Missouri,* 137.
23. Hafen, *Fremont's Fourth Expedition,* 162–63.
24. Ibid.; Young, *Wolves of North America,* 216.

25. DeVoto, *Across the Wide Missouri,* 372.

26. Hebard, *The Bozeman Trail,* 98.

27. Blevins, *Dictionary of the American West,* 212; Hutton, *The Custer Reader,* 157.

28. Burroughs, *The Natural History,* 87.

29. Report of Lt. J. W. Abert, *House Executive Documents,* 30th Cong., 1847–48, 543.

30. Schultz, *Blackfeet and Buffalo,* 165; Carrington, *My Army Life,* 97.

31. Sage, *Scenes in the Rocky Mountains,* 1:193; Condit, "The Hole-in-the-Wall," (October 1956): 158.

32. Matthiessen, *North American Indians,* 268; Schultz, *Many Strange Characters,* 6; Thomas, *People of the First Man,* 152; Thwaites, *Early American Travels,* 28: 284.

33. Russell, *Journal of a Trapper,* 129–30; Cox, *The Columbia River,* 241; Cowie, *The Company of Adventurers,* 250, 252.

34. Beard, "The American Black Wolf" (July 1892): 41.

35. Gohdes, *Hunting in the Old South,* 83–86 passim.

36. Dodge, *The Hunting Grounds,* 209.

37. Bogue, "An Agricultural Empire," in Milner, *The Oxford History of the American West,* 283.

38. Jenkinson, *Beasts Beyond the Fire,* 215.

39. Grinnell, *The Cheyenne Indians,* 2:174–75.

40. Gregg, *Commerce of the Prairies,* 376.

41. Ibid., 375.

42. DeVoto, *Across the Wide Missouri,* 104–6.

43. Dodge, *The Hunting Grounds,* 97–98.

44. Sage, *Scenes in the Rocky Mountains,* 1:193.

45. Blevins, *Dictionary of the American West,* 102–3; Hughes, *American Indians in Colorado,* 58.

46. Schultz, *Over the Earth I Come,* 258.

47. Wissler, *Societies of the Plains Indians,* 873; Josephy, *The Great West,* 156; Britton, *The Truth About Geronimo,* 50.

48. Burroughs, *The Natural History,* 86.

49. McHugh, *The Time of the Buffalo,* 240; Harper, *Paul Kane's Frontier,* 148.

50. U.S. Forest Service, *Assessment of the Forest and Range Land Situation in the United States* [gov't. doc.], 168. For a lower population estimate, see Dan Flores, "Bison Ecology and Bison Diplomacy," (September 1991): 465–81; Mech, *The Wolf,* 184.

51. Sage, *Scenes in the Rocky Mountains,* 1:194.

52. Ibid., 2:192.

53. Chittenden, *Life, Letters and Travels of Father DeSmet,* 2:603; Cox, *The Columbia River,* 214–15.

54. McHugh, *The Time of the Buffalo,* 225; Burroughs, *The Natural History,* 84; McHugh, *The Time of the Buffalo,* 227; ibid., 187.

55. Young, *Wolves of North America,* 230.

56. DeVoto, *Across the Wide Missouri,* 39.

57. Schultz, *Blackfeet and Buffalo,* 166–67.

58. Sage, *Scenes in the Rocky Mountains,* 1:194; Gregg, *Commerce of the Prairies,* 374–75.

59. Sage, *Scenes in the Rocky Mountains,* 1:194; Boller, *Among the Indians,* 270, 272.

60. Catlin, *Letters and Notes,* 257–58.

61. Ibid., 254.

6: CIVILIZATION'S ENEMY *(pages 102–126)*

1. Brown, *The Wolf in the Southwest,* 14; Wentworth, *America's Sheep Trails,* 471.

2. Ibid., 472; Peirce, "Great Hinckley Hunt," 43, 46, 47.

3. Wentworth, *America's Sheep Trails,* 472; Petersen, "Wolves in Iowa" (December 1960): 523; Young, *Wolves of North America,* 88.

4. Bryant, *Rocky Mountain Adventures,* 132; Jones, *Forty Years among the Indians,* 75–76.

5. Flint, *Diary,* 82–84.

6. Young, *Wolves of North America,* 258.

7. Hastings, *The Emigrant Guide,* 98; Young, *The Wolf in North American History,* 91, 94.

8. Alexander, "Stewardship and Enterprise" (Autumn 1994): 345, 354.

9. Dodge, *The Hunting Grounds,* 210.

10. McHugh, *The Time of the Buffalo,* 283.

11. Ibid., 254, 268.

12. Gregg, *Commerce of the Prairies,* 374–75.

13. McHugh, *The Time of the Buffalo,* 253; Dodge, *Hunting Grounds,* 133.

14. Matthiessen, *Wildlife in America,* 152; Koch, "Big Game in Montana" (October 1941): 365.

15. Schultz, *Many Strange Characters,* 6.

16. Young, *Wolves of North America,* 224.

17. McGowan, *Animals of the Canadian Rockies,* 28.

18. Curnow, "History" [master's thesis], 30.

19. Brown, *The Wolf in the Southwest,* 14; Young, *Wolves of North America,* 326–27.

20. Stelfox, "Wolves in Alberta" 12 (1969): 19.

21. Quaife, *Yellowstone Kelly,* 120.

22. Curnow, "History" [master's thesis], 30.

23. Brown, *The Frontier Years,* 80–81.

24. Seton, "Trail of an Artist-Naturalist," 74; Taylor, "Twenty Years on the Trap Line," 57–58.

25. Grinnell, *Two Great Scouts,* 28–31; Cowie, *The Company of Adventurers,* 250–52.

26. Grinnell, *The Wolf Hunters,* 150–63.

27. Hebard, *The Bozeman Trail,* 126; Carrington, *My Army Life,* 97.

28. MacInnes, *In the Shadow of the Rockies,* 66–67.

29. Ibid., 67.

30. Novak, *Furbearer Harvests* [gov't. doc.], 246; Matthiessen, *Wildlife in America,* 156.

31. Novak, *Furbearer Harvests* [gov't. doc.], 246; Grinnell, *The Wolf Hunters,* 286. Previously reported annual wolf harvests during this period of between 55,000 and 100,000 for Montana (Walter, "Wolf Wars," 23; Curnow, "History," 31) appear to be in error. Both estimates fail to provide sources, and may have inadvertently included coyote harvests. (D. Walter to author, 28 February 1995.)

32. Weaver, *The Wolves of Yellowstone* [gov't. doc.], 7.

33. Young, *Wolves of North America,* 333; Allen, "Notes" (1874): 45; Bennett, *Colorado Gray Wolf Recovery* [gov't. doc.], 180.

34. White, "Animals and Enterprise," 252, 257; Lee, *Last Grass Frontier,* 122.

35. Hassrick, "The Wyoming Cowboy's Evolving Image" (Winter 1993–94): 11; Lee, *Last Grass Frontier,* 12.

36. Stuart, *Forty Years on the Frontier,* 2:150.

37. Curnow, "History" [master's thesis], 46–49; White, "Animals and Enterprise," 266.

38. Ibid., 269.

39. Young, *Wolves of North America,* 151; Nelson, *The Cowman's Southwest,* 231; Novak, *Furbearer Harvests* [gov't. doc.], 246.

40. Brown, *The Wolf in the Southwest,* 41–42.

41. White, "Animals and Enterprise," 266–67.

42. King, *Reasons for the Decline,* 74; Bennett, *Colorado Gray Wolf Recovery* [gov't. doc.], 181; Young, *The Wolf in North American History,* 122.

43. Curnow, "History" (master's thesis), 60; Young, *The Wolf in North American History,* 117; Grinnell, *The Cheyenne Indians,* 2: 212; Young, *Wolves of North America,* 379.

44. Brown, *The Wolf in the Southwest,* 42.

45. *Wyoming Legislative History* [gov't. doc.], 1; Adams, "North Dakota Bounty Data" [manuscript], 1; Curnow, "History" [master's thesis], 42.

46. Curnow, "History" [master's thesis], 59; Corbin, *Corbin's Advice,* 22–23; *Big Horn Sentinel,* 29 November 1884.

47. Young, *Wolves of North America,* 360.

48. "Minutes of the Nineteenth Annual Convention of the Wyoming Woolgrowers Association, 1922," 37.

49. "Montana Wolves and Panthers" (July 1886): 508.

50. Stuart, *Forty Years,* 2:172.

51. Brown, *The Wolf in the Southwest,* 31.

52. Ibid., 36.

53. Grinnell, *The Cheyenne Indians,* 216–17.

54. Graham, *Animal Outlaws,* 42.

55. Carhart, "World Champion Wolfer" (September 1939): 22–23, 74–75.

56. Bowman, "Wolves" [manuscript], 30, 42, 47.

57. Palmer, "Extermination of Noxious Animals" [gov't. doc.], 58.

58. Wyoming. Session Laws . . . 1905 [gov't. doc.], 31, 33; Palmer, "Extermination of Noxious Animals," 63.

59. Huidekoper, "The Wolf Question" [manuscript], 2–4.

60. *Montana Bounty Certificate Record,* 1883–1918 passim; Wyoming State Auditor's Reports, 1895–1897 and 1900–1918 passim.
61. Hornaday, *The American Natural History,* 23; Roosevelt, *The Wilderness Hunter,* 532.
62. *The River Press* (Fort Benton, Montana), 5 December 1899.
63. Corbin, *Corbin's Advice,* ii.

7: KILLING FOR BLOOD LUST *(pages 127–146)*

1. Thornton, *American Indian Holocaust,* 133; U.S. Forest Service, *An Assessment of the Forest and Range Land Situation in the United States* [gov't. doc.], 168.
2. Burroughs, *Camping and Tramping,* 4.
3. Roosevelt, *The Wilderness Hunter,* 305; Hornaday, *Wild Animal Interviews,* 295; Hornaday, *The Minds and Manners of Wild Animals,* 223, 269; Hornaday, *The American Natural History,* 22.
4. Salt, *Animals' Rights,* 54.
5. Long, "The Sociology of a Wolf Pack" (June 1909): 1179–85; Mighetto, *Wild Animals,* 78.
6. Seton, "Lobo, King of the Currumpaw" (November 1894): 618–28.
7. Seton, *Great Historic Animals,* 236; Seton, *Lives of Game Animals,* 319. For a comprehensive review of early twentieth-century literature concerning animals see Dunlap, *Saving America's Wildlife,* 22–33, and Mighetto, *Wild Animals,* 1–26.
8. Bad, *The Life and Letters of John Muir,* 1:122; Ibid., 2:248–50; Muir, *John Muir: Wilderness Essays,* 23.
9. Hunt, "The Wake of the Wolves" (November 1901): 458–61.
10. Shoemaker, *Wolf Days in Pennsylvania,* 9, 11, 62.
11. USDA, *Report of the Secretary of Agriculture, 1906* [gov't. doc.], 7.
12. Bailey, Papers, Box 7, Folder 21; *Washington Post* 6 December 1908.
13. USDA, *Report of the Secretary of Agriculture, 1907* [gov't. doc.], 5.
14. Ibid., 1908, 4; Bailey, Papers, Box 7, Folder 21; ibid., Box 5, Folder 12.
15. *Chicago Sunday Tribune* (undated), Bailey, Papers, Box 6, Folder 5; Wilson, "The Wolves Are Always After Us!" (February 1937): 38.
16. *Chicago Record Herald,* 26 May 1908; *Woman's National Daily,* 23 May 1908.
17. Sterling, *Last of the Naturalists,* 339.
18. Matheson, "The Grey Wolf" 17 (1943): 15; USDA, *Yearbook of the Department of Agriculture, 1916* [gov't. doc.], 29.
19. "Resolutions Adopted at the 18th Annual Conference of the American National Livestock Association, 24, 25, and 26 March 1915," 6; USDA, *Report of the Secretary of Agriculture, 1916* [gov't. doc.], 1.
20. USDA, *Report of the Secretary of Agriculture, 1916* [gov't. doc.], 1.
21. King, *Reasons for the Decline,* 40.
22. USDA, *Yearbook of the Department of Agriculture, 1907* [gov't. doc.], 560–65; Wyoming State Auditor's Report 1913–14, 31; PARC Annual Reports 1915, 1916, RG 22, Entry 232, NARA; Wyoming Department of Agriculture, *Wyoming Legislative History* [gov't. doc.], 3; Huidekoper, "The Wolf Question" [manuscript], 3.

23. Young, *The Wolf in North American History,* 135; Petersen, "Wolves in Iowa" (December 1960): 558–59; Young, *Wolves of North America,* 338.

24. Curnow, "History" [master's thesis], 75–83.

25. *Wyoming State Journal,* 17 August 1917.

26. PARC Annual Reports 1915–1918, RG 22, Entry 232, NARA.

27. Mech, *The Wolf,* 285; USDA, *Report of the Secretary of Agriculture, 1922* [gov't. doc.], 6; Brown, *Wolf in the Southwest,* 69; USDA, *Weekly News Letter* (23 October 1918): 5.

28. USDA, *Report of the Secretary of Agriculture, 1920* [gov't. doc.], 2; Gerstell, *The Steel Trap,* 198, 203, 214, 297.

29. Brown, *The Wolf in the Southwest,* 58, 60, 64, 70.

30. USDA, *Report of the Secretary of Agriculture, 1922* [gov't. doc.], 4; USDA, *The Official Record* (5 March 1924): 6.

31. Grinnell, "Animal Life" (September 1916): 375–80.

32. Dunlap, *Saving America's Wildlife,* 50–51.

33. Ibid., 53–54.

34. A. Howell to P. Redington, undated letter, OMC, Box 265.

35. Cameron, *The Bureau of Biological Survey,* 177–78; Address delivered before PARC field agents 23 April 1928 in "Records of Conferences, 1928–1941," RG 22, Entry 158, NARA; Cameron, *The Bureau of Biological Survey,* 51–52.

36. Grinnell, *Hunting and Conservation,* 201–2.

37. Heller, "The Big Game Animals of Yellowstone" (1925): 430.

38. Skinner, "The Predatory and Fur-Bearing Animals," 292–296 passim.

39. Weaver, *The Wolves of Yellowstone* [gov't. doc.], 9; Bailey, *Animal Life,* 135; Yellowstone National Park, "Monthly Report for May 1922" [gov't. doc.], 18–19. .

40. Weaver, *The Wolves of Yellowstone* [gov't. doc.], 9; Albright, "The National Park Service's Policy" (May 1931): 185–86.

41. Wright, *Fauna* [gov't. doc.], 54, 2.

42. Redington, Address delivered before the convention of the National Wool Growers' Association, Colorado Springs, Colorado, 10–12 December 1930, in "Federal Program" (1931): 6–7; USDA, *Report of the Secretary of Agriculture, 1931* [gov't. doc.], 27.

43. *Cong. Rec.,* 71st Cong., 2d sess., 1929, 72, no. 12 (14 December 1929): 701–2.

44. Ibid.

45. Young, *The Wolf in North American History,* 7; S. Young to A. Carhart, 24 November 1930, SYC, Box 325.

46. Senate Committee on Agriculture and Forestry, *Hearings on Control of Predatory Animals (S. 3483),* 71st Cong., 2d and 3d sess., 8 May 1930 and 28, 29 January 1931, 21.

47. Ibid., 6–7; Day, *Wild Life Conservation* [gov't. doc.], 4.

48. Senate Committee on Agriculture and Forestry, *Hearings on Control of Predatory Animals (S. 3483),* 71st Cong., 2d and 3d sess., 8 May 1930 and 28, 29 January 1931, 98.

49. Ibid., 128.

50. PARC Annual Reports 1915–1964, RG 22, Entry 232, NARA.

8: TURNING THE TIDE *(pages 147–174)*

1. Limerick, *Legacy of Conquest,* 88.

2. Anthony, "The Control of Predatory Mammals" (September 1931): 288–90.

3. Goldman, "The Control of Injurious Animals" (March 1932): 309–11.

4. O. Murie, "Description of Game in Parts of Alaska" in OMC, Box 265, 7.

5. O. Murie, "Report on Investigations of Predatory Animal Poisoning in Wyoming and Colorado" in OMC, Box 265, 20, 22.

6. Kendrick, "An Environmental Spokesman," 259; A. Howell to O. Murie, 26 May 1931, 15 June 1931 and O. Murie to W. Henderson, 9 January 1931 in OMC, Box 265; O. Murie to A. Howell, 7 May 1931, Department of Mammology, AMNH.

7. O. Murie to M. Hildebrand, 28 August 1950 and O. Murie to W. Sanderson, 3 February 1935 in OMC, Box 265; O. Murie to O. Geist, 17 September 1936, Otto Geist Collection, Box 16.

8. Brandenburg, *Brother Wolf,* 134, 160, 159; Link, *The Collected Works of Sigurd F. Olson,* 103.

9. Leopold, "The Varmint Question," 188, 189; Leopold, "The Game Situation in the Southwest," *Bulletin of the American Game Protective Association,* (1920): 5.

10. Leopold, *A Sand County Almanac,* 138–39.

11. Dunlap, *Saving America's Wildlife,* 89; Leopold, *A Sand County Almanac,* 140.

12. Leopold, *Game Management,* 252; Leopold, *A Sand County Almanac,* 262; Leopold, "Review of *The Wolves of North America*" (1944): 928–29.

13. Flader, *Thinking Like a Mountain,* 211–12; Leopold, *A Sand County Almanac,* 137.

14. Dunlap, *Saving America's Wildlife,* 73–74.

15. Ibid., 65–67.

16. Graham, *Animal Outlaws,* 243; Stanwell-Fletcher, "Three Years in the Wolves' Wilderness" (March 1942): 103–9.

17. R. Stewart, untitled Alaska PARC report (1929), "Records relating to Alaska 1922–49," RG 22, Entry 181, NARA.

18. H. Albright to W. Bell, 16 November 1931, RG 79, Entry 7, Box 1415, Folder 719, NARA; Gabler, "The Wolf Pack" (January 1935): 16–17.

19. Wright, *Fauna* [gov't. doc.], 147–48.

20. R. Pough to V. Cahalane, 11 March 1938, RG 79, Entry 7, Box 1415, Folder 719, NARA; Rawson, "Adolph Murie, 1899–1974: A Master Naturalist" [manuscript], 6.

21. Klinghammer, "Introduction" in *Behavior and Ecology of Wolves,* n.p.; Murie, *Wolves of Mount McKinley* [gov't. doc.], 24–25, 26–27, 30–31, 230.

22. Dufresne, *Alaska's Animals and Fishes,* 80–83.

23. *Cong. Rec.,* 79th Cong., 1st sess., 1945, 91, pt. 3: 3283; G. Pearson to Regional Director, 5 November 1945, RG 79, Entry 7, Box 1414, Folder 715, NARA.

24. A. Murie, "Review of the Mountain Sheep Situation in Mount McKinley National Park, Alaska, 1945," 9 October 1945, Box 7, AMC; A. Murie journal, 12 September 1946, Box 12, Folder "1946 Alaska Trip," AMC; A. Leopold to N. Drury, 6 November 1945, N. Drury to H. Ickes, 31 October 1945, RG 79, Entry 7, Box 1414, Folder 715, NARA.

25. House Committee on the Public Lands, *Hearings on Protection of Wildlife in Mount McKinley National Park (H. R. 5004 and 5401),* 79th Cong., 2d sess., 3 April 1946 and 22 May 1946, 1, 20, 22, 51–55.

26. Rawson, "Alaska's First Wolf Controversy" [master's thesis], 228–29; A. Murie, "Wolf Diary '48–'50," 9 December 1949, Box "Field Notes on Wolves," AMC.

27. Rawson, "Alaska's First Wolf Controversy," [master's thesis], 245. Rawson's comprehensive thesis provides the best scholarly treatment of this period of wolf control in McKinley Park.

28. O'Connor, *Hunting in the Rockies,* 211, 214; Zepp, "America's Longest War" (May 1948): 38–41, 118–20.; Dufresne, "Ghosts That Kill Game," (April 1948): 37.

29. A. Williams to Supervisor, "Records relating to Alaska 1922–49," RG 22, Entry 181, NARA.

30. Rearden, "Alaska's Boom-to-Bust Reindeer Saga" (September 1974): 9; Rawson, "Alaska's First Wolf Controversy" [master's thesis], 64.

31. Fourteenth Annual Report (1938–1939) of the Alaska Game Commission [gov't. doc.], 90.

32. Washington, D.C., *Daily News,* 6 August 1943.

33. PARC Annual Report 1951, RG 22, Entry 232, NARA; Rearden, "Alaska's Boom-to-Bust Reindeer Saga" (September 1974): 76.

34. Rawson, "Alaska's First Wolf Controversy" [master's thesis], 240.

35. "Records relating to Alaska 1922–49," RG 22, Entry 158, NARA.

36. Dunlap, *Saving America's Wildlife,* 114, 117.

37. Brown, *The Wolf in the Southwest,* 107.

38. J. Buckley to author, 12 December 1993.

39. Hammond, "Strafing Arctic Killers" (February 1955): 37–39, 111–114.; R. Rausch to O. Murie, 10 January 1953, Box 265, OMC.

40. PARC Annual Reports 1915–1964, RG 22, Entry 232, NARA.

41. Nowak, "The Gray Wolf in North America" [manuscript], 90; Hillaby, "Wolf" (October 1967): 144.

42. Stelfox, "Wolves in Alberta" (1969): 21; Nowak, "The Gray Wolf in North America" [manuscript], 66–79.

43. Nowak, "The Gray Wolf in North America" [manuscript], 49–66; Pimlott, "Wolves and Men in North America" (January–March 1967): 40.

44. Nowak, "The Gray Wolf in North America" [manuscript], 15–42.

45. This figure is based primarily on a compilation of estimated wolf populations in both Alaska and Canada during the 1940s and 1950s in Nowak's "The Gray Wolf in North America." Nowak suggests that the continent's wolf population may have recovered by 1974 to as many as 35,000 animals (227); Pimlott, "Wolf Control in Canada" (1961): 145.

46. Carbyn, "Canada's 50,000 Wolves" (Winter 1994): 3.

47. Pimlott, "Wolf Control in Canada" (1961): 146.

48. Caras, *The Custer Wolf,* 30, 59.

49. Pimlott, "Wolves and Men in North America" (January–March 1967): 43.

50. Ibid., 40, 42, 43.

51. Dunlap, *Saving America's Wildlife,* 148.

52. PARC Annual Reports 1915–1964, RG 22, Entry 232, NARA.

53. Ibid.

54. R. Nowak to L. Parker, 27 December 1963, RG 22, Entry 230, Folder "General Correspondence," NARA; Young, "It's Red, But Truly All-American" (January 1968): 57.

55. Dunlap, *Saving America's Wildlife,* 127.

56. Leopold, "Predator and Rodent Control" [gov't. doc.], 6, 15.

57. Cain, *Predator Control—1971* [gov't. doc.], 2, 11, 29.

58. *Predator Project Newsletter* (Summer 1994): 11.

59. Dunlap, *Saving America's Wildlife,* 163–64.

9: RETURN OF THE NATIVE *(pages 175–193)*

1. Kellert, "Public Perceptions of Predators" (1985): 167–89.

2. Carbyn, "A Wolf Manifesto" (1979): 18–22; Joseph Fontaine, 10 March 1995, "Wolves and Humans 2000" wolf symposium, 9–11 March 1995, Duluth, Minnesota.

3. Chadwick, "Dead or Alive" (March 1995): 9.

4. Bierstedt, "Wolf Hatred" (October 1975): 72; the *New York Times,* 14 June 1972.

5. Dunlap, *Saving America's Wildlife,* 153–54.

6. Ibid., 154. According to the U.S. Fish and Wildlife Service, the cost of wolf recovery programs will total $36 million for the forty-year period from 1972 to 2012. (*Casper Star Tribune,* 1 February 1996.)

7. Ibid., 177–78 n. 2.

8. The following account of the red wolf is drawn primarily from: Nowak, "The Mysterious Wolf of the South" (January 1972): 50–53; Nowak, "Red Wolf" (August 1974): 9–12; Shaw, "The Wolf That Lost Its Genes" (December 1977): 80–88; Rennie, "Howls of Dismay" (October 1991): 18–19.

9. *Red Wolf Newsletter,* (Summer/Fall 1995): 5.

10. Wayne, "Mitochondrial DNA Variability of the Gray Wolf" (December 1992): 559–69; Manuel, "Red Wolf Showdown" (March/April 1995): 22–24; *Red Wolf Newsletter,* (Summer/Fall 1994): 1–2.

11. Manuel, "Red Wolf Showdown" (March/April 1995): 22–24. The only other two potential areas for red wolves—Georgia's Okefenokee Swamp and Florida's Everglades—have been temporarily rejected due to possible conflicts between red wolves and Florida panthers, a species scientists believe is even more at risk. (Dietz, "Initial Investigation of . . . Wolf Reintroduction," [manuscript], 22–23.)

12. The following account of the eastern gray wolf is drawn primarily from: Van Ballenberghe, "Wolf Management in Minnesota," 313–22; Fuller, "History and Current Estimate of Wolf Distribution" (1992): 42–55. Recently there has been a growing consensus that Minnesota's wolf population is more closely related to *nubilus* than to populations of *lycaon* in southeastern Canada. (Nowak, "Another Look at Wolf Taxonomy" [manuscript], 21.)

13. Kolenosky, "Morphological and Ecological Variation," 62–72; Nowak, "Another Look at Wolf Taxonomy" [manuscript], 3; Purrett, "The Last Cry of the Wolf" (February 1973): 109.

14. Fuller, "A History and Current Estimate of Wolf Distribution" (1992): 42.

15. Erickson, "The Wolf Men" (Fall 1972): 26–30.

16. Hook, "Attitudes of Michigan Citizens Toward Predators," 382–94.

17. Bierstedt, "Wolf Hatred" (October 1975): 67, 73–74; Schneider, "Is There Room for the Wolf?" (August 1980): 104; the *New York Times,* 30 July 1973.

18. USFWS, *Recovery Plan for the Eastern Timber Wolf* [gov't. doc.], preface; Bierstedt, "Wolf Hatred" (October 1975): 73–74; *Chicago Tribune,* 20 August 1978.

19. Nevin, "Revered and Reviled" (January 1985): 79–86.

20. Fritts, "Trends and Management of Wolf–Livestock Conflicts" [gov't. doc.], 1–28.

21. Paul, "Trends and Management," 8.

22. USFWS, *Mexican Wolf Recovery Plan* [gov't. doc.], 2.

23. Brown, *The Wolf in the Southwest,* 106.

24. Ibid., 114–15.

25. McBride, *The Mexican Wolf* [gov't. doc.], 33.

26. USFWS, *Mexican Wolf Recovery Plan* [gov't. doc.], 9–10, 23–24.

27. Ibid., 16–21.

28. Arizona Game and Fish Department, "Mexican Wolf Study Public Review Draft" [gov't. doc.], 3–4; *The Arizona Daily Star,* 22 July 1987.

29. *The Arizona Daily Star,* 22 July 1987. See Bednarz, *An Evaluation of the Ecological Potential of White Sands Missile Range* [gov't. doc.] for the initial study results.

30. Arizona Game and Fish Department, "Mexican Wolf Study Public Review Draft" [gov't. doc.], 5.

31. Ibid.

32. Ibid., 6.

33. Brown, "Back from the Brink of Extinction" (Spring 1995): 3–7.

34. USFWS, *Reintroduction of the Mexican Wolf Within Its Historic Range in the Southwestern United States—DEIS,* Washington, D.C.: GPO, 1995.

35. *High Country News,* 19 February 1996, 20 January 1997.

10: SYMBOL OF THE WEST *(pages 194–225)*

1. Investigation and Arrest Report No. 43626, Livingston Police Department, 22 May 1988, 1–2; *Casper Star Tribune,* 27 May 1988; D. Palmisciano to D. Johnson, 28 June 1988, Montana Department of Fish, Wildlife, and Parks, Helena.

2. R. Nowak to D. Palmisciano, 14 June 1988, Office of the Scientific Authority, USFWS; Bass, *The Ninemile Wolves,* 14.

3. R. Nowak to author, 15 March 1993; Day, "The Status and Distribution of Wolves" [master's thesis], 90–91; Ream, "Wolf Status in the Northern Rockies," 376–79.

4. Ream, "Wolf Status in the Northern Rockies," 364.

5. USFWS, *Northern Rocky Mountain Wolf Recovery Plan* [gov't. doc.], 1980.

6. Ibid.

7. Schneider, "Is There Room for the Wolf?" (August 1980): 52. For a synopsis of the grizzly controversy, see Clark, *Greater Yellowstone's Future,* 84–89.

8. J. Hoover to ADC State Supervisor Rightmire, 18 January 1982; H. Fischer to author, 10 July 1995.

9. Cole, "The Elk of Grand Teton" [manuscript], 134.

10. Cole, "Yellowstone Wolves" [manuscript], April 1971.

11. G. Cole to Superintendent, 11 April 1960, YNPRL; Steinhart, *The Company of Wolves,* 249.

12. Weaver, *The Wolves of Yellowstone* [gov't. doc.], 3, 15; G. Cole to Superintendent, 11 April 1960, YNPRL.

13. D. Randall to author, 26 May 1993; Steinhart, *The Company of Wolves,* 247–48.

14. A. S. Leopold to D. Allen, 7 January 1976, and D. Allen to A. S. Leopold, 15 January 1976 (obtained through the Freedom of Information Act from the NPS).

15. House Subcommittee on Public Lands and National Parks, *Public Land Management Policy,* 98th Cong., 1st sess., 24 February 1983, Serial no. 98-8, pt. 1., 15.

16. Davis, "Ranchers Want Right to Hunt Wolves" (19 March 1988): 707–8.

17. McNamee, "Yellowstone's Missing Element" (January 1986): 14.

18. Ibid.; Fischer, *Wolf Wars,* 74.

19. USFWS, *Northern Rocky Mountain Wolf Recovery Plan* [gov't. doc.], 1987.

20. Fischer, *Wolf Wars,* 85–86.

21. Chase, *Playing God in Yellowstone,* 140–41.

22. Fischer, "Deep Freeze for Wolf Recovery?" (November/December 1987): 29–33; Steinhart, "A Wolf in the Eye" (January 1988): 83.

23. *Casper Star Tribune,* 20 August 1987; Williams, "Bringing Back the Beast of Lore" (June/July 1988): 63.

24. Fischer, "Deep Freeze for Wolf Recovery?" (November/December 1987): 30.

25. Steinhart, "A Wolf in the Eye" (January 1988): 89; Fischer, "Deep Freeze for Wolf Recovery?" (November/December 1987): 30; Williams, "Confusion About Wolves" (1988): 145–6, 147.

26. Zumbo, "Should We Cry Wolf?" (December 1987): 100; Bath, "Attitudes of Interest Groups" (1989): 519–25; Fischer, *Wolf Wars,* 4; Sparano, "The Wolf Vote" (May 1994): 8.

27. Fischer, *Wolf Wars,* 100–102.

28. Davis, "Ranchers Want Right to Hunt Wolves" (19 March 1988): 707; *High Country News,* 16 May 1994.

29. Fischer, "Assuming Economic Responsibility," 11.

30. USFWS, *Interim Wolf-Control Plan* [gov't. doc.], 4; Fischer, "Deep Freeze for Wolf Recovery?" (November/December 1987): 32.

31. Davis, "Ranchers Want Right to Hunt Wolves" (19 March 1988): 707; Williams, "Waiting for Wolves to Howl" (November 1990): 36; Fischer, "Deep Freeze for Wolf Recovery?" (November/December 1987): 33; Fischer, "Wolves for Yellowstone?" (March/April 1988): 16.

32. Ridenour, *The National Parks Compromised,* 158; Williams, "Waiting for Wolves to Howl" (November 1990): 38.

33. USFWS, *Wolves for Yellowstone?* [gov't. doc.], 1990, 1:3–4, 31–36.

34. Davis, "Ranchers Want Right to Hunt Wolves" (19 March 1988): 707; Fischer, *Wolf Wars,* 127.

35. Fischer, *Wolf Wars,* 129–41.

36. *Casper Star Tribune,* 7 February 1991.

37. Ibid., 5 January, 9 August 1991; Fischer, *Wolf Wars,* 145.

38. *Casper Star Tribune,* 30 July 1991; S. Kearney [wilderness ranger] to author, 19 July 1995.

39. *Casper Star Tribune,* 1 March 1992.

40. Ibid., 29 February 1992.

41. Ibid., 14 August 1992.

42. Ibid., 8 October 1992; Bangs, "Wolf Hysteria" in McIntyre, *War Against the Wolf,* 406.

43. R. Nowak to S. Fain, 29 October 1992 (obtained through the Freedom of Information Act from the USFWS).

44. *High Country News,* 5 April 1993.

45. D. Pletscher to S. Fritts, 15 December 1992, USFWS Ecological Services Records, Helena, Montana.

46. S. Fritts to E. Bangs, 11 March 1994 in USFWS, *The Reintroduction of Gray Wolves,* FEIS [gov't. doc.], 6–66.

47. Link, *Following the Pack,* 99; *Casper Star Tribune,* 23 March 1993.

48. *Casper Star Tribune,* 23 April 1993.

49. Ibid., 19 October 1992.

50. *Riverton Ranger,* 11 December 1992; Brewster, "Taxonomy, Genetics, and Status" [gov't. doc.], 4: 3–35, 3–36.

51. *Riverton Ranger,* 10 December 1992; USFWS, *The Reintroduction of Gray Wolves,* FEIS [gov't. doc.], 6–92; *Casper Star Tribune,* 22 March and 2, 27 July 1993.

52. Bangs, "Wolf Hysteria," 403, 405; Williams, "Waiting for Wolves to Howl" (November 1990): 40.

53. *Wolves.* Riverton: Wyoming Public Television (KCWC-TV), 1993. Filmstrip.

54. USFWS, *The Reintroduction of Gray Wolves,* DEIS [gov't doc.]; *Casper Star Tribune,* 4, 18 July 1993.

55. Bangs, "Wolf Hysteria," 410.

56. *Casper Star Tribune,* 26 January 1995; Fischer, *Wolf Wars,* 154; *Denver Post,* 4 December 1994.

57. *Casper Star Tribune,* 13 November, 19 January 1995.

58. *Wyoming State Journal,* 20 September 1993.
59. *Casper Star Tribune,* 12 July 1993.
60. USFWS, *The Reintroduction of Gray Wolves,* DEIS [gov't. doc.], x.
61. *Casper Star Tribune,* 5 May 1994.
62. Ibid., 30 October, 19 April 1994.
63. Ibid., 13 November 1994, 21 March 1995.
64. Ibid., 22, 23 December 1994.
65. Ibid., 4 January 1995.
66. Grant, "Who's Afraid of the Big, Bad Wolf?" (Spring 1995): 4.
67. *Casper Star Tribune,* 13 January 1995.
68. Ibid., 19, 26 January 1995; Fischer, *Wolf Wars,* 153–54.
69. "Going Wild" (April 1995): 16.
70. *Casper Star Tribune,* 25 January, 2 February 1995.
71. Ibid., 27 January 1995; *Wyoming State Journal,* 3 April 1995.
72. *High Country News,* 2 October 1995.
73. Ibid., 27 November 1995.
74. Ibid., 15 May 1995.
75. *Canis Lupus Returns.* Laramie: Wyoming Public Television (UWTV), 1995. Filmstrip.

11: HUNTING THE HUNTERS *(pages 226–250)*

1. *Anchorage Daily News,* 23 October 1981.
2. Ibid.
3. Jorgensen, *Wolf Management* [gov't. doc.], 24; ADF&G 1958 Annual Report [gov't. doc.], 99; Harbo, "Historical and Current Perspectives" [gov't. doc.], 56.
4. Rearden, "A Tug-of-War With Facts and Feelings" (May 1980): 30; ADF&G, Federal Aid in Wildlife Restoration Project W-15-2 and 3 [gov't. doc.], 6–13.
5. ADF&G, Federal Aid in Wildlife Restoration Project W-6-R-5 [gov't. doc.], 32.
6. *16 United States Code* [gov't. doc.], 742j-1.
7. Rausch, "Wolf Management in Alaska," 151.
8. Ibid., 151–53; Ballard, "The Case of the Disappearing Moose" (January 1983): 22–23.
9. Ballard, "The Case of the Disappearing Moose" (January 1983): 24; Rausch, "Wolf Management in Alaska," 155.
10. Rausch, "Wolf Management in Alaska," 153.
11. Johnson, "Alaska Plans Aerial Hunt" (February 1976): 7; the *New York Times,* 23 February 1975.
12. Cooper, "The Wolves, the Courts, and the Big, Fat Truth" (April 1976): 134–35.
13. Yates, "Research on a Researcher" (May 1991): 30; Harbo, "Historical and Current Perspectives" [gov't. doc.], 57.
14. Mitchell, "Fear and Loathing in Wolf Country" (May 1976): 34.
15. Hammond, "The Wolves and the Furor" (June 1976): 29.
16. Mitchell, "Fear and Loathing in Wolf Country" (May 1976): 36.

17. Harbo, "Historical and Current Perspectives" [gov't. doc.], 58–59.

18. Ibid., 59; Ballard, "The Case of the Disappearing Moose" (March 1983): 42.

19. Rearden, "A Tug-of-War With Facts and Feelings" (May 1980): 30.

20. W. Hall to author, 19 September 1995.

21. *Alaska Wildlife Alliance Newsletter* (July 1984–October 1985), n.p.; Williams, "Confusion about Wolves" (1988): 132.

22. "FCC Stops Alaska's Aerial Wolf Hunt" (January 1985): 57.

23. *The New York Times,* 24 December 1982.

24. *Anchorage Daily News,* 12 January 1991.

25. *16 United States Code* [gov't. doc.], 742j-1.

26. Waterman, "Sheep's Clothing" (May 1993): 56; Williams, "Confusion About Wolves" (1988): 136;

27. *Alaska Wildlife Alliance Newsletter* (January/February 1986), 1–6.

28. "Indicted Wolf Hunter to Stand Trial" (March/April 1991): 3.

29. "Judge Accepts Frost's Plea Bargain" (July/August 1991): 1.

30. "Aerial Wolf Hunter Pleads Guilty" (May/June 1991): 1; Steinhart, *The Company of Wolves,* 290.

31. Stephenson, "An Alaskan Perspective" (Fall 1991): 3, 5.

32. J. Theberge to W. Hickel, 7 December 1992, Alaska Wildlife Alliance files.

33. P. Joslin to W. Hickel, 16 January 1993, Alaska Wildlife Alliance files; G. Haber, interview with author, 6 February 1993; Haber, "The Balancing Act of Moose and Wolves" (October 1980): 49–50.

34. Pope, "Brazen Wolf Plan," *Anchorage Daily News,* 12 December 1992.

35. "Strategic Wolf Management Plan for Alaska," *Alaska's Wildlife* (January/February 1992), 11.

36. Whittington-Evans, "Alaska's 1992 Wolf Control Plans" [manuscript], 67; *Anchorage Daily News,* 5 April 1991.

37. ADF&G, "Area Specific Wolf Management Plan" [gov't. doc.], 1991.

38. *The New York Times,* 19 November 1992.

39. Whittington-Evans, "Alaska's 1992 Wolf Control Plans" [manuscript], 54–55; van den Berg, "Center Condems Wolf Control Programs" (December 1992): 3.

40. N. Whittington-Evans, interview with author, 5 February 1993.

41. Pope, "Brazen Wolf Plan," *Anchorage Daily News,* 12 December 1992; Williams, "Alaska's War on the Wolves" (May/June 1993): 45.

42. Whittington-Evans, "Alaska's 1992 Wolf Control Plans" [manuscript], 4–5; Williams, "Alaska's War on the Wolves" (May/June 1993): 44.

43. Whittington-Evans, "Alaska's 1992 Wolf Control Plans" [manuscript], 12, 15; Capps, "Wolf Wars" (August 1994): 22; Sherwonit, "State Wildlife Management in the 1990s" [manuscript], 9.

44. Dittman Research Corporation, "Survey Among Alaska Residents" [manuscript], 4; Sherwonit, "State Wildlife Management in the 1990s" [manuscript], 20; Whittington-Evans, "Alaska's 1992 Wolf Control Plans" [manuscript], 9; *Anchorage Daily News,* 20 December, 18 December 1992.

45. *Anchorage Daily News,* 20 December 1992.

46. Ibid., 31 January 1993; Peterson, "Wolf Medicine," 446; N. Whittington-Evans, interview with author, 5 February 1993.

47. *Anchorage Daily News,* 19 February, 31 January 1993.

48. Ibid., 5 March 1995.

49. Ibid., 1 July 1993, 29 June 1993.

50. Whittington-Evans, "Alaska's 1992 Wolf Control Plans" [manuscript], 14.

51. Capps, "Wolf Wars" (August 1994): 22.

52. "Alaska Wolf Kill Update" (April–June 1994): 1, 3; W. Hall to author, 19 September 1995; Mark McNay, address delivered before the "Wolves and Humans 2000" wolf symposium, 10 March 1995, Duluth, Minnesota.

53. "Alaska National Parks: Open for Hunting and Trapping?" (Spring 1995): 12.

54. *Anchorage Daily News,* 1 December 1994.

55. Ibid.

56. Ibid., 4 December 1994; Whittington-Evans, "Alaska's 1992 Wolf Control Plans" [manuscript], 14; *Casper Star Tribune,* 5 February 1995; "State Suspends Wolf Kill" (Winter 1995): 1–2.

57. *Anchorage Daily News,* 13 April 1994, 28 October 1995.

58. Ibid., 5 May 1995.

59. R. Stephenson to F. Rue, 4 April 1995, ADF&G files, Fairbanks, Alaska.

60. W. Hall to author, 19 September 1995; *Anchorage Daily News,* 30 August 1995.

61. *Anchorage Daily News,* 19 July 1995.

EPILOGUE *(pages 251–255)*

1. Carbyn, "Canada's 50,000 Wolves" (Winter 1994): 3–8.

2. Court proceedings recorded by the author in Casper, Wyoming, on February 8 and 9, 1996; *Casper Star Tribune,* 27 March 1996.

3. Fritts, "Population Viability" (March 1995) 27.

4. Dietz, "Initial Investigation" [manuscript], 20; S. Rose (USFWS) to author, 28 November 1995; *Casper Star Tribune,* 24 November 1995.

5. Skeele, "A Look at Wolf Control in Minnesota" (Summer 1995): 10–11, 18.

6. Phillips, "Wolf Restoration Is a Touchstone" (Summer 1995): 26.

BIBLIOGRAPHY

MANUSCRIPTS

Adams, Arthur. "North Dakota Bounty Data." North Dakota Game and Fish Department, Bismarck, 1965.

American National Livestock Association. "Resolutions Adopted at the 18th Annual Conference of the American National Livestock Association, 24, 25, and 26 March 1915." Wyoming Woolgrowers Association Collection, American Heritage Center, University of Wyoming, Laramie.

Bailey, Vernon. Papers. The Smithsonian Institution Archives, Washington, D.C.

Bowman, Elbert F. "Wolves: Being Reminiscent of My Life on an Eastern Montana Ranch." Montana Historical Society, Helena, 1938.

Cole, Glen F. "The Elk of Grand Teton and Southern Yellowstone National Parks." National Park Service, Yellowstone National Park, 1969.

———. "Yellowstone Wolves." Research Note No. 4, April 1971. Yellowstone National Park Research Library.

Curnow, Edward. "The History of the Eradication of the Wolf in Montana." Master's thesis, University of Montana, Missoula, 1969.

Day, Gary L. "The Status and Distribution of Wolves in the Northern Rocky Mountains of the United States." Master's thesis, University of Montana, Missoula, 1981.

Dietz, Matthew S. "Initial Investigation of Potentially Suitable Locations for Wolf Reintroduction." Unpublished paper, Enivronmental Studies Department, University of Montana, Missoula, 1993.

Dittman Research Corporation. "Survey Among Alaska Residents Regarding Wolf Hunting." Alaska Wildlife Alliance, Anchorage, 1992.

Geist, Otto. Otto Geist Collection. Rasmuson Library, University of Alaska, Fairbanks.

Haber, Gordon C. "Wildlife Management in Alaska." Alaska Wildlife Alliance, Anchorage, 1992.

Huidekoper, Wallis. "The Wolf Question and What the Government Is Doing to Help." Address to Montana Stock Grower's Association, 18 April 1916. Montana Historical Society, Helena.

Kaminski, Timm, and Jerome Hansen. "Wolves of Central Idaho." Unpublished report, Montana Cooperative Wildlife Research Unit, Missoula, 1984.

Montana Bounty Certificate Records, 1883–1918. Montana Historical Society, Helena.

Murie, Adolph. Adolph Murie Collection. Rasmuson Library, University of Alaska, Fairbanks.

Murie, Olaus. Olaus Murie Collection. Conservation Center, Denver Public Library, Denver.

Nowak, Ronald M. "Another Look at Wolf Taxonomy." Unpublished paper, 1994.

————. "The Gray Wolf in North America: A Preliminary Report." Unpublished paper, March 1974.

Rawson, Timothy M. "Adolph Murie, 1899–1974: A Master Naturalist." Unpublished paper, 1995.

————. "Alaska's First Wolf Controversy: Predator and Prey in Mount McKinley National Park, 1930–1953." Master's thesis, University of Alaska, Fairbanks, 1994.

Sherwonit, William. "State Wildlife Management in the 1990s." Unpublished paper, Alaska Conservation Foundation, Anchorage, 1995.

Whittington-Evans, Nicole. "Alaska's 1992 Wolf Control Plans: Why They Failed—A Political, Biological and Ethical Analysis." Master's thesis, University of Montana, Missoula, 1995.

Wyoming Woolgrowers Association. "Minutes of the Nineteenth Annual Convention of the Wyoming Woolgrowers Association, 1922." Wyoming Woolgrowers Association Collection, American Heritage Center, University of Wyoming, Laramie.

Young, Stanley P. Stanley Young Collection. Conservation Center, Denver Public Library, Denver.

Young, Stanley P. Papers. The Smithsonian Institution Archives, Washington, D.C.

GOVERNMENT DOCUMENTS

Alaska Department of Fish and Game. Annual Reports, 1958–. Alaska Department of Fish and Game Library, Anchorage.

————. Annual Reports of Survey-Inventory Activities, 1970–1991. Alaska Department of Fish and Game Library, Anchorage.

————. Annual Survey Inventories, 1959–1993. Alaska Department of Fish and Game Library, Anchorage.

————. "Area Specific Wolf Management Plan for South Central/Interior Alaska." Fairbanks, 1991.

————. Federal Aid in Wildlife Restoration Projects 1964–1969. Alaska Department of Fish and Game Library, Anchorage.

Alaska Game Commission. Annual Reports. Washington, D.C., 1932–1958.

Arizona Game and Fish Department. "Mexican Wolf Study Public Review Draft." Phoenix, March 1922.

Bailey, Vernon. *Destruction of Deer by the Northern Timber Wolf.* U.S. Department of Agriculture, Bureau of Biological Survey Circular 58. Washington, D.C., 1907.

————. *Directions for the Destruction of Wolves and Coyotes.* U.S. Department of Agriculture, Bureau of Biological Survey Circular 55. Washington, D.C., 1907.

————. *Key to Animals on Which Wolf and Coyote Bounties Are Paid.* U.S. Department of Agriculture, Bureau of Biological Survey. Washington, D.C., 1909.

————. *Wolves in Relation to Stock, Game, and the National Forest Reserves.* U.S. Department of Agriculture, Forest Service Bulletin 72. Washington, D.C., 1907.

Bednarz, James C. *An Evaluation of the Ecological Potential of White Sands Missile Range to Support a Reintroduced Population of Mexican Wolves.* U.S. Fish and Wildlife Service, Endangered Species Report 19. Washington, D.C., 1989.

————. *The Mexican Wolf: Biology, History and Prospects for Re-establishment in New Mexico.* U.S. Fish and Wildlife Service, Endangered Species Report 18. Washington, D.C., 1988.

Bell, W. B. "Hunting Down Stock Killers." In *U.S. Department of Agriculture Yearbook 1920.* Washington, D.C., 1921.

Bennett, Larry E. *Colorado Gray Wolf Recovery: A Biological Feasibility Study.* United States Fish and Wildlife Service. Washington, D.C., 1994.

Brewster, Wayne, and Steven Fritts. "Taxonomy, Genetics, and Status of the Gray Wolf, *Canis lupus,* in Western North America: A Review." In vol. 4 of *Wolves for Yellowstone?* National Park Service. Washington, D.C., 1992.

British Columbia Ministry of Environment. *Wolf management in British Columbia: protecting predator & prey.* Victoria, 1985.

Cain, S. A., et al. *Predator Control—1971.* Council on Environmental Quality and U.S. Department of Interior. Washington, D.C., 1972.

Carbyn, Ludwig N., ed. *Wolves in Canada and Alaska: their status, biology, and management.* Canadian Wildlife Service Report Series No. 45. Ottawa: Canadian Wildlife Service, 1983.

Congressional Record. Washington, D.C., 1929, 1945.

Day, Albert M., and Almer P. Nelson. *Wild Life Conservation and Control in Wyoming under the Leadership of the United States Biological Survey.* Washington D.C., 1928.

Fritts, Steven H., et al. *Trends and Management of Wolf–Livestock Conflicts in Minnesota.* U.S. Fish and Wildlife Service, Resource Publication 181. Washington, D.C., 1992.

Gish, Dan M. *An Historical Look at the Mexican Gray Wolf (Canis lupus baileyi) in Early Arizona Territory and Since Statehood.* U.S. Fish and Wildlife Service. Washington, D.C., 1978.

Gunson, John R. "Status and Management of Wolves in Alberta." In *Wolves in Canada and Alaska,* edited by L. Carbyn. Ottawa: Canadian Wildlife Service, 1983.

Harbo, Jr., Samuel J., and Frederick C. Dean. "Historical and Current Perspectives on

Wolf Management in Alaska." In *Wolves in Canada and Alaska,* edited by L. Carbyn. Ottawa: Canadian Wildlife Service, 1983.

Jorgensen, S. E., et al, eds. *Wolf Management in Selected Areas of North America.* Twin Cities, Minnesota: USFWS, Region 3, 1970.

Leopold, A. Starker, et al. "Predator and Rodent Control in the United States." In *Transactions of the Twenty-ninth North American Wildlife and Natural Resources Conference.* Advisory Board on Wildlife Management. Washington, D.C., 1964.

McBride, Roy T. *The Mexican Wolf.* U.S. Fish and Wildlife Service, Endangered Species Report 8. Washington, D.C., 1980.

Mooney, James. *The Ghost-Dance Religion.* Bureau of American Ethnology, 14th Annual Report. Washington, D.C., 1896.

Murie, Adolph. *The Wolves of Mount McKinley.* National Park Service, Fauna Series No. 5. Washington, D.C., 1944.

Murray, Allan. *The Wild Dogs: A Story of Wolves in Manitoba.* Winnipeg: Manitoba Department of Natural Resources, 1969.

Musgrave, Mark E. "Predatory Animal Control." U.S. Department of the Interior, Bureau of Biological Survey, Arizona District, Annual Reports, Washington, D.C., 1919–1929.

Novak, Milan, et al. *Furbearer Harvests in North America, 1600–1984.* Toronto: Ontario Ministry of Natural Resources, 1987.

———. *Wild Furbearer Management and Conservation in North America.* Toronto: Ontario Ministry of Natural Resources, 1987.

Nunley, Gary L. *The Mexican Gray Wolf in New Mexico.* U.S. Fish and Wildlife Service, Division of Animal Damage Control. Albuquerque, 1977.

Palmer, T. S. "Extermination of Noxious Animals by Bounties." In *U.S. Department of Agriculture Yearbook 1896.* Washington, D.C., 1897.

Scudday, J. F. *The Mexican Gray Wolf in Texas.* U.S. Fish and Wildlife Service. Washington, D.C., 1977.

U.S. Biological Survey. Records of the U.S. Biological Survey. Record Group 22, Annual Reports (232), General Correspondence (230), Alaska (181), Special Reports (235), National Archives and Records Administration. Washington, D.C.

U.S. Bureau of American Ethnology. Annual Reports and Bulletins, 1881–1920. Washington, D.C.

U.S. Congress. House. Committee on the Public Lands. *Hearings on Protection of Wildlife in Mount McKinley National Park (H.R. 5004 and 5401).* 79th Cong., 2d sess., 3 April 1946 and 22 May 1946.

———. *Report of Lieut. J. W. Abert of His Examination of New Mexico in the Years 1846–1847.* 30th Cong., 1st sess., 1847–48. Executive Document no. 41, vol. 4.

———. Subcommittee on Public Lands and National Parks of the Committee on Interior and Insular Affairs. *Public Land Management Policy.* 98th Cong., 1st sess., 24 February 1983, Serial no. 98–8, pt. 1.

U.S. Congress. *Reintroduction and Management of Wolves in Yellowstone National Park and the Central Idaho Wilderness Area.* Report of the Wolf Management Committee to the United States Congress, [unpublished report], 1991.

U.S. Congress. Senate. Agriculture and Forestry Committee. *Hearings on Control of Predatory Animals (S. 3483)*. 71st Cong., 2d and 3d sess., 8 May 1930 and 28, 29 January 1931, respectively.

U.S. Department of Agriculture. *Animal Damage Control Program Draft Environmental Impact Statement*. Animal and Plant Health Inspection Service. Washington, D.C., 1990.

―――. Annual Reports of the Secretary of Agriculture, 1885–1922. Washington, D.C.

―――. *The Weekly News Letter* and *The Official Record,* 1919–1929. Washington, D.C.

U.S. Fish and Wildlife Service. *Interim Wolf Control Plan: Northern Rocky Mountains of Montana and Wyoming*. Washington, D.C., 1988.

―――. *Mexican Wolf Recovery Plan*. Washington, D.C., 1982.

―――. *Northern Rocky Mountain Wolf Recovery Plan*. Washington, D.C., 1980, 1987.

―――. *Recovery Plan for the Eastern Timber Wolf*. Washington, D.C., 1978.

―――. *The Reintroduction of Gray Wolves to Yellowstone National Park and Central Idaho*. Draft (DEIS) and Final Environmental Impact Statement (FEIS). Washington, D.C., 1993 and 1994, respectively.

―――. *Reintroduction of the Mexican Wolf Within Its Historic Range in the Southwestern United States—DEIS*. Washington D.C., 1995.

―――. *Wolves for Yellowstone? A Report to the United States Congress*. 4 vols. Washington, D.C., 1990–1992.

U.S. Forest Service. *An Assessment of the Forest and Range Land Situation in the United States*. Forest Resource Report No. 22. Washington, D.C., 1981.

Weaver, John. *The Wolves of Yellowstone*. National Park Service, Natural Resources Report No. 14. Washington, D.C., 1978.

Wright, George M., et al. *Fauna of the National Parks of the United States*. National Park Service. Washington, D.C., 1933.

Wyoming Department of Agriculture. *Wyoming Legislative History of Predator Control*. Cheyenne: n.d.

Wyoming. *Session Laws of Wyoming, 1905*. Wyoming State Archives, Cheyenne.

Wyoming State Auditor. Annual Reports, 1886–1918. Wyoming State Archives, Cheyenne.

Yellowstone National Park. "Monthly Report for May 1922." Yellowstone National Park Research Library.

NEWSPAPERS/NEWSLETTERS/PERIODICALS/FILM

Alaska Wildlife Alliance Newsletter (Anchorage, Alaska)
Anchorage Daily News
Casper Star Tribune (Casper, Wyoming)
Chicago Record Herald
Chicago Sunday Tribune
Daily News (Washington, D.C.)
Denver Post
High Country News (Paonia, Colorado)

Predator Project Newsletter (Bozeman, Montana)
Red Wolf Newsletter (Tacoma, Washington)
Riverton Ranger (Riverton, Wyoming)
The Arizona Daily Star (Tucson, Arizona)
The Billings Gazette (Billings, Montana)
The New York Times
The River Press (Fort Benton, Montana)
The Spirit (Alaska Wildlife Alliance, Anchorage, Alaska)
Washington Post
Woman's National Daily (Washington, D.C.)
Wyoming State Journal (Lander, Wyoming)

"Aerial Wolf Hunter Pleads Guilty." *The Spirit* (May/June 1991): 1.

"Alaska National Parks: Open for Hunting and Trapping?" *The Spirit* (Spring 1995): 12.

"Alaska Wolf Kill Update." *The Spirit* (April–June 1994): 1, 3.

Albright, Horace M. "The National Park Service's Policy on Predatory Mammals." *Journal of Mammology* 12, no. 2 (May 1931), 185–86.

Alexander, Thomas G. "Stewardship and Enterprise: The LDS Church and the Wasatch Oasis Environment, 1847–1930." *Western Historical Quarterly* 25, no. 3 (Autumn 1994): 340–64.

Allen, J. A. "Notes on the Mammals of Portions of Kansas, Colorado, Wyoming, and Utah." *Bulletin of the Essex Institute* 6, no. 3 (1874): 43–52.

Anthony, Harold E. "The Control of Predatory Mammals." *Science* 74, no. 1916 (18 September 1931): 288–90.

Aulerich, Richard. "The Wolf." *National Parks Magazine* 40, no. 230 (November 1966): 10–13.

Ballard, Warren B. "The Case of the Disappearing Moose." *Alaska* (January, February, and March 1983): 22–25, 36–39, 38–42, respectively.

Barton, Benjamin S. "On Indian Dogs." *Alexander Tillock's Philosophical Magazine* 15 (1803): 1–9, 136–42.

Bath, Alistair J., and Thomas Buchanan. "Attitudes of Interest Groups in Wyoming toward Wolf Restoration in Yellowstone National Park." *Wildlife Society Bulletin* 17, no. 4 (1989): 519–25.

Beard, J. Carter. "The American Black Wolf." *Scientific American* 67 (16 July 1892): 41.

Bierstedt, Karen. "Wolf Hatred." *Science Digest* 78, no. 4 (October 1975): 66–75.

Bower, Bruce. "Extinctions on Ice." *Science News* 132 (31 October 1987): 284–85.

Brown, Wendy. "Back from the Brink of Extinction: The Mexican Gray Wolf." *International Wolf* (Spring 1995): 3–7.

Budiansky, Stephen. "The Ancient Contract." *U. S. News & World Report* 106 (20 March 1989): 74–79.

Buys, C. J. "Predator Control and Ranchers' Attitudes." *Environment and Behavior* 7, no. 1 (1976): 81–98.

Canis Lupus Returns. Laramie: Wyoming Public Television (UWTV), 1995. Filmstrip.

Capps, Kris. "Wolf Wars." *Alaska* (August 1994): 20–27.

Carbyn, Ludwig N. "A Wolf Manifesto for the World." *Ontario Naturalist* 18, no. 5 (1979): 18–22.

————. "Canada's 50,000 Wolves." *International Wolf* (Winter 1994): 3–8.

Carhart, Arthur H. "World Champion Wolfer." *Outdoor Life* 84 (September 1939): 22–23, 74–75.

Chadwick, Douglas. "Dead or Alive: The Endangered Species Act." *National Geographic* 187, no. 3 (March 1995): 2–41.

Cohn, Jeffrey P. "Endangered Wolf Population Increases." *BioScience* 40, no. 9 (October 1990): 628–32.

Condit, Thelma G. "The Hole-in-the-Wall." *Annals of Wyoming* 28 (October 1956): 151–65.

Cooper, Toby. "The Wolves, the Courts, and the Big, Fat Truth." *Defenders* 51 (April 1976): 134–35.

Coues, Elliott. "The Quadrupeds of Arizona," *American Naturalist* 1, no. 6 (1867): 281–92.

Crichton, V. "A Record of a Timber Wolf Attacking a Man." *Journal of Mammology* 28, no. 3 (August 1947): 294–95.

Davis, Joseph A. "Ranchers Want Right to Hunt Wolves, Bears." *Congressional Quarterly* (19 March 1988): 707–8.

Dufresne, Frank. "Ghosts That Kill Game." *Outdoor Life* 101 (April 1948): 37.

Dutcher, William. "Old-time Natural History." *Forest and Stream* 28, no. 6 (March 1887): 105–6.

Erickson, David L., and G. Norman Van Tubergen. "The Wolf Men." *Journal of Environmental Education* 4, no. 1 (Fall 1972): 26–30.

"FCC Stops Alaska's Aerial Wolf Hunt." *Science News* 126 (26 January 1985): 57.

Fischer, Hank. "Deep Freeze for Wolf Recovery?" *Defenders* (November/December 1987): 29–33.

————. "Wolves for Yellowstone?" *Defenders* (March/April 1988): 16–17.

Flores, Dan. "Bison Ecology and Bison Diplomacy: The Southern Plains from 1800 to 1850." *The Journal of American History* 78 (September 1991): 465–81.

Fogleman, Valerie M. "American Attitudes Toward Wolves: A History of Misperception." *Environmental Review* 13, no. 1 (1989): 63–94.

Fritts, Steven H. "Wolves and Wolf Recovery Efforts in the Northwestern United States." *Western Wildlands* (Spring 1991): 2–6.

Fritts, Steven H., et al, "The Relationship of Wolf Recovery to Habitat Conservation and Biodiversity in the Northwestern United States." *Landscape and Urban Planning* 28 (1994): 24.

Fritts, Steven H., and Ludwig N. Carbyn. "Population Viability, Nature Reserves, and the Outlook for Gray Wolf Conservation in North America." *Restoration Ecology* 3, no. 1 (March 1995): 26–38.

Fuller, Todd, et al. "A History and Current Estimate of Wolf Distribution and Numbers in Minnesota." *Wildlife Society Bulletin* 20 (1992): 42–55.

Gabler, F. W. "The Wolf Pack." *The Alaska Sportsman,* 1 (January 1935): 16–17.

Goble, Dale D. "Of Wolves and Welfare Ranching." *The Harvard Environmental Law Review* 16, no. 1 (1992): 101–27.

"Going Wild." *Harpers* 290, no. 1739 (April 1995): 16.

Goldman, Edward. "The Control of Injurious Animals." *Science,* 75, no. 1942 (18 March 1932): 309–11.

Grant, Eric. "Who's Afraid of the Big, Bad Wolf?" *Range Magazine* 3, no. 2 (Spring 1995): 4–5.

Grinnell, Joseph, and Tracy Storer. "Animal Life as an Asset of National Parks." *Science* 44 (15 September 1916): 375–80.

Haber, Gordon C. "The Balancing Act of Moose and Wolves." *Natural History* 89 (October 1980): 38–51.

Hammond, Jay. "Strafing Arctic Killers." *Field & Stream* 49 (February 1955): 37–39, 111–14.

———. "The Wolves and the Furor." *Alaska* (June 1976): 28–29, 63–64.

Hassrick, Peter. "The Wyoming Cowboy's Evolving Image." *Annals of Wyoming* 65, no. 4 (Winter 1993–94): 8–19.

Hays, W. J. "Notes on Animals at Time of White Man's Arrival." *American Naturalist* 5, no. 7 (September 1871): 387–92.

Heller, Edmund. "The Big Game Animals of Yellowstone National Park." *Roosevelt Wildlife Bulletin* 2, no. 4 (1925): 430.

Hillaby, John. "Wolf: Victim of Calculated Slaughter." *Animal Kingdom* (October 1967): 143–45.

Hunt, Fred A. "The Wake of the Wolves." *Overland* 64 (November 1901): 458–61.

"Indicted Wolf Hunter to Stand Trial." *The Spirit* (March/April 1991): 3.

Johnson, Aubrey S. "Alaska Plans Aerial Hunt." *Defenders* 51 (February 1976): 4–7.

"Judge Accepts Frost's Plea Bargain." *The Spirit* (July/August 1991): 1.

Kellert, Stephen R. "Public Perceptions of Predators." *Biological Conservation* 31 (1985): 167–89.

Kendrick, Gregory D. "An Environmental Spokesman: Olaus J. Murie and a Democratic Defense of Wilderness." *Annals of Wyoming* 50, no. 2 (Fall 1978): 213–302.

Koch, Elers. "Big Game in Montana from Early Historical Records." *Journal of Wildlife Management* 5, no. 4 (October 1941): 357–70.

Leopold, Aldo. "The Game Situation in the Southwest." *Bulletin of the American Game Protective Association* 9, no. 2 (1920): 3–5.

———. "Review of *The Wolves of North America,* by S. P. Young and E. A. Goldman, 1944." *Journal of Forestry* 42 (1944): 928–29.

Licht, Dan. "Wolves Attempt to Colonize the Dakotas." *International Wolf* (Summer 1993): 21–22.

Long, William J. "The Sociology of a Wolf Pack." *Independent* 66 (3 June 1909): 1179–85.

Manuel, John. "Red Wolf Showdown." *Audubon* 97, no. 2 (March/April 1995): 22–24.

Matheson, Colin. "The Grey Wolf." *Antiquity* 17 (1943): 11–18.

Matteson, Mollie. "Unnatural Selection." *Wildlife Damage Review* 2 (Spring 1992): 10.

McNamee, Tom. "Yellowstone's Missing Element." *Audubon* 88 (January 1986): 12–19.

Merritt, Jim. "The Custer Wolf." *Field and Stream* 92 (March 1988): 44, 101–4.

Mitchell, John G. "Fear and Loathing in Wolf Country." *Audubon* 78 (May 1976): 20–39.

"Montana Wolves and Panthers." *Forest and Stream* 26 (22 July 1886): 508–9.

Nevin, David. "Revered and Reviled, Minnesota's Wolves are in Trouble Again." *Smithsonian* 15, no. 10 (January 1985): 79–86.

Nowak, Ronald M. "Red Wolf: Our Most Endangered Mammal." *National Parks Magazine* 48, no. 8 (August 1974): 9–12.

———. "The Mysterious Wolf of the South." *Natural History* 81 (January 1972): 50–53.

———. "Wolves: The Great Travelers of Evolution." *International Wolf* (Winter 1992): 3–7.

Petersen, William J. "Wolves in Iowa." *The Palimpsest* 41, no. 12 (December 1960): 517–64.

Phillips, Michael K. "Wolf Restoration Is a Touchstone." *International Wolf* (Summer 1995): 24–26.

Pimlott, Douglas H. "Wolf Control in Canada." *Canadian Audubon* 23 (1961): 145–52.

———. "Wolves and Men in North America." *Defenders of Wildlife News* 42, no. 1 (January–March 1967): 36–47.

Pope, Douglas. "Brazen Wolf Plan Spoils Hope for Compromise." *Anchorage Daily News* (12 December 1992).

Purrett, Louise A. "The Last Cry of the Wolf." *Science News* 103 (17 February 1973): 109–10.

Rearden, James. "Alaska's Boom-to-Bust Reindeer Saga." *Alaska* (September 1974): 8–11, 72, 73, 76–79.

———. "A Tug-of-War With Facts and Feelings." *Alaska* (May 1980): 30, 68, 71–72.

Redington, Paul. "Federal Program of Wild-Life Control." *The Producer* 12, no. 8 (1931): 6–7.

Rennie, John. "Howls of Dismay." *Scientific American* 265, no. 4 (October 1991): 18–19.

Roosevelt, Theodore. "A Wolf Hunt in Oklahoma." *Scribner's* 38, no. 5 (November 1905): 513–32.

Schmidt, Robert H. "Gray Wolves in California: Their Presence and Absence." *California Fish and Game.* 77, no. 2 (1991): 79–85.

Schneider, Bill. "Is There Room for the Wolf?" *Outdoor Life* 165 (20 August 1980): 51–53, 100, 103–4.

Seton, Ernest T. "Lobo, King of the Currumpaw." *Scribner's* 16 (November 1894): 618–28.

Shaw, James H., and Peter A. Jordan. "The Wolf That Lost Its Genes." *Natural History* 86 (December 1977): 80–88.

Shiras, George. "The Wild Life of Lake Superior, Past and Present." *National Geographic* 40, no. 2 (August 1921): 113–204.

Skeele, Tom. "A Look at Wolf Control in Minnesota and a Bit More." *Predator Project Newsletter* (Summer 1995): 10–11, 18.

Sparano, Vin T. "The Wolf Vote." *Outdoor Life* 193 (May 1994): 8.

Stanwell-Fletcher, John. "Three Years in the Wolves' Wilderness." *Natural History* 49 (March 1942): 103–9.

"State Suspends Wolf Kill." *The Spirit* (Winter 1995): 1–2.

Steinhart, Peter. "A Wolf in the Eye." *Audubon* 90 (January 1988): 79–89.

Stelfox, John G. "Wolves in Alberta: a history, 1800–1969." *Alberta Lands, Forests, Parks, and Wildlife* 12 (1969): 18–27.

Stephenson, Bob. "An Alaskan Perspective on Wolves." *International Wolf* (Fall 1991): 3–6.

"Strategic Wolf Management Plan for Alaska." *Alaska's Wildlife* (January/February 1992): 2–16.

Taylor, Zack. "Buffalo Wolves." *Sports Afield* (March 1983): 98, 99, 150, 151.

Tedford, Richard H. "Key to the Carnivores." *Natural History* 103 (April 1994): 74–76.

Trefethen, James B. "Another Vanishing American." *American Forests* 65, no. 1 (January 1959): 17, 48–49.

van den Berg, David. "Center Condems Wolf Control Programs." *The Northern Line* (16 December 1992): 3.

Van Valkenburgh, Blaire. "Tough Times in the Tar Pits." *Natural History* 103 (April 1994): 84–85.

Walker, Danny N., and George C. Frison. "Studies on Amerindian Dogs." *Journal of Archaeological Science* 9, no. 2 (1982): 125–72.

Walker, Tom. "Crimson Tundra." *Alaska* (May 1991): 26–27.

Walter, David. "Wolf Wars." *Montana, the Magazine of Western History* 75 (January–February 1986): 22–26.

Waterman, Jonathan. "Sheep's Clothing: Alaskan Wolf Control." *Outside* (May 1993): 51–60.

Wayne, Robert K., et al. "Mitochondrial DNA Variability of the Gray Wolf: Genetic Consequences of Population Decline and Habitat Fragmentation." *Conservation Biology* 6, no. 4 (December 1992): 559–69.

Williams, Harry P. "The Custer Wolf—Greatest Killer of Them All." *Denver Post* (24 September 1961): 10–11.

Williams, Ted. "Alaska's War on the Wolves." *Audubon* (May/June 1993): 44–50.

———. "Bringing Back the Beast of Lore." *Modern Maturity* (June/July 1988): 45–51.

———. "Confusion About Wolves." *Gray's Sporting Journal* 13 (1988): 132–55.

———. "Waiting for Wolves to Howl in Yellowstone." *Audubon* 92 (November 1990): 32–41.

Wilson, Clifford. "The Wolves Are Always After Us!" *Forest and Outdoors* (February 1937): 38.

"Wolves." *Littel's Living Age* 29 (1851): 265–71.

Wolves. Riverton: Wyoming Public Television (KCWC-TV), 1993. Filmstrip.

Yates, Doug. "Research on a Researcher." *Alaska* (May 1991): 30.

Young, Stanley P. "It's Red, But Truly All-American." *American Forests* 74, no. 1 (January 1968): 14–15, 56, 57.

Zepp, Fred R. "America's Longest War: The Battle with the Wolves." *Outdoor Life* 101 (May 1948): 38–41, 118–20.

Zumbo, Jim. "Should We Cry Wolf?" *Outdoor Life* 180 (December 1987): 50, 98–100.

BOOKS

Anderson, H. Allen. *The Chief: Ernest Thompson Seton and the Changing West.* College Station: Texas A & M University Press, 1986.

Arnold, Samuel G. *History of the State of Rhode Island.* 2 vols. New York: Privately published, 1859.

Astrov, Margot. *American Indian Prose and Poetry.* 1946. Reprint. New York: John Day Co., 1972.

Audubon, John J., and John Bachman. *The Quadrupeds of North America.* 3 vols. New York: V. G. Audubon, 1846–1854.

Bad, William, ed. *The Life and Letters of John Muir.* 2 vols. Boston: Houghton Mifflin, 1923–24.

Bailey, Vernon. *Animal Life of Yellowstone National Park.* Baltimore: Charles Thomas, Publisher, 1930.

Bangs, Ed. "Wolf Hysteria: Reintroducing Wolves to the West." In McIntyre, *War Against the Wolf.* Stillwater, Minn.: Voyageur Press, 1995.

Barclay, Donald A., et al. *Into the Wilderness Dream: Exploration Narratives of the American West, 1500–1805.* Salt Lake City: University of Utah Press, 1994.

Bartram, William. *Travels through North and South Carolina, Georgia, East and West Florida.* 1792. Reprint. Savannah: The Beehive Press, 1973.

Bass, Rick. *The Ninemile Wolves.* Livingston, Mont.: Clark City Press, 1992.

Beals, Charles E. *Passaconaway in the White Mountains.* Boston: Privately published, 1916.

Biggar, H. P. *The Works of Samuel De Champlain.* Vol. 1. Toronto: University of Toronto Press, 1922.

Blevins, Winfred. *Dictionary of the American West.* New York: Facts On File, 1993.

Bogue, Allan. "An Agricultural Empire." In Milner, *Oxford History of the American West.* New York: Oxford University Press, 1994.

Boller, Henry A. *Among the Indians.* Lincoln: University of Nebraska Press, 1972.

Brandenburg, Jim. *Brother Wolf.* Minocqua, Wis.: NorthWord Press, 1993.

Brightman, Robert A. *Grateful Prey: Rock Cree Human–Animal Relationships.* Berkeley: University of California Press, 1993.

Britton, Davis. *The Truth About Geronimo.* New Haven: Yale University Press, 1929.

Brown, David E., ed. *The Wolf in the Southwest: The Making of an Endangered Species.* Tucson: University of Arizona Press, 1983.

Brown, Mark, and W. R. Felton. *The Frontier Years.* New York: Bramhall House, 1955.

Bryant, Edwin. *Rocky Mountain Adventures.* New York: Hurst & Co., 1885.

Burbank, James C. *Vanishing Lobos: The Mexican Wolf and the Southwest.* Boulder, Colo.: Johnson Books, 1990.

Burland, Cottie. *North American Indian Mythology.* New York: Peter Bedrick Books, 1985.

Burroughs, John. *Camping and Tramping with Roosevelt.* Boston: Houghton Mifflin, 1879.

Burroughs, Raymond D. *The Natural History of the Lewis and Clark Expedition.* East Lansing: Michigan State University Press, 1961.

Byrd, William. *The Writings of Colonel William Byrd of Westover in Virginia.* New York: Doubleday, Page & Co., 1901.

Cahalane, Victor H. *A Preliminary Study of Distribution and Numbers of Cougar, Grizzly, and Wolf in North America.* New York: New York Zoological Society, 1964.

Cameron, Jenks. *The Bureau of Biological Survey: Its History, Activities and Organization.* Baltimore: Johns Hopkins Press, 1929.

Canetti, Elias. *Crowds and Power.* New York: Continuum Publishing Corporation, 1962.

Caras, Roger A. *Dangerous to Man.* New York: Holt, Rinehart and Winston, 1975.

————. *The Custer Wolf: Biography of an American Renegade.* Boston: Little, Brown, 1966.

Carhart, Arthur H., and Stanley P. Young. *The Last Stand of the Pack.* New York: J. H. Sears & Co., 1929.

Carrington, Frances. *My Army Life.* Philadelphia and London: J. B. Lippincott Co., 1911.

Carroll, Peter N. *Puritanism and the Wilderness.* New York: Columbia University Press, 1969.

Catlin, George. *Letters and Notes on the Manners, Customs, and Conditions of the North American Indians.* 1844. Reprint. New York: Dover Publications, 1973.

————. *North American Indians.* Edited by Peter Matthiessen. New York: Viking, 1989.

Chase, Alston. *Playing God in Yellowstone: The Destruction of America's First National Park.* New York: The Atlantic Monthly Press, 1986.

Chittenden, Hiram M. *The American Fur Trade.* 2 vols. 1902. Reprint. Stanford, Calif.: Academic Reprints. 1954.

Chittenden, Hiram M., and Alfred T. Richardson, eds. *Life, Letters and Travels of Father DeSmet.* 4 vols. 1904. Reprint. New York: Arno Press, 1969.

Clark, Ella. *Indian Legends from the Northern Rockies.* Norman: University of Oklahoma Press, 1966.

Clark, Tim W., and Steven Minta. *Greater Yellowstone's Future.* Moose, Wyo.: Homestead Publishing, 1994.

Clayton, John. *Clayton's Virginia: Letters of John Clayton.* 3 vols. Washington, D.C.: William Q. Force, 1844.

Cook, Ramsay. *The Voyages of Jacques Cartier.* Toronto: University of Toronto Press, 1993.

Cooper, William. *A Guide in the Wilderness: history of the first settlements in the western counties of New York.* Rochester: Privately published, 1810.

Corbin, Ben. *Corbin's Advice: or the Wolf Hunter's Guide.* Bismarck, N. Dak.: The Tribune Co., 1900.

Coues, Elliott, ed. *Manuscript Journals of Alexander Henry and David Thompson (1799–1814).* Vol. 1. 1897. Reprint. Minneapolis: Ross and Haines, Inc., 1965.

————. *The Journal of Jacob Fowler.* New York: Francis P. Harper, 1898.

Cowie, Issac. *The Company of Adventurers.* 1913. Reprint. Lincoln: University of Nebraska Press, 1993.

Cox, Ross. *The Columbia River.* Edited by Edgar I. Stewart. Norman: University of Oklahoma Press, 1957.

Crisler, Lois. *Arctic Wild.* New York: Harper & Row, 1958.

Cronon, William. *Changes in the Land.* New York: Hill and Wang, 1983.

Crosby, Alfred W. *Ecological Imperialism: The Biological Expansion of Europe, 900–1900.* Cambridge: Cambridge University Press, 1986.

Curtis, Edward S. *The North American Indian.* 20 vols. Seattle: E. S. Curtis, 1907–30.

Dary, David A. *The Buffalo Book.* Chicago: Avon Books, 1974.

Davies, K. G. *Peter Skene Ogden's Snake Country Jounral, 1826–1827.* London: Hudson's Bay Record Society, 1961.

Demos, John. *The Unredeemed Captive.* New York: Knopf, 1994.

DeVoto, Bernard. *Across the Wide Missouri.* Boston: Houghton Mifflin, 1947.

DiSilvestro, Roger L. *Fight for Survival.* New York: John Wiley and Sons, 1990.

Dodge, Richard I. *The Hunting Grounds of the Great West.* London: Chatto and Windus, 1878.

Dufresne, Frank. *Alaska's Animals and Fishes.* New York: A. S. Barnes, 1946.

Dunlap, Thomas R. *Saving America's Wildlife.* Princeton: Princeton University Press, 1988.

Durant, Mary, and Michael Harwood. *On the Road with John J. Audubon.* 1980. Reprint. New York: Dodd, Mead and Co., 1984.

Earle, Alice M. *Home Life In Colonial Days.* London: Macmillan, 1900.

Emmart, Emily W., ed. *The Badianus Manuscript.* Baltimore: The Johns Hopkins Press, 1940.

Emmons, George T. *The Tlingit Indians.* New York: American Museum of Natural History, 1991.

Ernst, Alice H. *The Wolf Ritual of the Northwest Coast.* Eugene: University of Oregon Press, 1952.

Errington, Paul. *Of Predation and Life.* Ames, Iowa: Iowa State University, 1967.

Faragher, John M. *Daniel Boone: The Life and Legend of an American Pioneer.* New York: Henry Holt, 1992.

Ferris, W. A. *Life in the Rocky Mountains.* Denver: The Old West Publishing Co., 1940.

Fischer, Hank. "Assuming Economic Responsibility for Wolf Depredation." In *Wolves and Humans 2000: Program and Abstracts of Wolf Symposium, 9–11 March 1995, Duluth, Minnesota.* Ely, Minn.: International Wolf Center, 1995.

―――. *Wolf Wars.* Helena, Mont.: Falcon Press, 1995.

Flader, Susan L. *Thinking Like a Mountain.* 1978. Reprint. Lincoln: University of Nebraska Press, 1974.

Flint, Thomas. *Diary of Dr. Thomas Flint.* Los Angeles: Historical Society of Southern California, 1923.

Fox, M. W., ed. *The Wild Canids.* New York: Van Nostrand Reinhold Co., 1975.

Freeman, Frederick. *The History of Cape Cod: The Annals of the Thirteen Towns of Barnstable County.* 2 vols. Boston: Rand and Avery, 1958–62.

Freuchen, Peter. *Book of the Eskimos.* 1961. Reprint. New York: Ballantine Books, 1983.

Garfield, Viola, and Linn Forrest. *The Wolf and the Raven: Totem Poles of Southeastern Alaska.* Seattle and London: University of Washington Press, 1961.

Genoways, Hugh, and Marion Burgwin, eds. *Natural History of the Dog.* Pittsburgh: Carnegie Museum of Natural History, 1984.

Gerstell, Richard. *The Steel Trap in North America.* Harrisburg, Pa.: Stackpole, 1985.

Gill, Sam D., and Irene F. Sullivan. *Dictionary of Native American Mythology.* New York: Oxford University Press, 1992.

Gipson, Philip. "Wolves and Wolf Literature: A Credibility Gap." In McIntyre, *War Against the Wolf.* Stillwater, Minn.: Voyageur Press, 1995.

Gohdes, Clarence. *Hunting in the Old South.* Baton Rouge: Louisiana State University Press, 1967.

Graham, Gideon. *Animal Outlaws.* Collinsville, Okla.: Privately published, 1939.

Greeley, Horace. *An Overland Journey from New York to San Francisco in the Summer of 1859.* San Francisco: H. H. Bancroft, 1860.

Gregg, Josiah. *Commerce of the Prairies.* Edited by Max Moorhead. Norman: University of Oklahoma Press, 1954.

Grinnell, George B. *Blackfoot Lodge Tales.* 1892. Reprint. Williamstown, Mass.: Corner House Publishers, 1972.

———. *By Cheyenne Campfires.* 1926. Reprint. Lincoln: University of Nebraska Press, 1971.

———. *Pawnee Hero Stories and Folk-tales.* Lincoln: University of Nebraska Press, 1961.

———. *The Cheyenne Indians.* 2 vols. New York: Cooper Square Publishers, 1962.

———. *The Wolf Hunters.* New York: Charles Scribner's Sons, 1914.

———. *Trail and Camp-fire.* New York: Harper & Brothers, 1914.

———. *Two Great Scouts and Their Pawnee Battalion.* 1928. Reprint. Lincoln: University of Nebraska Press, 1973.

———. *When Buffalo Ran.* 1920. Reprint. Norman: University of Oklahoma Press, 1966.

Grinnell, George B., and Charles Sheldon, eds. *Hunting and Conservation.* New Haven: Yale University Press, 1925.

Hafen, LeRoy, R., and Ann Hafen. *Fremont's Fourth Expedition.* Glendale, Calif.: The Arthur H. Clark Co., 1960.

Hall, Roberta. "Variability and Speciation in Canids and Hominids." In Hall, *Wolf and Man.* New York: Academic Press, 1978.

Hall, Roberta L., and Henry S. Sharp, eds. *Wolf and Man: Evolution in Parallel.* New York: Academic Press, 1978.

Hampton, Bruce. *Children of Grace: The Nez Perce War of 1877.* New York: Henry Holt, 1994.

Harding, A. R. *Wolf and Coyote Trapping.* Columbus, Ohio: A. R. Harding Publishing Co., 1909.

Harper, J. Russell. *Paul Kane's Frontier.* Austin: University of Texas Press, 1971.

Harrington, F. H., and P. C. Paquet, eds. *Wolves of the World: Perspectives of Behavior, Ecology, and Conservation.* Park Ridge, N.J.: Noyes Publishing Co., 1982.

Hassrick, Royal B. *The Sioux: Life and Customs of a Warrior Society.* Norman: University of Oklahoma Press, 1964.

Hastings, Lansford Warren. *The Emigrant Guide to Oregon and California.* Princeton: Princeton University Press, 1932.

Hebard, Grace, and E. A. Brininstool. *The Bozeman Trail.* Cleveland: The Arthur H. Clark Co., 1922.

Heckewelder, John. *History, Manners, and Customs of the Indian Nations Who Once Inhabited Pennsylvania and the Neighboring States.* 1876. Reprint. New York: Arno Press, 1971.

Hoffman, Charles F. *A Winter in the West.* 2 vols. New York: Harper and Bros., 1835.

Hook, Richard A., and William L. Robinson. "Attitudes of Michigan Citizens Toward Predators." In Harrington, *Wolves of the World.* Park Ridge, N.J.: Noyes Publishing Co., 1982.

Hornaday, William T. *Our Vanishing Wildlife: Its Extermination and Preservation.* 1913. Reprint. New York: Arno Press, 1970.

————. *The American Natural History.* New York: Charles Scribner's Sons, 1904.

————. *The Minds and Manners of Wild Animals: A Book of Personal Observation.* New York: Charles Scribner's Sons, 1922.

————. *Wild Animal Interviews and Wild Opinions of Us.* New York: Charles Scribner's Sons, 1929.

Hughes, J. Donald. *American Indians in Colorado.* Boulder: Pruett Publishing Company, 1977.

Hummel, Monte, and Sherry Pettigrew. *Wild Hunters: Predators in Peril.* Niwot, Colo.: Roberts Rinehart Publishers, 1991.

Humphreys, David. *An Essay on the Life of the Hon. Major General Putnam.* Boston: Samuel Avery, 1818.

Hutton, Paul A. *The Custer Reader.* Lincoln: University of Nebraska Press, 1992.

Jenkinson, Michael. *Beasts Beyond the Fire.* New York: E. P. Dutton, 1980.

Jonaitis, Aldona. *Art of the Northern Tlingit.* Seattle: University of Washington Press, 1986.

————. *Chiefly Feasts: The Enduring Kwakiutl Potlach.* New York: American Museum of Natural History, 1991.

Jones, Daniel. *Forty Years among the Indians.* Salt Lake City: Junior Instructor Office, 1890.

Josephy, Alvin, ed. *The Great West.* New York: American Heritage Publishing Co., 1965.

Kalm, Peter. *Peter Kalm's Travels in North America.* Edited by Adolph B. Benson. Vol. 1. 1770. Reprint. New York: Wilson-Erickson, 1937.

Keller, Betty. *Black Wolf: The Life of Ernest Thompson Seton.* Vancouver: Douglas and McIntyre, 1984.

King, Calvin L. *Reasons for the Decline of Game in the Bighorn Basin of Wyoming.* New York: Vantage Press, 1965.

Klinghammer, Erich, ed. *The Behavior and Ecology of Wolves.* New York: Garland STPM Press, 1979.

————. *Wolf Literature References: Scientific and General.* Battle Ground, Ind.: Wolf Park, 1990.

Kolenosky, G. B., and R. O. Standfield. "Morphological and Ecological Variation Among Gray Wolves of Ontario, Canada." In Fox, *The Wild Canids.* New York: Van Nostrand Reinhold Co., 1975.

Lee, Robert and Dick Williams. *Last Grass Frontier: The South Dakota Stock Grower Heritage.* Sturgis, S. Dak.: Black Hills Publishers, 1964.

Leopold, Aldo. *A Sand County Almanac.* 1949. Reprint. New York: Ballantine Books, 1974.

———. *Game Management.* New York: Charles Scribner's Sons, 1933.

———. "The Varmint Question." In McIntyre, *War Against the Wolf,* Stillwater, Minn.: Voyageur Press, 1995.

Lévi-Strauss, Claude. *The Naked Man.* New York: Harper & Row, 1981.

Limerick, Patricia. *Legacy of Conquest.* New York: Norton, 1987.

Linderman, Frank B. *Plenty-Coups, Chief of the Crows.* New York: Harper & Row, 1957.

———. *Pretty Shield.* 1932. Reprint. New York: John Day Co., 1972.

Link, Mike. *The Collected Works of Sigurd F. Olson.* Stillwater, Minn.: Voyageur Press, 1990.

Link, Mike, and Kate Crowley. *Following the Pack: The World of Wolf Research.* Stillwater, Minn.: Voyageur Press, 1994.

Lopez, Barry H. *Of Wolves and Men.* New York: Charles Scribner's Sons, 1978.

MacInnes, C. M. *In the Shadow of the Rockies.* London: Rivingtons, 1930.

Mails, Thomas E. *Plains Indians.* New York: Bonanza Books, 1973.

Martin, Calvin. *Keepers of the Game: Indian–Animal Relationship and the Fur Trade.* Berkeley: University of California Press, 1978.

Matthiessen, Peter. *North American Indians.* New York: Viking, 1989.

———. *Wildlife in America.* New York: Viking, 1987.

McClintock, Walter. *The Old North Trail: Life, Legends and Religion of the Blackfeet Indians.* Lincoln: University of Nebraska Press, 1968.

McDermott, John Francis. *Up the Missouri with Audubon: The Journal of Edward Harris.* Norman: University of Oklahoma Press, 1951.

McGowan, Dan. *Animals of the Canadian Rockies.* New York: Dodd, Mead & Co., 1936.

McHugh, Tom. *The Time of the Buffalo.* New York: Knopf, 1972.

McIlwraith, Thomas. *The Bella Coola Indians.* Vols. 1 and 2. Toronto: University of Toronto Press, 1948.

McIntyre, Rick, ed., *War Against the Wolf.* Stillwater, Minn.: Voyageur Press, 1995.

McKechnie, Jean, ed., *Webster's New Universal Unabridged Dictionary.* New York: Simon & Schuster, 1983.

Mech, David L. *The Wolf: The Ecology and Behavior of an Endangered Species.* New York: The American Museum of Natural History, 1970.

Merritt, John. *Baronets and Buffalo.* Missoula, Mont.: Mountain Press, 1985.

Mighetto, Lisa. *Wild Animals and American Environmental Ethics.* Tucson: University of Arizona Press, 1991.

Milner II, Clyde A. *The Oxford History of the American West.* New York: Oxford University Press, 1994.

Morgan, Ted. *Wilderness at Dawn: The Settling of the North American Continent.* New York: Simon & Schuster, 1993.

Muir, John. *John Muir: Wilderness Essays.* Edited by Frank Buske. Salt Lake City: Peregrine Smith, 1980.

———. *The Writings of John Muir.* 10 vols. Boston: Houghton Mifflin, 1916.

Nash, Roderick. *Wilderness and the American Mind.* New Haven: Yale University Press, 1967.

Nelson, Oliver. *The Cowman's Southwest.* Edited by Angie Debo. Glendale, Calif.: The Arthur H. Clark Co., 1953.

Nelson, Richard. *Hunters of the Northern Forest.* Chicago: University of Chicago Press, 1973.

———. *Make Prayers to the Raven.* Chicago: University of Chicago Press, 1983.

Nowak, Ronald M. "A Perspective on the Taxonomy of Wolves in North America." In Carbyn, *Wolves in Canada and Alaska.* Ottawa: Canadian Wildlife Service, 1983.

———. *North American Quaternary Canis.* Lawrence: University of Kansas, 1979.

O'Connor, Jack. *Hunting in the Rockies.* New York: Knopf, 1947.

Olsen, Stanley J. *Origins of the Domestic Dog, The Fossil Record.* Tucson: University of Arizona Press, 1985.

Paul, William. "Trends and Management of Wolf–Livestock Conflicts in Minnesota." In *Wolves and Humans 2000: Program and Abstracts of Wolf Symposium, 9–11 March 1995, Duluth, Minnesota.* Ely, Minn.: International Wolf Center, 1995.

Peattie, Donald Culross, ed. *Audubon's America: The Narratives and Experiences of John James Audubon.* Boston: Houghton Mifflin Co., 1940.

Peck, Robert M. *Land of the Eagle: A Natural History of North America.* New York: Summit Books, 1990.

Peirce, Milton P. "The Great Hinckley Hunt." In McIntyre, *War Against the Wolf.* Stillwater, Minn.: Voyageur Press, 1995.

Peters, Roger. "Communication, Cognitive Mapping, and Strategy in Wolves and Hominids." In Hall, *Wolf and Man.* New York: Academic Press, 1978.

Peterson, Brenda. "Wolf Medicine." In McIntyre, *War Against the Wolf.* Stillwater, Minn.: Voyageur Press, 1995.

Phillips, R. L., and C. Jonkel, eds. *Proceedings of the 1975 Predator Symposium.* Missoula: Montana Forestry and Conservation Experiment Station, 1975.

Pielou, E. C. *After the Ice Age: the return of life to glaciated North America.* Chicago and London: University of Chicago Press, 1991.

Quaife, M. M., ed. *Yellowstone Kelly: The Memoirs of Luther S. Kelly.* New Haven: Yale University Press, 1926.

Rausch, Robert, and R. A. Hinman. "Wolf Management in Alaska—an exercise in futility?" In Phillips, *Proceedings of the 1975 Predator Symposium.* Missoula: Montana Forestry and Conservation Experiment Station, 1975.

Ray, Dorothy J. *Eskimo Masks: Art and Ceremony.* Seattle: University of Washington Press, 1967.

Ream, Robert, and Ursula Mattson. "Wolf Status in the Northern Rockies." In Harrington, *Wolves of the World.* Park Ridge, N.J.: Noyes Publishing Co., 1982.

Ridenour, James M. *The National Parks Compromised: Pork Barrel Politics & America's Treasures.* Merrillville, Ind.: ICS Books, Inc., 1994.

Rider, Sidney. *The Lands of Rhode Island as They Were Known to Caunounicus and Miantunnomu when Roger Williams Came in 1636.* Providence: Privately published, 1904.

293

Robertson, Joe D. *The Gray Wolf: a story of wolf management in Manitoba.* Winnipeg: Wildlife Crusader and the Manitoba Wildlife Federation, 1984.

Roe, Frank G. *The North American Buffalo.* Toronto: University of Toronto Press, 1970.

Roosevelt, Theodore. *Good Hunting: in pursuit of big game in the West.* New York: Harper & Brothers, 1907.

———. *Hunting the Grisly and Other Sketches.* New York: Review of Reviews Co., 1904.

———. *The Wilderness Hunter.* 1893. Reprint. New York: Charles Scribner's Sons, 1926.

Ross, Alexander. *The Fur Hunters of the Far West.* Edited by Kenneth Spaulding. Norman: University of Oklahoma Press, 1956.

Rountree, Helen C. *Pocahontas's People.* Norman: University of Oklahoma Press, 1990.

Russell, Osborne. *Journal of a Trapper.* Lincoln: University of Nebraska Press, 1955.

Rutter, R. J., and D. H. Pimlott. *The World of the Wolf.* Philadelphia: J. P. Lippincott Co., 1968.

Ruxton, George F. *Life in the Far West.* Edited by Leroy Hafen. Norman: University of Oklahoma Press, 1951.

Sage, Rufus B. *Scenes in the Rocky Mountains.* Vols. 1 and 2. Glendale, Calif.: Arthur H. Clark Co., 1956.

Salt, Henry S. *Animals' Rights Considered in Relation to Social Progress.* New York: Macmillan, 1892.

Savage, Candace S. *Wolves.* San Francisco: Sierra Club Books, 1988.

Schlesier, Karl H. *The Wolves of Heaven: Cheyenne Shamanism, Ceremonies, and Prehistoric Origins.* Norman and London: University of Oklahoma Press, 1987.

Schoolcraft, Henry. *History of the Indian Tribes of the United States.* 5 vols. Philadelphia: J. B. Lippincott and Co., 1855.

Schultz, James W. *Blackfeet and Buffalo.* Edited by Keith Seele. Norman: University of Oklahoma Press, 1962.

———. *Many Strange Characters: Montana Frontier Tales.* Norman: University of Oklahoma Press, 1982.

———. *Recently Discovered Tales of Life Among the Indians.* Edited by Warren L. Hanna. Missoula, Mont.: Mountain Press Publishing Co., 1988.

Seton, Ernest T. *Great Historic Animals, Mainly About Wolves.* New York: Scribners, 1937.

———. *Lives of Game Animals.* Vol. 1, part 1. 1925. Reprint. Boston: Charles T. Branford Co., 1953.

———. "Trail of an Artist-Naturalist." In McIntyre, *War Against the Wolf.* Stillwater, Minn.: Voyageur Press, 1995.

Shoemaker, Henry W. *Wolf Days in Pennsylvania.* Altoona, Pa.: The Altoona Tribune Press, 1914.

Shultz, Duane. *Over the Earth I Come.* New York: St. Martin's Press, 1992.

Skinner, Milton P. "The Predatory and Fur-Bearing Animals of the Yellowstone National Park." In McIntyre, *War Against the Wolf.* Stillwater, Minn.: Voyageur Press, 1995.

Spencer, Paula U. *Who Speaks for Wolf?* Austin, Tex.: Tribe of Two Press, 1983.

Standing Bear, Luther. *Stories of the Sioux.* 1934. Reprint. Lincoln: University of Nebraska Press, 1988.

Steinhart, Peter. *The Company of Wolves.* New York: Knopf, 1995.

Sterling, Keir B. *Last of the Naturalists: The Career of C. Hart Merriam.* New York: Arno Press, 1974.

Stevenson, Marc. "Dire Wolf Systematics and Behavior." In Hall, *Wolf and Man.* New York: Academic Press, 1978.

Stuart, Granville. *Forty Years on the Frontier.* 2 vols. Cleveland: Arthur H. Clark, 1925.

Taylor, Joseph H. "Twenty Years on the Trap Line." In McIntyre, *War Against the Wolf.* Stillwater, Minn.: Voyageur Press, 1995.

Theberge, John B. *Wolves and Wilderness.* Toronto: J. M. Dent and Sons, 1975.

Thiel, Richard P. *The Timber Wolf in Wisconsin: The Death and Life of a Majestic Predator.* Madison: University of Wisconsin Press, 1993.

Thomas, Davis, and Karin Ronnefeldt. *People of the First Man.* New York: E. P. Dutton, 1976.

Thompson, Zadock. *Natural History of Vermont.* Burlington: Stacy & Jameson, 1853.

Thornton, Russell. *American Indian Holocaust and Survival: A Population History Since 1492.* Norman: University of Oklahoma Press, 1987.

Thwaites, Reuben. *Early American Travels 1748–1846.* 32 vols. Cleveland, Ohio: Arthur H. Clark Co., 1904–1907.

Trefethen, James B. *An American Crusade for Wildlife.* New York: Winchester Press and the Boone and Crockett Club, 1975.

Tyrell, J. B. *David Thompson's Narrative of His Explorations in Western America, 1784–1812.* Toronto: Champlain Society, 1916.

Utley, Robert M. *The Lance and the Shield: The Life and Times of Sitting Bull.* New York: Henry Holt, 1993.

Van Ballenberghe, Victor. "Wolf Management in Minnesota: An Endangered Species Case History." In *Transactions of the Thirty-Ninth North American Wildlife Conference.* Washington, D.C.: Wildlife Management Institute, 1974.

Walker, James R. *Lakota Belief and Ritual.* Lincoln: University of Nebraska Press, 1980.

Washington, George. *Letters from His Excellency General Washington to Arthur Young.* London: B. McMillan, 1801.

Webster, Noah. *A Compendious Dictionary of the English Language.* 1806. Reprint. New York: Crown Publishers, Inc., 1970.

Weltfish, Gene. *The Lost Universe.* New York: Basic Books, 1965.

Wentworth, Edward N. *America's Sheep Trails.* Ames, Iowa: Iowa State College Press, 1948.

Wherry, Joseph. *The Totem Pole Indians.* New York: Thomas Crowell Co., 1974.

White, Richard. "Animals and Enterprise." In Milner, *Oxford History of the American West.* New York: Oxford University Press, 1994.

Wissler, Clark, ed. *Societies of the Plains Indians.* Vol. 11 of *Anthropological Papers.* New York: American Museum of Natural History, 1916.

Wood, William. *New England's Prospect (1634).* Edited by Alden T. Vaughan. Amherst: University of Massachusetts Press, 1977.

Young, Stanley P. *The Last of the Loners.* London: Macmillan Co., 1970.

————. *The Wolf in North American History.* Caldwell, Idaho: The Caxton Printers, Ltd., 1946.

Young, Stanley P., and Edward A. Goldman. *The Wolves of North America.* Washington, D.C.: The American Wildlife Institute, 1944.

ACKNOWLEDGMENTS

Any author today who attempts to write about the wolf must pay homage to the rich literary heritage that exists concerning the animal; by one count the number of publications exceed many of these titles proved valuable, several thousand. Although many of these titles proved valuable in the course of researching and writing this book, some deserve special mention: Thomas Dunlap's *Saving America's Wildlife* and Barry Lopez's *Of Wolves and Men.* No less important was Tim Rawson's comprehensive master's thesis, "Alaska's First Wolf Controversy."

Special thanks to the helpful staffs of various state historical archives, in particular, those of Missouri, South and North Dakota, Arizona, New Mexico, Texas, Oklahoma, Nevada, Kansas, Nebraska, Iowa, Colorado, Idaho, Montana, and Wyoming. The Montana Historical Society's Dave Walter kindly shared much material about Montana's early wolf history. The National Archives's Jimmy Rush cheerfully assisted me in locating numerous government records concerning predator control. Also helpful were the staffs of the Smithsonian Institution, Amon Carter Museum, Yellowstone National Park, University of Alaska's Rasmuson Library, Denver Public Library, Central Wyoming College, and the University of Wyoming. As always, Barbara Oakleaf and the staff of Wyoming's Fremont County Library proved invaluable in tracking down numerous publications.

Acknowledgments

Alaska's premier conservation organization, the Alaska Conservation Foundation, led by its able director, Jan Konigsberg, contributed financial, logistical, and psychological support during the research phase of my writing, for which I am particularly grateful.

Two U.S. Fish and Wildlife Service scientists, Steve Fritts and Ron Nowak, provided scientific and historical material as well as many helpful suggestions. Photographer, writer, and filmmaker Bruce Weide furnished photographs and encouragement. Jim and Cat Urbigkit shared their interest and a wealth of material about wolves.

Thanks also to Rick McIntyre, Peter Steinhart, Pat Tucker, Nicole Whittington-Evans, Sandra Arnold, Wayne Hall, Wendy Brown, Sylvia Altman, Barbara Allen Bogart, Jaime Gonzalez, John Buckley, Paul Schullery, Norm Bishop, Dan Neal, Susan Mackreth, Hank Fischer, Tom Walker, John Schoen, Larry Loendorf, and Sharon Rose.

The University of Montana's Bob Ream first suggested the idea of this book to me nearly twenty years ago, and the eminent mammalogist Phil Wright gave me the tools to find my way.

Finally, my family offered their patience, assistance, and love, for which I am ever in their debt.

INDEX